HANDBOOK OF
POLYGRAPH TESTING

HANDBOOK OF
POLYGRAPH TESTING

Edited by Murray Kleiner

ACADEMIC PRESS
A Division of Harcourt, Inc.

San Diego   San Francisco   New York   Boston
London   Sydney   Tokyo

ACADEMIC PRESS
A division of Harcourt Inc.
Harcourt Place, 32 Jamestown Road, London NW1 7BY, UK
http://www.academicpress.com

ACADEMIC PRESS
A division of Harcourt Inc.
525 B Street, Suite 1900, San Diego, California 92101-4495, USA
http://www.academicpress.com

ISBN 0-12-413740-7

Library of Congress Control Number 2001096019
A catalogue record for this book is available from the British Library

Typeset by Kenneth Burnley, Wirral, Cheshire, England
Printed in the United Kingdom by Bath Press, a part of the CPI Group
02 03 04 05 06 07 BP 9 8 7 6 5 4 3 2 1

CONTENTS

CONTRIBUTORS

Susan L. Amato
Department of Psychology, Boise State University, 1910 University Drive, Boise, ID 83725, USA.

Professor Gershon Ben-Shakhar
Department of Psychology, The Hebrew University of Jerusalem, Jerusalem, 91905, Israel.

Captain John "Jack" E. Consigli
Massachusetts State Police.

Charles W. Daniels
Freedman Boyd Daniels Hollander Goldberg and Cline, PA, 20 First Plaza Suite 700, Albuquerque, NM 87102, USA.

Eitan Elaad
Israel National Police Headquarters, Division of Identification and Forensic Sciences, Jerusalem, 91906, Israel.

Dr Charles R. Honts
Chair, Department of Psychology, Boise State University, 1910 University Drive, Boise, ID 83725, USA.

Professor John C. Kircher
Department of Educational Psychology, University of Utah, Salt Lake City, UT 84112, USA.

Murray Kleiner
Israel National Police HQ, Division of Identification and Forensic Sciences, Behaviour Section, Jerusalem, 91906, Israel.

Donald J. Krapohl
Department of Defense Polygraphy Institute, Fort Jackson, South Caroline, USA.

Dennis C. Mitchell, PhD
4 Westview Drive, Canton, Connecticut, 06019, USA.

Makoto Nakayama
4-6-1-205, Kami-Ashiarai, Shizuoka-shi, Shizuokaken, 4200841, Japan.

David C. Raskin, PhD
Professor Emeritus, PO Box 2419, Homer, AK 99603, USA.

J. Peter Rosenfeld
Department of Psychology, Northwestern University, Evanston, IL 60208, USA.

INTRODUCTION

There is an aura of magic surrounding the polygraph. For the uninitiated, it is a kind of crystal ball, piercing the innermost soul to reveal secrets or illuminate exoneration apparent only to the magician. The parallel between polygraph and magic is eerily appropriate. Both are regarded as a special power, being beyond the ordinary human sphere. They are used to ensure a successful outcome when firm knowledge is missing or uncertain. Both may aim to prevent or remove danger and to protect an individual or community from the evil acts of others. Their use gives confidence to people aware of their practical limitations, which may also promote incentive and the efficient organization of effort. They may also be performed for expressive purposes – stating and maintaining the formal culture and organization of the society, so that "polygraph magic" has also the function of stressing the importance of integrity and the activities dependent upon it.

"Any sufficiently advanced technology is indistinguishable from magic," wrote Arthur C. Clarke. Magic and science can be seen as a philosophical continuum, overlapping ways of understanding the world around us. As scientific and technical understanding develop, some magic is recognized and incorporated as technology, while the rest retreats. We live with an abundance of technology, upon which we blindly rely – to send voices through the air, see pictures in crystal tubes, fly like a bird, and cure our ills – even though we seldom actually know just how this is done. We are content that the scientists and technicians, who devised the technology, understand it. On the other hand, everyone knows about lying. We all have experience of our own lies, and assume that others' is similar to ours. We are not content to leave the understanding of such an intimately known issue to the sole command of magicians or scientists – especially when polygraph testing is characterized in a confusing spectrum – from infallible and indispensable, to unpleasant and intrusive, which can ruin lives because it is inaccurate.

Polygraph occupies a special region in the balance between magic and science. Its instrumentation and procedures were devised for use in law enforcement, prior to advances in relevant scientific and technological realms of knowledge. This state of affairs is symbolized in the 1923 *Frye* legal standard, dealing with an early version of the polygraph, which ruled that a scientific technique is admissible only if that technique has gained "general acceptance" as reliable in the relevant scientific community; and the polygraph test had, at that time, not yet gained such standing and scientific recognition among physiological and psychological authorities. The utility of polygraph for law enforcement proved to be sufficiently robust to persist in its application and development, mainly by practitioners. Instrumentation, theory, and procedure have remained basically unchanged for decades, with minor variations, while psychological and psychophysiological research and theory have progressed, refining physiological monitoring and conceptualization of psychological processes. Even with years of scientific study following the 1950s, polygraph use had not yet gained "general acceptance" and continues to generate some heat within the scientific community. Consequently, its status has not been resolved within the legal community, despite the 1993 *Daubert* revision of admissibility standards of scientific evidence (see Daniels, this volume), and regularly emerges as a topic of public debate.

In part, this is due to the involvement of the scientific community with law enforcement, or lack thereof. The contribution of technological advance to forensic science has been extensive in the last half-century, for the most part in the realms of chemistry, physics, biology, and computer science. Paradoxically, although law enforcement deals with criminal behavior, the role of the behavioral sciences in forensic applications has been minor. Only in recent years has there been an increase of activity and effectiveness in research and applications on offender profiling, memory refreshment, and assessment of competence. In the area of polygraph, the challenge of psychological research has been accepted by a relatively small fraction of the community, a major portion of whom is represented in this book.

Forensic professionals often possess academic degrees in chemistry, physics, biology, engineering or computer science, whereas polygraph practitioners with a degree in psychology are quite rare. Understandably, polygraph has been taught, by and large, in the vocabulary of its non-psychologist developers rather than the specialized terminology and evolving concepts of psychology. Practitioners, while competent and experienced in their work, generally can't express it in a way that is accessible to psychologists, nor comprehend it in terms of contemporary psychological constructs. This has isolated the majority of research psychologists and psychophysiologists from the basic precepts and procedures of polygraph, and most scientific research has dealt with its accuracy, generating controversy regarding methodology, while leaving the theoretical basis of the phenomenon relatively unexplored. Few law enforcement agencies (the Department of Defense Polygraph Institute a notable exception) have polygraph practitioners with the background to recognize and articulate the need for research, or the funds to carry it out. The amount of polygraph research in the last half-century is but a fraction of that in other fields of behavioral forensic sciences. Polygraph examiners, conscious of academic reservations regarding their profession, and their difficulty in explaining and defending their procedures, are becoming aware of the need to upgrade the polygraph rationale.

The dissociation of the practitioners and academicians has gradually led to mutual unfamiliarity with the respective fields, their concerns and constraints. The polygraph application involves a rich and stimulating complement of psychological and physiological processes for empirical investigation, which has not been addressed in basic academic research. Similarly, useful psychological and physiological concepts and techniques, currently employed in research, have not impacted significantly on polygraph rationale, practice, and technology.

Polygraph is simply not understood: by scientists unaware of the application; by agencies that need the information it produces; by those who legislate its use and by those who are examined.

The start of the millennium is the right time to have a long, hard look at our present position, and recognize issues for our future research and development agenda. This should include reconsideration of the psychological and psychophysiological foundations of polygraph, in the light of modern advances in these fields.

A clear presentation of polygraph from a modern viewpoint, expanding the traditional perspective of the practitioner could foster progress in the field; promote understanding, cooperation, study and development. This book offers the opportunity for practitioners and academics to recognize the pertinence of their counterpart's disciplines, hoping to promote polygraph-relevant research, and evolution of polygraph consistent with modern scientific thought.

MURRAY KLEINER

CHAPTER 1

THE COMPARISON QUESTION TEST

David C. Raskin and Charles R. Honts

In this chapter, we describe and analyze the major method of physiological detection of deception, the comparison or control question test (CQT). We start with a discussion of the basic requirements of a psychological test for the assessment of the credibility of an individual. Since the CQT is a psychological and pyschophysiological test, we evaluate the extent to which each of the major polygraph techniques satisfies the general requirements of a psychological test, beginning with the early relevant–irrelevant test (RIT) and proceeding through the most recent development, the directed-lie test (DLT). For each technique, we describe and evaluate the basic test protocols, including the question structure, the pre-test interview, the development and review of the questions to be asked, the sequence of question presentation, and the methods for evaluating the outcome. We then present an analysis of the validity of the CQT based on laboratory and field research. We also describe some of the technical and practical issues surrounding their applications.

REQUIREMENTS OF A PSYCHOLOGICAL TEST

According to Gregory (1992:35), a psychological test is a "standardized procedure for sampling behavior." Standardization of a test is a prerequisite for results that are reliable (repeatable) and valid (accurate). The purpose of the test and its underlying rationale must be articulated, the procedures for conducting the test must be described in detail, the test protocol must relate directly to the purpose of the test and also provide that impression to the subject (face validity), the procedures for evaluating the test outcome must be specified, and data must be gathered regarding the criterion (empirical) validity of the test. Such data must be accompanied by a description of the populations and the contexts of their collection in order to define the extent of their applicability.

The basic principles underlying all polygraph tests for the assessment of credibility (detection of deception) are psychophysiological in nature. The test is based on the well-established "fight or flight" phenomenon. That is, a physical or psychological threat will automatically elicit a complex set of physiological reactions manifested as changes that are readily measured with a polygraph instrument (Thompson, 2000). These physiological changes include increases in palmar skin conductance and blood pressure and decreases in respiratory activity and peripheral circulation (Stern *et al.*, 1980). The various polygraph techniques generally rely on one or more psychological constructs as the causes of these physiological changes, such as fear of detection, enhanced attention, information processing, orienting reflexes, conflict, and arousal (see Podlesny and Raskin, 1977; Raskin, 1979). However, the assessment of the underlying causal nature of the physiological responses is a separate scientific question from determining the accuracy of a test. It is quite possible, and acceptable, to have a test validated as accurate for its specified purpose (internal and criterion validity) without having a complete theoretical understanding of the underlying theoretical constructs (construct validity, Cook and Campbell, 1979).

COMMON CHARACTERISTICS OF ALL DETECTION OF DECEPTION TESTS

All polygraph tests begin with a pre-test interview. The interview usually involves obtaining verbal or written consent from the subject to administer the test. Basic biographical information is obtained, such as personal data and a brief health history. The issues to be covered by the test are discussed, including the specific allegations, and the subject's version of the events is obtained. This interaction is usually followed by the examiner providing some type of description of the relevant psychophysiology, including how and why a person will react physiologically when engaging in deception and when answering truthfully. The physiological transducers are then attached to the subject, and the examiner may also conduct a demonstration test to accustom the subject to the recording procedures and to convince the subject that attempts to deceive will be accompanied by clear physiological changes, whereas truthful answers will not produce such changes. This usually is accomplished with a simple number or "stimulation test." Since detection of deception techniques vary greatly in the extent and manner in which these procedures are utilized and presented to the subject, they will be discussed in more detail with respect to each of the major techniques.

All polygraph tests for assessing credibility (which excludes the so-called guilty knowledge test) require the subject to answer direct questions concerning involvement or knowledge of a crime or incident. Questions are formulated so that the subject will answer "Yes" or "No" and are reviewed in detail with the subject during the pre-test interview. The relevant questions typically embody a major aspect of the incident, and other questions (e.g., comparison questions) are included for various purposes that depend on the type of test format employed (see below).

All polygraph techniques assume that the measured physiological reactions are automatic (autonomic) and will occur with greater strength to the questions that are most important to the individual, e.g., a crime-relevant question that is answered deceptively. However, techniques vary in psychophysiological sophistication and the extent to which they recognize and attempt to control factors that may produce relatively strong reactions to questions that are answered truthfully. This raises concerns about the internal validity of some techniques, a problem that has encouraged critics to claim that polygraph tests are invalid (see Iacono and Lykken, 1997). Therefore, the internal validity will be discussed as we consider each of the techniques below.

THE RELEVANT–IRRELEVANT TEST

The first widely used test for deception, the general questions test or relevant–irrelevant test (RIT), was developed from the research of Marston (1917) for use in law enforcement applications (Keeler, 1933; Larson, 1932). Although it was the dominant polygraph technique for about 20 years, it is now used infrequently in criminal investigation (Raskin, 1986).

TEST STRUCTURE AND ADMINISTRATION

The typical RIT employs a series of 10 to 15 questions comprised of crime-relevant questions (e.g., "Did you rob the Quick Mart last night?") and irrelevant (neutral) questions (e.g., "Are you sitting down?"). The rationale of the RIT predicts that since a guilty subject will answer the relevant questions deceptively, it is expected that the guilty person will exhibit relatively strong physiological reactions to the relevant as compared to the truthfully answered irrelevant questions. Conversely, the rationale of the RIT predicts that since an innocent subject will answer all questions truthfully, it is expected that there will be little difference in the strength of reactions to the two types of questions.

Since the RIT was developed in a law enforcement context, it tends to be oriented toward obtaining admissions and confessions. The pre-test interview is typically somewhat confrontational and may lead into an interrogation before the test is completed. The examination does not usually include a detailed explanation of the relevant psychophysiology or a number test.

The series of questions is usually presented twice in a mixed order with relevant and irrelevant questions interspersed and a brief pause between the two presentations. The early version of the test often included a surprise question known as the "emotional standard question" that took the form "In your entire life (pause), have you ever (pause) . . ." This question was designed to elicit a strong physiological reaction from relatively unresponsive subjects, but it was abandoned when licensing bodies and professional organizations began to require that all questions be reviewed in advance with the subject. A typical test sequence is shown in Table 1.1.

I1.	Is today Tuesday?
R1.	Do you intend to lie to me on this test?
I2.	Are you sitting down?
R2.	Did you rob the Quick Mart last night?
R3.	Did you use a gun to rob the Quick Mart last night?
I3.	Do you sometimes watch TV?
I4.	Is your name Bob?
R4.	Did you rob the cashier at the Quick Mart last night?
R5.	Did you take money from the cash register at the Quick Mart last night?
I5.	Do you like beer?
R6.	Have you lied to me today?
I6.	Do you live in the United States?

INTERPRETATION OF THE RIT

Relative strengths of physiological reactions to the relevant and irrelevant questions are used to determine whether or not the subject is truthful or deceptive in answering the relevant questions. Since most individuals display some autonomic reactivity to almost any type of question, neutral questions are used to establish a baseline of reactivity against which to compare the strength of the reactions produced by the relevant questions. Therefore, the polygraph examiner makes a global inspection and looks for heightened reactivity to the relevant questions. The presence of such a pattern of reactions leads to the conclusion that the subject was practicing deception on the relevant issues. This is usually followed by an interrogation for the purpose of obtaining a confession. If no difference in reactions to relevant and neutral questions is observed, the examiner concludes that the subject was truthful in answering the relevant questions. This evaluation procedure is impressionistic and lacks a systematic set of rules for its application.

EVALUATION OF THE RIT

The underlying assumption of the RIT is that the observed physiological reactions are produced by "fear" of being detected in deception. Since only guilty persons are expected to experience this "fear of detection," larger reactions to the relevant questions are considered a *direct* indication of deception. This assumption and the interpretations of the RIT are simplistic and psychophysiologically naive (Podlesny and Raskin, 1977.) It is generally accepted by psychophysiologists that there is no "specific-lie response" or pattern of reactions that is peculiar to deception (Raskin, 1979). That is to say, an inspection of the physiological responses of an individual to a particular question cannot provide the sole basis for concluding that the subject's answer was deceptive or truthful. Although some progress has been made in identifying patterns of reactions that may be helpful in this regard (Honts *et al.*, 1988a; Kircher and Raskin, 1982), considerably more research is needed before that approach can be applied successfully in detection of deception.

A variety of factors may cause subjects to react with greater strength to questions about crimes of which they are suspected than to the innocuous neutral questions. Serious accusations, the emotional impact of the questions (e.g., if they mention the death of a spouse or friend), the nervousness of the individual, the thought processes and images evoked by the content of the questions, distrust of the examiner, or anger and disgust concerning the accusation (e.g., sexual abuse of one's own child) may cause autonomic reactions to relevant questions even when they are answered truthfully. Neither polygraph examiners nor psychophysiologists are able to distinguish with any reasonable accuracy such reactions from those that occur as a result of deception. Therefore, the RIT lacks internal validity.

Problems with the RIT are compounded by low face validity. Since it is obvious to any subject that the relevant questions are the only important questions, there is reason to believe that most innocent subjects will react most strongly to the relevant questions. It is common experience that almost everyone who is presented with such a situation states that they would fail the test because of "nervousness" about being accused of a crime. The confrontational atmosphere of this approach further compounds these problems. The lack of face validity and internal validity coupled with inadequate and unsystematic methods for evaluating the test outcome would be expected to result in a substantial number of false positive errors. In fact, scientific research indicates that the RIT produces extremely high rates of false positive errors (Horowitz *et al.*, 1997; Horvath, 1988). The RIT suffers from fundamental flaws in internal, face, and criterion validity, along with lack of standardization of pre-test interviews, question sequencing, and procedures for evaluating the test outcome. Thus, the RIT does not satisfy the basic requirements of a psychophysiological test and should not be used.

COMPARISON QUESTION TESTS

Comparison question tests (CQT) are the most commonly used and generally applicable techniques for the investigation of criminal cases. They are also used in civil litigation, national security screening, and post-conviction assessments. The CQT is used to assess credibility concerning actions or events about which the subject has direct knowledge or experience and a clear memory (Raskin, 1986). In most cases, the relevant questions can be worded in simple, concrete terms that allow an unambiguous interpretation of their meaning. A relevant question that is ambiguous or that requires the subject to draw conclusions or make interpretations can cause problems in making inferences about truth or deception, regardless of the actual guilt or innocence of the person tested.

Lack of clear memory for an event (from intoxication, trauma, or other causes) may render a subject unsuitable for a test. Also, relevant questions should not attempt to directly assess a subject's state of mind during the incident or the subject's interpretation of the meaning of such acts or events. However, motives, intentions, or legal conclusions may sometimes be inferred from the content and the meaning of the questions that the examiner and subject discuss during the pre-test interview. For example, the subject accused of rape should not be asked "Did Mary voluntarily have sex with you on June fifth?" Instead, he might be asked, "Did you use physical force or threat to get Mary to have sex with you on June fifth?" The subject's veracity in denying a rape can be directly inferred from the test outcome on the use of physical force or threat. However, it is necessary for the examiner to discuss and define the meaning of *physical force* and *threat* in terms of the allegations and descriptions provided by the witness/victim. However, the subject should never be asked, "Did you rape Mary on June fifth?" This question is unsuitable because it requires the subject to draw a legal conclusion.

The CQT typically employs between two and four relevant questions in a test sequence of 10 to 12 questions that includes other types of questions. The nature and purposes of the other questions vary according to the type of technique and the purposes of the examination, and the methods for conducting the pre-test interview and evaluating test outcomes vary for different techniques. The evolution of the CQT together with the major variations in question sequences and pre-test interviews is described in the following sections.

THE REID CQT

The Reid CQT, also known as the modified general questions test (MGQT), was the first CQT test. It was the first test format designed to overcome problems inherent in the RIT by including comparison questions. The concept of comparison questions was first described by Summers (1939:341), who referred to them as "emotional standards" designed to "evoke within the individual rather intense psychogalvanic reactions due to surprise, anger, shame or anxiety over situations which he would ordinarily prefer to conceal." Reid (1947) further refined the concept and application of comparison questions. He modified examination procedures then in common use by incorporating what he termed the "comparative response question" and then discussing the questions in advance with the subject. Reid (1947:544) described the function of the comparative response question as follows:

> . . . because the magnitude of the response to that question is to be compared with responses to questions pertaining to the actual crime, and it may therefore serve to include or exclude definitely the subject as a suspect in the crime under investigation. If the examiner is fortunate enough to have in his possession certain information concerning a situation or offense involving the subject (but of less importance than the actual crime being investigated) which the examiner knows or feels reasonably sure the subject will lie about, a question based on such information and actually lied to will serve very well to indicate the subject's responsiveness when lying. Such a question thereby affords a basis for evaluating the nature of the response to the questions pertinent to the offense under investigation.

Comparison questions are designed to provide the innocent suspect with an opportunity to become more concerned about questions other than the relevant questions, thereby causing the innocent suspect to react more strongly to the comparison than to the relevant questions. If the subject does react with greater strength to the control questions, the result is interpreted as truthful. On the other hand, stronger reactions to the relevant questions are interpreted as indicating that the subject was deceptive to the relevant questions. The problem of no specific lie response is circumvented by the procedure of drawing inferences about truth or deception by comparing the relative strength of this particular subject's reactions to relevant and control questions.

Although the concept of the comparison question is simple and its effectiveness is an empirical question, some have argued that it cannot possibly work because it is based on a scientifically faulty premise (Ben-Shakhar and Furedy, 1990; Furedy and Heslegrave, 1991; Lykken, 1979). Because Backster (1963) erroneously renamed comparison questions "control" questions, they have argued that the comparison question is not a control in the scientific sense, because a true control would provide "a reasonable estimate of what the subject's response to the relevant question ought to be if he is answering truthfully [to the relevant question]" (Lykken, 1979:49). This argument reveals a lack of understanding of the nature and function of the comparison question. This question actually serves to determine whether the subject is more concerned or less concerned about the relevant question, and it comes closer to providing an estimate of what the reaction to the *relevant* question would be if the subject answered it *deceptively* (Raskin *et al.*, 1997b; Raskin and Kircher, 1991).

Test structure and administration

The Reid version of the MGQT (Reid and Inbau, 1977) typically includes an extensive pre-test interview about the issues under investigation, which provides the basis for introducing and reviewing the relevant questions. There are four relevant questions that vary in the strength of the issue and may encompass different possible levels of involvement in the event under investigation. This is followed by an in-depth discussion of the background and moral values of the subject. The latter is designed to establish the context for introducing the comparison questions to the subject and arousing concerns that will lead the subject to deny any acts embodied in the comparison questions. This approach may cause the subject to experience considerable discomfort and anxiety, which may be counterproductive and increase the risk of false positive errors.

Comparison questions usually encompass the subject matter of the alleged offense but are broader and more general in nature. For example, a person accused of a theft is given a brief lecture about the importance of honesty and how they were brought up by their parents to respect the property of others and would not be expected to steal or engage in other dishonest acts. After gaining agreement on these points, the examiner then poses the question "Have you ever stolen anything?" At this point, the subject has usually been led to believe that a "No" answer is expected and usually answers that way even if it is untruthful. Another comparison might be similarly posed, such as "Have you ever cheated anyone?" This procedure increases the face validity of the test, which should increase its effectiveness. The comparison questions are placed at positions 6 and 10, as shown in Table 1.2 for a theft case.

Table 1.2

The Reid CQT question sequence.

1.	Irrelevant:	Is today Tuesday?
2.	Irrelevant:	Are you sitting down?
3.	Relevant:	Did you rob the Quick Mart last night?
4.	Irrelevant:	Do you sometimes watch TV?
5.	Relevant:	Did you use a gun to rob the Quick Mart last night?
6.	Comparison:	Have you ever stolen anything?
7.	Irrelevant:	Is your name Bob?
8.	Relevant:	Did you take money from the cash register at the Quick Mart last night?
9.	Relevant:	Did you drive the getaway car at the Quick Mart robbery last night?
10.	Comparison:	Have you ever cheated anyone?

There are two problems with the Reid approach to formulating comparison questions. First, the examiner must develop a question to which the subject's denial is known to be deceptive. This requires the independent development of comparison question information. Unfortunately, such information is usually difficult or impossible to obtain. Therefore, the Reid examiner must choose a very general question to which the subject answers "No" and is assumed to be deceiving. This is risky because a subject who actually answers the question truthfully would not have the benefit of an adequate comparison question and could fail the test even when answering truthfully to the relevant questions. Second, the Reid type comparison question frequently encompasses the relevant issue of the test (see question sequence in Table 1.2). This situation should tend to increase the risk of a false negative error. Podlesny and Raskin (1978) reported that comparison questions worded so as to exclude the incident under investigation were more effective in detecting deception than questions that encompassed the relevant issue. However, Horvath (1988) reported the opposite result. Having maneuvered the subject into answering "No" to the comparison questions, the question sequence is presented three times, the last time in a mixed order. A "stimulation" test is usually inserted between the first and second presentation. The Reid approach to the stimulation test consists of having the subject pick a card from a set of cards presented face down by the examiner. Unknown to the subject, the cards were marked so that the examiner knows which card is chosen. The examiner then asks the subject to deny picking each card when asked about each card during the test. After completing the questions, the examiner informs the subject that he or she produced a strong reaction to the chosen card, leading the subject to believe that deception was clearly indicated on the polygraph recording (chart). Even though this procedure has been shown to increase the effectiveness of the polygraph test (Bradley and Janisse, 1981; but see Elaad and Kleiner, 1986 who failed to find effects), a deceptive card trick runs the risk of losing the trust of the subject. A simpler, straightforward method is discussed later in this chapter.

Interpretation of the result

The Reid examiner performs a global evaluation of the recordings to determine if the physiological reactions to the relevant questions are stronger or weaker than those to the comparison questions. Global evaluation includes an overall inspection of the polygraph charts to form a general impression concerning the relative strengths of reactions to the various questions. This subjective impression is somehow integrated with information derived from the case reports, observations of the subject's demeanor and verbal behavior, and other sources of information that may be idiosyncratic to the particular examiner. Although Reid described qualitative criteria for determining if a reaction is relatively strong or weak (Reid and Inbau, 1977), he provided no formal rules or procedures for evaluating the polygraph recordings and generally ignored the electrodermal response, which has been repeatedly demonstrated to be the most useful measure (e.g., Kircher and Raskin, 1988).

Research by the Reid organization (e.g., Horvath and Reid, 1971; Hunter and Ash, 1973; Slowik and Buckley, 1975; Wicklander and Hunter, 1975) has indicated relatively high interrater reliability and validity of their chart interpretation. However, field research has shown that the global method of chart interpretation produces substantially more error than the more systematic method known as numerical scoring (see below). Raskin *et al.* (1978) reported that blind numerical interpretations of polygraph charts from confirmed criminal cases produced only 1% errors, but global evaluations yielded 12% errors on the same charts. This finding is consistent with the large body of literature concerning statistical versus clinical judgment and argues for the use of systematic methods such as numerical scoring (see Kircher and Raskin, 1983).

Evaluation of the Reid CQT
This early CQT has considerably more face validity than the RIT, and its use of comparison questions is more closely related to the underlying principles of psychophysiology and has increased internal validity. However, this approach does not provide the subject with an adequate explanation of the psychophysiological reasons for stronger reactions when questions are answered deceptively as compared to truthful answers. Instead, it relies more on a mildly moralistic approach to setting up the comparison questions. The stimulation test is rigged and not presented until one chart has been collected, thereby reducing its effectiveness. The test may also be weakened by the use of general comparison questions that encompass the relevant issues and the need to assume that the subject is deceptively answering the comparison questions. Because of the difficulty of introducing and explaining the comparison questions to the subject, there is great variability in the pre-test interview, which is relatively unstandardized. The lack of a systematic method for evaluating the test outcome is another serious deficiency.

The Reid CQT represented a major advance in polygraph technique and is undoubtedly superior to the RIT in almost every respect. Although the face validity of the Reid CQT seems adequate, its internal validity is limited and empirical validity has not been well established. Subsequent developments in CQT techniques have produced more systematic and effective methods that are validated by scientific studies.

THE BACKSTER ZONE COMPARISON TEST

Backster (1963) modified the Reid CQT and named it the zone comparison test (ZCT). The name is derived from Backster's conceptualization of three basic zones: the red zone comprised relevant questions; the green zone comprised probable-lie (comparison) questions; and the black zone comprised outside issue questions. Backster renamed the comparison questions "probable-lie questions" because the underlying concept of relatively stronger reaction to the greater perceived threat requires the assumption that the subject is probably lying to the comparison questions. Probable-lie questions deal with acts that are similar to the issue of the investigation. However, they should be more general in nature, deliberately vague, and cover long periods of time in the life history of the subject. When properly formulated, most individuals would have difficulty in unequivocally and truthfully answering "No" to them.

Test structure and administration

An example of a Backster ZCT questions sequence regarding a theft is shown in Table 1.3. The Backster ZCT employs only two relevant questions that are slightly different wordings of essentially the same question. The set of questions is asked only twice, usually in the same order, and there is no discussion between the two runs. Backster handled the problem of overlap between relevant and comparison questions by prefacing each probable-lie question with a phrase such as "Before 1997" in order to exclude the incident under investigation from the comparison question. However, the Backster approach is mildly confrontational owing to its law enforcement orientation and typically uses comparison question wording that embodies specific offenses, such as "steal from a place where you worked" or "physically injure someone who loved and trusted you." Such comparison questions are frequently too specific and increase the probability that the subject's denial is truthful, thereby increasing the risk of a false positive error. In addition, Backster severely reduced the amount of pre-test discussion of the comparison questions to simply telling the subject that certain other questions needed to be asked. He also minimized the pre-test explanation of the psychophysiological reasons why stronger reactions occur during deception. The latter changes reduce the face validity and accuracy of the test.

1. Irrelevant:	Is today Tuesday?
2. Sacrifice relevant:	Regarding whether you robbed the Quick Mart last night, do you intend to answer truthfully each question about that?
3. Outside issue:	Do you believe me when I say that I won't ask you a question we have not already reviewed?
4. Probable lie:	Before 1997, did you ever steal from a place where you worked?
5. Relevant:	Did you rob the Quick Mart at Fourth and Main last night?
6. Probable lie:	Before age 27, did you ever cheat someone who loved and trusted you?
7. Relevant:	Did you use a gun to rob the Quick Mart at Fourth and Main last night?
8. Outside issue:	Are you afraid I will ask you a surprise question even though I told you I would not?

Table 1.3

Backster ZCT question sequence.

Backster made other modifications to the CQT. He added what he called a sacrifice relevant question. This is a weak overall question such as "Regarding whether you robbed the Quick Mart last night, do you intend to answer truthfully each question about that?" It is placed early in the sequence to absorb the general impact of being confronted with the relevant issue and is not included in the evaluation of the test outcome. Backster also added what he called outside issues questions that are designed to determine if the subject is more concerned about something other than the issue of the test (e.g., selling illegal drugs). Backster assumed that such outside issues can so dominate the subject's psychological set as to reduce reactivity to the relevant questions and cause a false negative error. However, recent research by Honts *et al.* (2000a) demonstrates just the opposite, i.e., the presence of an outside issue causes an increase in false positive errors but has no significant effect on the false negative rate. Honts *et al.* (2000a) also reported that the outside issue questions were not useful in detecting the presence of outside issues.

Interpretation of the result

Backster (1963) introduced a numerical scoring system for evaluating the polygraph charts. This was a major advance in test evaluation. Numerical scoring involves a systematic comparison of the reactions to each relevant question and the surrounding comparison questions. This process involves the assignment of numerical values on a 7-point scale ranging from scores of –3 when the reaction to the relevant question is dramatically stronger, through 0 when there is no difference, to +3 when the reaction to the comparison question is dramatically stronger. This scoring is performed for each physiological measure for each relevant question in the entire test. There is a complex set of rules for this procedure, but they are extremely difficult to follow and are biased against the innocent subject (see the research by Honts *et al.*, 1992; Raskin, 1986; Weaver, 1985).

Evaluation of the Backster ZCT

In some respects, the Backster ZCT was a major advance in polygraph technique; in other respects it was a step backward. The introduction of the numerical scoring system for evaluating the test outcome was its most important improvement, but the complex scoring rules and their bias against the innocent suspect weaken its usefulness. Although he acknowledged the probabilistic nature of the subject's lying to the comparison questions, Backster failed to recognize the weaknesses of the probable-lie comparison question and used an inadequate method of introducing them to the subject.

Backster assumed that if the test results are inconclusive, the "probable-lie questions are perfectly formulated" and the problem is the wording of the relevant questions, which need to be strengthened (Backster, 1973). This automatic strengthening of the relevant questions rather than the probable-lie questions increases the risk of false positive errors. His use of the time exclusion in the probable-lie questions to eliminate the problem of overlap between the comparison and relevant questions is also an improvement. However, he weakened the power of the probable-lie questions to establish the truthfulness of the innocent suspect by including behaviors and terminology that would allow more subjects to truthfully answer with a denial. He further weakened them by reducing the amount of introductory rationale for the comparison questions and by providing only a minimal explanation of the psychophysiology underlying reactions evoked by attempts to deceive. His way of using probable-lie questions makes it difficult to standardize the pre-test interview.

The changes introduced by Backster resulted in an overall reduction in the internal and face validity of the CQT. Further, there is no scientific research to support the empirical validity of the pure Backster ZCT, and the demonstrated risk of false positive errors argues against its use.

SCIENTIFIC DEVELOPMENT AND REFINEMENT OF THE CQT

There are numerous variants of the Reid and Backster approaches, notably those developed by the U.S. federal government (see Barland and Raskin, 1973). Although some aspects of these other approaches represent improvements and others represent regressions, none was explicitly based on principles of psychophysiology and developed and tested with scientific research. In order to increase the internal and empirical validity of the CQT, it was re-conceptualized within the framework of current concepts of psychological science and psychophysiology (see Raskin 1979, 1982, 1986) and subjected to rigorous scientific testing in laboratory and field contexts (see the review in Raskin *et al.*, 1997).

In 1970, Raskin and his colleagues at the University of Utah (see the review in Raskin *et al.*, 1997) embarked on a research program to evaluate the CQT and to improve its conceptual and empirical validity. This effort stimulated considerable research in many university and government laboratories, and similar research continues at the University of Utah and Boise State University. The initial research at Utah dealt with the probable-lie CQT, and later research has been devoted to development of a CQT that utilizes directed-lie comparison questions. Since the techniques developed at Utah and Boise State Universities are based on three decades of scientific research and represent the state of the art, they are described here in some detail.

UTAH PROBABLE-LIE TEST

The Utah probable-lie test (PLT) begins with a detailed pre-test interview that usually requires at least 1 h to complete. Prior to meeting the subject, the examiner becomes familiar with the case facts by reading incident reports and/or meeting with the relevant investigators or attorneys. At the outset of the pre-test interview, the subject is informed of the purpose and issues of the examination, is given a full advisement of legal rights, and gives written consent to undergo the examination. This formal advisement of rights, even when not required by law, creates a serious, professional atmosphere that blunts the argument of the "friendly polygrapher" advanced by polygraph critics (see Raskin, 1986; Honts, 1997).

The examiner should tape-record the entire examination, including the advisement of rights, and the subject should be informed at the outset that such a recording will be made. A complete recording provides a record for later review, as well as protection for the subject and the examiner if any questions are subsequently raised about the manner in which the examination was conducted and its specific contents. The recording is very useful for an independent evaluation of the examination and for training polygraph examiners.

Test structure and administration

The pre-test interview is a low-key approach designed to obtain information from the subject without pressure or confrontation. As such, it is an investigative psychological interview rather than an interrogation. The examiner does not lecture the subject or provide morality examples or personal anecdotes. The examiner never challenges the subject's version of the events during the pre-test interview. The interview begins by obtaining basic biographical information from the subject, including a brief medical and psychiatric history designed to uncover any serious physical or mental problems that might affect the validity of the test. The examiner then discusses the allegations or issues of the test and encourages the subject to freely describe and relate any events or knowledge that may be important for the examiner to know. This provides an opportunity for the subject to describe the incident from their own point of view and to clarify any ambiguities or misunderstandings that might interfere with a valid test. This helps to reduce the subject's general anxiety and assists in establishing an atmosphere of professional objectivity and trust.

The examiner then places the polygraph transducers on the subject and provides a general explanation of the psychophysiology that underlies the polygraph test. A rationale is provided as to why people show strong involuntary physiological reactions when they are deceptive and do not exhibit such reactions when they are truthful. A demonstration (stimulation) test is then performed to convince the subject that the polygraph is effective at detecting deception and verifying truthfulness. This takes the form of a number test in which the subject is asked to choose a number between 2 and 6, to disclose the number to the examiner, and to deny having chosen any of the numbers 1 through 7 while recordings are made with the polygraph.

After completing the number test, the subject is informed that a clear reaction occurred to the deception on the chosen number and that little change was observed in response to the truthful answers given to the other numbers. The subject is also told that the examiner now knows the individual characteristics of the subject's physiological reactions during deception and truthfulness and that there should be no problem on the test as long as the subject replies completely truthfully to every question. The subject is also told that any deception to any question on the test will produce even larger reactions than the reaction on the number test because such deception is more serious. Number tests have been shown to increase the accuracy of the polygraph test (Bradley and Janisse, 1981; but see contrary results by Elaad and Kleiner, 1986), and they should be used with all polygraph tests. The specific wording of each question is then reviewed and discussed with the subject to ensure that no ambiguities are present in the relevant questions. The probable-lie questions are then introduced. Probable-lie questions deal with acts that are similar to the issue of the investigation. However, they are more general in nature, deliberately vague, and cover long periods of time in the life history of the subject. Virtually every criminal suspect has difficulty in unequivocally answering them with a simple, truthful "No." An example of a probable-lie question in an examination regarding a robbery is "Prior to 1987, did you ever take something that did not belong to you?" The PLT includes two or three comparison questions that are reviewed with the subject after the relevant questions have been discussed and reviewed, and they are presented in a manner designed to encourage the subject to answer them with a denial. A typical introduction of the comparison questions by the examiner during the pre-test interview is as follows:

> Since this is a matter of a theft, I need to ask you some general questions about yourself in order to assess your basic character with regard to honesty and trustworthiness. I need to make sure that you have never done anything of a similar nature in the past and that you are not the type of person who would do something like robbing that Quick Mart and then would lie about it. Therefore, I need to ask you some questions for that purpose. So, if I ask you, "Before age 27, did you ever do anything that was dishonest or illegal?" you could answer that "No," couldn't you?

Most subjects initially answer "No" to the probable-lie questions. If the subject answers "Yes," the examiner asks for an explanation. The typical response is a minor admission, such as lying about taking some trivial item at an early age. The examiner then responds by saying, "Well, that was when you were a child and didn't know better. You never did anything like that when you were older and knew better, did you?" Most subjects then answer in the negative, and the question is used in its original form or reworded to "Other than what you told me, before age 27 did you ever do anything that was dishonest or illegal?" If the subject makes further admissions, the examiner continues to minimize and discourage admissions until a "No" answer is obtained. The goal is to get to the denial as quickly as possible.

The manner of introducing and explaining the probable-lie questions is designed to pose a dilemma for the subject. It leads the subject to believe that admissions will cause the examiner to form the opinion that the subject is dishonest and is therefore guilty. This discourages admissions and maximizes the likelihood that the negative answer is untruthful. However, the manner of introducing and explaining the probable-lie questions also causes the subject to believe that deceptive answers to them will result in strong physiological reactions during the test and will lead the examiner to conclude that the subject was deceptive with respect to the relevant issues concerning the robbery. In fact, the converse is true.

There are two forms of the Utah PLT. The first version, shown in Table 1.4, is often used when there is a single issue.

Table 1.4

Utah PLT single-issue question sequence.

I.	Introductory:	Do you understand that I will ask only the questions we have discussed?
SR.	Sacrifice relevant:	Regarding whether you robbed the Quick Mart last night, do you intend to answer all of the questions truthfully?
N1.	Neutral:	Do you live in the United States?
C1.	Probable lie:	During the first 27 years of your life, did you ever take something that did not belong to you?
R1.	Relevant:	Did you rob the Quick Mart at Fourth and Main last night?
N2.	Neutral:	Is your name Rick?
C2.	Probable lie:	Prior to 1987, did you ever do anything dishonest or illegal?
R2.	Relevant:	Did you use a gun to rob the Quick Mart at Fourth and Main last night?
N3.	Neutral:	Were you born in the month of November?
C3.	Probable lie:	Before age 27, did you ever lie to get out of trouble or to cause a problem for someone else?
R3.	Relevant:	Did you rob the cashier at the Quick Mart at Fourth and Main last night?

The sequence includes three relevant questions, three probable-lie questions (C1, C2, C3), and three neutral questions (N1, N2, N3). The first two questions (I, SR) are buffers designed to habituate the reactions that normally occur to the question that is presented first and to the first presentation of a question that embodies the relevant issue of the test. The introductory question also serves to reassure the subject that there will be no surprises. The reactions to these buffer questions are not evaluated.

The other version, shown in Table 1.5, is employed when there are multiple issues to be tested.

I.	Introductory:	Do you understand that I will ask only the questions we have discussed?
SR.	Sacrifice relevant:	Regarding whether you were involved in robbing the Quick Mart last night, do you intend to answer all of the questions truthfully?
N1.	Neutral:	Do you live in the United States?
C1.	Probable lie:	During the first 27 years of your life, did you ever take something that did not belong to you?
R1.	Relevant:	Did you rob the Quick Mart at Fourth and Main last night?
R2.	Relevant:	Did you use a gun to rob the Quick Mart at Fourth and Main last night?
C2.	Probable lie:	Prior to 1987, did you ever do something dishonest or illegal?
R3.	Relevant:	Did you take the money from the cash register at the Quick Mart at Fourth and Main last night?
R4.	Relevant:	Did you participate in any way in the robbery of the Quick Mart at Fourth and Main last night?
C3.	Probable lie:	Before age 27, did you ever lie to get out of trouble or to cause a problem for someone else?
N2.	Neutral:	Were you born in the month of November?

Table 1.5

Utah PLT multiple-issue question sequence.

This format is very flexible and can accommodate almost any set of issues in a case. Because of its flexibility, it is also very useful for single-issue tests. It has the advantage of bracketing each pair of relevant questions with surrounding comparison questions for purposes of numerical scoring (see below).

Just before beginning data collection, the subject is instructed not to move around or talk during the asking of questions, except to answer each question simply "Yes" or "No." Just before asking the questions, the examiner reminds the subject to answer every question truthfully. The examiner also instructs the subject that if anything else comes to mind during the test, it should be mentioned right after the test, not during the test. The questions are presented at a rate of one question every 25–35 s while physiological activity is recorded on the polygraph charts. The sequence is repeated at least three times. The neutral and comparison questions, and possibly the relevant questions, are rotated through their respective locations across repetitions of the question sequence in order to prevent the subject from producing anticipatory reactions caused by expecting the questions to be presented in a particular order. If the results are not conclusive after three repetitions, two additional repetitions may be administered.

After each presentation of the question sequence, the examiner asks the subject if there were any problems and discusses any concerns that the subject expressed. The examiner then reviews the relevant and probable-lie questions in order to ensure that the relevant questions are clear and straightforward and the comparison questions remain salient. If the subject makes an admission to a probable-lie question or provides additional information that changes the meaning of a relevant question, this is discussed and appropriate adjustments are made in the affected questions. Abrams (1999) and Matte (2000) claimed that the between-charts discussion and review of questions places undue emphasis on the comparison questions and increases the risk of a false negative error. However, Honts (1999) analyzed data from 19 studies that involved 1092 polygraph tests. The results of the Honts (1999) analysis clearly demonstrate that between-charts discussion, even when limited only to the comparison questions, *decreases* the risk of error (see additional discussion in Honts, 2000 and Honts *et al.*, 2000b). However, the subject should not be given any information about the physiological reactions observed to the specific questions nor provided with any indication of how the subject is doing on the test. Any specific information given during the test concerning the subject's reactions can affect the outcome and interfere with the integrity of the test.

It is critical that the polygraph examiner's demeanor and behavior be professional and objective. If the subject is suspicious of the examiner or feels that the examiner is not competent or is biased, the accuracy of the test may be compromised. Some examiners are psychologically insensitive and abusive, and they sometimes convey an impression of disbelief in the subject's version of the events or attempt to interrogate the subject prior to completion of the test. Such behaviors increase the risk of a false positive error and are inappropriate (an example is presented by Raskin, 1986, p.70 and see the discussion in Honts and Perry, 1992).

Interpretation of the results
Numerical evaluation
The outcome of the Utah PLT is numerically evaluated by comparing the relative strengths of physiological reactions to relevant and comparison questions. This analysis is performed using a method of numerical evaluation that was originally developed by Backster (see above) and modified by the US Government (USAMPS, 1970; Swinford, 1999). The Utah group further modified the scoring system on the basis of scientific research conducted at the University of Utah (for

a discussion of the basic approaches and differences in results obtained with these three systems, see Weaver, 1980, 1985, see also Honts *et al.*, 2000a for a direct comparison of the accuracy of the Utah and Department of Defense approaches). The Utah numerical evaluation is a systematic approach that utilizes only the information obtained from the polygraph charts. All other sources of information, such as verbal and non-verbal behavior and case information, are formally excluded from the decision-making process. As compared to the Backster and USAMPS/DoDPI systems, the criteria for assessing the strength of reaction were substantially reduced and refined on the basis of the principles of psychophysiology and extensive laboratory and field research. A detailed description of this scoring system is presented in Bell *et al.* (1999).

Numerical evaluation begins with an inspection of the polygraph charts to form an impression of their overall quality and the range of reactivity in the various physiological measures. Against this background, comparisons are then made of the relative strengths of reactions to the relevant and comparison questions. Starting with the first relevant question (R1), a score is assigned for each of the physiological parameters (electrodermal activity, blood pressure, peripheral vasomotor activity, and respiration). This score can range from –3 to +3 depending on the direction and magnitude of the observed difference in the reactions elicited by the relevant question and the comparison question.

For the single-issue sequence in Table 1.4, each relevant question is compared to its adjacent comparison question. For the multiple-issue sequence in Table 1.5, each relevant question is compared to the stronger reaction produced by one of the two bracketing comparison questions. If there is an artifact or distortion in the physiological recording for the comparison question, another comparison question is used for assigning that score. Occasionally, the subject answers "Yes" to a comparison question even though the reviewed answer was "No." Research has shown that using this comparison question in the scoring is a valid procedure (Honts *et al.*, 1992). The procedure of choosing the stronger reaction from the surrounding comparison questions has also been validated by field research (Honts, 1996; Raskin *et al.*, 1988).

If the observed reaction is stronger to the relevant question, a negative score is assigned. A positive score is assigned when the reaction is greater to the comparison question, and a zero is assigned if there is no real difference. The magnitude of scores can vary from 1 for a noticeable difference, to 2 for a strong difference, to 3 for a dramatic difference. Most assigned scores are 0 or 1. Scores of 2 are less common, and scores of 3 are unusual (Bell *et al.*, 1999). The examiner proceeds through the polygraph charts, independently assigning a score for each physiological parameter for each comparison of the responses to the relevant question and the appropriate comparison question. This is repeated for each relevant question on the chart and for each chart. The scores are then summed to provide a total score for the test, and the outcome is based on this total. If the total is –6 or lower, the outcome is deceptive; if the total is +6 or higher, the outcome is truthful; totals between –5 and +5 indicate an inconclusive outcome. These decision rules apply to tests that consist of three charts or five charts.

If the information obtained in the investigation indicates that the subject must answer all of the questions truthfully or all deceptively, the overall total for the test is used as the basis for the decision. For example, if the case information indicates that a single person robbed the Quick Mart, the subject is assumed to be deceptive or truthful to all of the questions and the total score is used for the decision. However, if it is possible for the subject to answer some relevant questions truthfully and others deceptively in the same test, more complex decision criteria are employed. If the total scores for the individual relevant questions are all in the same direction (all positive or all negative, ignoring totals of 0), then the overall total can be used as the outcome for all questions. If there are conflicts among the questions, with some question totals being positive and others negative, a different rule is used. Under the latter circumstance, total scores of at least –3 or +3 for a particular relevant question are required for a definite decision of deception or truthfulness, respectively. For example, the suspect in the Quick Mart robbery might have played one of several different roles, such as the gunman, the accomplice who took the money from the cash register, or the driver of the getaway car. Assume that the subject was the driver of the car and did not enter the store. When asked relevant questions about each of these possibilities, the subject would be truthful when denying being the gunman or taking the money (e.g., +4 and +5, respectively), but deceptive when denying robbing or being involved in the robbery (e.g., –3 and –6, respectively). The outcome of such a test would be evaluated separately for each of the three relevant questions, using cutoff scores of –3 and +3 for the totals on each of the three relevant questions.

Research has shown that there is no penalty or advantage to addressing multiple issues in a single question list (Barland et al., 1989). However, when subjects are truthful to some questions and deceptive to others, the accuracy rates for decisions on the individual questions is lower than for tests where the subject is either completely truthful or deceptive (Barland et al., 1989; Honts et al., 1988b; Raskin et al., 1988).

The reliability of the Utah system of numerical evaluation has been determined by having different raters independently interpret the same sets of polygraph charts. Correlations among the total numerical scores assigned by the original examiner and by blind raters tend to be very high. In laboratory studies that used mock crime paradigms and field polygraph methods (e.g., Kircher and Raskin, 1983, 1988; Podlesny and Raskin, 1978; Raskin and Hare,

1978; Rovner *et al.*, 1979), interrater reliabilities are typically in excess of 0.90. Similar results have been obtained in field studies (Honts, 1996; Raskin *et al.*, 1978; Raskin *et al.*, 1988). Numerical scoring by adequately trained and experienced interpreters produces extremely high reliability that compares favorably with any psychological test interpreted by humans.

Computer interpretations

In order to provide more powerful, objective, and totally reliable polygraph chart interpretation and decision making, computer methods were developed at the University of Utah (Kircher and Raskin, 1981, 1988). The computer methods were validated on data from confirmed polygraph examinations of criminal suspects (Raskin *et al.*, 1988), and they are based on extensive analyses of features extracted from physiological recordings obtained from guilty and innocent subjects. Discriminant functions were developed to yield optimal separation of the groups based on linear combinations of the physiological data. The discriminant scores for individual subjects are entered into Bayes' Theorem to calculate the probability (ranging from 0 to 1.0) that the obtained physiological data indicate that the subject was truthful.

Results obtained with the computer model are quite encouraging (Kircher and Raskin, 1988; Raskin *et al.*, 1988). The computer diagnoses were somewhat more accurate than blind interpretations by skilled numerical evaluators, although the field study showed that the original examiners were slightly more accurate than the computer model. Apparently, the original examiners used the case information and their interactions with the subjects to adjust their numerical scoring to be more accurate. However, in terms of interpretations based solely on the polygraph charts, the computer outperformed the human interpreters. The results of these studies indicate that computer evaluations are extremely useful. Kircher and Raskin provide a detailed discussion of computer evaluation in Chapter 11.

Evaluation of the Utah PLT

The Utah PLT is the first polygraph technique developed by psychologists who explicitly incorporated basic knowledge and principles from psychological science and psychophysiology into the pre-test interview, question structure, recording methods, and evaluation methods. Research has consistently shown it to have high reliability and validity (see the review in Raskin *et al.*, 1997 and the section on the general validity of the CQT below).

UTAH DIRECTED-LIE TEST

The directed-lie question has been proposed as a remedy for most of the problems inherent in the probable-lie comparison question (Fuse, 1982; Honts, 1994; Honts and Raskin, 1988; Horowitz *et al.*, 1997). The PLT can be difficult to administer and requires psychological sensitivity, sophistication, and skill on the part of the examiner in order to obtain an accurate outcome. Unfortunately, many polygraph examiners lack adequate training in psychological methods and do not understand the basic concepts and requirements of a standardized psychological test. These problems are exacerbated when the examiner formulates and introduces the comparison questions to the subject, because it is difficult to standardize the wording and discussion of the questions. A great deal depends on how the subject perceives and responds to the probable-lie questions when they are introduced and discussed during the pre-test interview.

The difficulties with probable-lie comparison questions are compounded by problems related to the characteristics of examinees. Some examinees are very anxious about the subject matter of the probable-lie questions, making it difficult for the examiner to establish effective comparison questions. These questions may be personally intrusive and offensive to some subjects. For other subjects, they may encompass prior criminal behavior of a serious nature that poses problems for the subjects, some of whom may refuse to answer the questions. If a person is administered more than one test or tested on multiple occasions, it may become difficult to formulate new probable-lie questions that continue to be effective for the subject. It is difficult to explain the functions of probable-lie questions and their role in interpreting the outcome of the test to those who use the results of polygraph tests (investigators, lawyers, judges, and juries) and to laypersons. They may not understand the rationale of the PLT and may interpret strong physiological reactions to probable-lie questions as indicating that the subject is dishonest and guilty. For all of these reasons, the directed-lie test (DLT) was developed.

Test structure and administration

A common directed-lie question is "Before age 27, did you ever tell even one lie?" A typical directed lie question sequence is shown in Table 1.6. The subject is instructed to answer "No" to the directed-lie questions, and it is made clear that anyone who gives a negative answer to those questions would be lying.

Table 1.6

Utah DLT question sequence.

I.	Introductory:	You understand that I will ask only the questions we have discussed?
SR.	Sacrifice relevant:	Regarding whether you were involved in robbing the Quick Mart last night, do you intend to answer all of the questions truthfully?
N1.	Neutral:	Do you live in the United States?
C1.	Directed lie:	During the first 27 years of your life, did you ever tell even one lie?
R1.	Relevant:	Did you rob the Quick Mart at Fourth and Main last night?
R2.	Relevant	Did you use a gun to rob the Quick Mart at Fourth and Main last night?
C2.	Directed lie:	Prior to 1987, did you ever break even one rule or regulation?
R3.	Relevant:	Did you take the money from the cash register at the Quick Mart at Fourth and Main last night?
R4.	Relevant:	Did you participate in any way in the robbery of the Quick Mart at Fourth and Main last night?
C3.	Directed lie:	Before age 27, did you ever make even one mistake?
N2.	Neutral:	Were you born in the month of November?

The interview in a directed-lie test is similar to that described above for the PLT up to the end of the subject's description of the incident. At that point the subject is attached to the instrument, the psychophysiology of deception is described, and the number test is conducted. Subjects are told that it is critical that they respond appropriately when they lie or they will not be a suitable subject for testing. As in the PLT, the subjects are told that they did respond appropriately on the stimulation tests and that they are suitable subjects for a detection of deception test. The relevant questions are then reviewed with the subject. The review of the relevant questions is followed by the introduction of the directed-lie questions. The purpose of the directed-lie questions is explained to the subject as follows:

On this test I need to ask you some questions to which I want you to lie. Just as on the number test, I need to have questions to which you and I both know you are lying and some that you and I know you are answering truthfully. That way, I can see the difference in your reactions when you lie and when you tell the truth, and I will be able to see if your reactions on the questions about the robbery are the same or different compared to the questions I know you answered with a lie. Therefore, I am going to ask you, "During the first 27 years of your life, did you ever tell even one lie?" I want you to lie to that question. Also, I want you to think of a particular time when you did lie in the past, and I want you to have that in mind when you answer this question on the test. Do you have a particular instance in mind? . . . All right, I do not want you to tell me what it is. When I ask you that question on the test, I want you to lie by answering "No." When you answer, I want you to think about the time when you lied. That way, you and I will be sure that you are lying when you answer that question on the test, and I can make sure that you react appropriately and that you continue to be a suitable subject.

The rationale for using directed-lie questions is similar to the rationale for probable-lie questions. It is assumed that the subject's concern will be focused on the questions that pose the greatest risk of failing the test. For guilty subjects, the focus will be on the relevant questions that are answered deceptively, especially because the examiner has stated that the number test clearly demonstrated how the examinee reacts when lying. Thus, guilty subjects should show stronger reactions to the relevant questions. However, subjects who are truthful in response to the relevant questions will be most concerned about their reactions to the directed-lie questions. They will focus on showing that they are suitable subjects and on clearly demonstrating that their reactions when lying are different from when they are truthful and are different from their reactions to the relevant questions. This focus of concern should enhance the reactions of truthful subjects to the directed-lie questions, making them stronger than reactions to the relevant questions.

The DLT is administered and interpreted in the same way as the probable-lie comparison question test, except for the introduction of the directed-lie questions and the discussion between charts. Just prior to asking the questions, the examiner says to the subject, "Be sure that you answer every question truthfully, except those questions to which I want you to lie. Be sure that you lie to them and think about the specific incident in your past when you did lie." Following the presentation of the questions, the examiner discusses any problems the subject may raise and asks if the subject was aware that the answers to the directed-lie questions were actually lies.

The substitution of directed-lie for probable-lie questions makes it easier to administer the test and allows greater standardization of the pre-test interview. Except for adjustment in the year and the subject's age, the same directed lies can be used for any type of crime and every subject. In addition, they are not intrusive, do not embarrass the subject, do not elicit admissions that require rewording of the questions, are readily answered by all subjects, and are less likely to cause the type of problems encountered when probable-lie comparison questions encompass a past criminal act of serious magnitude. Directed lies require less psychological manipulation of the subject and less examiner skill and sophistication. From the standpoint of standardization and ease of administration, directed-lie questions are clearly preferable to probable-lie comparison questions.

Validity of the directed-lie test

Since the DLT is relatively new, there are fewer studies of its validity. As with the PLT, both a laboratory (Department of Defense Polygraph Institute (DODPI) Research Staff, 1997, 1998; Horowitz *et al.*, 1997; Reed, 1994) and one field validity study (Honts and Raskin, 1988) have been conducted. The Horowitz *et al.* (1997) study used a mock crime that closely approximated the field situation, similar to those described in the section on Laboratory Studies that follows. It compared the effectiveness of the DLT with the PLT and RIT. Different groups received one of two types of directed lies, personally relevant directed lies using the procedures previously described or simple directed lies to three of the neutral questions that were used in the RIT. The results of the Horowitz et al. (1997) study indicate that compared to the other three conditions, the personal DLT produced the highest accuracy, except for the RIT with guilty subjects. The outcomes for the four types of tests are presented in Table 1.7.

Experimental groups	Test outcomes (%)			
	Correct	Wrong	Inconclusive	% correct decisions
Guilty				
Relevant–irrelevant	100	0	0	100
Trivial directed lie	53	20	27	73
Personal directed lie	73	14	13	84
Probable lie comparison	53	20	27	73
Innocent				
Relevant–irrelevant	20	73	7	22
Trivial directed lie	67	13	20	84
Personal directed lie	87	13	0	87
Probable lie comparison	80	13	7	86

Table 1.7

Test outcomes on the Horowitz et al. (1997) study.

$n = 15$ for each of the experimental groups.
The percentage of correct decisions was calculated by excluding inconclusive outcomes.

Among all question structures, the personal directed lie produced the highest number of correct decisions on innocent subjects and among the three tests that employed comparison questions, it produced the highest number of correct decisions on guilty subjects.

The U.S. Department of Defense has conducted three sets of studies concerning the validity of the directed-lie comparison question. Barland (1981) examined the validity of the Military Intelligence version of the DLT in a mock screening setting with 26 truthful subjects and 30 subjects who attempted deception. All subjects were tested with the directed-lie comparison; no other techniques were examined. Excluding inconclusive outcomes, Barland's evaluators correctly classified 79% of the subjects. Although this might be considered a modest performance in comparison to that obtained in the University of Utah studies, it must be remembered that Barland's (1981) study was in a screening setting. When compared with other mock-screening studies, which have often produced near chance performance with probable lie tests (e.g., Barland *et al.*, 1989; Honts, 1992), the performance of the directed-lie comparison in Barland (1981) was actually quite strong.

The other two sets of studies on the DLT concern a new test, the test of espionage and sabotage (TES) developed by DODPI for use in national security screening tests. Reed (1994; also published as DODPI Research Staff 1997) reported three laboratory mock screening studies. Following a series of studies that indicated that the national security screening tests of the time were making an unacceptably high number of false negative errors (Barland *et al.*, 1989; Honts, 1991, 1992, 1994) the DODPI attempted to develop a more accurate screening test. It should be noted that the primary concern in conducting national security screening tests is a desire not to make false negative errors. Following a series of studies that are not publicly available, Reed (1994) described the product of the DODPI's efforts. In the first study reported by Reed (1994), the TES test format with only directed-lie comparison questions was tested against two versions of the Counterintelligence Scope Polygraph (CSP) test. One version of the CSP used probable-lie comparison questions while the other used directed-lie comparison questions. The TES outperformed both of the CSP formats in terms of correctly identifying guilty subjects. The CSP with directed-lie comparisons was slightly, but not significantly, better at identifying guilty subjects than was the CSP with probable-lie comparisons. A second study was reported that produced even higher accuracy for the TES, a directed-lie comparison test format. Little information is provided about the third study, but it also appears to show considerable accuracy for the directed-lie TES.

DODPI Research Staff (1998) reported a mock espionage/sabotage study that involved 82 subjects. All subjects were tested with the TES. Excluding one inconclusive outcome, the examiners correctly identified 98% of the innocent subjects and 83.3% of the guilty subjects. This study also indicates that the directed-lie TES is extremely successful in discriminating between innocent and guilty subjects.

Abrams (1991) reported the only other laboratory study of the directed lie. Unfortunately that study was so poorly designed and so methodologically flawed that the data are meaningless. Abrams and Matte have become outspoken critics of the DLT, but their criticisms have consistently been shown to be without merit and essentially all of their attacks are baseless. Interested readers are referred to the research and commentary by Honts and his colleagues (Honts, 1999, 2000; Honts and Gordon, 1998; Honts *et al.*, 2000b).

To date, Honts and Raskin (1988) have reported the only field study of the DLT. They conducted polygraph tests of criminal suspects over a 4-year period and obtained 25 confirmed tests in which one personal directed lie was included along with probable-lie comparison questions. Each of the investigators then performed blind interpretations of the charts obtained by the other investigator, scoring them with and without the use of the directed-lie question. The results of the Honts and Raskin study indicated that inclusion of the directed-lie question in the numerical evaluation of the charts had a noticeable effect on the confirmed innocent suspects, reducing the false positive rate from 20% to 0%. For the confirmed guilty suspects, it had the slight effect of changing one inconclusive outcome to a false negative. The effects of the directed-lie question on the numerical scores were more dramatic. Inclusion of the directed-lie comparisons almost doubled the size of the total numerical scores for the confirmed innocent suspects, raising the mean score from +4.7 to +9.0. It had a lesser effect on the scores of the confirmed guilty suspects, lowering them from −13.8 to −11.5. Thus, the directed-lie question had the effect of raising the mean score for innocent suspects from the inconclusive range into the definite truthful area, while leaving the mean score for guilty suspects clearly in the deceptive area. The main impact of the directed-lie question was a reduction in false positive errors.

The results from the laboratory and the field are consistent with the proposition that the DLT represents a substantial advance over the PLT. It is more standardized in its structure; it is easier to administer; it requires less manipulation of the subject and creates fewer problems for the subject; it is more readily explained to laypersons, lawyers, judges, and juries. Most importantly, it reduces the number of errors associated with the PLT.

OVERALL VALIDITY OF COMPARISON QUESTION TESTS

The validity of comparison question polygraph tests is the subject of intense debate among scientists (Iacono and Lykken, 1997; Raskin *et al.*, 1997a). Although the majority of psychophysiologists have expressed generally positive attitudes concerning the usefulness of polygraph tests for assessment of credibility (Amato and Honts, 1994; Gallup, 1984), the American Psychological Association expressed serious concerns about their scientific basis and some of their specific applications (see Raskin, 1986: p 73). A detailed examination of the scientific literature is necessary to provide answers to this complex empirical question. In the last 30 years, there has been a great deal of research, development, and experience with various techniques that employ physiological measures for assessing credibility with regard to specific acts, events, or knowledge (Raskin *et al.*, 1997a). Interestingly, the first laboratory study of the comparison question technique was conducted less than 30 years ago (Barland and Raskin, 1972), although the technique has been in widespread use since it was introduced more than 50 years ago by Reid (1947).

The debate about the accuracy of comparison question tests for investigative and forensic purposes centers on two general sources of data from which the accuracy of such tests may be estimated. Data may be obtained either from laboratory simulations of criminal situations (mock crime studies) or studies of actual cases that include testing of one or more suspects in a criminal investigation. Each type of study has advantages and disadvantages, and both types are needed to provide an overall picture of test accuracy.

LABORATORY STUDIES

Laboratory research has traditionally been an attractive alternative because the scientist can control the environment. Moreover, with regard to credibility assessment studies, by randomly assigning subjects to conditions, the scientist can know with certainty who is telling the truth and who is lying. Laboratory research on credibility assessment has typically made subjects deceivers by having them commit a mock crime (e.g., "steal" a watch from an office), and then instructing them to lie about it during a subsequent test. From a scientific viewpoint, random assignment to conditions is highly desirable because it controls for the influence of extraneous variables that might confound the results of the experiment (Cook and Campbell, 1979). The most accepted type of laboratory study realistically simulates a crime in which some subjects commit an overt transaction, such as a theft (Raskin, 1982). While the guilty subjects enact a realistic crime, the innocent subjects are merely told about the nature of the crime and do not enact it. All subjects are motivated to produce a truthful outcome, usually by the offer of a cash bonus for passing the test. For example, one such study used prison inmates who were offered a bonus equal to one month's wages if they could produce a truthful outcome (Raskin and Hare, 1978).

The advantages of careful laboratory simulations include total control over the issues that are investigated and the types of tests that are used, consistency in test administration and interpretation, specification of the subject populations that are studied, control over the skill and training of the examiners, and absolute verification of the accuracy of test results. Carefully designed and conducted studies that closely approximate the methods and conditions characteristic of high-quality practice by polygraph professionals and that use subjects similar to the target population, such as convicted felons or a cross-section of the general community, provide the most generalizable results (Kircher *et al.*, 1988).

Laboratory research in general, and credibility assessment in particular, can be criticized for a lack of realism. This lack of realism may limit the ability of the scientist to apply the results of the laboratory to real-world settings. However, a recent study reported by Anderson *et al.* (1999) examined a broad range of laboratory-based psychological research. They concluded that "Correspondence between lab- and field-based effect sizes of conceptually similar independent and dependent variables was considerable. In brief, the psychological laboratory has generally produced truths, rather than trivialities" (p. 3). Our position with regard to the high-quality studies of the CQT is similar. We believe that these studies produce important information about the validity of such tests (see Raskin *et al.*, 1989) and not trivial information as some of the critics have claimed (e.g., Iacono and Lykken, 1997).

A Committee of Concerned Social Scientists filed a brief for amicus curiae (Honts and Peterson, 1997) with the Supreme Court of the United States in the case of *United States v. Scheffer 1998*. They found eight high-quality laboratory studies of the CQT. The results of those laboratory studies are illustrated in Table 1.8. The high-quality laboratory studies indicate that the CQT is a very accurate discriminator of truth tellers and deceivers. Over all of these studies, the CQT correctly classified about 91% of the subjects and produced approximately equal numbers of false positive and false negative errors.

Study	Guilty				Innocent			
	n	% correct	% wrong	% inc.	n	% correct	% wrong	% inc.
Driscoll *et al.* (1987)[b]	20	90	0	10	20	90	0	10
Ginton *et al.* (1982)	2	100	0	0	13	85	15	0
Honts *et al.* (1994)[a]	20	70	20	10	20	75	10	15
Horowitz *et al.* (1997)[b]	15	53	20	27	15	80	13	7
Kircher and Raskin (1988)	50	88	6	6	50	86	6	8
Podlesny and Raskin (1978)	20	70	15	15	20	90	5	5
Podlesny and Truslow (1993)	72	69	13	18	24	75	4	21
Raskin and Hare (1978)	24	88	0	12	24	88	8	4
Rovner *et al.* (1979)[a]	24	88	0	12	24	88	8	4
Means	247	80	8	12	210	84	8	8
Precent decisions		90	10			92	8	

a Countermeasure subjects excluded.
b Traditional control question subjects only.

Table 1.8

The results of high-quality laboratory studies of the control question test.

■ The credibility of the subject must be determined by information that is independent of the specific test. Confessions substantiated by physical evidence are presently the best criterion available.

Unfortunately, there are few field studies from which we can estimate the accuracy of properly conducted comparison question tests. In 1983, the Office of Technology Assessment of the United States Congress selected 10 field studies that they felt had at least some degree of scientific merit. The overall accuracy of the polygraph decisions was 90% on criterion-guilty suspects and 80% on criterion-innocent suspects. In spite of the inclusion of many studies with serious methodological problems, accuracy in field cases was higher than is claimed by some of the most vocal critics (Lykken, 1997).

A more recent survey of the available field studies was performed by the Committee of Concerned Social Scientists (Honts and Peterson, 1997). They were able to find four field studies that met the criteria for meaningful field studies of psychophysiological credibility assessment tests (see above). The results of the independent evaluations for those studies are illustrated in Table 1.9. Overall, the independent evaluations of the field studies produced results that are quite similar to the results of the high-quality laboratory studies. The average accuracy of field decisions for the CQT was 90.5%. However, with the field studies nearly all of the errors made by the CQT were false positive errors.

Table 1.9

The accuracy of independent evaluations in high-quality field studies.

Study	Guilty				Innocent			
	n	% correct	% wrong	% inc.	*n*	% correct	% wrong	% inc.
Honts (1996)[a]	7	100	0	0	6	83	0	17
Honts and Raskin (1988)[b]	12	92	0	8	13	62	15	23
Patrick and Iacono (1991)[c]	52	92	2	6	37	30	24	46
Raskin *et al.* (1989)[d]	37	73	0	27	26	61	8	31
Means	108	89	1	10	82	59	12	29
Precent decisions		98	2			75	25	

a Subgroup of subjects confirmed by confession and evidence.
b Decision based only on comparisons to traditional comparison questions.
c Results from mean blind rescoring of the cases "verified with maximum certainty" (p. 235).
d These results are from an independent evaluation of the "Pure verification" cases.

Although the high-quality field studies indicate a high accuracy rate for the CQT, all of the data represented in Table 1.9 were derived from independent evaluations of the physiological data. This is a desirable practice from a scientific viewpoint, because it eliminates possible contamination (e.g., knowledge of the case facts, and the overt behaviors of the subject during the examination) that might be included in the decisions of the original examiners. However, independent evaluators rarely testify in legal proceedings, nor do they make decisions in most applied settings. It is usually the original examiner who makes the decision on how to proceed in an actual case and provides court testimony. Thus, accuracy rates based on the decisions of independent evaluators may not be the true figure of merit for legal proceedings and most applications. The Committee of Concerned Social Scientists summarized the data from the original examiners in the studies reported in Table 1.9, and for two additional studies that are often cited by critics of the CQT. The data for the original examiners are presented in Table 1.10. These data clearly indicate that the original examiners were even more accurate than the independent evaluators.

Study	Innocent	Guilty
Horvath (1977)	100	100
Honts and Raskin (1988)	100	92
Kleinmuntz and Szucko (1984)	100	100
Raskin et al. (1988)[a]	96	95
Patrick and Iacono (1991)	90	100
Honts (1996)[b]	100	94
Means	**98**	**97**

Table 1.10

Per cent correct decisions by original examiners in field cases.

a Cases where all questions were confirmed.
b Includes all cases with some confirmation.

The scientific data concerning the validity of the polygraph can be summarized as indicating that high-quality scientific research from the laboratory and the field converge on the conclusion that a properly conducted CQT is a highly accurate discriminator of truth tellers and deceivers. The results converge on an accuracy estimate that exceeds 90%. Moreover, original examiners, who are most likely to offer testimony, produce even higher accuracy. There may be a tendency for the CQT to produce more false positive than false negative errors, but this trend in the current literature is not particularly strong. Moreover, no tendency toward false positive errors is seen in the decisions of the original examiners. If there is a tendency for the polygraph to produce more false positive than false negative outcomes, then triers of fact should weight negative outcomes (passed polygraphs) more heavily than positive outcomes (failed polygraphs). The scientific validity of a properly administered polygraph examination in a real-life case compares favorably with other forms of scientific evidence, such as X-ray films, electrocardiograms, fiber analysis, ballistics comparison tests, and blood analysis. Polygraph evidence is far more reliable than some other types of expert testimony (e.g., psychiatric and psychological opinions as to sanity, diminished capacity, dangerousness and many of the post-traumatic stress/recovered memory syndromes; see the discussion in Honts and Perry (1992) and in Honts and Quick (1995).

APPLIED ISSUES

As the uses of polygraph techniques have grown in criminal investigation and evidence, there is increasing concern about factors that may adversely affect their accuracy and their uses in administrative and judicial proceedings (Raskin, 1986). Critics have pointed to potential problems of physical and mental countermeasures, such as drugs, physical maneuvers, and mental states, as well as to personality characteristics such as psychopathy or sociopathy, and the testing of victims (Orne, 1983). Some have raised questions about the value of tests conducted confidentially by defense counsel (Orne, 1975), and the possibly prejudicial effect of polygraph evidence on jurors (Abbell, 1977). This section discusses the scientific and practical aspects of some of these questions (for a detailed discussion of countermeasures, see Chapter 9).

PERSONALITY FACTORS

Mental status and personality are important considerations in deciding whether a person is a suitable subject for a polygraph examination. The small amount of available evidence indicates that psychotic and other seriously disturbed individuals present higher risks of error (see Abrams, 1977). Fortunately, the problems of concern are so extreme that most examiners should be able to identify them during the pre-test interview. Other types of personality factors, such as psychopathy, may not be as apparent.

It is commonly believed that poorly socialized individuals and psychopaths can defeat polygraph tests because they are adept at lying and are deficient in moral development and social conscience (Waid and Orne, 1982). Waid *et al.* (1979) reported that three college students who scored lower in socialization than other college students were undetected in deception on a single presentation of a comparison question sequence. They concluded that poorly socialized individuals can beat the test; however, their study had major methodological deficiencies that rendered the results meaningless (Honts, *et al.*, 1985; Raskin, 1986).

Careful laboratory and field research has clearly demonstrated that poor socialization and psychopathy do not reduce the accuracy of comparison question tests. These studies have been conducted with college students and volunteers from the general community (Honts *et al.*, 1985), convicted felons and clinically diagnosed psychopaths (Patrick and Iacono, 1986; Raskin and Hare, 1978), and psychopathic criminal suspects who were given polygraph tests in actual investigations (Barland and Raskin, 1975). Other investigators have produced similar results with concealed knowledge and comparison question tests (see Office of Technology Assessment, 1983). The extensive scientific literature demonstrates that polygraph techniques are highly effective in detecting deception in poorly socialized and psychopathic individuals, but highly socialized individuals and even psychopaths may be subject to false positive errors (Honts *et al.*, 1985; Patrick and Iacono, 1986).

CONFIDENTIAL TESTS FOR DEFENSE ATTORNEYS

A major challenge to the validity of polygraph evidence offered by the defense in criminal cases is known as the "friendly polygrapher" hypothesis (Orne, 1975: p. 114). Orne proposed that a guilty criminal defendant or accused who takes a polygraph test is more likely to pass the test if it is confidential and requested by the defense attorney than if the subject is informed that adverse as well as favorable results will be disclosed to the prosecution. Orne's argument assumes that under the confidential or privileged situation, the guilty subject has little at stake and little to fear. Therefore, the guilty subject will be more confident, the examiner will be more supportive, and the results are more likely to be favorable. Orne based this hypothesis on the results of a weak laboratory study with college students who were administered card tests in an unrealistic setting (Gustafson and Orne, 1965).

The principles and procedures of comparison question polygraph tests argue against the friendly polygrapher notion (Honts, 1997; Raskin, 1986). First, the advisement of rights at the outset of the examination warns the subject that the results may be used as adverse evidence in court. In addition, the subject has a great deal at stake in the outcome. A deceptive result precludes the opportunity to use the polygraph to obtain a dismissal of the case or an acquittal at trial, as well as increased legal costs and a fear of disruption of the subject's relationship with the defense attorney. In order to pass a comparison question test, the subject must show larger reactions to the comparison questions, and the friendly polygrapher hypothesis offers no explanation of how reduced concern can result in larger reactions to the comparison than to the relevant questions. One study (Timm, 1982) showed no effects of increased confidence in beating the test, even when subjects were given a drug (placebo) that they were told would help them to beat the test and a number test that indicated that their lie was not detected.

Beyond the logical failings of the friendly polygrapher notion, none of the available data support Orne's supposition. Laboratory studies where there is little at stake routinely produce detection rates of in excess of 90% (See Table 1.8, above). If Orne's hypothesis were correct, one would expect laboratory studies of the CQT to produce relatively more false negative than false positive errors. This is clearly not supported by the data. Honts (1997) reviewed 20 laboratory studies of the CQT with a total of 567 guilty subjects and 490 innocent subjects. The false negative rate was 12% and the false positive rate was 16%. This outcome is opposite to the prediction generated by the friendly examiner hypothesis. Notably, 6 of the 20 laboratory studies examined in Honts (1997) reported no errors with guilty subjects, despite a lack of fear of any negative sanctions associated with failing the test.

Similarly, data from actual cases do not support the friendly polygrapher notion. There are two published sets of data from tests of criminal suspects that also contradict the friendly examiner hypothesis. Raskin (1986) presented complete data from 12 years of his confidential CQT examinations for defense attorneys and non-confidential tests for law enforcement, courts, and stipulated situations. He reported that 58% of suspects who were informed that the results would be provided to the prosecution passed their tests, but only 34% of those who took confidential defense tests were able to pass. In addition, the numerical scores were significantly more negative (in the deceptive direction) for confidential tests compared to the more positive scores (in the truthful direction) for non-confidential tests. Honts (1997) presented a similar complete set of data from 14 years of confidential and non-confidential examinations. He reported that 44% of the confidential tests were passed, while 70% of the non-confidential tests were passed. These recent data are the opposite of the effects predicted by the friendly examiner hypothesis. The foregoing analysis and these data clearly demonstrate that the friendly examiner hypothesis fails on all counts. It is illogical, unsupported by laboratory studies, and is contradicted by data from actual field cases.

TESTING VICTIMS

Suspects and defendants are not the only subjects of polygraph examinations. In some jurisdictions for some types of cases (e.g., suspicious robberies, questionable sexual assaults), the complaining witness may be asked to take a polygraph examination to demonstrate the veracity of the allegations. Because there is trauma associated with such events, actual victims are more likely than other suspects to show reactions to the relevant questions when they answer truthfully. The problem is compounded by the anger and indignation experienced by many victims who are asked to prove that they really were assaulted.

In a field study of comparison question polygraph examinations conducted by a law enforcement agency (Horvath, 1977), all but one of the false positive errors occurred on victims of sexual or physical assault or robbery (G. H. Barland, personal communication, September 18, 1982). Because of these problems, the American Psychological Association has raised concerns about administering polygraph tests to victims of crimes (Mervis, 1986). Such applications should be approached with great caution and only when there is a strong basis for suspicion. The alleged perpetrator is usually a more suitable and appropriate subject for a polygraph test.

IMPACTS ON JURORS

Opponents of polygraph evidence have argued that it should not be admitted at trial because it will have an undue influence on the jury owing to its scientific aura (Abbell, 1977). The scientific literature and experience with the use of polygraph evidence in court argue against such a view. A number of studies have been conducted on the topic of the impact of polygraph testimony on juries (Brekke *et al.*, 1991; Carlson *et al.*, 1977; Cavoukian and Heslegrave, 1979; Markwart and Lynch, 1979; Meyers and Arbuthnot, 1997). Research has been conducted both as experimental work with mock juries and by conducting post-trial interviews with jury members who had been presented with polygraph testimony. This literature is consistent in showing that juries are not inclined to give undue weight to polygraph evidence. The research provides strong evidence that juries are capable of weighing and evaluating all evidence. Moreover, they are also capable of rendering verdicts that may be inconsistent with polygraph results. In no case did research suggest that polygraph testimony strongly or overwhelmingly affected the jury decision-making process.

Typical of the research on jury impact is the study done by Cavoukian and Heslegrave (1979). They reported two experiments where cases were presented to mock juries either with or without polygraph evidence. Their mock jurors were asked to give ratings of their perceptions of the likelihood of the defendant's guilt and they were asked to render verdicts. In both experiments, in the absence of polygraph evidence, subjects tended to rate the defendant near the middle (uncertain) portion of the rating scale. This indicates that the evidence was relatively equivocal, the very type of case where polygraph evidence is likely to be offered. The addition of evidence that the defendant had passed a polygraph did shift subjects' ratings in the not guilty direction, but the effect was relatively small, shifting from a mean rating of approximately 3 to a mean rating of approximately 4 (7-point scale) in one experiment and from a mean rating of about 5 to a mean rating of about 6 (9-point scale) in the other experiment. Polygraph evidence had a significant effect on verdicts in one experiment, but polygraph testimony did not have a significant effect on verdicts in a second study. In addition, all effects of polygraph testimony were eliminated by the introduction of negative testimony by an opposing witness who testified that polygraph tests were only 80% accurate and that the results of polygraph tests should be viewed with skepticism. Cavoukian and Heslegrave concluded that concerns about blind acceptance and overwhelming impact of polygraph tests are unjustified.

Research conducted by Honts and his colleagues replicated the findings of the research described above (Devitt *et al.*, 1993; Honts and Devitt, 1992; Honts *et al.*, 1993; Vondergeest *et al.*, 1993). In the context of mock trials, they contrasted polygraph testimony with testimony concerning identification based on a blood test. Consistently, they found that jurors were more skeptical of polygraph testimony than they were of blood-test testimony, even when the experts reported them to be of the same level of accuracy. There were no indications in any of the studies that polygraph evidence overwhelmed jurors or that they were unable to use and value evidence that ran contrary to the polygraph outcome.

It seems reasonable to conclude that no compelling data or arguments support the proposition that polygraph evidence should be treated differently than any other type of scientific evidence presented through the testimony of an expert. It should be treated just as other types of expert testimony, such as ballistics, blood tests, eyewitness evidence, or questioned documents. Many of these are similar in terms of their "scientific aura" and they often have greater error rates (see Peterson *et al.*, 1978; Widacki and Horvath, 1978).

SUMMARY AND CONCLUSIONS

CQT polygraph techniques are complex and controversial methods that are extensively employed in investigations and administrative and evidentiary proceedings. The voluminous scientific literature indicates that they can be highly accurate when properly employed in appropriate circumstances, but they are also subject to abuse and misinterpretation. There are also many myths concerning their accuracy and effectiveness and the ways in which they are employed. This chapter has attempted to describe the various methods, along with their strengths and weaknesses, and the scientific evidence concerning their validity. Careful consideration of these features, combined with thorough analysis of each particular case in which they have been or might be applied, should result in judicious decisions about when and how the CQT should be used.

ACKNOWLEDGMENT

A great deal of the research described in this chapter was conducted with the assistance and collaboration of John C. Kircher and Steven W. Horowitz, whose help is gratefully acknowledged.

REFERENCES

Abbell, M. (1977) Polygraph evidence: The case against admissibility in federal criminal trials. *American Criminal Law Review,* 15, 29–62.

Abrams, S. (1977) *A Polygraph Handbook for Attorneys.* Lexington, MA: Lexington Books.

Abrams, S. (1991) The directed lie control question. *Polygraph*, 20, 26–31.

Abrams, S. (1999) A response to Honts on the issue of the discussion of questions between charts. *Polygraph,* 28, 223–229.

Amato, S. L. and Honts, C. R. (1994) What do psychophysiologists think about polygraph tests? A survey of the membership of SPR. *Psychophysiology*, 31, S22 (Abstract).

Anderson, C. A., Lindsay, J. J. and Bushman, B. J. (1999) Research in the psychological laboratory: Truth or triviality? *Current Directions in Psychological Science*, 8, 3–9.

Backster, C. (1963) The Backster chart reliability rating method. *Law and Order*, 1, 63–64.

Backster, C. (1973) *Polygraph Examiner's Training Manual.* New York, NY: Backster School of Lie Detection.

Barland, G. H. (1981) *A Validity and Reliability Study of Counterintelligence Screening Tests.* Unpublished manuscript, Security Support Battalion, 902nd Military Intelligence Group, Fort George G. Meade, Maryland.

Barland, G. H. and Raskin, D. C. (1972) An experimental study of field techniques in "lie detection". *Psychophysiology,* 9, 275.

Barland. G. H. and Raskin, D. C. (1973) Detection of deception. In: W. F. Prokasy and D. C. Raskin (eds) *Electrodermal Activity in Psychological Research*, (pp. 417–477). New York: Academic Press.

Barland, G. H. and Raskin, D. C. (1975) Psychopathy and detection of deception in criminal suspects. *Psychophysiology,* 12, 224.

Barland, G. H., Honts, C. R.,and Barger, S. D. (1989) *Studies of the Accuracy of Security Screening Polygraph Examinations*. Department of Defense Polygraph Institute, Fort McClellan, Alabama. Available online: http://truth.boisestate.edu/raredocuments/bhb.html

Bell, B. G., Raskin, D. C., Honts, C. R. and Kircher, J. C. (1999) The Utah numerical scoring system. *Polygraph,* 28, 1–9.

Ben-Shakhar, G. and Furedy, J. J. (1990) *Theories and Applications in the Detection of Deception.* New York: Springer-Verlag.

Bersh, P. L (1969) A validation study of polygraph examiner judgments. *Journal of Applied Psychology,* 53, 399–403.

Bradley, M. T. and Janisse, M. P. (1981) Accuracy demonstrations, threat, and the detection of deception: Cardiovascular, electrodermal, and pupillary measures. *Psychophysiology,* 18, 307–315.

Brekke, N. J., Enko, P. J., Clavet, G. and Seelau, E. (1991) The impact of nonadversarial versus adversarial expert testimony. *Law and Human Behavior,* 15, 451–475.

Carlson, S. C., Passano M. S. and Jannunzzo, J. A. (1977) The effect of lie detector evidence on jury deliberations: An empirical study. *Journal of Police Science and Administration,* 5, 148–154.

Cavoukian, A. and Heslegrave, R. J. (1979) The admissibility of polygraph evidence in court: Some empirical findings. *Law and Human Behavior,* 4, 117–131.

Cook, T. D. and Campbell, D. T. (1979) *Quasi-experimentation: Design and Analysis Issues for Field Settings.* Boston: Houghton Mifflin.

Department of Defense Polygraph Institute Research Division Staff (1997) A comparison of psychophysiological detection of deception accuracy rates obtained using the Counter-intelligence Scope Polygraph (CSP) and the Test for Espionage and Sabotage (TES) question formats. *Polygraph,* 26, 79–106.

Department of Defense Polygraph Institute Research Division Staff (1998) Psychophysiological detection of deception accuracy rates obtained using the Test for Espionage and Sabotage (TES). *Polygraph,* 27, 68–73.

Devitt, M. K., Honts, C. R. and Gillund, B. (1993) *Stealing Thunder Does Not Ameliorate the Effects of the Hired Gun Cross-examination Tactic.* Paper presented at the annual meeting of the American Association for Applied and Preventive Psychology, Chicago, June, 1993.

Driscoll, L. N., Honts, C. R. and Jones D. (1987) The validity of the positive control physiological detection of deception technique. *Journal of Police Science and Administration,* 15, 46–50.

Elaad, E. and Kleiner, M. (1986) The stimulation test in polygraph field examinations: A case study. *Journal of Police Science and Administration,* 14, 328–333.

Furedy, J. J. and Heslegrave, R. J. (1991) The forensic use of the polygraph: A psychophysiological analysis of current trends and future prospects. In: P. K. Ackles, J. R. Jennings
and M. G. H. Coles (eds) *Advances in Psychophysiology,* Vol. 4, pp. 157–189. Greenwich,
CT: Jessica Kingsley Publishers.

Fuse, L. S. (1982) *Directed Lie Control Testing Technique.* Unpublished manuscript.

The Gallup Organization (1984) Survey of the members of the Society for Psychophysiological Research concerning their opinions of polygraph test interpretations. *Polygraph,* 12,
153–165.

Gregory, R. J. (1992) *Psychological testing: History, Principles, and Applications.* Boston:
Allyn and Bacon.

Ginton, A., Netzer, D., Elaad, E. and Ben-Shakhar, G. (1982) A method for evaluating the use
of the polygraph in a real-life situation. *Journal of Applied Psychology*, 67, 131–137.

Gustafson, L. A. and Orne, M. T. (1965) Effects of perceived role and role success on the
detection of deception. *Journal of Applied Psychology,* 49, 412–417.

Honts, C. R. (1991) The emperor's new clothes: Application of polygraph tests in the
American workplace. *Forensic Reports,* 4, 91–116.

Honts, C. R. (1992) Counterintelligence scope polygraph (CSP) test found to be a poor discriminator. *Forensic Reports,* 5, 215–218.

Honts, C. R. (1994) The psychophysiological detection of deception. *Current Directions in
Psychological Science,* 3, 77–82.

Honts, C. R. (1996) Criterion development and validity of the control question test in field
application. *The Journal of General Psychology,* 123, 309–324.

Honts, C. R. (1997) *Is It Time to Reject the Friendly Polygraph Examiner Hypothesis (FPEH)?*
Paper presented at the annual meeting of the American Psychological Society, Washington, DC, May, 1997. Available online:
http://truth.boisestate.edu/polygraph/fpeh.html

Honts, C. R. (1999) The discussion of comparison questions between list repetitions (charts)
is associated with increased test accuracy. *Polygraph,* 28, 117–123.

Honts, C. R. (2000) A brief note on the misleading and the inaccurate: a rejoinder to Matte
(2000) with critical comments on Matte and Reuss (1999) *Polygraph,* 29, 321–325.

Honts, C. R., Amato, S. and Gordon, A. (2000a) *Validity of Outside-issue Questions in the
Control Question Test: Final Report on Grant No. N00014-98-1-0725.* Submitted to the
Office of Naval Research and the Department of Defense Polygraph Institute. Applied
Cognition Research Institute, Boise State University.

Honts, C. R. and Devitt, M. K. (1992) *The Hired Gun Cross-examination Tactic Reduced Mock Jurors' Perception of Expert Witness' Credibility*. Paper presented at the biennial meeting of the American Psychology–Law Society/Division 41 San Diego, CA, March, 1992.

Honts, C. R., Devitt, M. K. and Amato, S. L. (1993) *Explanatory Style Predicts Perceptions of Expert Witness Believability*. Paper presented at the annual meeting of the American Association of Applied and Preventive Psychology, Chicago, June, 1993.

Honts, C. R. and Gordon, A. (1998) A critical analysis of Matte's analysis of the directed lie. *Polygraph,* 27, 241–252.

Honts, C. R., Kircher, J. C. and Raskin, D. C. (1988a) Patterns of activation and deception. *Psychophysiology,* 25, 455 (Abstract).

Honts, C. R. and Perry, M. V. (1992) Polygraph admissibility: Changes and challenges. *Law and Human Behavior,* 16, 357–379.

Honts, C. R. and Peterson, C. F. (1997) *Brief of the Committee of Concerned Social Scientists as Amicus Curiae. United States v. Scheffer*, in the Supreme Court of the United States. Available from the author.

Honts, C. R. and Quick, B. D. (1995) The polygraph in 1995: Progress in science and the law. *North Dakota Law Review,* 71, 987–1020.

Honts, C. R. and Raskin, D. C. (1988) A field study of the validity of the directed lie control question. *Journal of Police Science and Administration,* 16, 56–61.

Honts, C. R., Raskin, D. C., Amato, S. L., Gordon, A. and Devitt, M. K. (2000b) The hybrid directed lie test, the overemphasized comparison question, chimeras and other inventions: A rejoinder to Abrams (1999) *Polygraph,* 29, 156–168.

Honts, C. R., Raskin, D. C. and Kircher, J. C. (1985) Effects of socialization on the physiological detection of deception. *Journal of Research in Personality,* 19, 373–385.

Honts, C. R., Raskin, D. C. and Kircher, J. C. (1992) Effectiveness of control questions answered "Yes": Dispelling a polygraph myth. *Forensic Reports,* 5, 265–272.

Honts, C. R., Raskin, D. C. and Kircher, J. C. (1994) Mental and physical countermeasures reduce the accuracy of polygraph tests. *Journal of Applied Psychology,* 79, 252–259.

Honts, C. R., Raskin, D. C., Kircher, J. C. and Horowitz, S. W. (1988b) *A Field Validity Study of the Control Question Test*. Paper presented at the American Psychology and Law Society/Division 41 Midyear Conference, Miami, Florida, March, 1988.

Horowitz, S. W., Kircher, J. C., Honts, C. R. and Raskin, D. C. (1997) The role of comparison questions in physiological detection of deception. *Psychophysiology,* 34, 108–115.

Horvath, F. S. (1977) The effect of selected variables on interpretation of polygraph records. *Journal of Applied Psychology,* 62, 127–136.

Horvath, F. S. (1988) The utility of control questions and the effects of two control question types in field polygraph techniques. *Journal of Police Science and Administration,* 16, 198–209.

Horvath, F. S. and Reid, J. E. (1971) The reliability of polygraph examiner diagnosis of truth and deception. *Journal of Criminal Law, Criminology and Police Science,* 62, 276–281.

Hunter, F. L. and Ash, P. (1973) The accuracy and consistency of polygraph examiners' diagnoses. *Journal of Police Science and Administration,* 1, 370–375.

Iacono, W. G., and Lykken, D. T. (1997) The scientific status of research on polygraph techniques: The case against polygraph tests. In: D. L. Faigman, D. Kaye, M. J. Saks and J. Sanders (eds) *Modern Scientific Evidence: The Law and Science of Expert Testimony,* pp. 582–618. St Paul, Minnesota: West Publishing.

Keeler, L. (1933) Scientific methods of criminal detection with the polygraph. *Kansas Bar Association,* 2, 22–31.

Kircher, J. C., Horowitz, S. W. and Raskin, D. C. (1988) Meta-analysis of mock crime studies of the control question polygraph technique. *Law and Human Behavior,* 12, 79–90.

Kircher, J. C. and Raskin, D. C. (1981) Computerized decision-making in the detection of deception. *Psychophysiology,* 18, 204–205.

Kircher, J. C. and Raskin, D. C. (1982) Cross-validation of a computerized diagnostic procedure for detection of deception. *Psychophysiology,* 9, 568–569.

Kircher, J. C. and Raskin, D. C. (1983) Clinical versus statistical lie detection revisited: Through a lens sharply. *Psychophysiology,* 20, 452.

Kircher, J. C. and Raskin, D. C. (1988) Human versus computerized evaluations of polygraph data in a laboratory setting. *Journal of Applied Psychology,* 73, 291–302.

Kleinmuntz, B. and Szucko, J. (1984) A field study of the fallibility of polygraphic lie detection. *Nature,* 308, 449–450.

Larson, J. A. (1932) *Lying and its Detection.* Chicago: University of Chicago Press.

Lykken, D. T. (1979) The detection of deception. *Psychological Bulletin,* 86, 47–53.

Markwart, A. and Lynch, B. E. (1979) The effect of polygraph evidence on mock jury decision-making. *Journal of Police Science and Administration,* 7, 324–332.

Marston, W. M. (1917) Systolic blood pressure symptoms of deception. *Journal of Experimental Psychology,* 2, 117–163.

Matte, J. A. (2000) A critical analysis of Honts' study: The discussion (stimulation) of Comparison Questions. *Polygraph,* 29, 146–149.

Mervis, J. (1986) Council takes stand on AIDS, polygraph; creates science post. *American Psychological Association Monitor,* March 11.

Meyers, B. and Arbuthnot, J. (1997) Polygraph testimony and juror judgments: A comparison of the guilty knowledge test and the control question test. *Journal of Applied Social Psychology,* 27, 1421–1437.

Office of Technology Assessment (1983) *Scientific Validity of Polygraph Testing: A Research Review and Evaluation.* Washington, DC: US Government Printing Office.

Orne, M. T. (1975) Implications of laboratory research for the detection of deception. In: N. Ansley (ed.) *Legal Admissibility of the Polygraph* (pp. 94–119). Springfield, IL: Charles C. Thomas.

Orne, M. T. (1983) *Proceedings of the Polygraph Validity Advisory Panel of the Office of Technology Assessment,* Washington, DC, August, 1983, unpublished.

Patrick, C. J. and Iacono, W. G. (1986) The validity of lie detection with criminal psychopaths. *Psychophysiology,* 23, 452–453.

Patrick, C. J. and Iacono, W. G. (1991) Validity of the control question polygraph test: The problem of sampling bias. *Journal of Applied Psychology,* 76, 229–238.

Peterson, J. L, Fabricant, B. L, Field, K. and Thornton, J. (1978) *Crime Laboratory Proficiency Testing Research Program.* Washington, DC: US Government Printing Office.

Podlesny, J. A. and Raskin, D. C. (1977) Physiological measures and the detection of deception. *Psychological Bulletin,* 84, 782–799.

Podlesny, J. A. and Raskin, D. C. (1978) Effectiveness of techniques and physiological measures in the detection of deception. *Psychophysiology,* 15, 344–358.

Podlesny, J. A. and Truslow, C. M. (1993) Validity of an expanded-issue (modified general question) polygraph technique in a simulated distributed-crime-roles context. *Journal of Applied Psychology,* 78, 788–797.

Raskin, D. C. (1979) Orienting and defensive reflexes in the detection of deception. In: H. D. Kimmel, E. H. van Olst and J. F. Orlebeke (eds) *The Orienting Reflex in Humans* (pp. 587–605). Hillsdale, NJ: Erlbaum.

Raskin, D. C. (1982) The scientific basis of polygraph techniques and their uses in the judicial process. In: A. Trankell (ed.) *Reconstructing the Past: The Role of Psychologists in Criminal Trials* (pp. 317–371). Stockholm: Norstedt and Soners.

Raskin, D. C. (1986) The polygraph in 1986: Scientific, professional, and legal issues surrounding applications and acceptance of polygraph evidence. *Utah Law Review*, 1986, 29–74.

Raskin, D. C. (1987) Methodological issues In estimating polygraph accuracy in field applications. *Canadian Journal of Behavioural Science*, 19, 389–404.

Raskin, D. C., Barland, G. H. and Podlesny, J. A. (1978) *Validity and Reliability of Detection of Deception*, Contract 75- NI-99-0OOI, US Department of Justice. Washington, DC: US Government Printing Office.

Raskin, D. C. and Hare, R. D. (1978) Psychopathy and detection of deception in a prison population. *Psychophysiology,* 15, 121–136.

Raskin, D. C., Honts, C. R. and Kircher, J. C. (1997a) The scientific status of research on polygraph techniques: The case for polygraph tests. In: D. L. Faigman, D. Kaye, M. J. Saks and J. Sanders (eds) *Modern Scientific Evidence: The Law and Science of Expert Testimony,* pp. 565–582. St Paul, Minnesota: West Publishing.

Raskin, D. C., Honts, C. R. and Kircher, J. C. (1997b) A response to professors Iacono and Lykken. In: D. L. Faigman, D. Kaye, M. J. Saks and J. Sanders (eds) *Modern Scientific Evidence: The Law and Science of Expert Testimony,* pp. 619–627. St Paul, Minnesota: West Publishing.

Raskin, D. C. and Kircher, J. C. (1991) Comments on Furedy and Heslegrave: Misconceptions, misdescriptions, and misdirections. In: P. K. Ackles, J. R. Jennings, and M. G. H. Coles (eds) *Advances in Psychophysiology,* Vol. 4, (pp. 215–223). Greenwich, CT: Jessica Kingsley Publishers.

Raskin, D. C., Kircher, J. C., Honts, C. R. and Horowitz, S. W. (1988) *A Study of the Validity of Polygraph Examinations in Criminal Investigation*, Grant No. 85-IJ-CX-0040. Salt Lake City: Department of Psychology, University of Utah.

Raskin, D. C., Kircher, J. C., Horowitz, S. W. and Honts, C. R. (1989) Recent laboratory and field research on polygraph techniques. In: J. C. Yuille (ed) *Credibility Assessment,* (pp. 1–24). Deventer, The Netherlands: Kluwer.

Reed, S. (1994) A new psychophysiological detection of deception examination for security screening. *Psychophysiology*, 31, S80, (Abstract).

Reid, J. E. (1947) A revised questioning technique In lie detection tests. *Journal of Criminal Law, Criminology and Police Science,* 37, 542–547.

Reid, J. E. and Inbau, F. B. (1977) *Truth and Deception: The Polygraph ("Lie Detector") Technique.* Baltimore: Williams and Wilkins.

Rovner, L. I., Raskin, D. C. and Kircher, J. C. (1979) Effects of information and practice on detection of deception. *Psychophysiology,* 16, 197–198.

Slowik, S. M. and Buckley, J. P. (1975) Relative accuracy of polygraph examiner diagnosis of respiration, blood pressure, and GSR recordings. *Journal of Police Science and Administration,* 3, 305–309.

Stern, R. M., Ray, W. J. and Davis, C. M. (1980) *Psychophysiological Recording.* New York: Oxford Press.

Swinford, J. (1999) Manually scoring polygraph charts utilizing the seven-position numerical analysis scale at the Department of Defense Polygraph Institute. *Polygraph,* 28, 10–28.

Summers, W. G. (1939) Science can get the confession. *Fordham Law Review,* 5, 334–354.

Thompson, R. F. (2000) *The Brain: A Neuroscience Primer,* 3rd edn. New York: Worth.

Timm, H. W. (1982) Effect of altered outcome expectancies stemming from placebo and feedback treatments on the validity of the guilty knowledge technique. *Journal of Applied Psychology,* 67, 391–400.

United States v. Scheffer (1998) 118 S. Ct. 1261.

United States Army Military Police School (USAMPS), Polygraph Branch (1970) *Chart Interpretation (CI551L).* Fort Gordon, Georgia: USAMPS.

Vondergeest, L., Honts, C. R. and Devitt, M. K. (1993) Effects of juror and expert witness gender on jurors' perceptions of an expert witness. *Modern Psychological Studies,* 1, 1–6.

Waid, W. M. and Orne, M. T. (1982) The physiological detection of deception. *American Scientist,* 70, 402–409.

Waid, W. M., Orne, M. T. and Wilson, S. K. (1979) Effects of level of socialization on electrodermal detection of deception. *Psychophysiology,* 16, 15–22.

Weaver, R. S. (1980) The numerical evaluation of polygraph charts: Evolution and comparison of three major systems. *Polygraph,* 9, 94–108.

Weaver, R. S. (1985) Effects of differing numerical chart evaluation systems on polygraph examination result. *Polygraph,* 14, 34–41.

Wicklander, D. K. and Hunter, F. L (1975) The influence of auxiliary sources of information in polygraph diagnoses. *Journal of Police Science and Administration,* 3, 405–409.

Widacki, J. and Horvath, F. S. (1978) An experimental investigation of the relative validity and utility of the polygraph technique and three other common methods of criminal identification. *Journal of Forensic Sciences,* 23, 596–601.

CHAPTER 2

PRACTICAL USE OF THE CONCEALED INFORMATION TEST FOR CRIMINAL INVESTIGATION IN JAPAN

Makoto Nakayama

About 5000 polygraph examinations are conducted in Japan each year, mainly concerning issues of homicide, burglary, theft, and the like. Japanese police polygraph examiners use the concealed information test (CIT) exclusively in actual criminal investigations and consider it to be of greater value than the control question test (CQT). The CIT is regarded as a kind of recognition test in Japan and examiners use it to verify whether or not the subject identifies a crime-related detail.

CIT AND CRIMINAL INVESTIGATION

THE QUESTION SEQUENCE STRUCTURE OF THE CIT

According to Lykken (1998), the CIT is composed of a series of multiple choice questions, each having one crime relevant alternative (e.g., a feature of the crime under investigation) and several neutral alternatives. If a subject has committed the crime, he or she will be able to distinguish the critical item among non-critical items during the polygraph test, while an innocent subject will not. When the deceptive subject discovers the critical item in the question sequence, specific involuntary changes are triggered in the autonomic nervous system. Therefore, a direct question such as "Did you kill John?" is not considered necessary; instead, information about the murder is used to construct a concrete question. For example, if the case involved murder by strangling the victim with a rope, a question series could be:

1. Did you shoot him with a handgun?
2. Did you hit him with a stone?
3. Did you stab him with a knife?
4. Did you strangle him with a rope?
5. Did you push him off a bridge?

In this case, alternative 4 is the critical question and the others are non-critical questions.

As long as information about the event was not made public, the critical item will not cause any physiological responses for an innocent subject. However, when the circumstances of a homicide are reported in detail by newspaper and TV news, the cause of death cannot be considered to be concealed information because it has become "common knowledge." In this event, the examiner must go to the crime scene and search for critical items for use in the CIT that were not reported by the mass media.

AN EXAMPLE OF CIT IN AN ACTUAL BURGLARY CASE

The case facts are as follows. A masked man entered a residence, where the victim was watching TV. After threatening her with a jackknife, he covered her mouth with packing tape. Then, he took 36 000 yen in cash and her wristwatch. Before he fled, he said to her, "Take care of yourself." His knife was found on the road near her house. Eight series of CIT questions were constructed and used to test a suspect:

Question 1: Where was the place of entry? Was it a:

   1. front entrance?
   2. kitchen door?
*3. bathroom window?
   4. balcony?
   5. room on the second floor?

In this case, the suspect had broken a bathroom window and crept through it, so alternative 3 is the critical item in this sequence.

Question 2: When the intruder entered the house, what was the victim doing? Was she:

   1. reading a magazine?
   2. taking a shower?
   3. sleeping?
*4. watching TV?
   5. talking on the phone?

The victim was watching TV at that time, so the critical item is number 4.

Question 3: What kind of weapon did the intruder have? Did he have a:

    1. carving knife?
    2. gun?
  *3. jackknife?
    4. pair of scissors?
    5. ice pick?

The intruder had a jackknife, and number 3 is the critical item.

Question 4: With what did the intruder cover his face? Did he cover his face with:

    1. a flu mask?
  *2. panty hose?
    3. a muffler?
    4. a gorilla mask?
    5. a towel?

The intruder covered his face with panty hose during the crime, so the critical question is number 2.

Question 5: What did the intruder do? Did he:

    1. put handcuffs on her?
    2. bind her ankles with wire?
    3. put a bandage over her eyes?
  *4. cover her mouth with packing tape?
    5. strike her on the head?

He covered her mouth with a packing tape actually, so the critical question is number 4.

Question 6: What did the intruder take? Did he take:

    1. 54 000 yen and her bag?
    2. 45 000 yen and her necklace?
  *3. 36 000 yen and her wristwatch?
    4. 27 000 yen and her ring?
    5. 18 000 yen and her car key?

The intruder took 36 000 yen and her wristwatch, so the critical question is number 3.

Question 7: What did he say to her before he escaped? Did he say:

1. "See you next time"?
2. "Have a nice day"?
3. "You are safe now"?
*4. "Take care of yourself"?
5. "Thank you for a good job"?

He said, "take care of yourself", so 4 is the critical question.

Question 8: Which way did he escape?

Police found a jackknife on the street near the victim's house and deduced that the intruder ran along this street. The questions regarding the escape route were presented using a map.

PREPARATION OF AN EFFECTIVE CIT

When a police chief or the HQ detective section requests a polygraph test, a polygraph examiner visits the crime site, where the detective explains the circumstances of the scene to the examiner. The examiner carefully reads the case file with photographs of the site, and, when possible, should meet the victim or the witnesses, to get a grasp of the course of events. This enables the examiner to experience what the offender had done and seen. The examiner attempts to select crime scene details that the offender could not fail to remember, for use as critical items, and to exclude details that the offender may not be able to recall during the polygraph examination.

SELECTION OF THE CIT QUESTION

The CIT differs from a memory test in a laboratory experiment. The offender's experience at the crime scene is retained as episodic memory, specified spatially and temporally, and associated with emotion. Therefore, the memory is very vivid for the culprit, with rich information processing, and consequently is recalled as a whole. Episodic memory is a kind of incidental learning or implicit memory (Shacter, 1987) and culprits neither try to memorize the event during the crime nor need any effort to recall it during the examination. The polygraph examiner must detect whether the suspect has previous experience and memory regarding the crime site by means of CIT, taking many factors into consideration.

Offenders might not remember objects they saw by chance at the crime site, but will often recall the tools they prepared before breaking into a residence. For instance, the kinds of weapon and facial cover used by the offender are very effective critical questions. Details concerning actions planned before the offense, such as binding the victim or cutting the telephone line, will also be recollected easily during examination, and are suitable for selection as critical questions.

Circumstances encountered in the course of the offense that directly affect the actions of the offender are also remembered well. For example, while burgling an office the offender found that the safe was obstructed by a large stuffed bear. Not knowing that this stuffed animal was the company mascot, the offender wondered at its presence. It was not only conspicuous but was also an obstacle to the safe, and the criminal was forced to move it. If a photograph of the stuffed animal is presented during the examination, the offender will recall it. However, even a prominent picture on the wall may not be recognized, especially if the burglary occurred at night.

According to Kasuya (1999), the context of the offender's goal is remembered accurately. In cases of theft, details concerning the sum of money and the type of jewelry are remembered by the offender during the test. This is also true for the place or state of items stolen ("Was the ring in a desk drawer?," "in a bag?," "in a box?" . . . "Was the stolen money in an envelope?," "in an account book?" . . .). These types of questions are often asked in such cases. Kiriu (1991) found that questions concerning location produced better detection than those concerning numbers (date, time, sum of money stolen, or the number of offenders).

A habitual criminal often has a script or schema. For example, searching for homes where no car is parked during the day, forcing the kitchen door with a crowbar, then searching the bedroom for jewelry. This is a typical burglary.

Occasionally, the burglar is interrupted by an unexpected turn of events, for instance, the unforeseen return of the occupant. The criminal cannot anticipate the state of affairs, nor cope with the situation in his or her habitual script, and must first analyze circumstances for a safe escape. If the offender presented a successful excuse, an effective question to this event might be, "what did the burglar explain to the occupant?"

The more attention culprits pay to aspects of their offence, the better those aspects are remembered. If the culprit copes with unexpected events, he or she needs to process information about the circumstances more deeply. In general, memory is related to depth of information processing (Craik and Lockhart, 1972).

Before the examination, the examiner reviews all questions with the subject, explaining the context of the various alternatives. If the context is not established, and the questions are presented without reviewing, the subject may not understand them. This is also related to the encoding specificity principle (Tulving, 1983). For example, the examiner informs the subject of some feature contexts of the event and tells him or her that these questions are related to "stolen objects" or "things left at the site". Then the questions are reviewed: "was it a lighter?," "was it a necklace?," "was it a ballpoint pen?," "was it a watch?," "was it a key?"

We cannot know precisely what the culprit has retained in memory before the examination. Therefore, it is very difficult to decide upon criteria for selecting CIT questions. As mentioned above, suspects never fail to recall what they prepared beforehand. However, if a detective found a cigarette lighter at the murder site, we cannot know if it was the murderer's lighter or not. Consequently even if the subject's responses to the item are not indicative of recognition, we will not be able to decide their innocence. A polygraph examination is always composed of seven or more series of CIT questions. However, it is uncommon to observe clear responses to all items that are designated as critical. To some degree, it depends on the likelihood of choosing appropriate critical items. The advantage of the CIT is in presenting many question sequences about one crime from its various component aspects – in comparison to the CQT, which is a single sequence of questions. In the CIT, several sequences are prepared, and the overall responses are considered for a decision.

THE SIMILARITY BETWEEN QUESTION ITEMS

The selection of non-critical items is also important in composing an effective CIT question sequence. When a suspect is asked about stolen objects in the theft case, the most likely items to be stolen, or prototypes, such as cash and a wallet, should not be included because an innocent person would expect those to be critical questions. If prototypes are used as critical items, false positive errors may result.

In a case where a bracelet is stolen, non-critical items are often selected from the same category, such as a ring, necklace, earrings, and brooch. However, if a subject does not know that an item of jewelry was stolen, non-critical items could be selected from higher order categories of valuables, such as a camera, a handbag, a floppy disk, or a credit card, etc. It is preferable to select non-critical questions from different, suitable categories. If the content of different items is highly similar, orienting responses do not discriminate between them (Ben-Shakhar et al., 1995; Gati and Ben-Shakhar 1990).

Accordingly, in the case of a threatening letter written with a green marker, if the color of the text is not discriminative, it is possible to compose a question sequence concerning the type of writing implement. That is, the critical item is a marker, and non-criticals are pen-and-ink, pencil, ballpoint pen, or brush.

Lykken (1998) suggested that a "good critical question" may involve the type or color of clothing. However, Yokoi (1999) pointed out that a suspect's memory in relation to color was not accurate in the experimental situation. If the crime was committed at night, the culprit may not see the color accurately. Furthermore, numbers, such as amount of money stolen or the time or date of the crime, may not be recalled exactly during the examination. Also, a victim may not know the sum of money stolen, and human memory for numbers is easily disrupted. Because color and number vary in the same dimension and sometimes lack salient contexts, it is difficult to encode in long-term memory (Kiriu, 1991).

Ideally, the critical questions and non-critical questions should present neutral contents for the innocent subject, whereas the critical item should be significant only for the culprit, and only in relation to the event. Clearly, the use of affectively laden words concerning forbidden sexual acts (Manning and Melochiori, 1974; Schwartz, 1971; Stelmack and Mandelzys, 1975), fear (Hare, 1973; Klorman *et al.*, 1975), or personal preference of the individual, is not appropriate in a critical item because it easily arouses a subject's feelings, whether innocent or guilty, and produces physiological reactions. It is also necessary to avoid technical terms, and questions should suit the subject's intellectual level and age.

THE USE OF VISUAL MATERIALS WITH ORAL QUESTIONS

Visual materials, such as maps, floor plans, photographs, and real objects, are frequently used in CITs in Japan (Kasuya, 1999). A simple map of the vicinity of the crime scene, upon which locations have been marked by numerals, is often used to observe if a suspect recognizes the position of a victim's house in a theft or burglary. In arson cases, we can also examine whether the subject recognizes the specific place on a map or floor plan where the fire was started. Similarly, the place of entry and position of stolen items in a theft case, or the location of a corpse in a homicide case, can also be subject to examination. If the culprit left tools used during the crime (weapon, gloves, or mask) at the site, photographs of such tools, or occasionally a collection of actual objects, may be used to ask the subject questions about those items. Because the examiner doesn't name the items and just indicates the number on the map or the number of the photograph, verbal significance and connotation are neutralized.

Using real objects and photographs often makes their features more available to the subject than possible by words alone. In these cases, care must be taken that the items, critical and non-critical, are worn, new, soiled, or clean to the same degree. The visual presentation of items retrieves the deceptive subject's memory of the crime more vividly, which is designed to induce a prominent response owing to to its subjectively stressful character.

INTERFERENCE OF SERIAL OFFENSES ON MEMORY

The repetitive character of serial offenses, such as theft or burglary, may present difficulties for the culprit to recall details about each crime incident precisely. Although each culprit has episodic memories that are specified spatially and temporally, he or she may not recognize some correct alternatives in critical questions because he or she committed the same kind of offense many times, causing interference in memory.

For example, an offender may repeatedly steal valuables from parked cars, a quick and simple crime, not too lucrative, and usually committed many times a day. Therefore, the culprit may not recall what items or how much money, he or she stole, and from what type of car, in every case. Similarly, if the culprit is a serial arsonist, he or she may not understand which specific arson case is the topic of the examination because he or she repeatedly set fire to houses.

To avoid interference effects on memory, the newest or the most impressive event should be selected as an object of the CIT polygraph test. Subjects will recall the crime they committed last month more easily than a similar kind of crime committed a few months ago, all other things being equal. Unusual or noteworthy events will also be remembered in more detail, for instance, a burglary in which much more money was found than expected.

Ordinarily, the sequences of CITs are presented in order of the culprit's behavior during the course of the offense, from the entry to the escape. For serial offenses, it is preferable to start with the issue concerning the most distinctive feature of the crime, which may trigger the subjects' memory as a whole.

Occasionally the same person is suspected of several, similar crimes. When examining such suspects, it is customary to omit features common to more than one crime as critical items, in order to enable an independent decision regarding the commission of each offense.

TYPICAL CIT QUESTION TOPICS

Homicide

The most important CIT items are place, method, lethal weapon, final location of corpse, and disposal of corpse. If the site was the victim's home, questions regarding the point and method of entry are also presented. Questions are asked regarding details when stolen objects are known, or the culprit left something at the scene. For example, if a suspect left tools or belongings on the floor, he or she will recall it easily at the presentation of the real object. Or if three wine glasses had been left on the table, only the person who had committed the crime would be aware of them. Moreover, if a blanket was put on the corpse, it is an effective question. In a homicide case without the corpse, a searching peak of tension test (SPOT – see below) may be used (Kiriu, 1991) in an attempt to locate the body.

Burglary and sexual assault

Adequate critical questions concern weapon, tool (type of mask, gloves, or burglar tool), criminal's peculiar act or word, victim's words, amount of money stolen, and stolen objects. If the site was the victim's home, questions regarding the point of entry may be presented visually. An eyewitness report of the culprit's getaway by car may enable presentation of question sequences about the kind of car, the position of parking, or the direction of the escape using a map.

Arson

The location, type of place, or materials used to start the fire can be questioned using a map or photograph. If the offender first set fire to a towel and then put it into a trash bin, these are effective CIT items. Arson materials found at the crime site (candle, gasoline, kerosene, timer, a battery, or powder) are items that should be included in CIT sequences as critical questions.

Theft

The location of money, types of stolen objects, place and method of entry, sum of money stolen, and the state of affairs are questioned by CIT.

Kidnapping

CIT sequences may be constructed about the place of abduction, the sum of demanded money, and the kidnapper's words over the phone. A demand that money be brought to a specific location may also be the subject of a CIT sequence.

Hit and run

The accident location on a city map, accurate position on a road diagram, and collision point of car are examined using visual materials. Eyewitness reports may enable presentation of questions about the make of the car, direction of escape, or the suspect's actions after collision.

SEARCHING PEAK OF TENSION TEST (SPOT) AND CQT IN JAPAN

Many psychologists accept that CIT is the most scientifically effective method for the detection of deception (Iacono and Lykken, 1997), but the CIT is not always applicable to the event in field situations. When we cannot find appropriate critical questions at the crime scene, SPOT and CQT are also used in Japan.

When suspects know detailed information about the crime, it is no longer "concealed." In a homicide case, the person who discovers the body cannot be examined, because he or she has seen the details of the event and learned them legitimately. Furthermore, even if they are suspected of knowing the information because they committed the offense, and not because they discovered the body, the CIT cannot differentiate the two roles. Possible contradictions between forensic evidence and the suspect's account may leave an insufficient number of CIT sequences for an adequate examination.

In a case of arson, where the house was totally destroyed, the location and method of ignition may be unknown. In a hit and run, two people were seen in the offending car. The examination for distinguishing which person was driving is quite difficult using only CIT. There are occasional instances in which the manager opens the office safe to discover that all the money is missing. The safe can't be opened without its key and combination. The manager questioned the employees before calling the police, leaking all critical information. In investigations of sexual assault where the accounts of the complainant and the suspect correspond, except that the woman charges rape while the man argues consensual sex, CIT is not the appropriate method to indicate whether the event was consensual or not.

SPOT

If appropriate critical questions are not available, SPOTs are often conducted in Japan. When a person disappears suddenly and motives of suicide or escape have been ruled out, police investigators must consider the possibility of homicide. Detectives investigate the existence of motives and suspects. Though it is difficult to compose CIT sequences in these circumstances, SPOT-containing questions about the date, place, method, manner of murder, and disposal of the corpse may be utilized. However, we cannot be certain that the sequences contain correct items of critical information because they are unknown, except to the culprit.

Here are several examples:

Question 1: When was he killed? Was he killed in:

1. January?
2. February?
3. March?
4. April?
5. May?

Question 2: Where was he killed? Was he killed:

1. in a house?
2. in a car?
3. in the mountains?
4. by the seaside?
5. in an office?

Question 3: How did you kill him? Did you:

1. shoot him with a handgun?
2. hit him with a stone?
3. stab him with a knife?
4. strangle him with a rope?
5. push him off a bridge?

Question 4: Did you know how the corpse was disposed of? Was the corpse:

1. left on the street?
2. buried?
3. hidden under water?
4. burnt?
5. hidden in a building?

Question 5: Do you know where the corpse is (on this map)? Was the corpse left in:

1. area A?
2. area B?
3. area C?
4. area D?
5. area E?

Question 6: How many persons were involved in the murder? Was it:

1. only one person?
2. two persons?
3. three persons?
4. four persons?
5. five persons or more?

The SPOT regarding the date of the homicide starts at the date when the victim was last seen and ends with the date just previous to the examination. A map of the area, clearly partitioned into several parts, is used to examine suspects regarding locations. Date and region are limited to some degree by constraints, but method or motivation is not, so that "correct alternatives" may not be included in these sequences. In this case, many alternatives are possible in a sequence. If seven or more questions are included in the sequence, it will be divided in two.

Some examiners include a catchall question such as "another place than those mentioned" at the end of the sequence. This is very different from the other questions and the reaction to the question is not meaningful.

CQT

The control question test (CQT) is used in the overwhelming majority of polygraph examinations in North America, while the concealed information test (CIT) is not considered useful in actual criminal cases (Ben-Shakhar and Furedy, 1990; Lykken, 1998; Matte, 1997). In contrast, Japanese police polygraph examiners use the CIT exclusively in actual criminal investigations and consider it to be of greater value than the CQT.

Although it is recognized that the court may sometimes mistakenly find a culprit to be innocent, the Japanese people recoil from the opposite error, i.e., mistaking an innocent person for the culprit. For this reason, Japanese police polygraphers are especially motivated to avoid false positive decisions in the detection of deception. Therefore, when use of the CIT is not possible, SPOT, a related procedure, is willingly used. However, examiners are very reluctant to use the CQT as the sole examination method. About 40% of examiners in Japan have never used CQT, even if the number of critical items is insufficient for CIT.

Japanese examiners have never learned about pre-test interview procedures for directing the subject's attention to the control question of CQT, in the same way that North American examiners have relatively little experience with CIT. In Japan, the CQT is a kind of supplementary method and is used for preventing a false negative error with CIT. In cases where the investigation produces a strong suspicion toward the subject, but specific responses to critical questions were not conclusive during CIT, CQT may be conducted reluctantly, following the CIT. If the subject's responses to the relevant question (Did you kill John?) are insignificant, it will be inferred that he or she is not deceptive. Therefore, the CQT is valued as a supporting indication of innocence; however, a distinct reaction to the relevant question is not regarded as significant by Japanese examiners.

Yamamura and Miyata (1990) proposed a revised CQT quite different from that used in North America. Their control questions are very similar to relevant questions, and are required to have the same characteristics concerning the issue under investigation, but include aspects of the crime that are known to be incorrect or impossible. For example, the control question may focus on the suspicion that the subject was an accomplice – when his or her alibi is known, or a fictitious crime, or the time when the crime was committed, etc. If a relevant question is "Did you ask him to kill your husband?," an example of a control question might be "Did you assist him to kill your husband?"

USEFULNESS OF CIT

A BRIEF REVIEW OF PSYCHOPHYSIOLOGICAL THEORY SUPPORTING CIT POLYGRAPH PRACTICE

As psychologists in the laboratory examine the unknown effects of the known experimental condition by measuring physiological indices, polygraph examiners decide whether or not the suspect experienced the condition of crime by their known distribution of physiological responses to the CIT questions. An intention to deceive is not necessary with CIT (Lykken, 1998), however, the results regarding the effect of verbal answers are not totally consistent. For example, no differences were found between "No" and "Yes" verbal response conditions in Kugelmass et al.'s (1967) study. However, Elaad and Ben-Shakhar (1989), Gustafson and Orne (1965), and Horneman and O'Gorman (1985) reported that responding "No" to all questions produces a better detection rate in comparison with a "Yes" response.

Bando and Nakayama (1999) conducted an experiment to examine the role of verbal response in CIT. Twenty subjects were asked to give affirming ("yes"), denying ("no"), or no verbal responses to a question about the object which they previously stole in the mock crime. This experiment was designed within-subjects-factorial-design and three types of answering condition were repeated two times, respectively. All subjects were promised a monetary reward if they could produce a truthful outcome. Skin resistance response (SRR) to the critical question was consistently larger than that to non-critical items and there were no differences between verbal response conditions. Additionally, in the silent answer condition, differential responsivity was most enhanced owing to the remarkable decline of SCR amplitude to non-critical items (Figure 2.1).

Nakayama *et al.* (1988) used a delayed answering procedure to separate the skin conductance response (SCR) induced by the presentation of questions from that by the act of answering deceptively. Subjects in the delayed answer group were asked to be silent at the visual presentation of question, and to delay their answers until presentation of a tone. Subjects in the immediate answer group replied to the question in the ordinary manner and did not reply to the tone. As a result, the effect of deception emerged significantly: responsivity at

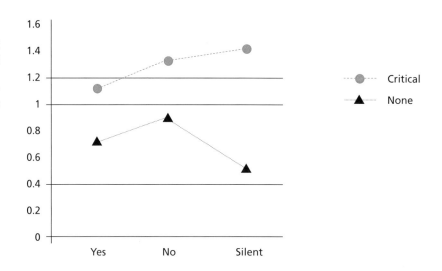

Figure 2.1

Mean standardized SRR elicited by the critical (●) and non-critical (▲) questions under the three verbal answer conditions (Bando and Nakayama, 1999).

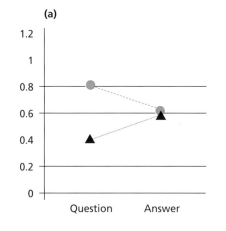
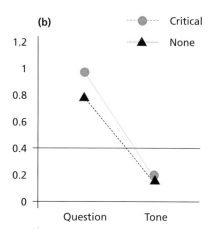

Figure 2.2

Mean SCR elicited by the critical (●) and non-critical (▲) questions with (a) the delayed and (b) immediate answering procedure (Nakayama et al., 1988).

the time of question presentation for the delayed answer group was better than that for the immediate answer group. SCRs produced by answering, to critical and non-critical questions, displayed no differences in the delayed answer group (Figure 2.2).

Bando and Nakayama (1999) and Nakayama *et al.* (1988) suggested that a deceptive answer was neither a necessary nor a sufficient condition for CIT. Specifically, deception did not play any role in the CIT's efficacy to detect the critical question. This is because electrodermal amplitude in no-answer and delayed-answer conditions was larger than that in deceptive ("No") or truthful ("Yes") answer conditions, suggesting that the response to non-critical items in the silent or delayed answering was selectively suppressed.

The verbal answer to a question is motor response, which generates an SCR in itself, and thus amplifies the SCR in both types of questions. However, the SCR to non-critical items is distinctively inhibited in the silent or delayed answers. Therefore, although emotional factors were emphasized in early research on detection of deception, a deceptive answer to the critical question in CIT is not a crucial factor. If the deceptive answer does not cause the specific response, fear of test (Davis 1961), motivation to avoid detection (Gustafson and Orne, 1965), and conflict associated with the act of lying (Davis, 1961) are not sufficient conditions for CIT.

Later research has focused on cognitive factors. Lykken (1974) pointed out that the "correct alternative" has added "signal value," so that a stronger orienting reflex is produced. Raskin (1979) has suggested that the effectiveness of CIT depends on the evocation of orienting responses (OR) to the critical items, but it depends on the evocation of defensive responses to the relevant question in CQT.

According to Maltzman (1979), the subject's previous experiences, history, and stimulus context establish a psychological set, and the significant stimulus in a sequence evokes OR. Before conducting a CIT, all questions are reviewed with the subject in advance. Only deceptive subjects have the specific experience of the crime, and find that the critical question is related to the act they previously committed. Therefore, deceptive subjects can discover the critical question during the question review and recognize it as a significant stimulus, evoking a voluntary OR to the critical question during the examination phase (Pendery and Maltzman, 1977). In other words, if an OR is evoked by the critical question, the subject has the guilty knowledge, which indicates that previous criminal experience. Stimulus change from a non-significant stimulus to a significant stimulus produces an OR, but stimulus change from a significant to a non-significant stimulus does not (Bernstein, 1979, Maltzman, 1979). Correspondingly, stimulus change from a non-critical question to a critical question produces an OR, but stimulus change from a critical to a non-critical question does not produce an OR in CIT (Nakayama and Kizaki, 1990). Reviewing questions is also important to remove the novelty of non-critical items.

Ben-Shakhar (1977) proposed the dichotomization theory to account for the phenomenon of differential responsivity to the critical question. If a silver bracelet, a diamond ring, a pearl necklace, a gold watch, and ruby earrings are presented as questions about stolen objects, an innocent subject regards the question sequence as a single category, composed of jewelry. Both critical and non-critical questions should be apparently neutral for such subjects. However, for the guilty subject there are dual categories in the CIT sequence, because they distinguish "a correct alternative" from "incorrect alternatives." This suggests that the two stimulus categories (critical and non-critical) produce independent habituation processes, and therefore differential responsivity is enhanced by generalization of habituation among non-critical questions.

If the suspect's memory does not access long-term memory, or encode events precisely owing to memory interference, or influences of alcohol or drugs (Bradley and Ainsworth, 1984; Iacono et al., 1984; O'Tool et al., 1994), a false negative error may occur on CIT. Ben-Shakhar and Furedy (1990) reviewed the entire countermeasure literature and concluded that CIT can be made "immune to such (countermeasure) manipulation" if Lykken's (1960) scoring method is applied. However, Honts et al. (1996) reported that mental counter-measures (counting backwards by sevens) and physical ones (pressing the toes to the floor) were equally effective on CIT. Elaad and Ben-Shakhar (1991) also found that electrodermal differentiation was somewhat reduced by "counting sheep" continuously. On the other hand, in field CIT situations innocent subjects have no need for countermeasures. Even if a deceptive subject used physical countermeasures for enhancing responses to non-critical items, these responses would be apparently unnatural. For example, pressing the toes to the floor would cause a rapid rise time of SRR, which would be obviously different from a natural wave produced by the psychological process.

COMPARISON OF CIT AND CQT

The CQT has been controversial mainly because it utilizes "control questions" that are not true controls in the usual scientific sense of the term (Ben-Shakhar and Furedy, 1990). In the CQT, control questions are designed to embarrass the subjects or elicit a lie. "Did you ever do anything you are ashamed of?" or "During the first 18 years of your life, did you ever take something that didn't belong to you?" may be a typical control question. These types of question are designed to be deliberately vague so that the subject cannot answer "No" with confidence. If the subject answers "Yes" to a question during the pre-test interview, it is reworded slightly so that the subject will answer "No" during the examination. However, there is no certainty that the attention of the subject is effectively directed to the control question, even if the examiner attempts manipulation during the pre-test interview. Therefore, even for an innocent examinee, it is at least arguable that the significance of the relevant question would exceed that of the control question (Furedy *et al.*, 1988). If the innocent subject denies the control question with complete confidence during the examination, and is not concerned with its significance, they are expected to respond more to the relevant questions than the control questions, and to produce a deceptive result.

In contrast to the CQT, an innocent subject need not lie during a CIT examination, which has no questions of the "control" type, so it takes less time to conduct a pre-test interview to develop the subject's attention set. The CIT is an examination of the subjects' memory for features of the investigated crime, and the response to a critical item is the orienting response to significant stimulus rather than lability of attention or anxiety.

Each CIT sequence is composed of a multiple-choice question. When the correct alternative and four plausible items are presented to a guilty subject, control alternatives should be easily distinguished from the critical item, so that the subject unequivocally responds to the key information of the event. However, the innocent subject responds to all alternatives by chance, so the probability of response to the critical item is less than 20%. The major merit of CIT is that we can present many sequences on a variety of features about a single crime scene in comparison with CQT. If the cutoff score is set at 4 with 10 CITs, fewer than one innocent suspect in 100 would be expected to be mistaken as guilty (Lykken, 1998).

Elaad and Ben-Shakhar (1997) proposed that several different CITs should be formulated, because the use of multiple and independent questions provides better protection to innocent subjects. They suggested that even if there were few CITs, those stimulus sequences should be presented several times. Especially for innocent subjects, the use of many repetitions of a single good question may be more desirable than use of a single CQT.

Iacono and Lykken (1997) conducted a mail survey to obtain the opinions of members of the Society for Psychophysiological Research and Fellows of the American Psychological Association. Almost three quarters of those who responded viewed the CIT as scientifically sound, in contrast to their doubts about CQT.

PHYSIOLOGICAL CHANGES DURING DECEPTION

Recognition of the critical question causes physiological reactions such as an occurrence of SRR, respiratory amplitude reduction, and a rise in blood pressure. The following example of CIT in the field was conducted in the Shizuoka Prefecture Police Headquarters. The record of channels, from top to bottom, shows the thoracic respiration, abdominal respiration, SRR, blood pressure, and marker line. The most reliable pattern as an index of deception is a simultaneous occurrence of a cessation of respiration and the largest amplitude in SRR to the critical item (Figure 2.3). Respiratory suppression (Figure 2.4) and baseline change of respiration (Figure 2.5) at the critical item are also frequently observed.

Changes preceding and following the critical item are also important in the CIT. For example, the amplitude of SRR following presentation of the critical item was drastically diminished in comparison with that preceding it (Figure 2.6). The reduction of tension after the critical item might cause this kind of change. Occasionally, when the respiration amplitude is decreased during a presentation of critical question, the amplitude to the next item is often larger than that to preceding non-critical items (Figures 2.4 and 2.5). Furthermore, there may be an anticipatory response before the critical item if the subject anticipates the serial position of the critical item in a CIT sequence. The rate of respiration may decrease (Figure 2.7) when subjects are aware of the serial position of the critical question.

To investigate the effect of habituation to the critical item, the same sequence was repeated seven times. A voluntary SRR occurred before the presentation of the critical item because at the second and fourth repetition the subject was informed of the question order (Figures 2.8 and 2.9). However, when questions were presented randomly at the fifth repetition, the subject could not anticipate the critical item and consequently an anticipatory response was not found in this sequence (Figure 2.10). After the question sequence was repeated five times, SRR to the critical question was still observed (Figure 2.10) but after six times the response was not specific in comparison with other items (Figures 2.11 and 2.12).

The last example was a case of sexual assault. The victim complained that she was threatened in the suspects' car and he touched her privates but did not have sex with her. There were five questions as follows: 1. "Did you force her to clasp your penis?;" 2. "Did you force her to lick your body?;" 3. "Did you touch her privates?;" 4. "Did you lick her privates?;" 5. "Did you have sex with her?" These sexual questions are not usually asked in CIT because sexual content might induce a subjective, idiosyncratic response in the subject, whether it is a critical or non-critical question. In such circumstances, we would expect response

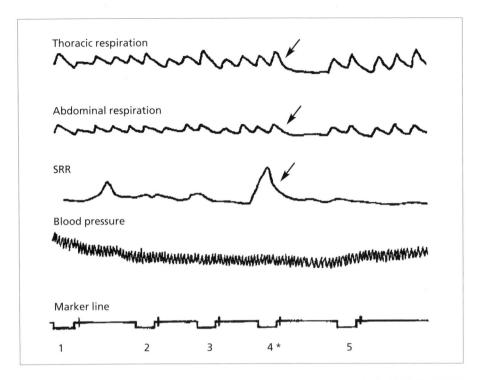

Figure 2.3

A record of CIT for a 29-year-old female suspected of committing a theft. Prior to the test, no investigator has disclosed to the subject what was stolen in the house. The subject was asked whether (1) a watch, (2) a ring, (3) a necklace, (4) a bracelet, or (5) a brooch was stolen. In this case, the critical item was 4. Both respiration amplitudes ceased after the answer to the critical question and the largest SRR occurred at this point.

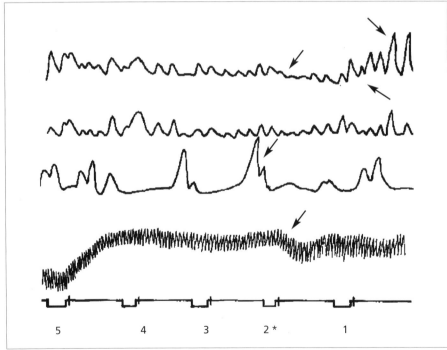

Figure 2.4

A record of CIT for a 23-year-old male suspected of committing a theft. During a pre-test interview, the subject told the examiner that he would not know where the stolen object (a brooch) was. The subject was asked whether it was (1) on a bed-side table, (2) in a drawer of the dresser, (3) in a jewel box, (4) on a jacket, or (5) in a shoulder bag. The critical question was 2 on the chart. The thoracic respiration amplitude was suppressed remarkably and consequently physiological rebound for the oxygen in the post-critical item may induce deeper breathing.

Figure 2.5

A record of CIT for a 57-year-old male suspected of committing a homicide. Both newspaper and TV news did not report where the corpse was found. The subject was asked whether the corpse was disposed at (1) city A, (2) city B, (3) city C, (4) city D, or (5) city E. The critical question was 2 on the chart. The thoracic respiration amplitude was suppressed and the baseline of the tracing fell slightly.

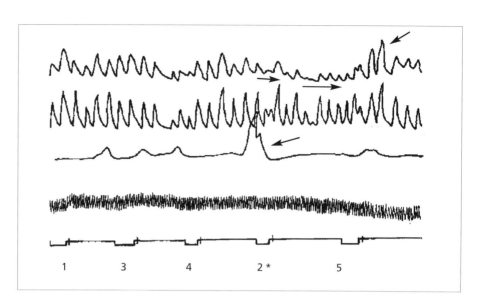

Figure 2.6

A record of CIT for a 34-year-old female suspected of committing a theft. The subject was asked what was stolen using photographs. The critical question was 3. The SRR tracing for questions 1 to 3 remained equal but the amplitude suddenly disappeared at the fourth question. It was thought to be the result of a reduction of tension after the critical item. Although the baseline blood pressure rose rapidly during the critical item, the rise or fall of this tracing was not frequently observed in CIT.

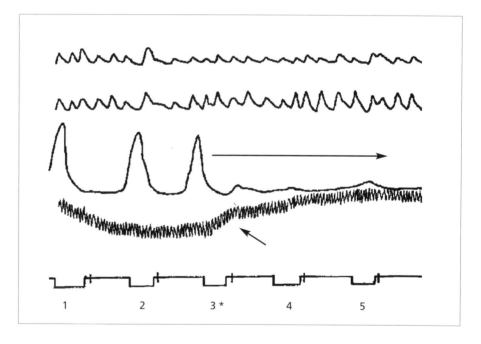

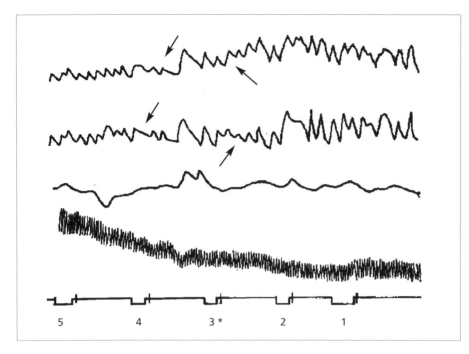

Figure 2.7

A record of CIT for a 42-year-old male suspected of committing a bank robbery. The subject was asked where the suspect's car was parked using a picture of the area around the bank. The critical question was 3. The baseline of thoracic respiration rose, while the baseline of abdominal respiration fell. Both amplitudes of respiration before the critical question were depressed. The decrease in the rate of respiration was caused by expectation of the critical question, because the subject could predict the serial position of the critical item on the picture.

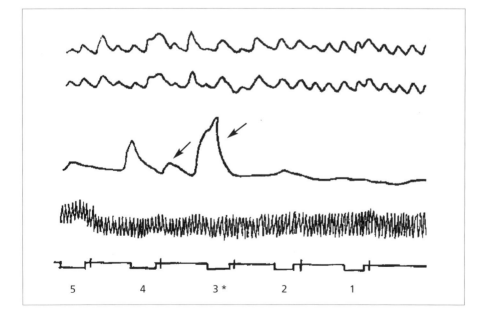

Figure 2.8

A record of CIT for a 49-year-old male suspected of committing a sexual assault. The subject was asked where the place of entry was using a ground plan. The critical question was 3. This sequence was repeated seven times and this is the first presentation. A prominent SRR to the critical item occurred and a voluntary SRR was induced immediately before the presentation of the critical item subject. This was also caused by the subject's expectation of seeing the critical item on the picture.

Figure 2.9

*This is the fourth
presentation for the same
person as in Figure 2.8.
The SRR to the critical
item and the anticipatory
response preceding the
critical item were observed.*

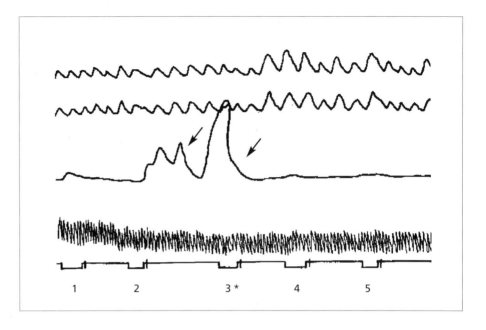

Figure 2.10

*This is the fifth
presentation for the same
person as in Figure 2.8.
The SRR to the critical
item was still clear. In
contrast to Figures 2.8
and 2.9, the anticipatory
response was not observed
because the subject was
not informed of the
question order in this
sequence.*

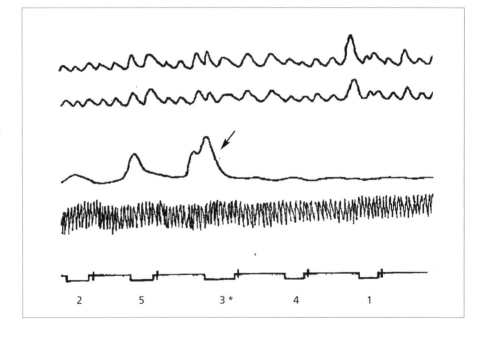

REQUEST FOR EXAMINATION

When the head of the police station requests a polygraph examination from the forensic science laboratory, the chief of the laboratory dispatches a polygraph examiner to the event site. The examiner visits the crime scene and searches for critical items that only the culprit will recognize during the test. Therefore, the matter of identification in the examination is "Does the subject recognize the crime details or not?" rather than "Is the subject deceptive or not?"

After the examiner finds several effective critical questions by researching the crime site deliberately, he returns to the laboratory and composes CIT sequences. These are often presented with visual materials, necessitating the preparation of a map, ground plan, photograph, and/or real objects, which takes at least 2 or 3 days. It is impossible to administer the polygraph examination on the day of the request. The examiner makes detailed arrangements with the investigator for the examination beforehand regarding the basis for suspicion, suspect statement, investigative information given to suspect, health of suspect, rest before examination, etc.

In many cases, the examination is requested upon identifying a possible suspect in the course of the police search. However, the question sequences are sometimes prepared beforehand, immediately after the occurrence of the serious event such as a homicide or bank robbery. It is advantageous for the examiner to see the fresh circumstances immediately following the offense.

EXECUTION OF EXAMINATION

The polygraph examination is contingent upon the consent of the suspect. If the subject refuses, he or she will not be examined. Polygraph examinations after arrest are very rare because the police must inform the suspect of the crime facts, exposing much information that includes effective critical questions. After the subject consents to the polygraph test, the examiner first explains the measuring of physiological responses and the procedure of polygraph examination. The goal of the pre-test interview is that the examiner confirms the subject's alleged unawareness of the crime details and to reduce the subject's anxiety for the examination. If the subject knows some critical items from the media or another information source, those questions are excluded or replaced with others. Moreover, if the suspects' colleagues, friends, or family had knowledge of the crime, as victims or the vicinity of victims, the suspect may have learned about details from them. Also, the subject might have visited the crime site and become acquainted with the place, although he or she was not there during the crime.

It takes about 30 min to conduct the pre-test interview, and examination time depends on the number of CIT sequences. For example, about 10 min are needed for a CIT sequence, and seven or more sequences are usually prepared for a test, taking at least an hour and a half. If there are too few questions (three sequences), the examiner cannot judge accurately. In contrast, if there are too many CITs, the subject's fatigue may interfere with adequate physiological responses. In such instances, it is necessary that the subject rest after several CIT sets, rather than testing 10 question sequences for 2 h consecutively.

There are four or five (usually four) non-critical items compared with a critical item in one question sequence, and the interval between questions is about 20–25 s. The first question of each sequence is always one of the non-critical items, to act as a buffer. Each question sequence is usually repeated three times.

According to Matte (1997), the North American version of the peak of tension test (POT) often includes a second key question that serves as a kind of control question in the form of "false key" to protect innocent subjects. However, Japanese polygraph examiners never use such a question in CIT.

When the examination ends, the subject is returned to the police investigator. Since polygraph examiners are not police officers, they do not have the right to investigate the subject, nor to conduct a "post-test interview." After the polygraph test, the examiner first informs the head of the police station of the results and then prepares the written report. If salient responses are observed to some critical items but not to others in the same examination, we must consider the weight of question sequences. An innocent subject might be able to infer or guess the critical item by chance, and guilty subjects may not recall the critical item or may not have noted it at the time of the crime. However, when there are no responses to critical items that the culprit never forgets, it should be judged that he is innocent.

Polygraph testing is prohibited for pregnant women, psychopaths, the mentally retarded, narcotic addicts, and intoxicated persons.

FIELD STUDIES AND EXPERIMENTAL DATA ON CIT IN JAPAN

COMPUTERIZED INSTRUMENTATION AND TEST EVALUATION

In the CIT, response indices (e.g., respiration rate, SRR amplitude, and heart rate change) are repeatedly measured for each question. The objective of statistical algorithms is to analyze the response record and classify a subject as either guilty or innocent – to decide whether the subject has knowledge about the critical question or not.

Statistical methods have recently been introduced in Japan (Adachi, 1995;

Tokuda, 1993). These methods commonly assume that the responses are distributed according to multivariate normal distributions, and are divided into two approaches: training data and within-subject approaches. In the training-data approach, a database (a set of training data) is used as the reference for classification (Adachi, 1995; Tokuda, 1993). The database is a collection of the records of subjects who have been verified to be either innocent or guilty. The subject under the current examination is judged in terms of whether his or her record is statistically similar to the sample of guilty subjects in the database or to the sample of innocents. That is, the subject is classified as having guilty knowledge if higher similarity is seen to the guilty sample, while classified as innocent otherwise. This procedure is a kind of linear discriminant analysis (e.g., McLachlan, 1992). In the within-subject approach, the database of the past records is not utilized and only the record from the current subject is analyzed (Adachi, 1995). This approach is equivalent to statistical hypothesis testing (e.g., Anderson, 1984), i.e., testing whether the responses to the critical questions are significantly different from those for the non-critical questions. The subject is classified as having guilty knowledge if significant differences are observed, and is classified as innocent otherwise.

In both approaches, the Akaike's Information Criterion (AIC) statistic (Akaike, 1974) is used for the final decision of guilt or innocence. Furthermore, the soundness of the final decision can be numerically expressed by posterior probabilities of the subject's innocence or guilt in the training-data approach, and by the level of significance in the within-subject approach. These indicate to what extent we can believe the innocent or guilty decision provided by the statistical analysis.

The statistical algorithms have been empirically examined with laboratory data (Adachi, 1995) and indicate that the classification accuracy for the within-subject approach is satisfactory for the data; however, as the number of question sets decreases, accuracy also decreases. These findings can be predicted from the fact that the within-subject approach is based on the data obtained from the subject under examination. In contrast, the number of repetitions does not affect the training-data approach, which may thus be recommended for field settings with comparatively few repetitions.

Iwami and Tsuji (1998) examined the accuracy of Adachi's statistical diagnostic algorithms in actual polygraph tests using computer analysis of 14 confirmed guilty subjects in three question sequences. In the training-data approach, the classification of four combined indices (i.e., respiration rate, SCR amplitude, and heart rate change) was correct for 91.3% of the sequences. The correct classification rate of each index was respiration rate 67.4%, SCR amplitude 50.0% and heart rate change 73.9%. On the other hand, in the within-subject approach, the correct classification rate of the four indices was

63.0%, and that of each index was respiration rate 39.1%, SCR amplitude 28.3%, and heart rate change 31.9%. In both statistical algorithms, respiration rate and heat rate changes were more accurate than SCR amplitude. Consequently, Adachi's computerized detection of CIT was found to be very effective in actual polygraph conditions.

Adachi and Suzuki (1994) found the training-data approach more accurate than the within-subject approach. This suggested that the conditions with three question sequences in field polygraph tests were less effective than experimental polygraph tests with five question sequences.

DISSIMILARITY BETWEEN CRIMINAL FACTS AND PROBING ITEMS ON SPOT

Kiriu (1991) investigated the relationship between question content and detection accuracy on the SPOT. Analysis of SPOT records for 74 subjects in the field polygraph tests indicated that questions about location produced better detection accuracy in comparison with questions about numbers (date, time, sum of money stolen, or the number of offenders). An association test (12 subjects) and a free recall test (14 subjects) on information about place and numbers were conducted to examine the above result in an experimental situation and confirmed the field observations. Subjects encoded information of location more elaborately than they did for numbers.

Detection accuracy in SPOT is not better than that in CIT. However, because the examiner does not know which item was the most similar to the criminal fact, there may be a mismatch between question contents and the actual critical facts. In an experiment designed to examine the effects of the similarity between CIT questions and crime details, Kiriu (1993) confirmed that detection rate was better for questions similar to crime details than for dissimilar questions. Moreover, Kiriu (1996) examined the effect of plausibility experimentally, and found a better detection rate in the high-plausibility condition.

From these experiments regarding SPOT, the most accurate result was obtained in questions about place. The more similar the critical question was to the actual crime detail the higher the detection rate.

PLAUSIBILITY OF ITEMS AND DETECTION RATE IN CIT

Yokoi (1997) investigated the effect of homogeneity among items as an index of SRR on CIT. Twenty-five participants, all of whom were assigned to innocent role, were presented a CIT multiple-choice question including five items, one of which was more likely than the other four, as indicated in pre-test rating by the test participants. When the highly plausible item was the critical one, it was expected that participants would be classified as having guilty knowledge (i.e., false positive error). The results, however, did not support this prediction; there was no significant difference between the highly plausible item and less plausible ones in mean rank scores of SRR, nor was a significant correlation found between plausibility ratings of items and the mean ranks of elicited responses. Even when highly plausible items were assumed to be the critical item, detection rate did not significantly exceed chance expectancy. It was suggested that homogeneity among items does not cause false positive errors, at least in experimental situations.

RESPIRATION CHANGES TO CRITICAL QUESTIONS

Nakayama (1987) investigated changes of respiration curves in CIT in field situations. A typical respiratory cycle may be viewed as the sum of three components: inspiration, expiration, and post-expiratory pause periods (Cohen *et al.*, 1975). Those periods and respiration amplitude (of inspiration and of expiration) following the critical, pre-critical and post-critical items were examined by computer processing for 50 field charts verified as guilty. Significantly longer expiration periods were found during the critical question; however, inspiration periods did not show any definite change over items. It was concluded that the decreased respiration rate during the critical question depended on the expiration period. Nakayama and Yamamura (1990) confirmed that expiration period is the most effective index of deception in field situations. Further observations from the same study showed decreased respiration amplitude following critical items and increased amplitude following post-critical items. Expiratory amplitude was found to vary more distinctly, the increased amplitude during the post-critical item was assumed to be related to compensation for respiratory suppression following critical questions.

Similarly Nakayama and Mizutani (1988) studied expiration period as an index of deception in the experimental setting. Twelve subjects were requested to select a computer image of the place of entry to a house in a burglary and deny all presented questions during visual presentation of the stimuli. Decrease of expiratory amplitude and increase of expiration period following the presentation of the critical item was consistently observed. Accordingly, Nakayama (1996) suggested that CIT using visual materials such as a map or photograph produces superior detection rates in respiration compared to presentation of an oral question.

STIMULUS REPETITIONS AND HABITUATION

Nakayama and Kizaki (1990) conducted two experiments to assess the usefulness of repeated questions on CIT. Twenty-four female subjects were instructed to conceal the critical item which they had previously selected, and their SCRs were recorded. In experiment 1, the amplitude of SCR to both the critical and non-critical items tended to decrease with the number of repetitions. However, responses to critical items were consistently larger than those to non-critical items during the total nine repetitions. In experiment 2, each item was presented three times successively, and SCR was enhanced at the first presentation of the critical items compared with experiment 1, while habituation processes were not different in the two experiments. These results suggested that the repetitive presentation of stimuli in CIT would be effective to distinguish the responses to the critical item from non-critical items because SCRs to non-critical items are remarkably inhibited.

EVENT-RELATED POTENTIAL ON THE EXPERIMENTAL CIT

The CIT procedure is closely related to the oddball paradigm that elicits the P3 event-related brain potential (ERP). Therefore, many Japanese researchers are interested in the use of ERP as a detection measure.

Detection of deception using ERP was first reported by Miyake *et al.* (1986) in Japan. They compared P3 produced in response to the critical item (subject's own name) with P3 produced in response to the non-critical items (other names). They reported that P3 amplitude was larger for the critical item than for the non-critical items. Similar studies reported that the critical item elicited a large P3 amplitude (Miyake *et al.*, 1987; Neshige *et al.*, 1991a; Neshige *et al.*, 1991b). These results indicate that P3 can be an effective indicator of "guilty knowledge." Furthermore, Miyake *et al.* (1993) used P3 for detection in 18 field examinees.

Besides P3 amplitude, the contingent negative variation (CNV) amplitude can be a useful psychophysiological index of the detection of deception (Hira *et al.*, 1989; Matsuda *et al.*, 1990). Hira and Matsuda (1998) examined the possible use of CNV as an index of detection of deception in a serial presentation of pictures. Twelve subjects were required to complete both an innocent and a guilty condition in that order. In the innocent condition, a series of six pictures, two of which depicted different landscapes and four others that depicted different female faces, was presented repeatedly on a computer display. Subjects responded by pressing a button following the landscape picture (target stimulus), which was presented last in the sequence. In the guilty condition, the procedures were the same except that subjects were also required not to detect one of the female pictures (critical item), which they had chosen after the completion of the innocent condition. As compared with the innocent condition, the CNV amplitudes decreased significantly immediately before the target stimulus in the guilty condition where subjects had to conceal the critical item. Not only P3 but also CNV can be an effective indicator of "guilty knowledge."

Recently, Hira (1998) reviewed ERP-based detection studies in England, Japan, and the United States. He found several advantages of using the ERP component as a detection index: (1) advancement and elaboration in judgment of test results because ERPs are specifically time-locked to an event; (2) an improvement of the correct detection rate; (3) an improvement of test objectivity and reliability; and (4) counteracting countermeasures. However, before ERPs can be used practically in the psychophysiological detection of deception, a method of artifact-free measurement of ERPs and a definite criterion of judgment for individuals must be established.

REFERENCES

Adachi, K. (1995) Statistical classification procedures for polygraph tests of guilty knowledge. *Behaviormetrika*, 22, 49–66.

Adachi, K. and Suzuki, A. (1994) A comparison of parameter estimation methods in statistical lie detection algorithm. *Reports of the National Research Institute of Police Science: Research on Forensic Science*, 47, 84 (text in Japanese with an English summary).

Akaike, H. (1974) A new look at the statistical model identification. *IEEE Transactions on Automatic Control*, 19, 716–723.

Anderson, T. W. (1984) *An Introduction to Multivariate Statistical Analysis*, 2nd edn. New York: Wiley.

Bando, E. and Nakayama, M. (1999) *The Effect of Verbal Answer on the Guilty Knowledge Test.* Proceedings of the 63rd annual meeting of the Japanese Psychological Association (text in Japanese).

Ben-Shakhar, G. (1977) Psychophysiological detection through the guilty knowledge technique: effects of mental countermeasures. *Journal of Applied Psychology*, 81, 273–281.

Ben-Shakhar, G. and Furedy, J. J. (1990) *Theories and Applications in the Detection of Deception: Psychophysiological and International Perspectives.* New York: Springer-Verlag.

Ben-Shakhar, G., Gati, I., and Salamon, N. (1995) Generalization of the orienting response to significant stimuli: The roles of common and distinctive stimulus components. *Psychophysiology*, 32, 36–42.

Bernstein, A. (1979) The orienting response as a novelty and significance detector: Reply to O'Gorman. *Psychophysiology*, 16, 263–273.

Bradley, M. T. and Ainsworth, D. (1984) Alcohol and the psychophysiological detection of deception. *Psychophysiology*, 21, 63–71.

Cohen, H. D., Goodenough, D. R., Witkin, H. A., Oltman, W. P., Gould, H. and Shulman, E. (1975) The effects of the stress component of the respiration cycle. *Psychophysiology*, 12, 377–380.

Craik, F. I. M. and Lockhart, R. S. (1972) Level of processing. A framework for memory research. *Journal of Verbal Learning and Verbal Behavior*, 11, 671–684.

Davis, R. C. (1961) Physiological responses as a means of evaluating information. In: A. D. Biderman, and H. Zimmer (eds) *The Manipulation of Human Behavior*, chapter 4, pp. 142–168. New York: Wiley.

Elaad, E. and Ben-Shakhar, G. (1989) Effects of motivation and verbal-response type on psychophysiological detection of information. *Psychophysiology*, 26, 442–451.

Elaad, E. and Ben-Shakhar, G. (1991) Effects of mental countermeasures on psychophysiological detection in the guilty knowledge test. *International Journal of Psychophysiology*, 11, 99–108.

Elaad, E. and Ben-Shakhar, G. (1997) Effects of item repetitions and variations on the efficiency of the guilty knowledge test. *Psychophysiology*, 34, 587–596.

Elaad, E., Ginton, A. and Jungman, N. (1992) Detection measure in real-life criminal guilty knowledge tests. *Journal of Applied Psychology*, 77, 757–767.

Fukumoto, J. (1980) A case in which the Polygraph was the sole evidence for conviction. *Polygraph*, 9, 42–44.

Fukumoto, J. (1982) Psychophysiological detection of deception in Japan: The past and the present. *Polygraph*, 11, 234–238.

Furedy, J. J. and Ben-Shakhar, G. (1990) The roles of deception, intention to deceive, and motivation to avoid detection in the psychophysiological detection of guilty knowledge. *Pychophysiology*, 28, 163–171.

Furedy, J. J., Davis, C. and Gurevich, M. (1988) Differentiation of deception as psychophysiological process: A psychophysiological approach. *Psychophysiology*, 25, 683–688.

Gati, I. and Ben-Shakhar, G. (1990) Novelty and significance in orientation and habituation: a feature-matching approach. *Journal of Experimental Psychology: General*, 1990, 251–263.

Gustafson, L. A. and Orne, M. T. (1965) The effects of verbal responses on the laboratory detection of deception. *Psychophysiology*, 2, 10–13.

Hare, R. D. (1973) Orienting and defensive responses to visual stimuli. *Psychophysiology*,10, 453–464.

Hikita, Y. (1971) The effectiveness of the polygraphic truth test. *Report of National Institute Police Science*, 24, 230–235 (text in Japanese).

Hira, S. (1998) Detection of deception with event-related brain potentials. *Japanese Journal of Science and Technology for Identification*, 3, 21–35 (text in Japanese with an English summary).

Hira, S. and Matsuda, T. (1998) Contingent negative variation (CNV) in the detection of deception task using a serial presentation of pictures. *Japanese Journal of Psychology*, 69, 149–155 (text in Japanese with an English summary).

Hira, S., Nakata,M., Matsuda,T. and Kakigi, S. (1989) Event related potential (P3 and CNV) as an index of detection of deception. *Japanese Journal of Physiological Psychology and Psychophysiology*, 7, 11–17 (text in Japanese with an English summary).

Honts, C. R., Devitt, M. K., Winbush, M. and Kircher, J. C. (1996) Mental and physical coun-termeasures reduce the accuracy of the concealed knowledge test. *Psychophysiology*, 33, 84–92.

Horneman, C. J. and O'Gorman, J. G. (1985) Detectability in the card test as a function of the subject's verbal response. *Psychophysiology*, 22, 331–333.

Iacono, W. G., Boisvenu,G. A. and Fleming, J. A. (1984) Effects of diazepam and methylphenidate on electrodermal detection of guilty knowledge. *Journal of Applied Psychology*, 69, 289–299.

Iacono, W. G., Cerri, A. M., Patrick, C. J. and Fleming, J. A. (1984) The use of antianxiety drugs as countermeasures in the detection of guilty knowledge. *Journal of Applied Psychology*, 77, 60–64.

Iacono, W. G. and Lykken, D. T. (1997) The validity of the lie detector: Two surveys of scientific opinion. *Journal of Applied Psychology*, 82, 426–433.

Iwami, H. and Tsuji, N. (1998) An examination of Adachi's statistical diagnosis algorithm in a practical polygraph test. *Japanese Journal of Science and Technology for Identification*, 3(2), A34 (text in Japanese).

Kasuya, T. (1999) *Practical Aspects of Polygraph Examination.* Tachibana Shobo (Tokyo) (text in Japanese).

Kiriu, M. (1991) Evaluation of question contents and memory of the critical question in the detection of deception. *Reports of National Research Institute of Police Science: Research on Forensic Science*, 44, 67–72 (text in Japanese with an English summary).

Kiriu, M. (1993) Dissimilarity between critical stimuli and criminal facts in the guilty knowledge test. *Reports of National Research Institute of Police Science: Research on Forensic Science*, 46, 6–10 (text in Japanese with an English summary).

Kiriu, M. (1996) The effect of correlation between criminal facts and non-critical stimuli in detection of deception. *The Japanese Journal of Criminal Psychology*, 34, 15–23 (text in Japanese).

Klorman, R., Wiesenfeld, A. R. and Austin, M. L. (1975) Automatic responses to affective visual stimuli. *Psychophysiology*, 12, 553–560.

Kugelmass, S., Liebilich, I. and Bergman, Z. (1967) The role of "lying" in psychophysiological detection. *Psychophysiology*, 31, 2–315.

Lykken, D. T. (1960) The validity of the guilty knowledge technique: The effect of faking. *Journal of Applied Psychology*, 44, 258–262.

Lykken, D. T. (1974) Psychology and the lie detector industry. *American Psychologist*, 29, 725–739.

Lykken, D. T. (1998) *A Tremor in the Blood: Uses and Abuses of the Lie Detector*, 2nd edn. New York: Plenum Press.

Maltzman, I. (1979) Orienting reflexes and significance: A reply to O'Gorman. *Psychophysiology*, 1979, 16, 274–282.

McLachlan, G. J. (1992) *Discriminant Analysis and Statistical Pattern Recognition*. New York: Wiley.

Manning, S. A. and Melchiori, M. P. (1974) Words that upset urban college students: Measured with GSRs and roting scales. *Journal of Social Psychology*, 94, 304–306.

Matsuda, T., Hira, S., Nakata, M. and Kakigi, S. (1990) The effect of one's own name upon event related potentials: Event related potential (P3 and CNV) as an index of detection of deception (2). *Japanese Journal of Physiological Psychology and Psychophysiology*, 8, 9–18 (text in Japanese with an English summary).

Matte, J. A. (1997) *Forensic Psychophysiology Using The Polygraph. Scientific Truth Verification – Lie Detection*. Williamsville, New York: Matte Polygraph Service.

Miyake, Y., Mizutani, M. and Yamamura, T. (1993) Event-related potentials as an indicator of detecting information in field polygraph examinations. *Polygraph*, 22, 131–149.

Miyake, Y., Okita, T. and Konishi, K. (1987) Effect of self-relevancy of stimuli of event-related brain potentials as an index of detection of deception. *Reports of National Research Institute of Police Science: Research on Forensic Science*, 40, 90–94 (text in Japanese with an English summary).

Miyake, Y., Okita, T., Konishi, K. and Matsunaga, I. (1986) Event-related brain potentials as an index of detection of deception. *Reports of National Research Institute of Police Science: Research on Forensic Science,* 39, 132–138 (text in Japanese with an English summary).

Nakayama, M. (1987) Suppression of respiration on the critical item and the rebound component. *Reports of National Research Institute of Police Science*, 40 (1), 32–37 (text in Japanese with an English summary).

Nakayama, M. (1996) Respiration curve. In: Y. Miyata, K. Yamazaki, K. Fujisawa and S. Kakigi (eds) *New Psychophysiology 2*, chapter 24, pp. 286–290. Kitaoji-Shobo (Japan) (text in Japanese).

Nakayama, M. and Kizaki, H. (1990) Usefulness of the repeated presentation of questions on the psychological detection of deception. *Japanese Journal of Psychology*, 60, 390–393 (text in Japanese with an English summary).

Nakayama, M. and Mizutani, M. (1988) The assessment of respiratory change evoked by the critical question. *Reports of National Research Institute of Police Science*, 41(1), 27–34 (text in Japanese with an English summary).

Nakayama, M., Mizutani, M. and Kizaki, H. (1988) The effects of delayed answers on the detection of deception. *Japanese Journal of Physiological Psychology and Psychophysiology*, 6, 35–40 (text in Japanese with an English summary).

Nakayama, M. and Yamamura, T. (1990) Changes of respiration pattern to the critical question on guilty knowledge technique. *Polygraph*, 19, 188–198.

Neshige, R., Kuroda, Y., Kakigi, R., Fujiyama, F. and Yarita, M. (1991a) Task-irrelevant event-related potentials related to recognition of a photograph. *Japanese Journal of Electroencephalography and Electromyography*, 19, 25–31 (text in Japanese with an English summary).

Neshige, R., Kuroda, Y., Kakigi, R., Fujiyama, F., Matoba, R., Yarita, M., Luders, H. and Shibasaki, H. (1991b) Event-related brain potentials as indicators of visual recognition and detection of criminals by their use. *Forensic Science International*, 51, 95–103.

Nihei, K. and Tateno, S. (1982) Credibility of polygraph tests in Ibaraki prefectural police. *Reports of National Research Institute of Police Science*, 36, 43–45 (text in Japanese).

O'Tool, D., Yuille, J. C., Patrick, C. J. and Iacono, W. (1994) Alcohol and the physiological detection of deception: Arousal and memory influences. *Psychophysiology*, 31, 253–263.

Pendery, M. and Maltzman, I. (1977) Instruction and the orienting reflex in "Semantic Conditioning" of the galvanic skin response in an innocuous situation. *Journal of Experimental Psychology: General*, 106, 120–140.

Raskin, D. C. (1979) Orienting and defensive reflexes in the detection of deception. In: H. D. Kimmel, E. H. van Olst and J. F. Orleveke (eds) *The Human Orienting Reflex in Humans*, chapter 34, pp. 587–605. Hillsdale, NJ: Lawrence Erlbaum Associates.

Schwartz, G. E. (1971) Cardiac responses to self-induced thoughts. *Psychophysiology*, 8, 462–467.

Shacter, D. L. (1987) Implicit memory: history and current status. *Journal of Experimental Psychology: Learning, Memory and Cognition*, 13, 501–518.

Stelmack, R. T. and Mandelzys, N. (1975) Extraversion and pupillary response to affective and taboo words. *Psychophysiology*, 12, 536–540.

Tokuda, Y. (1993) An approach to practical use of an automated diagnostic system for the polygraph test. *Reports of National Research Institute of Police Science: Research on Forensic Science*, 46, 22–26 (in Japanese).

Tulving, E. (1983) *Elements of Episodic Memory.* Oxford: Oxford University Press.

Yamamura, T. and Miyake, Y. (1980) Influences of the audio GSR feedback in the detection of deception. *Report of National Institute Police Science*, 29, 24–28 (text in Japanese with an English summary).

Yamamura, T. and Miyata, Y. (1990) Development of the polygraph technique in Japan for detection of deception. *Forensic Science International*, 44, 257–271.

Yokoi, Y. (1997) The effect of item plausibility on the concealed information test. *Japanese Journal of Science and Technology for Identification*, 2, 79 (text in Japanese).

Yokoi, Y. (1999) *The Relation Between Intention to Act and Memory of an Object in a Study of the Guilty Knowledge Test.* Proceedings of the 63rd Annual Meeting of the Japanese Psychological Association (text in Japanese).

CHAPTER 3

THE GUILTY KNOWLEDGE TEST (GKT) AS AN APPLICATION OF PSYCHOPHYSIOLOGY: FUTURE PROSPECTS AND OBSTACLES

Gershon Ben-Shakhar and Eitan Elaad

INTRODUCTION

The controversy surrounding the polygraph has been focused almost exclusively on the validity and application of the "control questions test" (see, e.g., Ben-Shakhar and Furedy, 1990; Furedy and Heslegrave, 1991; Iacono and Lykken, 1997, 1999; Lykken, 1974, 1978; Raskin, 1982, 1989; Raskin *et al.*, 1997, 1999; Saxe *et al.*, 1983, 1985). Unfortunately too little attention has been paid to research and discussions of other methods of psychophysiological detection. In particular, we are referring to the guilty knowledge test (GKT), also called the concealed information test (CIT).

The GKT (Lykken, 1959, 1960) utilizes a series of multiple-choice questions, each having one relevant alternative (e.g., a feature of the crime under investigation) and several neutral (control) alternatives, chosen so that an innocent suspect would not be able to discriminate them from the relevant alternative (Lykken, 1998). Typically, if the suspect's physiological responses to the relevant alternative are consistently larger than to the neutral alternatives, knowledge about the event (e.g., crime) is inferred. As long as information about the event has not leaked out, the probability that an innocent suspect would show consistently larger responses to the relevant than to the neutral alternatives depends only on the number of questions and the number of alternative answers per question. Thus, the rate of false positive errors (innocent examinees classified as guilty) can be controlled such that maximal protection for the innocent is provided.

Indeed, laboratory research has supported this hypothesis, and most studies conducted to estimate the validity of the GKT have reported high accuracy rates, particularly among innocent examinees. For example, Ben-Shakhar and Furedy (1990) reviewed and summarized 10 GKT laboratory experiments and showed that across these studies, 83.9% of 248 guilty examinees and 94.2% of 208 innocent examinees were correctly classified. They acknowledged that the number of studies they analyzed was too small to allow for a statistical examination of the sources of the between-studies variability, but they speculated that the number of GKT questions used is a natural candidate for accounting for at least some of this variability. They noted that the two studies that used the largest number of questions (Bradley and Ainsworth, 1984; Bradley and Warfield, 1984, nine and ten, respectively) demonstrated the largest rates of correct classifications. Ben-Shakhar and Furedy (1990) concluded that with a sufficiently large number of GKT questions the method could be used quite efficiently. More recently, Elaad (1998) reviewed 15 mock crime studies attempting to estimate the validity of the GKT and reached similar conclusions. Elaad (1998) estimated the accuracy rates among guilty and innocent examinees as 80.6% and 95.9%, respectively, and noted that in 11 of these 15 studies no false positive errors were documented.

In spite of the research findings, which suggest that the GKT can be efficiently applied for detecting relevant information, this method is not being used very much in actual investigations. Furthermore, almost no advances have been made toward an implementation of the GKT. This is particularly surprising because the GKT is protected against most of the criticisms that have been directed toward the control question test (CQT), which is a widely used method of psychophysiological detection. The purpose of this chapter is to call for a shift in our research efforts. In particular, we should explore ways to make the GKT more usable. In the next section, we shall discuss several features of the GKT, which highlight the potential of this method as an applied technique for detecting involvement in criminal events. Then, we shall discuss the weaknesses of the GKT, and the reasons for its infrequent usage. The concluding section will be devoted to various means that should be adopted to overcome the weaknesses of the GKT and to broaden its usage as an aid in criminal investigation, and possibly in legal proceedings.

FEATURES OF THE GKT THAT MAKE IT AN ATTRACTIVE METHOD FOR FORENSIC APPLICATIONS

Several features of the GKT make this method an attractive application of psychophysiology. Furthermore, some of these features highlight the advantages of the GKT over alternative methods of psychophysiological detection. In this section we shall review and discuss these features.

THE GKT IS BASED ON PROPER CONTROL QUESTIONS, AND THUS IT SUPPLIES SUFFICIENT PROTECTION FOR INNOCENT SUSPECTS

As described above, the GKT is structured such that as long as relevant information has not leaked, innocent examinees could not discriminate between the critical and the neutral, control items. Thus, if sufficient number of questions are used, the probability that an innocent (uninformed) examinee will show consistently larger physiological responses to the relevant than to the neutral, control items could be minimized. This feature of the GKT does not characterize any of the alternative methods of psychophysiological detection, in which the relevant and control questions differ on several dimensions.

THE GKT STANDS ON WELL-ESTABLISHED PSYCHOPHYSIOLOGICAL FOUNDATIONS

Any scientifically based technology must be based on sound theoretical foundations. In this respect, the case of the GKT, unlike other methods of psychophysiological detection, is relatively simple. This method is based on extensive research and theory on orienting responses (ORs) and habituation processes in humans (e.g., Siddle, 1991; Sokolov, 1963, 1966). OR is a complex of physiological and behavioral reactions evoked by any novel stimulus or by any change in stimulation (e.g., Berlyne, 1960; Sokolov, 1963). In principle, each item presented to the subject, whether guilty or innocent, in the course of the GKT is capable of evoking an OR. Naturally, these ORs will display a habituation process – a gradual decline in response magnitude with repeated presentations of the stimuli (Sokolov, 1963). The interesting feature of orientation, which provides this concept with an explanatory power for the detection phenomenon, is that significant stimuli (i.e., stimuli that have a signal value) evoke enhanced ORs (Gati and Ben-Shakhar, 1990). Lykken (1974:728) made the connection arguing that: "... for the guilty subject only, the 'correct' alternative will have a special significance, an added 'signal value' which will tend to produce a stronger orienting reflex than that subject will show to other alternatives". In other words, it is assumed that the guilty knowledge endows a subset of the items with significance, or signal value, and therefore those items will evoke stronger ORs. Clearly, for subjects who do not possess the guilty knowledge, all items are equivalent and evoke similar ORs that will habituate with repetitions.

Ben-Shakhar and Furedy (1990) labeled this approach to psychophysiological detection a cognitive approach, because it emphasizes the fact that an individual knows something, rather than the individual's emotions, concerns, fears, conditioned responses, or deception. This approach is compatible with findings that demonstrate how relevant information can be detected even under mild conditions where no motivational instructions are given to the subjects and where no verbal response is required (e.g., Ben-Shakhar, 1977; Ben-Shakhar and Lieblich, 1982; Elaad and Ben-Shakhar, 1989). It is compatible also with the surprising detection without awareness effect reported by Thackray and Orne (1968).

THE GKT IS BASED ON A STANDARDIZED PROCEDURE

Standardization is another important feature of scientifically based techniques and tests, because it guarantees that the different examinees undergo the same experience. Only when a given test is based on standardized procedures do the resulting scores (or evaluations) have a uniform meaning, allowing comparisons between different people who took the test. The GKT can be designed in a standardized fashion, and once salient features of the event are identified, it is easy to formulate the relevant and control alternatives. Furthermore, it is easy to check whether the alternative items formulated for each question are equivalent (see, e.g., Lykken, 1998). Unlike alternative psychophysiological detection methods, the choice of relevant and control items in the GKT does not depend on a pre-test interview with the examinee and on the examiner–examinee interaction. They can be formulated before the polygraph investigation, and used uniformly to test all the suspects in a given case. Finally, the GKT can easily be administered using a "blind" procedure (i.e., by an examiner who is unaware of the critical items).

CONTAMINATION WITH NON-PHYSIOLOGICAL INFORMATION CAN BE AVOIDED WITH THE GKT

One of the major criticisms expressed toward the use of the polygraph test as an aid in legal proceedings is the fact that judgments made on the basis of their results are based on more information than is contained in the physiological measures alone (e.g., the opinion of the examiner formed during the pre-test interview, rumors the examiner heard prior to the administration of the test). In addition, during the investigation the polygraphist is in a position to watch and monitor the totality of a suspect's behavior, and not just the physiological changes alone. An experienced interrogator might well use these characteristics. Thus, it is always uncertain whether, and to what extent, a given judgment made by a polygraph examiner results from the physiological responses to the questions, or from other factors. This feature, which characterizes all polygraph investigations conducted by law-enforcement agencies, was labeled "contamination" (Ben-Shakhar, 1991; Ben-Shakhar et al., 1986; Elaad et al., 1994, but see also Elaad et al., 1998). The damaging consequences of contaminated polygraph examination, from a legal perspective, were discussed by Ben-Shakhar et al. (1986). They argued that the use of contaminated polygraph test results as admissible evidence could open the door for a type of "laundering" of inadmissible evidence, or evidence obtained through illegal means, without legal checks. Such evidence could accrue unknown weight through the influence it exerts on the opinions of the polygraphist, who has prior acquaintance with it.

But, while it may be difficult to decontaminate the CQT, contamination can be completely avoided with the GKT, because there is no need for a pre-test interview, and the test can be designed and administered by experts unfamiliar with the case or the suspects. Furthermore, the questions can be pre-recorded by someone who has no information about the case under investigation. In addition, interpretation, quantification, and integration of the physiological data can be conducted with the GKT in an objective way using mechanical, computerized rules (in principle, this can be achieved with the CQT as well, see Kircher and Raskin 1988, but it is not typically the case in practice). Thus, the interpretation of the GKT outcomes and the conclusions drawn from them would not be affected in any way by the prior knowledge and the impressions formed by the investigators prior to conducting the GKT.

THE ACCURACY OF THE GKT CAN BE ESTIMATED FROM LABORATORY STUDIES

So far we have discussed various features of the GKT that were derived from the structure of this procedure. But, the crucial question regarding all methods of psychophysiological detection is whether they can discriminate between guilty (those that were actually involved with a criminal act) and innocent individuals. An extensive body of research attempting to estimate the accuracy of the various detection methods has been conducted in the past three decades (for reviews see Ben-Shakhar and Furedy, 1990; Elaad, 1998; Kircher et al., 1988; Saxe et al., 1983 1985). However, several methodological questions have been raised regarding this research (e.g., Ben-Shakhar and Furedy, 1990). One of the major problems is whether the results of controlled experiments conducted in laboratory settings can be generalized to the realistic context of criminal investigations. In the typical laboratory experiment, subjects designated as "guilty" are asked by the experimenter to steal an envelope containing money, or some other item. Then, all the participants (both "guilty" who are asked by the experimenter to hide their connection to the simulated crime and "innocent" who did not commit the mock crime) are examined by a polygraph interrogator. When the experiment is over, they are given a monetary reward, thanked, and sent on their way. Obviously, these conditions do not begin to resemble the conditions of a real life investigation. There is no deception in the conventional sense of the word, and there is no anxiety about the consequences of the examination (either for the "guilty" or for the "innocent").

However, while this problem is particularly acute in the case of the CQT, it seems that results of laboratory studies, conducted to assess the validity of the GKT, can, at least partially, be generalized to the realistic context. This view is based on the nature of the GKT as a method, which does not depend on factors

THE PROBLEM OF COUNTERMEASURES

A number of experiments (e.g., Ben-Shakhar and Dolev, 1996; Elaad and Ben-Shakhar, 1991; Honts *et al.*, 1987, 1994, 1996; Kubis, 1962) have indicated that it is possible, indeed quite easy, to train guilty examinees and prepare them for a polygraph examination (either CQT or GKT) in such a way that they will be found truthful with a high probability. This can be done by adopting some rather simple techniques (that can be picked up with little effort), which can cause very strong reactions to the control questions. These techniques rely either on the use of physical means (such as biting one's tongue), or mental means (calling to mind an exciting or frightening event, or engaging in mental activities that require effort) each time a control question is asked. A series of experiments conducted by Honts and his colleagues demonstrated that the use of such countermeasures could be most effective. They showed in different experiments that the error rate produced by polygraphists testing "guilty" examinees who were using countermeasures ranged between 50% and 70%. Clearly, countermeasures may increase false negative outcomes (guilty suspects classified as "innocents"), but they have no effect on innocent examinees.

It should be pointed out that the type of countermeasures that are most detrimental for all psychophysiological detection techniques are mental countermeasures, because mental manipulations cannot be detected even by the most experienced examiners. Two recent studies demonstrated that mental countermeasures can be used effectively under both the GKT and the CQT (Ben-Shakhar and Dolev, 1996; Honts *et al.*, 1996).

FUTURE DIRECTIONS IN GKT RESEARCH: ATTEMPTING TO OVERCOME THE WEAKNESSES AND INCREASE ITS POTENTIAL USAGE

In this section, we shall discuss various ideas and some recent research results that show how the weaknesses of the GKT could be dealt with, so that a wider application of this technique could be achieved.

THE GKT MUST RELY ON A SUFFICIENT NUMBER OF PROPER GKT QUESTIONS

Identification of a sufficient number of GKT questions is clearly necessary for a successful implementation of this technique. Typically, it has been assumed that at least four different questions are necessary (e.g., Podlesny, 1993). But this assumption has not been tested empirically. It is clear that a single presentation of a GKT question with five or six alternative answers would be insufficient because an innocent, uninformed examinee would show the largest response to the critical alternative with a fairly large probability (0.16 or 0.20, in our example). But in principle it is possible to reduce the probability of a false positive error by using many repetitions of just one or two different questions, and by using several physiological measures.

Recently, we conducted two studies to test the efficiency of the GKT, based on a single question repeated several times, with two physiological measures (changes in skin conductance and respiration). Our first study (Elaad and Ben-Shakhar, 1997) produced very encouraging results and suggested that a single GKT question can produce an efficient discrimination between guilty and innocent examinees. Specifically, two experiments were conducted, in which a GKT based on four different questions, each repeated three times, was compared with a GKT based on 12 repetitions of a single question. Both experiments revealed that similar detection efficiencies were observed in these two conditions (for example, in the first experiment a combination of the two physiological measures yielded an area under the Receiver Operating Characteristics – ROC – of 0.86 for the single-question condition, and 0.88 for the multiple-questions condition).

This result was rather unexpected; therefore, we decided to conduct a constructive replication of the Elaad and Ben-Shakhar (1997) study. In this replication (Ben-Shakhar and Elaad, 2001), we added a third experimental condition, in which 12 different questions were used. In addition, instead of a mock-crime experiment we used a list of biographical details (e.g., mother's name, place of birth). The results of this study differed from those reported by Elaad and Ben-Shakhar (1997) and a clear advantage for the multiple-questions condition emerged in this experiment with the electrodermal measure, but not with the respiration measure. Although statistically significant differentiation between "guilty" and "innocent" individuals was observed under all three conditions, the use of multiple questions produced higher detection efficiencies (the areas under the ROC curves, obtained with a combination of the electrodermal and respiration measures, were 0.80, 0.88, and 0.99 in the single-question, 4-questions and 12-questions conditions, respectively).

Clearly, these results indicate that using several GKT questions is desirable. But at the same time, it seems that relatively high levels of detection efficiency could be obtained, even with a single question, provided that it is repeated many times and that several physiological measures are used. Further research is required to examine this issue in the real-life context. If this research shows similar results, it would mean that GKT could be more widely applied.

Another direction that also points out that a single GKT question may be sufficient was taken by MacLaren (1998), who demonstrated that expectancy conditioning might allow effective guilt discrimination using a single item of concealed information.

DEALING WITH THE PROBLEM OF INFORMATION LEAKAGE

The results of the field studies reported by Elaad and his colleagues (Elaad, 1990; Elaad *et al.*, 1992) suggest that leakage of relevant (crime-related) information did not affect the results of GKTs administered by the Israeli police. But the issue of information leakage and its effect on the outcomes of the GKT must be carefully examined before a wider application of the GKT can be recommended.

The effects of leakage of relevant information to innocent examinees have been studied extensively by Bradley and his colleagues (Bradley *et al.*, 1996; Bradley and Rettinger, 1992; Bradley and Warfield, 1984). These studies demonstrated that although informed innocent participants show larger responsivity to the critical items, as compared with uninformed innocents, they could be differentiated from guilty participants. In other words, other factors in addition to knowledge of the critical items play a role in determining differential responsivity to the critical items. In addition, Bradley and his colleagues showed that an alternative formulation of the GKT questions (the guilty action test) could reduce false positive outcomes among informed innocent suspects.

A recent study conducted in our laboratory (Ben-Shakhar *et al.*, 1999) demonstrated that introducing an additional task (responding to target items, which are unrelated to the event under investigation, while answering the GKT questions) may differentially attract the attention of informed innocent participants and reduce false positive outcomes in this group. These studies suggest that the risk associated with false positive outcomes, owing to leakage of relevant information, may be reduced by introducing new variations and improvements to the GKT.

A different approach to the problem of information leakage is to modify police practices, such that critical features of the event are identified and concealed at the outset of the investigation, as a standard investigative practice. Furthermore, GKTs could be conducted by investigators who are familiar with the scene of the crime and are trained to look for salient features that could be utilized as GKT questions. The fact that the GKT has been used for many years by Japanese law enforcement agencies as the preferred method of psychophysiological detection (Ben-Shakhar and Furedy, 1990; Fukumoto, 1980; Yamamura, and Miyata, 1990) demonstrates that these changes are possible.

DEALING WITH THE PROBLEM OF COUNTERMEASURES

Finally, the problem of countermeasures that has been shown to affect the GKT as much as it affects the CQT (Honts *et al.*, 1996) must be dealt with. A possible approach for dealing with countermeasure manipulations is the use of GKTs that are based on event-related potentials (ERPs) instead of autonomic measures. Several studies have demonstrated that guilty and innocent participants can be differentiated quite effectively with ERPs (e.g., Allen *et al.*, 1992; Farwell and Donchin, 1991; Rosenfeld *et al.*, 1988, 1991). ERP measures seem to be immune to countermeasures because they are based on a repeated rapid presentation of the items (e.g., one item per second). When items are presented at such a rapid pace, it is virtually impossible to execute countermeasures to the control items. This idea may require additional research, but it could lead to a GKT, which would be protected against countermeasures.

SUMMARY AND CONCLUSIONS

In this chapter we analyzed the GKT and discussed both its advantages over alternative methods of psychophysiological detection and its weaknesses. We showed that the GKT is based on proper controls, such that if the critical, crime-related information has not been leaked, maximal protection can be provided for innocent suspects. This feature of the GKT makes it an attractive aid in criminal investigations and possibly in legal proceedings (see a recent discussion of the possible use of GKT results as admissible evidence in criminal trials in Ben-Shakhar *et al.*, 2001). In addition, the GKT can be designed in a standardized manner, and the interpretation of its results can be made on the basis of objective and quantified measurement procedures. These features of the GKT guarantee that it can be administered in a non-contaminated manner. Finally, the GKT is based on well-established psychophysiological research and theory.

Our discussion also reveals three weaknesses of the GKT that may explain why this method is not being used very much as an aid in criminal investigations in North America. In many cases, it is difficult to identify a sufficient number of salient features of the event (features that are likely to be noticed and remembered by guilty individuals). Once such features have been identified, it is difficult to keep them concealed from the general public and from innocent suspects. Leakage of critical items might increase the likelihood of false positive outcomes. Finally, the use of mental or physical countermeasures might affect the outcome of the GKT and increase the rate of false negative outcomes.

In the final section, we reviewed recent studies that examined various means that can be used to modify the GKT, such that the effects of its weaknesses would be limited. First, it seems that the use of just one or two proper GKT questions with many repetitions and several physiological measures may produce relatively high levels of detection efficiency. Second, a modification of police investigation procedures may minimize the possibility that critical information would be leaked out. Furthermore, changes in the structure of the GKT and in the formulation of its questions may reduce the effects of information leakage. Finally, we argued that the use of ERPs in addition to the standard autonomic measures might be an important protection against the use of countermeasures.

Clearly, further research is required to examine whether these ideas can indeed be applied, in order that the GKT can become an efficient and feasible forensic method. In particular, more field studies are needed to examine how the GKT, with the various modifications, would function in realistic conditions. But we are certain that such efforts will be fruitful because we believe that the GKT has excellent potential as a forensic application of psychophysiology.

REFERENCES

Allen, J. J., Iacono, W. G. and Danielson, K. D. (1992) The development and validation of an event-related-potential memory assessment procedure: A methodology for prediction in the face of individual differences. *Psychophysiology*, 29, 504–522.

Ben-Shakhar, G. (1977) A further study of dichotomization theory in detection of information. *Psychophysiology*, 14, 408–413.

Ben-Shakhar, G. (1991) Clinical judgment and decision making in CQT polygraphy: A comparison with other pseudoscientific applications in psychology. *Integrative Physiological and Behavioral Science*, 26, 232–240.

Ben-Shakhar, G., Bar-Hillel, M. and Kremnitzer, M. (2001) Trial by polygraph: Reconsidering the use of the Guilty Knowledge Technique in court. Manuscript in preparation.

Ben-Shakhar, G., Bar-Hillel, M. and Lieblich, I. (1986) Trial by polygraph: Scientific and juridical issues in lie detection. *Behavioral Science and the Law*, 4, 459–479.

Ben-Shakhar, G. and Dolev, K. (1996) Psychophysiological detection through the guilty knowledge technique: the effects of mental countermeasures. *Journal of Applied Psychology*, 81, 273–281.

Ben-Shakhar, G. and Elaad, E. (2001) Effects of questions' repetition on the efficiency of the guilty knowledge test: A reexamination. Manuscript in preparation.

Ben-Shakhar, G., and Furedy, J.J. (1990) *Theories and Applications in the Detection of Deception: A Psychophysiological and International Perspective*. New York: Springer-Verlag.

Ben-Shakhar, G., Gronau, N. and Elaad, E. (1999) Leakage of relevant information to innocent examinees in the GKT: An attempt to reduce false-positive outcomes by introducing target stimuli. *Journal of Applied Psychology*, 84, 651–660.

Ben-Shakhar, G. and Lieblich, I. (1982) The dichotimization theory for differential autonomic responsivity reconsidered. *Psychophysiology*, 19, 277–281.

Berlyne, D. E. (1960) *Conflict, Arousal and Curiosity.* New York, NY: McGraw-Hill.

Bradley, M. T. and Ainsworth D. (1984) Alcohol and psychophysiological detection of deception. *Psychophysiology*, 21, 63–71.

Bradley. M. T., MacLaren, V. V. and Carle, S. B. (1996) Deception and nondeception in guilty knowledge and guilty actions polygraph tests. *Journal of Applied Psychology*, 81, 153–160.

Bradley, M. T. and Rettinger, J. (1992) Awareness of crime relevant information and the guilty knowledge test. *Journal of Applied Psychology*, 77, 55–59.

Bradley, M. T. and Warfield, J. F. (1984) Innocence, information, and the guilty knowledge test in the detection of deception. *Psychophysiology*, 21, 683–689.

Elaad, E. (1990) Detection of guilty knowledge in real-life criminal investigations. *Journal of Applied Psychology*, 75, 521–529.

Elaad, E. (1998) The challenge of the concealed knowledge polygraph test. *Expert Evidence*, 6, 161–187.

Elaad, E. (1999) A comparative study of polygraph tests and other forensic methods. In: D. Canter and L. Alison (eds) *Offender Profiling Series, Vol. 1: Interviewing and Deception*, pp. 209–231. Aldershot, England: Ashgate Publishing.

Elaad, E. and Ben-Shakhar, G. (1989) Effects of motivation and verbal response type on psychophysiological detection of information. *Psychophysiology*, 26, 442–451.

Elaad, E. and Ben-Shakhar, G. (1991) Effects of mental countermeasures on psychophysiological detection in the guilty knowledge test. *International Journal of Psychophysiology*, 11, 99–108.

Elaad, E. and Ben-Shakhar, G. (1997) Effects of item repetitions and variations on the efficiency of the guilty knowledge test. *Psychophysiology*, 34, 587–596.

Elaad, E., Ginton, A. and Ben-Shakhar, G. (1994) The effects of prior expectations and outcome knowledge on polygraph examiners' decisions. *Journal of Behavioral Decision Making*, 7, 279–292.

Elaad, E., Ginton, A. and Ben-Shakhar, G. (1998) The role of prior expectations in polygraph examiners' decisions. *Psychology, Crime and Law*, 4, 1–16.

Elaad, E., Ginton, A. and Jungman., N. (1992) Detection measures in real-life criminal guilty knowledge tests. *Journal of Applied Psychology*, 77, 757–767.

Farwell, L. A. and Donchin, E. (1991).The truth will out: Interrogative polygraphy ("lie detection") with event-related brain potentials. *Psychophysiology*, 28, 531–547.

Fukumoto, J. (1980) A case in which the polygraph was the sole evidence for conviction. *Polygraph*, 9, 42–44.

Furedy, J. J. and Heslegrave, R. J. (1991) The forensic use of the polygraph: A psychophysiological analysis of current trends and future prospects. In: J. R. Jennings, P. K. Ackles and M. G. H. Coles (eds) *Advances in Psychophysiology*, vol. 4. Greenwich, CT: Jessica Kingsley Publishers.

Gati, I. and Ben-Shakhar, G. (1990) Novelty and significance in orientation and habituation: A feature-matching approach. *Journal of Experimental Psychology: General*, 119, 251–263.

Honts, C. R., Devitt, M. K, Winbush, M. and Kircher, J. C. (1996) Mental and physical countermeasures reduce the accuracy of the concealed knowledge test. *Psychophysiology*, 33, 84–92.

Honts, C. R., Raskin, D. C. and Kircher, J. C. (1987) Effects of physical countermeasures and their electromyographic detection during polygraph tests for deception. *Journal of Psychophysiology*, 1, 241–247.

Honts, C. R., Raskin, D. C. and Kircher, J. C. (1994) Mental and physical countermeasures reduce the accuracy of polygraph tests. *Journal of Applied Psychology*, 79, 252–259.

Iacono, W. G. and Lykken, D. T. (1997) The scientific status of research on polygraph techniques: The case against polygraph tests. In: D. L. Faigman, D. Kaye, M. J. Saks, and J. Sanders (eds) *Modern Scientific Evidence: The Law and Science of Expert Testimony*. St. Paul, MN: West Law.

Iacono, W. G. and Lykken, D. T. (1999) Update: The scientific status of research on polygraph techniques: The case against polygraph tests. In: D. L. Faigman, D. H. Kaye, M. J. Saks and J. Sanders (eds) *Modern Scientific Evidence: The Law and Science of Expert Testimony*. St. Paul, MN: West Publishing, pp. 174–184.

Kircher, J. C. and Raskin, D.C. (1988) Human versus computerized evaluations of polygraph data in laboratory setting. *Journal of Applied Psychology*, 73, 291–302.

Kircher, J. C., Horowitz, S. W. and Raskin, D.C. (1988) Meta-analysis of mock crime studies of the control question polygraph technique. *Law and Human Behavior*, 12, 78–90.

Kubis, J. F. (1962) *Studies in Lie Detection: Computer Feasibility Considerations*. Technical Report #62-205, prepared for the Air Force Systems Command. Contract No. AF 30 (602)-2270, project No. 5534, Fordham University.

Lykken, D. T. (1959) The GSR in the detection of guilt. *Journal of Applied Psychology*, 43, 385–388.

Lykken, D. T. (1960) The validity of the guilty knowledge technique: The effects of faking. *Journal of Applied Psychology*, 44, 258–262.

Lykken, D. T. (1974) Psychology and the lie detection industry. *American Psychologist*, 29, 725–739.

Lykken, D. T. (1978) Uses and abuses of the polygraph. In: H. L. Pick (ed.) *Psychology: From Research to Practice*. New York: Plenum Press.

Lykken, D. T. (1998) *A Tremor in the Blood: Uses and Abuses of the Lie Detector.* New York: Plenum Trade.

MacLaren, V. (1998) *Detection of Concealed Information Using Manipulated Expectations.* A paper presented at a symposium entitled "Towards a Scientifically Based Forensic Psychophysiology", The 24th International Congress of Applied Psychology, San Francisco, California, August, 1998.

Podlesny, J. A. (1993) Is the guilty knowledge polygraph technique applicable in criminal investigations? A review of FBI case records. *Crime Laboratory Digest*, 20, 57–61.

Raskin, D. C. (1982) The scientific basis of polygraph techniques and their uses in the judicial process. In: A. Trankell (ed.) *Reconstructing the Past: The Role of Psychologists in the Criminal Trial*. Stockholm: Norsted and Soners.

Raskin, D. C. (1989) Polygraph techniques for the detection of deception. In: D. C. Raskin (ed.). *Psychological Methods in Criminal Investigation and Evidence*. New York: Springer-Verlag.

Raskin, D. C., Honts, C. R., Amato, S. L. and Kircher, J. C. (1999) Update: The scientific status of research on polygraph techniques: The case for the admissibility of the results of polygraph examinations. In: D. L. Faigman, D. H. Kaye, M. J. Saks, and J. Sanders (eds) *Modern Scientific Evidence: The Law and Science of Expert Testimony*, vol. 1. Pocket Part, pp. 160–174. St. Paul, MN: West Publishing.

Raskin, D. C., Honts, C. R. and Kircher, J. C. (1997) The scientific status of research on polygraph techniques: The case for polygraph tests. In: D. L. Faigman, D. Kaye, M. J. Saks and J. Sanders (eds) *Modern Scientific Evidence: The Law and Science of Expert Testimony*. St. Paul, MN: West Law.

Rosenfeld, J. P., Angell, A., Johnson, M. and Qian, J. H. (1991) An ERP based, control-question lie detector analog: Algorithms for discriminating effects within individuals' average wave forms. *Psychophysiology*, 32, 319–335.

Rosenfeld, J. P., Cantwell, B., Nasman, V. T., Wojdac, V., Ivanov, S. and Mazzeiri, L. (1988) A modified event-related potential-based guilty-knowledge test. *International Journal of Neuroscience*, 24, 157–161.

Saxe, L., Dougherty, D. and Cross, T. P. (1983) *Scientific Validity of Polygraph Testing (OTA-TM-H-15)*. (Report for the U.S. Congress Office of Technology Assessment). Washington, DC: U.S. Government Printing Office.

Saxe, L., Dougherty, D. and Cross, T. P. (1985) The validity of polygraph testing: Scientific analysis and public controversy. *American Psychologist,* 40, 355–366.

Siddle, D. A. T. (1991) Orienting, habituation, and resource allocation: An associative analysis. *Psychophysiology*, 28, 245–259.

Sokolov, E. N. (1963) *Perception and the Conditioned Reflex*. New York, NY: Macmillan.

Sokolov, E. N. (1966) Orienting reflex as information regulator. In: A. Leontyev, A. Luria and A. Smirnov (eds) *Psychological Research in the U.S.S.R.*, pp. 334–360. Moscow: Progress Publishers.

Thackray, R. I. and Orne, M. T. (1968) A comparison of physiological indices in detection of deception. *Psychophysiology*, 4, 329–339.

Yamamura, T. and Miyata, Y. (1990) Development of the polygraph technique in Japan for detection of deception. *Forensic Science International*, 44, 257–271.

CHAPTER 4

A CRITICAL REVIEW OF THE CONTROL QUESTIONS TEST (CQT)

Gershon Ben-Shakhar

INTRODUCTION

The control questions technique (CQT) is the most widely used method of psychophysiological detection and is currently used for various purposes (e.g., criminal investigations, employee screening and selection) in several countries, most notably in North America and Israel. Although the scientific basis and validity of the CQT have been debated in the scientific literature (e.g., Ben-Shakhar and Furedy, 1990; Iacono and Lykken, 1997, 1999; Lykken, 1974, 1998; Raskin, 1986, 1989; Raskin *et al.*, 1997, 1999), its extensive use continues. The purpose of this chapter is to present a critical analysis of the CQT, which demonstrates that this method does not have a sound scientific foundation, and that decisions made on the basis of its results may suffer from several flaws and biases. This does not necessarily mean that the CQT cannot serve as an aid to law-enforcement agencies, which use other non-scientific investigative methods, but it definitely means that it should not be used as admissible evidence in legal proceedings.

The chapter opens with a very brief description of the CQT. The next sections focus on the major problematic aspects of the CQT: (1) inadequate theoretical and logical rationale; (2) inadequate standardization; (3) lack of objective quantification procedures of the physiological responses; (4) the implications of contamination with other sources of information; (5) the problem of countermeasures. The empirical questions regarding the reliability and validity of the CQT will be discussed in the next section, and it will be argued that the available research is insufficient for estimating the accuracy of CQT outcomes that would be obtained in realistic criminal investigations. Finally, conclusions will be drawn regarding the various applications of the CQT.

A BRIEF DESCRIPTION OF THE CQT

Detailed descriptions of the CQT can be found in various sources (e.g., Raskin, 1989; Reid and Inbau, 1977; Saxe *et al.*, 1983). For the purposes of this chapter, actions based on test scores. In other words, in the process of validating a test or a method, it is not sufficient to demonstrate that its results correlate with a relevant criterion (i.e., predictive or criterion validity). A theoretical foundation is particularly important for validating the CQT because we need to generalize from experimental situations to realistic settings and this is virtually impossible without a theory.

Recently, Saxe and Ben-Shakhar (1999) analyzed the CQT in the light of Messick's (1989, 1995) approach and showed that it cannot be regarded as a valid test of deception. Specifically, there is no theory that can establish the relationships between physiological changes and deception. Furthermore, there is a general consensus, even among CQT proponents, that there is no specific "lie response." For example, Raskin (1986:31) wrote: "No known physiological response or pattern of responses is unique to deception." Thus, Saxe and Ben-Shakhar (1999) argued that the two major sources of invalidity noted by Messick (1995) affect CQT polygraph testing. First, the construct of deception is underrepresented by the CQT results, because there is neither a theoretical rationale, nor empirical evidence to support the relationship between the physiological measures monitored during the CQT examination and deceptive behavior. Second, CQT results may reflect other constructs, such as surprise, anxiety, and stress. Consequently, it suffers from the second major threat to validity suggested by Messick, namely "construct-irrelevant variance" – the assessment is too broad, and contains excess reliable variance associated with other distinct constructs.

But even if we abandoned the idea of psychophysiological detection of deception and restricted ourselves to more modest goals, such as detection of involvement with a criminal event, the CQT would still need to have a theoretical basis, or at least a logical rationale. Indeed, many CQT proponents (e.g., Raskin, 1986) have abandoned the notion of "a specific lie response," but argued that inferences about truth or deception could be made by comparing the relative strength of the subject's responses to relevant and control questions. However, no convincing rationale for such inferences has been given so far.

The major problem stems from the nature of the control questions used in the CQT. The phrase "control questions" gives the impression that true controls are being exercised. From a logical perspective, true controls require a perfect match between all factors other than the factor being tested (in this case, the factor of deception or involvement in a crime). Hence, the control questions ought to be just like the relevant questions in all details, though only the relevant questions should tie the suspect to the crime. In other words, from the perspective of an innocent suspect there ought to be no differences whatsoever between the two types of questions. Whereas this kind of control is exercised in another psychophysiological detection method, the guilty knowledge technique (GKT), it does not exist in the CQT. As explained earlier, in the CQT the relevant questions are questions that relate directly to the specific event being investigated, while the control questions relate to general, non-specific crimes. Thus, in the CQT both relevant and control questions are relevant to all examinees, but to different and unknown degrees. Clearly, one cannot assume that these questions are equivalent. Because of these obvious differences, it has been argued that the term "control" is misleading in this context (see, e.g., Ben-Shakhar and Furedy, 1990; Furedy and Heslegrave, 1991). The differences between the two types of questions are obvious, and even an innocent suspect can easily distinguish between a question that relates directly to the focal event around which the investigation revolves (the event that provided the impetus for conducting an investigation), and general questions related to hypothetical events from the examinee's past. Moreover, once an examinee is aware of the CQT rationale and inference rule, it becomes obvious to him or her that only the relevant questions pose a real threat. It should be stressed that the problematic nature of the control questions is not merely semantic, and calling these questions "comparison questions," as has been recently proposed by many CQT proponents, would not make the CQT's inference rule more reasonable and would not provide better protection against false positive outcomes.

Supporters of the CQT claim that a skilled interrogator is capable of choosing control questions while interviewing the suspect, and of creating an atmosphere that leads innocent examinees to be more concerned with the control than the relevant questions, while guilty suspects become more concerned with the relevant than the control questions. The following citation from Honts and Perry (1992:360) demonstrates how the logical basis of the CQT is explicated by its proponents:

> It is assumed that all subjects will be concerned about the veracity of their denial to the control questions. Innocent individuals are expected to produce larger physiological responses to control questions than to relevant questions since they are sure of the veracity of their response to the relevant questions, but they are assumed to be either lying or at least uncertain about the veracity of their response to the control questions.

Unfortunately, other than the polygraphists' strong belief in this assumption, it has no grounding in psychological or psychophysiological research, nor is it convincing in its inner logic. Honts and Perry's reasoning rests on the assumption that "belief in the veracity of their answers to the relevant questions" *is sufficient* to guarantee that innocent suspects will show larger physiological responses to the control questions. This might have made sense, if such beliefs were the only factor determining physiological reactions. But as indicated earlier, many other factors affect physiological responsivity. Particularly, fear of being falsely classified as guilty and bearing the consequences of such an error is one salient factor that may cause strong reactions to the relevant, crime-related questions among innocent suspects, even if they believe in the veracity of their answers to the relevant questions.

Indeed, numerous researchers (e.g., Ben-Shakhar and Furedy, 1990; Lykken, 1974, 1998) have expressed a concern that this technique is biased against the innocent suspect, because relevant questions could be readily perceived as more threatening and agitating than control questions to all examinees. Moreover, the rationale of the CQT creates an advantage for dishonest examinees. According to this rationale a control question elicits a strong reaction inasmuch as an examinee answers it falsely, or at the very least is unsure of the truthfulness of his answer. If we take this rationale at face value, the higher the chances that the examinee's answer is false, the higher his reactions to the control questions should be. According to this logic, a dishonest examinee who frequently steals, lies, or injures his fellow men will show stronger responses to a control question regarding the aforementioned activities than a virtuous person. Therefore, paradoxically, the chance that a CQT test will incriminate the honest examinee (who doesn't tend to react to the control questions) is greater than the chance that a dishonest examinee will be incriminated. Indeed, the very logic of the CQT points out the danger that the honest man's version will be judged untrue.

Recently, a new variation of the CQT, called the directed-lie test (DLT), has been endorsed by Raskin and his colleagues (e.g., Horowitz *et al.*, 1997; Raskin *et al.*, 1997). In the DLT, the traditional control questions are replaced with directed lies (i.e., questions that both the examiner and the examinee agree are deliberate lies). However, even these control questions are clearly distinct from the relevant questions and therefore cannot function as true controls. Thus, the weaknesses of the CQT are not going to be resolved by the DLT. Furthermore, the DLT has been disputed even among CQT supporters. For example, Abrams (1999) recently argued that the excessive emphasis placed on the directed lies could lead to false negative outcomes. A more general criticism of the DLT was made by Iacono and Lykken (1999) who argued that the directed-lie questions may create an additional difficulty because explaining the purpose of these questions to the examinees clarifies the importance of giving strong responses to these questions, thereby making the test even easier to beat than the CQT.

INADEQUATE STANDARDIZATION

Many regard the polygraph examination as a test. However this expression (like the expression "control questions") is misleading when applied to the CQT. A review of the scientific literature dealing with psychological testing reveals that a basic requirement of a "test" is standardization. This requirement is essential to guarantee that all examinees undergo the same experience. Only when it is fulfilled do the resulting scores (or evaluations) have a uniform meaning, allowing comparisons between different people who took the test. The CQT procedure is poorly standardized. The pre-test interview with the examinee, conducted by the interrogator, is an essential part of every CQT examination. This part is completely subjective, but the control questions, which later form the basis of the polygraphist's inferences, are determined in its course. The selection of control questions depends solely on the interrogator's intuition, and the relationship that forms between him (or her) and the examinee.

In addition, the testing conditions may also be a function of the examiner and the relationship he or she forms with the examinee. For example, an examiner may present the questions in a different manner when he believes that the examinee is deceptive than when he believes he is testing a truthful suspect. This feature of the CQT has been acknowledged by several supporters of this technique. For example, Honts and Perry (1992:372) wrote:

> . . . an examiner who was motivated to produce a deceptive result might ask overgeneral or provocative relevant questions, and spend a great deal of time on their review and presentation. Subsequently, this unethical examiner could ask very narrow, specific, or inappropriate control questions and spend very little time on their review and presentation. An examiner predisposed to produce a truthful result could take the opposite approach, overemphasizing the control questions and minimizing the relevant questions.

Honts and Perry (1992) raised this possibility in relation to an unethical and dishonest examiner, but decades of research in social psychology teaches us that honest persons could be unintentionally affected by their prior beliefs (e.g., Chapman and Chapman, 1982; Klayman and Ha, 1987; Snyder and Swann, 1978a, b). More recently, Abrams (1999:224) made a similar comment and wrote that,

> . . . there is a delicate balance that exists between the comparison and relevant questions and many variables can tip this balance in either of those two directions. Too much discussion of one or the other during the pretest, a difference in inflection or loudness when the questions are being asked, any discussion between charts that stresses either the relevant or comparison questions, or any mental activity on one question versus another can weigh the balance in the direction of that particular emphasis.

These citations clarify the implications of the unstandardized nature of the CQT. It is therefore clear that, by and large, polygraph examinations conducted by different interrogators (even for a given case and suspect) are liable to be quite different from one another.

In contrast, consider tests of cognitive abilities, such as intelligence tests. Despite all the criticism leveled at these tests, it would be inconceivable for each examinee to be tested on questions created especially for him or her, and for each tester to construct the questions for a particular examinee based on the best of his or her intuitive judgment.

Because the CQT is poorly standardized, one can regard the conclusions of an interrogator who employs this technique as more or less on a par with the opinions of an interviewer, rather than objective results of a scientifically based technique.

LACK OF OBJECTIVE QUANTIFICATION OF THE PHYSIOLOGICAL RESPONSES

Lack of standardization characterizes not only the choice and presentation of the CQT questions, but also the measurement and quantification of the physiological responses. This is rather surprising because the type of physiological responses monitored during a typical CQT test can be easily measured in an objective manner, using computerized procedures. Such an objective quantification is a routine procedure in psychophysiological experiments, and computer algorithms have been developed for measuring the responses in the CQT (e.g., Kircher and Raskin, 1988). However, objective, quantified measurement procedures are rare in CQT practice. Some polygraph agencies rely on an overall evaluation of the polygraph charts. This approach is clearly impressionistic and subjective and, as such, vulnerable to various judgment biases (e.g., the confirmation bias, which will be discussed in the next section). Others, use the semi-objective procedure proposed originally by Backster (1963). According to this procedure, two or three pairs of relevant-control questions are identified in each polygraph chart, and numbers (−3, −2, −1, 0, 1, 2, 3) are assigned to each pair for each physiological measure. The absolute value of the assigned number reflects the magnitude of the difference between the responses evoked by the two questions within the pair (e.g., −3 or +3 reflect a very large difference, −1 or +1 reflect a small difference, and 0 reflects no difference) and the sign of the assigned number reflects the direction of the difference, in a way that positive numbers are associated with a pattern of larger physiological reactivity to the control question and negative numbers reflect the opposite pattern. These numbers are then summed across question pairs, across physiological measures, and across polygraph charts to yield a global score. Thus, if, for example, a polygraph examination is based on three charts and three physiological measures and if two pairs of relevant-control questions are identified for each chart, then the global score will range between –54 and +54. Typically, the following classification rule is used: if the global score exceeds +5, an NDI ("no deception indicated") classification is reached; if the global score is less than –5, the polygraph record is classified as DI ("deception indicated"); and if the global score ranges between –5 and +5, the record is classified as inconclusive.

While the Backster (1963) procedure is certainly an improvement over the overall evaluation approach, it is still subjective because it is often unclear whether a given pair of responses reflects a large, medium, or small difference between the responses to relevant and control questions. Thus, this approach too may be vulnerable to judgment biases.

THE PROBLEM OF CONTAMINATION

Polygraphists who employ the CQT believe that it is vital that the same interrogator construct the questions and conduct the questioning. Often that interrogator also tallies up the results of the examination. This approach introduces contamination into the investigative process: judgments made on the basis of the CQT are based on more information than is contained in the physiological measures alone, such as the examinee's criminal records and the information contained therein. In addition, during the investigation the polygraphist is in a position to watch and monitor the totality of a suspect's behavior, and not just his physiological changes. An experienced interrogator might well use these characteristics. While such rich information could enhance the accuracy of the polygraphist's final judgment, it also contaminates "objective" evidence with mere impressions.

The distinction between an objective lie detector based on physiological responses and the subjective impressions of human investigators must not be blurred. If we confuse the validity of the polygraphist's judgment with the validity of the polygraph, we are liable to overestimate the validity of the machine. Furthermore, contamination may introduce a bias into the polygraph examiner's final judgment. This bias was labeled "confirmation bias" (e.g., Ben-Shakhar, 1991a; Elaad et al., 1994) because the knowledge gathered prior to the polygraph investigation may induce certain expectations in the examiner. The polygraph investigation and chart interpretation may be biased in favor of these prior expectations.

Darley and Gross (1983) made a distinction between two types of confirmation bias, both of which may play a role in polygraph examiners' judgments: (1) The "cognitive confirmation effect," which occurs in the absence of any interaction between the perceiver (in this case the polygraph examiner) and the target person (the suspect). This effect is relevant for the chart interpretation phase of polygraph investigation, and its impact depends on the subjectivity of the chart interpretation process. (2) The "behavioral confirmation effect," which refers to the effect of expectations on the behavior of the examiner toward the suspect (e.g., the manner in which the relevant and control questions are presented to the suspect).

It should be noted that the "behavioral confirmation effect" is not eliminated even if the polygraph charts are evaluated by polygraphists who are "blind" to the case and the details of the investigation. Contamination could still enter the measurements through what psychologists call the "interpersonal expectations" effect (Rosenthal and Rubin, 1978). This effect was first discovered in the context of psychological experiments, and is related to the experimenters often arousing in their subjects patterns of behavior that support their expectations – a sort of self-fulfilling prophecy. These effects are also known in medicine, for instance in the evaluation of the efficacy of new drugs. In the context of polygraphy, the effect occurs when an investigator, in the light of a previous examination, for example, develops a certain hunch about the suspect's guilt or innocence, and can subconsciously influence the measurements to match this belief. It should be noted that the physiological measures recorded by the polygraph are very sensitive to changes in the volume of the interrogator's voice, emphases, speech pauses, and the like.

An interesting and impressive demonstration of the contamination effect and the type of bias to which it could lead was presented in a television program produced by CBS in the United States. It was first shown in 1986, in the *60 Minutes* program, as an informal experiment conducted by its producers. As part of the experiment, the program makers independently approached three polygraphists with a request to conduct an investigation for a firm from which some photographic equipment had allegedly been stolen. The polygraphists were told that only four employees had access to the equipment, and therefore it must have been stolen by one of them. They were also told which employee was suspected of being the thief, but that there was no evidence to support this suspicion. In truth, no equipment had been stolen, but each polygraph interrogator was given a different name for the name of the suspected thief (unbeknownst to the employees themselves). Each of the polygraph interrogators examined the four employees using CQT procedures, and each of the three investigators reached the confident conclusion that the employee that had been named to them as the suspected thief had lied during the polygraph investigation, while the three other employees had spoken the truth. This demonstration gives a very vivid illustration of the confirmation bias that may result from contaminated CQT examinations.

Ethical as well as practical problems make it difficult to conduct controlled experiments on the effect of contamination on polygraph examiners' judgment. This is why only two studies that examined this issue have been published so far. However, their results are inconsistent. Elaad *et al.* (1994) showed that the cognitive confirmation effect does play a role in CQT chart interpretation, even when the semi-objective method proposed by Backster (1963) was adopted. They demonstrated that the prior expectations of polygraph examiners affected the way in which they interpreted CQT polygraph charts, when in reality these charts were inconclusive. No significant effect was obtained in this study for conclusive charts. In a subsequent study, Elaad *et al.* (1998) manipulated expectations and examined the effect of these expectations on the entire CQT examination. No effect was obtained in this study, but it is not entirely clear whether the manipulation was effective.

Ben-Shakhar *et al.* (1986) discussed the implications of contaminated CQT examinations for the legal usage of CQT results. They argued that the problem with the judgments of CQT examiners does not only rest in the subjectivity of their assessments, since subjectivity characterizes other categories of expert testimony as well. Rather, the laws of evidence sometimes deliberately constrain the evidence that can be presented in court. These constraints do not hold for polygraphists, who may have access to all the information that reaches the police. The ethical and legal regulations that guide and limit a polygraph examination are far less rigorous than those that guide court proceedings and there is no guarantee that polygraphists adhere even to these limited regulations. Unlike court actions, polygraph investigations are typically not conducted in the presence of a lawyer, and often provide only limited legal protection for the suspects. Therefore, the presentation of CQT results in court deprives the suspect of many of the legal protections provided to him in regular court proceedings. This is an opening for a type of "laundering" of inadmissible evidence, or evidence obtained through illegal means, without legal checks. Such evidence could accrue unknown weight through the influence it exerts on the opinions of the polygraphist, who has prior acquaintance with it.

This problem is especially acute when results obtained from CQT tests are presented as objective and scientific, when in fact the CQT is just a tool aiding the investigator in collecting impressions. The way a "lie detector" works carries an aura of mystery, but the true mystery is not in the function of the polygraph machine, but in the function of the mind of the human polygraphist behind the machine. Once we acknowledge this fact, we have to deal with the question of whether there is sufficient reason to believe that the polygraphist as a human lie detector is superior and should be preferred over other people in general, and judges in particular.

THE PROBLEM OF COUNTERMEASURES

A number of experiments (e.g., Ben-Shakhar and Dolev, 1996; Elaad and Ben-Shakhar, 1991; Honts *et al.*, 1987, 1994, 1996; Kubis, 1962) have indicated that it is possible, indeed quite easy, to train guilty examinees and prepare them for a polygraph examination (either CQT or GKT) in such a way that with a high probability they will be found truthful. This can be done by adopting some rather simple techniques, which can be picked up with little effort and can cause very strong reactions to the control questions. These techniques rely either on the use of physical means (such as biting one's tongue), or mental means (calling to mind an exciting or frightening event, or engaging in mental activities that require effort) each time a control question is asked. A series of experiments conducted by Honts and his colleagues demonstrated that the use of such countermeasures could be most effective. They showed in different experiments that the rate of mistakes made by polygraphists testing "guilty" examinees who were using countermeasures ranged between 50% and 70%.

These countermeasures may increase false negative outcomes (guilty suspects classified as "innocents"), but they have no effect on innocent examinees. Thus, from the legal perspective this problem may be less severe than the problematic nature of the control questions used in the CQT, because the legal system puts more weight on protecting the innocent than the guilty suspects. On the other hand, it is clear that if the results of the laboratory studies on the effects of countermeasures on false negative outcomes generalize to realistic polygraph examinations, they will have a restricted utility. It should be pointed out that the type of countermeasures that are most detrimental for all psychophysiological detection techniques are mental countermeasures, because mental manipulations cannot be detected even by the most experienced examiners. Two recent studies demonstrated that mental countermeasures can be used effectively under both the GKT and the CQT (Ben-Shakhar and Dolev, 1996; Honts *et al.*, 1996).

THE EMPIRICAL STATUS OF THE CQT

The primary question that arises in all debates about the CQT is of course the question of criterion validity. That is to say, to what degree can one really distinguish between liars and truth tellers (or between examinees who are informed regarding a certain event to those who are not), based on their physiological responses to questions presented to them during a CQT examination. This may seem to be an empirical question that could be checked through research and experimentation; and if the results of such experimentation were to indicate a high degree of accuracy, then many of the previously raised concerns would become less important. In actuality, matters are more complicated, and it turns out that the research conducted to date cannot provide a simple, clear-cut answer to the question of the CQT's validity. In order to allow conclusions about the value of the CQT, as typically conducted in real-life conditions, an experiment should fulfill the following requirements (see Ben-Shakhar and Furedy, 1990; Ginton *et al.*, 1982):

1. The existence of a clear, conclusive and irrefutable criterion for the guilt or innocence of the research participants. Clearly, without such a criterion there is no way to determine whether the CQT interrogator was right or wrong in a particular case.
2. A representative sampling of examinees and of the situations in which CQTs are employed.
3. Independence between the criterion and the polygrapher's judgment (which may be affected by all the information at his disposal).
4. Testing conditions in the experiment, which resemble those of a true examination. In particular, it is important that the examinees be anxious about the consequences of the test and take it seriously, and that the lie or the transgression be real.

A review of the literature reveals that no existing experiments (perhaps with the exception of the Ginton *et al.*, 1982 study) meet all these requirements. In particular, there are no experiments that simultaneously fulfill both the first and the last requirement. All the experiments providing a satisfactory criterion are simulations, so-called "mock crimes," in which the subjects know that they are participating in a role-playing game. The subjects designated as "guilty" are asked by the experimenter to steal an envelope containing money, or some other item. Then, all the participants (both "guilty" and "innocent") are examined by a polygraph interrogator. Participants are asked by the experimenter to hide their connection to the "simulated crime." When the experiment is over, they are given a monetary reward, thanked, and sent on their way. Obviously these conditions do not begin to resemble the conditions of a real-life criminal investigation. There is no deception in the conventional sense of the word, and there is no anxiety about the consequences of the test (either for the "guilty" or for the "innocent").

A different category of studies uses real investigations, but samples only cases in which the truth was later revealed when a suspect confessed to the crime. Even if we choose to ignore the possibility of a false confession, we are faced with the problem of a severely biased sample, since there is liable to be a direct causal relationship between the results of the polygraph examination and the confessions. It is well known that polygraph examinations are used not only to reveal the truth but also as an investigative tool and a lever for inducing suspects to confess (see Furedy and Liss, 1986). The chances are obviously higher that a polygraph interrogator will try to extract a confession from a suspect showing "signs of lying" in his or her polygraph chart, than from a suspect who has not shown such signs. Therefore, a sample of confessors is liable to include an inflated representation of cases in which the responses revealed obvious signs of guilt, and to underrepresent cases of judgmental error. This point was demonstrated by Iacono (1991) who showed that, in principle, in a sample based on confessions it should be possible to get nearly perfect accuracy rates, even if the true accuracy of the polygraph is at chance level (see also Iacono and Lykken, 1999). Even if the assumptions made by Iacono are not fully met, it is clear that samples of confessed suspects might be seriously biased. Thus, confession studies do not satisfy the second and third conditions mentioned above. In addition, confession studies, which are based on real-life CQT investigations, suffer from the problem of contamination, discussed above. Thus, it is doubtful whether a given accuracy rate obtained in a confession study can be attributed to the physiological information.

The studies that used the confession criterion yielded inconsistent results, but the overall picture indicates a rather high occurrence of "false incriminations." In at least two CQT field studies (Barland and Raskin, 1976; Horvath, 1977) the accuracy rate among the "innocents" was no higher than chance (i.e., the same accuracy that would have resulted from tossing a coin). The mock-crime studies attempting to validate the CQT usually lead to better results; however, as previously stated, these are hard to take seriously, because of the difficulty of generalizing from such artificial conditions to true-life examinations.

It should be noted that the problem of generalization is particularly acute in the case of the CQT because of the danger that even innocent suspects, when being interrogated about a real crime with possible severe consequences, might be more aroused by the relevant questions, which focus on the main issue under investigation, than by the control questions, that deal with much less threatening issues. This factor is completely missing from the simulated crimes.

As indicated earlier, the study reported by Ginton et al. (1982) is the only one that came close to fulfilling all four requirements. However, no generalizations can be drawn even from this study because the realistic setup resulted in a large rate of dropouts, particularly of guilty participants. Most of the guilty participants either refused to take the polygraph test, or confessed just before taking it. Thus, in the end, there were only two guilty participants who actually took the CQT, and clearly this sample does not allow for any generalizations.

The Ginton et al. (1982) study demonstrates the difficulties in estimating the validity of the CQT as a tool for detecting deception in real criminal investigations. But from a psychometric perspective, there is another important and necessary, though not sufficient condition, that any test must meet, namely reliability. Reliability, which can be estimated more easily than validity, refers to the consistency (or reproducibility) of the test scores. A test is considered reliable if its results tend to be replicated when the same individuals are tested several times under similar circumstances. In classical reliability theory, reliability is estimated by a correlation between two sets of equivalent measurements, such as administering the same test twice to the same group of subjects or administering two equivalent forms of the same test. In some circumstances reliability is estimated by correlating two sets of scores obtained from two independent observers (or judges) evaluating the performance of a given group in a specified condition. The different types of reliability estimates focus on different sources of inconsistencies, or measurement errors, and the choice of an appropriate reliability coefficient depends on the purposes of the specific measurement and on the desired range of generalizability. Sometimes more than one type of reliability estimate will be required.

Reliability of polygraph-based scores, whether expressed by numbers (e.g., the "quantified" method suggested by Backster, 1963) or by qualitative categories (guilty, innocent, or inconclusive), refers to the degree to which these scores tend to be stable across measurement situations. Stability could be estimated by using one of two approaches: (1) testing the same individual twice on the same issue, using the same polygraphic method, but having two independent examiners administer the test; or (2) testing the subject just once, but letting two independent experts score the charts. Clearly, the second method yields reliability estimates of very limited use for evaluating the CQT because two independent examiners could, in principle, reach a complete agreement (especially if they were trained by the same polygraph school and if they used a quantified scoring method) despite a very low test–retest consistency. In other words, the second approach relates to just one source of measurement error – errors in chart scoring and interpretation. But the crucial question is not whether two CQT examiners could be trained to read a given polygraph chart consistently, but whether the procedure as a whole (including the most critical stage of constructing proper relevant and control questions) is reliable. In order to obtain proper estimates of the polygraph's reliability – estimates of measurement errors related to the test as a whole – one must use the first approach and administer the whole polygraph-based interrogation twice, using two independent examiners.

Unfortunately, reliability studies of polygraph-based classifications are scarce and, incredibly enough, those that have been conducted have employed only the between-examiners agreement approach (e.g., Barland, 1975; Horvath and Reid, 1971). Thus, it is impossible to conclude from the available data whether a given subject interrogated twice by independent examiners will be similarly classified.

SUMMARY AND CONCLUSIONS

Six major arguments indicating basic flaws in CQT polygraph examinations were raised. These flaws undermine the scientific basis of this technique.

1. There is a basic flaw in the rationale of the CQT; a flaw related to the selection of "Control Questions," and their lack of equivalence to the relevant questions. This flaw is liable to introduce a systematic bias, which might increase the rate of false positive outcomes (innocent suspects classified as "guilty") into CQT examinations. It should be stressed that this bias is particularly damaging from a legal perspective because false positive errors are just the type of mistake that criminal courts are particularly anxious to avoid.

2. The CQT is not a standardized test, and therefore it is unjustified to use it as a basis for comparisons of any sort. Thus, its results should be regarded as no more than subjective-impressionistic conjecture.

3. The CQT does not rely upon objective methods of quantifying the physiological measures. This feature of the CQT opens the door to biases in interpreting CQT outcomes and in drawing conclusions from them.

4. The CQT contains an element of "contamination." In other words it is possible that the conclusions made by a CQT examiner are based on information that was in his hands prior to conducting the examination, rather than the physiological measurements recorded by the machine. This feature of the CQT, which might introduce a confirmation bias (i.e., a bias favoring the prior hypothesis over the alternatives), is particularly damaging from a legal perspective. The influence of a priori information and of behavioral impressions could result in the polygraphist reaching conclusions on the basis of elements that would not be admissible as court evidence, and that are now introduced under the cover of a "truth machine."

5. The CQT is vulnerable to both physical and mental countermeasures. These manipulations, that are relatively easy to learn, may increase the false negative error rate. Mental countermeasures are particularly problematic because they cannot be detected by the examiners.

6. Finally, there is neither sound empirical, research-based evidence that indicates any kind of validity for CQT polygraph tests under the realistic interrogative situation, nor are there good reliability studies demonstrating consistent outcomes derived from independent CQT examinations.

From all the above it appears that one cannot consider a CQT as an objective test, or tool based on scientific principles. In fact, there is no evidence that the CQT is more than another aid for interrogators who form subjective impressions based on many factors. Moreover, it is far from clear that the impressions of a CQT investigator are superior to those of any other investigator who questions suspects without the benefit of the polygraph. In particular, the use of the CQT can cause several judgmental biases, some of which mitigate against innocent suspects and against truthful respondents. A CQT polygraph test depends on the interrogator and his interaction with the examinee and could be influenced by personal inclinations of the interrogator and the premises of his investigation.

Once all the problematic aspects of the CQT are acknowledged, we must turn to the question of its applications. Currently, applications of the CQT can be classified into the following three general classes: (1) the CQT can be introduced as admissible evidence in courts; (2) it can be used by law-enforcement agencies as an aid in their investigations of specific acts (e.g., criminal acts); and (3) it can be used for selection and screening of employees. A brief discussion of each of these possible applications is given below.

Although there have been various attempts to introduce CQT results as admissible evidence in U.S. courts (e.g., *Commonwealth of Massachusetts v. Woodward*, 1998; *United States v. Cordoba*, 1998; *United States v. Scheffer*, 1998), the present analysis indicates that this application is highly problematic. We have stressed that at least two features of the CQT are particularly problematic from the legal perspective. The nature of the control questions, and the inference rule used to classify examinees as deceptive or truth-tellers, might increase the risk of false positive errors, and this in itself is a sufficient reason to prohibit the use of the CQT in criminal trials. Contamination is the second problematic feature of the CQT from the legal perspective. As indicated by Ben-Shakhar *et al.* (1986) this feature of the CQT might open a back door for all kinds of inadmissible evidence, which may enter the courtroom unchecked and unchallenged through their influence on the knowledgeable CQT examiner.

In addition, the non-standardized nature of the CQT and the fact that it is not based on scientific principles make it a poor candidate for assisting the trier of fact. Recently, Saxe and Ben-Shakhar (1999) analyzed the admissibility of CQT results in the Federal Courts of the United States, in light of the new guidelines set by the U.S. Supreme Court in *Daubert v. Merrell Dow Pharmaceuticals* (1993). This analysis demonstrated that the concepts of reliability and validity as commonly used by behavioral scientists (e.g., Brennan, 1992; Messick, 1995) are not applicable to the CQT. In other words, the CQT does not satisfy the major Daubert criteria (testability and known error rate, as well as reliability and validity) and therefore its outcomes should not be used as admissible evidence.

Some have suggested that CQT results might be ruled admissible in civil cases, provided both sides have agreed to this in advance. However, even this application is very problematic, because the phrase "lie detector" and the mystery it evokes could mislead many people and cause them to agree to a polygraph test without having any idea of its real nature. People could agree to the test under the impression that it is indeed a serious scientific tool for determining truth or lies, when in fact, as I have tried to show, this is not at all the case. The very suggestion that someone should undergo a "lie detection" test might be misleading and unfair. This practice could undermine innocent people.

The second possible application of the CQT as an aid to the police and other law-enforcement agencies in their investigations differs drastically from the legal usage of the CQT. First, police investigations do not need to rely on scientifically based tools, and many other investigation methods that are not necessarily scientific are being constantly used. Second, the consequences of police interrogations differ drastically from those of legal procedures. Typically, police interrogations end in a decision either to press charges, or not. As long as CQT results are inadmissible in Criminal Courts, the police cannot rely on it, as the only evidence, when deciding to press charges against a suspect. Consequently, the emphasis on false positive errors, which characterizes the legal system, does not hold for police investigations, and therefore many of the problematic features of the CQT, which may increase false positive errors, are less damaging in the context of police interrogations. A more detailed discussion of these issues, from a decision-theoretic perspective can be found in Ben-Shakhar *et al.* (1982).

Thus, from a psychophysiological perspective, there are no compelling reasons to object to the use of the CQT as an aid in police investigations, provided that it would be acknowledged that CQT results constitute no more than an opinion of an investigator. In addition, it should be pointed out that an alternative method of psychophysiological detection that does rest on sound scientific principles is available. I am referring to the GKT, which was originally endorsed by Lykken (e.g., 1974, 1998), and subsequently by many others (e.g., Ben-Shakhar, 1991b; Ben-Shakhar and Furedy, 1990; Elaad, 1998; Elaad and Ben-Shakhar, 1997). Currently, the GKT is rarely applied by law enforcement agencies in North America and Israel (see Podlesney, 1993). It has been argued that it is difficult to apply this technique, because it requires that salient features of the event under investigation will be concealed from the suspects. On the other hand, the GKT has been used for many years by Japanese law enforcement agencies as the preferred method of psychophysiological detection (Ben-Shakhar and Furedy, 1990; Fukumoto, 1980; Yamamura, and Miyata, 1990). This fact implies that the feasibility of the GKT is greater than the current beliefs of North American and Israeli experts, and it is highly recommended that greater efforts will be made to replace the CQT by the more standardized and better controlled method of the GKT. Recently, Ben-Shakhar *et al.* (2001) discussed the possibility of using the GKT as admissible evidence, but this is beyond the scope of this chapter.

The third possible application of the CQT, as a tool for personnel selection and screening is entirely different from the previously discussed applications. Contrary to criminal investigations, selection and screening does not revolve around a specific and known event (e.g., crime). Rather, an attempt is being made to detect dishonest behavioral tendencies. Such an attempt is based on an additional assumption, namely that dishonest behaviors exhibit a cross-situational consistency. This assumption has been questioned by several researchers (e.g., Mischel and Peake, 1982).

Ben-Shakhar (1989) labeled this kind of application (e.g., screening) as an event-free usage of the CQT, as opposed to the more typical event-related usage. He argued that all the problematic features of the CQT become even more severe under the event-free application, because this method cannot be used in a straightforward manner. Recall that the relevant questions used in the CQT pertain to a specific event (crime). In order to use it for detecting hypothetical (or future) crimes, control questions (which relate to general misdeeds) must play the role of the relevant questions. In other words, enhanced physiological reactions to the typical control question (e.g., 'Have you ever stolen from your employer?') are now taken as an indication of deception and a consistent responding to those questions might mean that an applicant to a certain job will be rejected on the grounds of failing the polygraph test. But to make such inferences, one must compare the responses to those new relevant questions with the responses to equivalent control questions. Unfortunately, it is impossible to construct such control questions, because they must relate to other hypothetical crimes of similar importance, and naturally a consistent responding to those questions is not going to make the applicant more attractive as a future employee.

Finally, there is no empirical evidence to support the event-free application of the CQT. Thus, it is not surprising that the United States Congress outlawed the use of polygraphs for screening of employees in the private sector (Employee Polygraph Protection Act, 1988). Similarly, it is not surprising that even keen supporters of the event-related applications of the CQT, including its use as admissible evidence, are opposed to its use for screening and selection (e.g., Honts, 1991, 1992).

ACKNOWLEDGMENT

I would like to thank Professor Leonard Saxe for his helpful and constructive comments.

Raskin, D. C., Honts, C. R., Amato, S. L. and Kircher, J. C. (1999) Update: The scientific status of research on polygraph techniques: The case for the admissibility of the results of polygraph examinations. In: D. L. Faigman, D. H. Kaye, M. J. Saks, and J. Sanders (eds) *Modern Scientific Evidence: The Law and Science of Expert Testimony*, vol. 1, pp. 160–174. Pocket Part. St. Paul, MN: West Publishing.

Raskin, D. C., Honts, C. R. and Kircher, J. C. (1997) The scientific status of research on polygraph techniques: The case for polygraph tests. In: D. L. Faigman, D. H. Kaye, M. J. Saks, and J. Sanders (eds) *Modern Scientific Evidence: The Law and Science of Expert Testimony*. St. Paul, MN: West Law.

Raskin, D. C. and Podlesny, J. A. (1979) Truth and deception: A reply to Lykken. *Psychological Bulletin*, 86, 54–58.

Reid, J. E. and Inbau, F. E. (1977) *Truth and Deception: The Polygraph ("Lie Detection") Technique*. Baltimore: Williams and Wilkins.

Rosenthal, R. and Rubin, D. B. (1978) Interpersonal expectancy effects: The first 345 studies. *Behavioral Brain Sciences,* 1, 377–415.

Saxe, L. (1991) Lying: Thoughts of an applied social psychologist. *American Psychologist,* 46, 409–415.

Saxe L. and Ben-Shakhar, G. (1999) Admissibility of polygraph tests: The application of scientific standards post-Daubert. *Psychology, Public Policy and Law,* 5, 203–223.

Saxe, L., Dougherty, D. and Cross, T. P. (1983) *Scientific Validity of Polygraph Testing (OTA-TM-H-15)*. (Report for the U.S. Congress Office of Technology Assessment). Washington, DC: U.S. Government Printing Office.

Saxe, L., Dougherty, D. and Cross, T. P. (1985) The validity of polygraph testing: Scientific analysis and public controversy. *American Psychologist,* 40, 355–366.

Snyder, M. and Swann, W. B., Jr. (1978a) Behavioral confirmation in social interaction: From social perception to social reality. *Journal of Experimental Psychology*, 14, 148–162.

Snyder, M. and Swann, W. B., Jr. (1978b) Hypothesis-testing processes in social interaction. *Journal of Personality and Social Psychology*, 36, 1202–1212.

United States v. Frank Javier Cordoba (1998) 158, D. California, 1998, *aff'd*, SA CR 95-39-GLT[SF].

United States v. Scheffer (1998) 118 S. Ct. Supp. 1261, D. Washington, 1998, *aff'd, USCA Dkt. No. 95-0521/AF* (US Court of Appeals for the Armed Forces).

Yamamura, T. and Miyata, Y. (1990) Development of the polygraph technique in Japan for detection of deception. *Forensic Science International*, 44, 257–271.

CHAPTER 5

PHYSIOLOGICAL DETECTION OF DECEPTION IN PSYCHOLOGICAL PERSPECTIVES: A THEORETICAL PROPOSAL

Murray Kleiner

Polygraph testing has been used extensively by law enforcement and private agencies over the last 30 years, yet has not received universal acceptance by scientific and legal (see chapter 12) standards. This technique has been criticized on the basis of non-standard physiological measurement, inadequate instrumentation, lack of specific deception response, contamination via interpersonal interaction, flawed methodology and insufficient validity (Ben-Shakhar and Furedy, 1990; Lykken, 1998; also see Ben-Shakhar, chapter 4, this volume).

However, the objection to polygraph use by its opponents has not been total. Use of the guilty knowledge technique (GKT) of polygraph testing (Lykken, 1959, 1998) has been accepted academically and recommended as being theoretically and empirically valid, deriving from orienting response theory and research (Ben-Shakhar and Furedy, 1990; Lykken, 1998; see also chapters 2 and 3 in this volume); however, the control question technique (more appropriately termed the comparison question test (CQT)), the most widely used polygraph procedure (Reid and Inbau, 1977), has been emphatically rejected as being devoid of any theoretical and empirical foundation (Ben-Shakhar and Furedy, 1990; Lykken, 1974, 1979, 1981, 1998; see also chapter 4, this volume). Indeed, the continuing controversy surrounding CQT polygraph practice has been irreconcilable and heated (Lykken, 1974, 1979, 1981; Raskin and Podlesny, 1979; also see Furedy and Heslegrave, 1989; and comments by Raskin and Kircher, 1989), culminating in a US Federal law which, in effect, limited employment-related polygraph testing to law-enforcement and Federal agencies from 1990 onwards.

Outwardly, the GKT and CQT test procedures are quite different in form and content. In the guilty knowledge technique of polygraph testing, the examinee is a suspect who denies commission of the crime as well as knowledge of crime-relevant details that only the perpetrator could possess. The GKT is covered in depth in this volume: see Nakayama, Chapter 2; and Ben-Shakhar and Elaad, Chapter 3. For each item of crime-related information documented by the investigation, the polygraph examiner composes a series of several alternative items, only one of which originates in the actual case at hand. The series is composed so that the crime-related alternative may be easily distinguished by the perpetrator of the crime, and by him only. The items in the series are presented to the examinee in the form of questions regarding his knowledge of the crime-related alternative, for example, "Do you know that the amount of money stolen from Jones' office was $100, $200, . . . ,$900?". The examinee, whose physiological activity is continuously monitored on the polygraph, replies "no" to each alternative, and the series is repeated several times. If the examinee's physiological response to the crime-related alternative is consistently greater than those to the other alternatives, he or she is considered to possess guilty knowledge. The GKT has been proved effective in many laboratory studies (Lykken, 1981, 1998), and to a lesser extent in the field (Elaad *et al.*, 1988; Elaad, 1990). The main reason for the scientific acceptance of the GKT as a potentially accurate procedure for the detection of deception (Ben-Shakhar and Furedy, 1990) is its manifest logic and the consistency of its basic underlying premises with orienting response (OR) theory, which is based upon an extensive body of empirical investigation.

In the comparison question technique, the examination begins with a pre-test interview, during which the test questions are formulated together with the examinee, who is a suspect who denies commission of the crime. Following the interview, the question series is presented a minimum of three times to the examinee, whose physiological and verbal responses are continuously recorded on the polygraph. The question series in the CQT is comprised of relevant questions, such as "Did you take the $700 from Jones' office?," directly related to the focus of a crime, and comparison questions, such as "Before 1989, did you ever steal anything of value?," which are used for purposes of comparison. Comparison questions are designed to provoke greater responses in truthful examinees, so as to cause them to be doubtful and concerned about the truthfulness of their answer to an issue similar in type to that of the relevant issue (Raskin, 1979). The test criterion utilized in the CQT assumes that the responses of deceptive examinees to relevant questions will be greater than those to comparison questions ($R > C$), *and* the responses of truthful examinees to comparison questions will be greater than those to relevant questions ($C > R$).

The main objection to the CQT concerns its test criterion, which determines the whole procedure. Specifically, people find it difficult to conceive that an innocent person, suspected of a serious crime, is capable of producing greater responses to comparison questions than to relevant questions in the polygraph setting. Lykken (1974) directly challenged the basis of the comparison question technique polygraph examination: "As a general rule, one would expect most subjects to be more concerned about the relevant questions than about the comparisons, whether they answer (the former) deceptively or truthfully, because it is the relevant questions that refer directly to the source of their immediate jeopardy." Ben-Shakhar and Furedy (1990:13) doubted "the unlikely assumption . . . that each polygraph CQT examiner can manipulate the arousal value of the comparison question in the innocent in such a way that its arousal value will exceed that of the relevant question in the innocent". In chapter 4, Ben-Shakhar, states about this counterintuitive criterion: " Unfortunately, other than the polygraphists' strong belief in this assumption, it has no grounding in psychological or psychophysiological research, nor is it convincing in its inner logic."

These critical opinions of the CQT imply that, regardless of guilt or innocence, all polygraph examinees will produce deceptive results by respond-ing to the relevant questions to a greater degree than to the comparison questions. However, data on polygraph decisions do not support this assump-tion. Examination results in the Israel National Police polygraph laboratories over the last 20 years have indicated truthfulness in 70% of the conclusive decisions, consistently, employing the CQT decision criterion. The technical memorandum of the Office of Technological Assessment (OTA) of the United States Congress (Saxe, 1983) reviewed and evaluated available research on the validity of CQT polygraph testing in the field and analog laboratory situation. The data from the response distribution in the studies selected by the OTA are presented in Table 5.1.

	"Ground truth"			
	In field studies (*n* = 624)		In analog studies (*n* = 1009)	
	Guilty	Innocent	Guilty	Innocent
Diagnosis				
Deceptive (R > C)	86.3 +	19.1 x	63.7 +	14.1 x
Non-deceptive (C > R)	10.2 x	76.0 +	10.4 x	57.9 +
Inconclusive (C = R)	3.5	4.9	25.9	28.0
Total	100.0	100.0	100.0	100.0

Table 5.1

Response distribution to comparison questions and relevant questions according to guilt/innocence (detection rates).

+ = correct decisions, x = incorrect decisions.
R = evaluated magnitude of recorded physiological responses to relevant questions.
C = evaluated magnitude of recorded physiological responses to comparison questions.

The observations of the response distribution in Table 5.1 demonstrate that the response magnitudes to relevant and comparison questions actually do discrim-inate between guilty and innocent examinees in the CQT setting, notwithstand-ing Lykken's expectation to the contrary. Saxe (1983) found that, relative to base rates, the results of CQT polygraph examinations conducted in field and analog CQT laboratory studies improved the prediction of deception and non-deception by 65% and 43% above chance, respectively, and do exhibit counterintuitive psychophysiological phenomena in innocent examinees, especially in field conditions. Similar response distributions have been observed in more recent field studies (Raskin *et al.*, 1988), and analog studies (Kircher *et al.*, 1988; Patrick and Iacono, 1989) utilizing relatively severe rules of physiological evaluation (see chapter 1). Despite Saxe's (1983) conclusion that "the controversy surrounding the CQT calls for a serious attempt to understand the processes involved within existing psychological theory," opponents of the CQT have apparently been oblivious to the theoretical significance of truthful polygraph results.

Are there, in fact, any psychological or psychophysiological theories that could explain why some polygraph examinees respond to comparison questions to a greater degree than to relevant questions, and how this may be related to deception or truthfulness? This chapter presents a basic model of orienting response (OR) as a theoretical framework in an attempt to reconcile both GKT and CQT procedures with current theory and research. The OR model will then be elaborated by additional psychological theories which are consistent with the operation of the CQT. An appropriate starting point is to consider the OR approach to the GKT expressed by Ben-Shakhar (Ben-Shakhar *et al.*, 1996; Gati and Ben-Shakhar, 1990).

ORIENTING RESPONSE

Pavlov (1927) found that stimuli chosen for use as conditioned stimuli evoked a response of directing attention toward the stimulus, or orienting response (OR), before the initiation of the conditioning process, and that only stimuli attracting attention in this manner could be used as conditioned stimuli. Pavlov originally described OR as the investigatory, or "What-is-it?" reflex. The orienting response has motor components, such as changes of posture directing receptor organs toward the stimulus; physiological components, such as the phasic changes in skin resistance and heart rate; and cognitive components (Maltzman and Raskin, 1965) – the focus of attention toward the stimulus event. While these components, especially the electrodermal response, have been the object of empirical study over the years (Raskin, 1973), a consensus has yet to be achieved regarding the underlying basis responsible for the phenomena observed (Bernstein, 1979; Maltzman, 1979; O'Gorman, 1979). Recently Williams *et al.* (2000) employed functional magnetic resonance imaging to study brain activity associated with visual stimuli that did or did not evoke simultaneously recorded electrodermal ORs (using skin conductance recording). Their results suggest that potentially significant stimuli (with OR) activate different functional networks to familiar (without OR) stimuli. Critchley *et al.* (2000) also used functional magnetic resonance imaging to study brain activity associated with spontaneous fluctuations in amplitude of electro-dermal activity, and activity corresponding to generation and afferent represen-tation of discrete electrodermal events. Their results suggest that areas implicated in emotion and attention are differentially involved in peripheral electrodermal responses. They proposed that this functional arrangement enables integration of adaptive bodily responses with ongoing emotional and attentional states of the organism.

Two stimulus characteristics are each recognized as sufficient conditions in order to observe the physiological components of the orienting response: novelty and signal value (Lynn, 1966). Sokolov (1963, 1966) postulated that sensory input from the environment is compared to a "neuronal model" con-taining a representation of the current environment in memory. The compari-son enables the detection of environmental novelty as a **mismatch** between the input and the neuronal model. The characteristics of the OR (Stern, 1972) are consonant with the notion of novelty: habituation or decay over repetitions; reappearance with each change of stimulus; specificity to stimulus qualities; not limited to a specific organ; equal magnitude to stimulus appearance or disap-pearance, or when stimulus series varies with respect to expectations, or when there is a change in the series of stimuli; contingent in time to the stimulus.

Berlyne (1961) and Sokolov (1963) used the term "signal value" to describe learned characteristics of a stimulus that constitute a signal, evoking an OR stronger and more resistant to habituation compared to a neutral stimulus that evokes an OR by novelty. Lynn (1966) found that it is possible to change a neutral stimulus (a non-novel stimulus which does not elicit an OR) – for example, the blue light is a series of variously colored lights – to a signal stimulus by (1) instructing the subject to attend to the stimulus, (2) instructing the subject to act when a certain stimulus is presented, and (3) classical condi-tioning.

Kahneman (1973) described the direction of attention and selection of infor-mation as "an exertion of effort" and demonstrated that it is a limited resource, so that investment of attention to one stimulus is at the expense of others, leaving less attentional resources available to other competing stimuli. Callicott *et al.* (1999) identified characteristics of working memory capacity using functional magnetic resonance imaging in healthy subjects. Memory capacity was studied using a working memory task involving increasing cognitive load and ultimately decreasing task performance. Loci within the prefrontal cortex produced an "inverted-U"-shaped neurophysiological response from lowest to highest load, consistent with a capacity-constrained response. These results demonstrated that regionally specific nodes within the working memory network are capacity-con-strained in the physiological domain, providing a missing link in current explo-rations of the capacity characteristics of working memory.

Gati and Ben Shakhar (1990) proposed a model analogous to that of Sokolov, capable of distinguishing signal stimuli from non-signal stimuli. In their model, sensory input from the environment is compared to a memory representation of the preceding stimuli, and to an additional memory representation of the signal. They used the feature-matching function from Tversky's (1977) contrast model of similarity to accomplish the comparison.

Utilizing a GKT paradigm, subjects were presented with a compound significant stimulus comprising four components, either a schematic face or a verbal description, and were told that the person had been the victim of a crime and were requested to memorize the stimulus. Subsequently, a sequence of stimuli was presented to the subjects while their skin conductance was recorded. The sequence always included the learned significant stimulus which was preceded by several control stimuli, each sharing no, one, two or three common components with the significant stimulus. Novelty was defined as the degree of **dissimilarity** between a stimulus and the stimuli preceding it, and significance as the degree of **similarity** between a stimulus and the signal stored in memory. They found that the OR magnitude corresponded to these definitions of novelty and significance. This finding was reinforced and refined in a study in which the similarity of test stimuli to significant stimuli was varied by adding or deleting common and distinctive features of schematic faces (Ben-Shakhar *et al.*, 1995), where it was found that both types of features affected OR generalization as predicted by the feature-matching theory of similarity.

Using a related approach, Ben-Shakhar *et al.* (1996) obtained an OR generalization gradient for test stimuli which presented the subjects with no common features to the signal stimulus, other than the **category relationship** between them. Test stimuli that were distinct coordinates – instances of the same verbal category as the signal (i.e., violin–piano) – exhibited no OR generalization, and increasing OR responsivity was observed for the signal:test stimuli relationships: instance: superordinate category (i.e., apple–fruit), synonyms (i.e., carpet–rug), and intermodal verbal:pictorial (i.e., signal–picture of apple: test–"apple", or vice versa), which exhibited perfect OR generalization. These results are in accordance with Tversky's similarity theory which views similarity as "a relation of proximity that holds between two objects. There exist other proximity relations . . . that hold between an object and a class." Tversky and Hutchinson (1986) cite data showing that instances (i.e., apple, orange) of a superordinate category (i.e., fruits, birds, clothes, etc.) are rated as more highly related to the category than to each other.

The model proposed by Ben-Shakhar and Gati advances OR theory considerably, demonstrating how the **similarity relation**, operating between stimulus input and two memory representations, can determine the magnitude of the is crime-irrelevant indicates the innocence of the examinee. The probability of the crime-relevant item to evoke an OR because of trivially diagnostic crime-irrelevant features is a function of the number of items in the series. In the example above, the probability that a maximal response to the crime-relevant item is due to the chance correspondence of an identical feature in a crime-irrelevant context, rather than the crime-relevant context, is at most 11%. The probability of this type of false positive error decreases with the number of GKT tests for additional crime-relevant details.

Innocent examinees may, for various reasons, deny knowledge of crime-relevant information that they have acquired. The GKT enables detection of crime-relevant information possessed by examinees, but not the source of the information, or the degree of involvement in the crime. Therefore, polygraph examiners do not use information that has been available to the examinee from legitimate sources (from the media, interrogation, the victim) as a basis for GKT tests, but rather limit the test issue to crime-relevant details that are not available from legitimate sources (commission of the crime, communication from the culprit, or as a witness to the crime). This limitation occasionally results in the use of crime-relevant information that the guilty examinee doesn't possess, because the detail was not perceived or attended at the time of the crime, or was forgotten afterwards. In such a case, the information is not stored in memory. In highly emotional experiences, people process more elaborately those critical details that were the source of the emotional arousal, and they maintain or restrict the scene's boundaries. The resultant "tunnel memory" may explain the superior recognition and recall of central, emotion-arousing details in such events (Christianson, 1992; Safer *et al.*, 1998). For an extreme, but true, example, two examinees were tested regarding two crime-relevant details: which floor of a six-story building was the site of the robbery, and which part of the victim's body was struck by the bullet. Both examinees participated in the same robbery, but responded only to one of the crime-relevant details, different for each examinee. The probability of this type of false negative error decreases with the number of GKT tests for additional crime-relevant details, essential to the examinee for commission of the crime.

To recapitulate, in the guilty knowledge technique the question series topic (a category of the crime-relevant detail) is assessed by the subject for significance by reference to enduring memory, after which the subject is tested for retrieval of the crime-relevant item utilizing the signal detector to identify the relevant stimulus among irrelevant stimuli as his or her ORs are monitored. The act of lying, *per se*, is **incidental** to the process, and is not a necessary condition for diagnostic responding in polygraph tests (Dawson, 1980; Elaad and Ben-Shakhar, 1989; Gustafson and Orne, 1965; Kugelmass *et al.*, 1967).

crime (relevant issues) at the high end of the scale, but are not specific only to the crime. At the low end of the scale, the same traits characterize universal misconduct of all persons (i.e., regrettable behavior, transgressions, white lies, negligence, etc.), not related to the crime (comparison issues).

3. The relevant and the comparison issues of the category are discussed with reference to the examinee, establishing **self-reference** as a diagnostic feature, i.e., "Are you capable of . . . (relevant/comparison)?, Did you do . . . ? Does this describe you . . . ? Have you ever . . . ?," etc.

The information establishes an implicit examination criterion, by which the category "the culprit," describes the examinee if he shares **any** of the criterion behaviors and attributes, producing a negative evaluation for examinees if they identify themself in **any** of the test questions, relevant or comparison. In essence, this procedure performs a **context shift**, enabling the examinee to conduct a self-referent comparison with respect to the culprit rather than a "crime-related" criterion.

The context shift derives from Tversky's (1977) "diagnostically principle," in which the similarity relation depends on the implicit context, and may change with the context of the objects compared.

The use of the self as a feature of the category "culprit" is especially effective in accomplishing the context shift. Any negative evaluative self-referent characteristic is highly motivating and therefore significant (Cantor and Kihlstrom, 1986). Evaluation apprehension (Rosenberg, 1965, 1980), is an anxiety-toned concern that the subject win a positive evaluation from the experimenter, or at least that he or she provide no grounds for a negative one. Evaluation apprehension was originally investigated as an extraneous influence in psychology experiments, and was subsequently observed to occur spontaneously whenever a negative evaluation by another person is possible, affecting performance in public speaking, group brainstorming, and demanding tasks in the presence of others. This phenomenon is expected to be stronger and more specific when the evaluation is explicit, its consequences are extreme, and the judged characteristic is overtly indicated.

Self-discrepancy theory proposes that we are motivated to sustain a condition where our self-concept matches our personally relevant self-guides (Higgins, 1987). In this theory, individuals maintain a system of beliefs about themselves: one's "actual" self (attributes one believes he/she actually possesses), "ought" self (attributes one believes he/she should or ought to possess), and "ideal" self (attributes one would ideally like to possess). The complement of relevant attributes in each view is ideographic, varying among individuals – one person may have "bravery" as an important attribute of his or her "ought" self, while another may have "friendliness" – but all persons share this belief structure. When one's failings are made salient, although not necessarily consciously, by relevant events – for one person "I am not as brave as I should be," for another "I am not as friendly as I ought to be" – the "actual-ought" self-discrepancy produces anxiety or agitation-related emotions when activated (Higgins, 1987, 1989). Moreover, in addition to the self views there are representations for views of significant others – mother, friend, teacher, coworker, manager, police officer, etc. When a person experiences self-discrepancy between actual/own and ought/other viewpoints, considerable discomfort may ensue considering attribute/other possibilities, such as cleanliness/mother, loyalty/friend, or honesty/police officer. In the CQT the examiner serves as a "significant other," conveying to the subject the salient and relevant self-guide – not to possess the negative attributes characterizing the culprit.

The importance and the prevalence of self-reference makes that feature of the test questions highly diagnostic, and tends to act as the basis for the classification of the subject with reference to the test questions; the combination of motivational and diagnostic factors enables the similarity outcome of the subject to the test questions to reflect the features retrieved by the subject from the enduring memory.

During the pre-test interview, the examinee often initiates the culprit category by spontaneously claiming "I've never done such a thing in my life. I'm an honest person." For the examiner, expressions of this type verify the establishment of the culprit category. In any case, examinees deny possessing the category attributes. The examiner ends the pre-test interview by formulating the test questions, together with the examinee, regarding the attributes of the culprit – the features of the superordinate category. The questions are structured to fulfill certain requirements:

1. All the questions are phrased to be self-referent for the examinee.
2. The features of relevant questions (i.e., Did you take the money from Jones' office last Tuesday?) are crime-specific, restricting the matching function to only one event in the enduring memory representation because of their distinctiveness (the money, Jones' office, last Tuesday).
3. The features of comparison questions (e.g., Did you ever do something dishonest to acquire something of value before 1990?),
   (a) are categories of behavioral traits which describe the crime as well as the culprit.
   (b) enable similarity to, and retrieval of, a wide range of significant events because of their indistinctiveness (something of value, dishonestly, before 1990), and
   (c) are crime-distinct, exclusive of the investigated crime, through the

use of a time bar (e.g. Before 1990, before age 24, etc.) or location bar (e.g. in other places of work).

The features of the category are prototypical misconducts (dishonesty, deceit, illegal, etc.) which are compared to representations of the self stored in the examinee's enduring memory. Essentially, the examinee asks him or herself "Am I like the person who did this?"

For all examinees, stored events that are similar to the culprit category features are accessed and retrieved from the enduring memory representation to working memory. Moreover, events accessed via similarity are retrieved according to their importance – represented by the magnitude of the motivational feature stored as part of the event – ensuring that the most significant instance of the category is retrieved to working memory.

This diagnostic and motivational context ensures that all examinees retrieve self-referent events stored in their enduring memory representations that match the comparison question category, consisting of crime-distinct instances of past misconduct, not related to the crime. Only guilty examinees can retrieve self-referent events containing crime-specific features that match the relevant question, from enduring memory representations.

TEST PHASE

The motivational features (fear of exposure, punishment) of the category are the examinee's "momentary motives" whose features (crime-specific and/or crime-distinct features), retrieved from the enduring memory representations to working memory, define the examinee's "momentary set" of significant events. As the test questions are presented in sequence, the examinee, denying the characteristics of the culprit category, replies "no" to each question, while his or her physiological activity is continuously monitored on the polygraph. The series is repeated several times.

The examinee – automatically, unconsciously, and involuntarily – conducts the feature matching function between the momentary set in working memory and the relevant and comparison test questions. The product determines the similarity between the himself and the features of each question. Therefore, for deceptive and truthful examinees, the identical set of relevant and comparison questions will result in different degrees of subject:question similarity and attribution of significance, and corresponding differences in the OR evoked by each.

As the test questions are presented, their significance is differentially assessed. For the examinee who is the culprit, the momentary set includes the crime-specific diagnostic features of his criminal act (date, time, place, $700, etc.), as well as crime-distinct diagnostic features of instances of his past misconduct, not related to the crime. In this instance, the correspondence between the relevant question and the criminal act in working memory produces a greater similarity result than the match between the comparison question and instances of past misconduct. Essentially, the guilty examinee identifies him or herself in the relevant question to a greater degree than in the comparison question. These similarity relations attribute a greater degree of significance to the relevant question (R) than to the comparison question (C), distributing ORs accordingly so that **R > C**.

For examinees who are innocent of the crime, working memory includes crime-distinct diagnostic features of their past misconduct, but not crime-specific diagnostic features of their criminal act. Therefore, the innocent examinee identifies himself in the comparison questions to a greater degree than in the relevant questions. This similarity relation attributes a greater degree of significance to the comparison question than to the relevant question, and produces an opposite distribution of ORs, **C > R**. As in the GKT, for both guilty and innocent examinees the act of lying, *per se*, is **incidental** to this process.

The model of orienting response has apparent descriptive value with respect to the comparison question technique criterion of lie detection, and explains the underlying psychological processes common to both GKT and CQT. Most importantly, the model presents a coherent system of mainstream psychological concepts that could explain why some polygraph examinees respond to comparison questions to a greater degree than to relevant questions, and how this may be related to deception or truthfulness.

However, the apparent descriptive value of the OR model is marred by its mechanistic, schematic character, lacking the evocative vividness to satisfy the need for intuitive comprehension of its operation, as experienced by polygraph examinees. People are more than just orienting machines, and consideration of the wealth of psychological study helps understand related dynamics in the CQT.

THE OR MODEL OF POLYGRAPH AND CONGRUENT PSYCHOLOGICAL THEORY

EMOTION AND MEMORY

The richness of human recollective experience is, in part, related to evocation of previously experienced emotions. Cahill *et al.* (1996) presented human subjects with video clips of emotionally neutral (N) or aversively emotionally arousing (E) content, while observing the activity of the amygdala using positron emission tomography. The amygdala is a brain structure in the limbic system, central to the response to danger and threat. They found that the emotional reaction immediately following each was higher for E clips than for N clips. Three weeks later subjects recalled significantly more E films than N films. Activity of the right amygdaloid complex while viewing the E films was highly correlated with the number of E films recalled, but not with the number of N films recalled. The findings support the view derived from both animal and human investigations that the amygdala is selectively involved with the formation of enhanced long-term memory associated with emotionally arousing events.

Furthermore, Hamann *et al.* (1997) found that amnesic patients with intact amygdalae demonstrate enhanced memory for emotional material despite their overall impaired memory performance. Amnesic patients and controls viewed a slide presentation while listening to an accompanying emotionally arousing story. In both groups, recognition memory was enhanced for the emotionally arousing story elements. The magnitude of the enhancement was proportional for both amnesic patients and controls. Emotional reactions to the story were also equivalent. The results suggest that the enhancement of declarative memory associated with emotional arousal is intact in amnesia. Together with findings from patients with bilateral amygdala lesions, the results indicate that the amygdala is responsible for the enhancement effect.

Cahill and McGaugh (1998) concluded that the adrenal hormones epinephrine and corticosterone appear to share two important adaptive functions in response to stressful experiences. First, they aid immediate responses to the stressful event. Second, they aid future responses by enhancing memory of the arousing experience. This perspective on the influence of emotional arousal upon memory presents an extreme, but representative, example of how significance, or signal value, may be acquired in real-life circumstances.

Committing a crime is an arousing experience, involving risk and fear, even for career burglars, who often admit and can accurately describe scores of burglaries. This enhanced memory is readily accessed and retrieved by guilty, but not innocent examinees. Furthermore, *all* people have arousing experiences arising from occasional breaches of conduct that are not crimes, but are sources of regret, shame, or disgrace. These transgressions – taking something without permission, ignoring rules, fabricating excuses, neglecting responsibility, avoiding effort, evading restrictions, offensive speech, adversary confrontations – are stressful events for which memory is enhanced and are readily accessed and retrieved by comparison questions. The correspondence of stress and memory enhancement ensures that the most stressful transgression episode is revived by comparison questions to working memory.

Research of brain activity (Isenberg *et al.*, 1999) has demonstrated that the amygdala actively participates in the processing of danger elicited by words. Subjects were instructed to name the color of words of either threat or neutral valence, presented in different color fonts, while neural activity was measured by using positron emission tomography. Bilateral amygdala activation was significantly greater during color naming of threat words than during color naming of neutral words. This demonstrates the amygdala's role in the processing of danger elicited by language. This may originate in early child–caretaker interactions in which misconducts resulted in punishment, and in general situations reflecting the presence of negative outcomes (Higgins, 1989), which are accompanied by verbal disapproval, and condemnation of negative behavioral attributes. Consistent with this perspective, Phelps *et al.* (2001) examined the neural substrates involved when subjects encountered an event linked verbally, but not experientially, to an aversive outcome, using an instructed fear task to model a primary way humans learn about the emotional nature of events. They told subjects that one stimulus (threat) represents an aversive event (a shock may be given), whereas another (safe) represents safety (no shock will be given). Using functional magnetic resonance imaging, activation of the left amygdala was observed in response to threat versus safe conditions, which correlated with the expression of the fear response as measured by skin conductance. These results suggest that the neural substrates that support conditioned fear across species have a similar role in more abstract representations of fear in humans. In this way, past events that included verbal expressions of censure are stressful events for which memory is enhanced, and are available to access by comparison questions in the present, operating via the amygdala.

LeDoux (1996) proposes that the memory enhancement of stress-evoked hormones acts not only upon the amygdala (implicit, emotional memory system), but also through it, on the hippocampus (explicit, conscious, and declarative memory system) as well. When the event is remembered at a later date, hippocampal-dependent memory of the past event details (which include the "fact" that it was stressful), as well as current amygdala-dependent emotional arousal, are both represented in working memory – leading to immediate conscious experience of the past event.

LeDoux's account is analogous to the OR model. Significance is engendered by the presence of motivational, emotional features in conjunction with diagnostic event features. In recall or recognition, diagnostic and motivational features of a significant past event are accessed in enduring memory and retrieved to working memory, where they are re-experienced, model motivational goals and initiate attentional mechanisms toward the environment. This is applicable for events indicated by comparison, as well as relevant questions. The correspondence with the ideas of Lang *et al.* (1997) above, Wheeler *et al.* (1997), and Damasio's (1991) below is notable.

EPISODIC AND SEMANTIC MEMORY

The distinction of episodic memory from semantic memory as separate and dissociable systems (Nyberg and Tulving, 1996; Schacter and Tulving, 1994) is pertinent to the relation between relevant and comparison questions in the CQT. With episodic memory, the subject not only has the memory, but can remember something about the setting in which the remembered information was learned – a system of context-specific memories personally experienced (event memory, personal, autobiographical). Conversely, with semantic memory, the subject cannot recall the context of the initial learning – a system of impersonal non-context-specific memories (generic, factual, knowledge).

Semantic memory supports the acquisition of general knowledge – maintaining classification categories, schemata, and stereotypes, together with evaluative information concerning each. In this knowledge system, the criminal act, the culprit, and the dispositional tendency of the culprit for generic similar activities are united in the same evaluated category, schema, and stereotype. Relevant questions refer to a specific episode in which the culprit committed a particular crime, whereas comparison questions refer to the assumed dispositional tendency of the culprit to activities of the same type as the crime. Comprehension of these involves the function of semantic memory.

However, in the polygraph setting, the relevant and comparison questions are discussed and presented in a self-referent context; therefore, they also mobilize the episodic memory system, involving autobiographical knowledge.

RELIVING THE EPISODE

Wheeler *et al.* (1997) describe episodic memory as the type of awareness experienced when one thinks back to a specific moment in one's personal past and consciously recollects some prior episode or state as it was previously experienced. Recollection of episodic information, in contrast to semantic memory, is not merely an objective account of what is, what has happened, or what one has seen, heard or thought. It involves remembering by re-experiencing and mentally traveling back in time. Its essence lies in the subjective feeling that, in the present experience, one is re-experiencing something that has happened before in one's life. This recollection is considered to be rooted in autonoetic (self-knowledge) awareness and in the belief that the self doing the experiencing now is the same self that did it originally, which may contribute to the observed robustness (Symons and Johnson, 1997) of the self-reference effect in memory. Duzel *et al.* (1997) reported an event-related potential experiment of human recognition memory that explored the relation between "remember" and "know" recognition judgments about previously seen words, reflecting "autonoetic" and "noetic" awareness, respectively. Their results provide physiological evidence for these two types of conscious awareness in episodic memory retrieval. Baddeley (2000) has proposed a fourth component to the original three-component model of working memory (Baddeley and Hitch, 1974), the episodic buffer. It comprises a limited capacity system that provides temporary storage of information held in a multimodal code, which is capable of binding information from the subsidiary systems, and from long-term memory, into a unitary episodic representation. Correspondingly, LePage *et al.* (2000) have data identified a network of brain sites, where neuronal activity is correlated with the maintenance of episodic memory retrieval mode, a basic and necessary condition of remembering past experiences.

Damasio and colleagues' (1991) somatic marker hypothesis, presents a similar view, including the following components. (1) There are structures in the prefrontal cortex that are involved in learning the association between complex social situations and the expressed emotional (somatic) state elicited when the situation is experienced by the individual. The somatic state includes all aspects of emotion from the evoked feeling to the musculoskeletal, visceral, and internal changes that occur. (2) When the situation occurs again in future time, the memory of the situation stored in the prefrontal cortex, triggers the associated link between the previous experience of the situation and the somatic state, thus reactivating the somatosensory emotional pattern that was elicited previously by a similar situation. This process may either be overt (conscious) or covert (nonconscious). Finally, (3) the reactivation of an emotional pattern from the knowledge of previous experience allows the individual to make a judgment on the predicted outcome of the experience when a similar situation occurs again; and depending on the outcome (consequence) of the situation, it is "marked" (labeled) as either 'good' or 'bad' in terms of personal benefits and losses. If this process is conscious, the triggered somatic state acts as an alarm signal to avoid a potentially damaging social situation, or to react in such a way as to reduce the adverse effects of the situation. If the situation is appraised as healthy, the somatic state acts as an incentive signal (cue) that encourages continued interaction in the situation.

Remembering an event involves not only what happened, but also concurrent context features regarding where and when the event occurred. Using positron emission tomography (PET) to study brain activity, Nyberg *et al.* (1996) found that initial encoding and subsequent retrieval of item-specific event information reactivates brain regions involving location and time information as well as those involved in item memory. Similarly, Nyberg *et al.* (2000) showed that that retrieval of specific event information reactivates brain regions that were active during encoding of this information. Remembering that words, presented visually, had been paired with sounds at encoding activated some of the auditory brain regions that were engaged during encoding. After word-sound encoding, activation of auditory brain regions was also observed during visual word recognition, when there was no demand to retrieve auditory information. Nilsson *et al.* (2000) also found that remembering actions involves reactivation of brain regions operating during encoding. Memory-related activity in the right motor cortex was maximal following encoding enactment of action events, intermediate following imaginary encoding enactment, and lowest following verbal encoding of the action command.

Correspondingly, Fabiani *et al.* (2000) presented strongly associated lists of words to one or the other cerebral hemisphere at study. This led to lateralized evoked-response potential brain activity for these words during a centrally presented recognition test, reflecting their lateralized encoding. This activity was absent for non-studied but strongly associated words falsely recognized as studied items. These results indicate that studied words leave sensory signatures of study experiences that are absent for false memories.

Dolan *et al.* (2000) conducted a PET study comparing patterns of brain activation associated with retrieving previously studied emotional and neutral pictorial material. Analysis identified a left amygdala response sensitive to actual retrieval of emotional items. He concluded that brain regions involved in episodic memory retrieval reflect not only physical attributes of stimulus material, for example, their verbal or visual qualities, but also their affective significance. In another PET study, Maguire and Mummery (1999) focused on the retrieval of real-world memories utilizing recollection of four memory subtypes–autobiographical events, public events, autobiographical facts, and general knowledge. These represent the factors of personal relevance and temporal context. They found that each of these was associated with activation of a common network of brain regions. Within this system, however, personal and temporal contexts affected region activity. For retrieval of personally relevant, time-specific memories enhanced activity was observed in a subset of brain regions, while for personal memories, regardless of time specificity, other regions were activated preferentially, and another set of regions was involved in memory retrieval irrespective of person or time.

Rolls (2000) has described the operation of different brain systems involved in different types of memory. One is a system in the primate orbitofrontal cortex and amygdala involved in representing rewards and punishers, and in learning stimulus–reinforcer associations. This system is involved in emotion and motivation. A second system in the temporal cortical visual areas is involved in learning invariant representations of objects. A third system in the hippocampus is implicated in episodic memory and in spatial function. Fourth, brain systems in the frontal and temporal cortices are involved in short-term memory.

Collectively, these observations demonstrate the power of part of an encoded event to reactivate memory of the whole experience: the event features, along with features representing the situated context, sensory experience, time, location, and emotion. These depictions indicate an experience of greater emotional impact, richness of detail and context and sensory vividness than the mechanistic portrayal in the OR model. The retrieval of the specific event to working memory essentially revives the original experience, of the whole complement of diagnostic and motivational features, retained in enduring memory representations. The relived episode is the reference for the comparisons conducted with the GKT and CQT test questions, determining OR magnitude. The actions and emotions experienced by the culprit during the crime – planning actions and preparing tools, breaking and entering, evasion, violence, danger, fear, gain – are also features of the event specific to the relevant alternative item for deceptive, but not for truthful, examinees in both test techniques.

Can we assume that this is so for actions and emotions embodied in comparison questions of broad scope? Do they retrieve autobiographical episodes, or perhaps general information lacking in motivational relevance?

SITUATED CONCEPTUALIZATION

A concept is often viewed as a detached description of a category's instances or statistical structure. Alternatively, Barsalou (Barsalou, 2001; Yeh and Barsalou, 2001) has demonstrated that a concept is a simulator that produces diverse simulations of "being there" with a category's instances. Across the episodic memory and conceptual processing literatures, the same pattern of results emerges. People do not store concepts in isolation – they store them with their background situations. When representing a category on a given occasion, a specific instance is simulated, not a generic exemplar, nor an exhaustive instance set. Furthermore, the instance is simulated in a background setting, not in isolation. Potential actions and mental perspectives on the instance are simulated as well – the instance is not simulated as detached. Thus, meaningful situations produce stronger situation effects than arbitrary situations. Conversely, when situations become active, they activate their associated concepts.

AFFECTIVE EQUIVALENCE OF EPISODIC AND SUMMARY MEMORIES

Singer and Moffitt (1992) requested autobiographical memories and personally significant "self-defining" memories relevant to one's self-understanding, in a non-clinical sample with no specification of the type of event. The mean percentage of episodic memories (discrete moment of time) and summary memories (no discrete moment of time, larger time frame and/or blend of events) was determined, recording subjects' affective responses to each memory type. The mean frequency of recall of episodic memory narratives was 78% versus summary memory narratives 22%, for both written and face-to-face verbal response. Request for personally significant memories increased the number of summary memory narratives retrieved, relative to autobiographical memories. However, summary and single event memories were not significantly different in affective quality.

Apparently, the activation of memory for specific episodes predominates over summaries, yet, the equivalence in affective quality of both ensures the motivational magnitude, or significance, of the memory contents retrieved to the comparison questions.

According to Klein and Loftus (1993), the distinction between specific and summary behavioral memories parallels that between specific and generic autobiographical memories: a specific memory is a representation of a single personal event that includes details about the time and place of that event; a generic memory is derived from multiple exposures to similar events but does not include details of the individual experiences from which it is derived – it's a representation of a general kind of event. Long-term self-knowledge of traits represented in abstract, summary form is independent of the representation of behavioral episodes. Episodes and abstract self-knowledge appear to be accessed independently, and also may be stored separately in memory. The retrieval of summary generic memories was found to facilitate trait judgments of self-descriptiveness (Klein *et al.*, 1993) and can serve as a basis for trait self-judgments even when the trait-relevant experience is low (Klein *et al.*, 1996). This reinforces the CQT assumption that comparison questions can effectively induce evaluative judgments of self-descriptiveness by activating summary memories or traits (e.g., "Did you ever tell a lie in order to avoid responsibility"), enabling them to compete with relevant questions.

A study by Kircher *et al.* (2000) has begun to lay the neurological basis for self-relevance. In their study, subjects made decisions about psychological trait adjectives previously categorized as describing their own attributes. A reaction time advantage was present when subjects responded to self-relevant words. The main area showing signal changes during self-reference processing, regardless of the type of stimulus, was the left fusiform gyrus. The self-relevant stimuli engaged, to a differential extent, long-term and working memory, semantic and emotional processes. Kircher *et al.* suggested that regions activated by these stimuli are engaged in self-processing.

Indeed, Gusnard *et al.* (2001), on the basis of a recent brain activity imaging study, proposed that both self-referential mental activity and emotional processing represent elements of an organized mode of default brain function as represented by activity in the medial prefrontal cortex.

One of the objections to the CQT doubts the capacity of the polygraph subject to perceive the importance of the comparison questions. Actually, phenomena observed in the study of social perception indicate the opposite.

THE ACTOR–OBSERVER DIFFERENCE

Observers, lacking well-developed trait knowledge about the actor, are likely to see individual behaviors as diagnostic of the actor's dispositions, and thus draw correspondent inferences regarding those personal tendencies (Jones and Gerard, 1967). The actor–observer difference (reviewed by Ross and Nisbett, 1991) is a robust phenomenon where people show a pervasive tendency to attribute their own behavior to external or situational causes, while attributing the behavior of others to internal dispositional factors (Jones and Nisbet, 1972).

This process contributes to its diagnostic ability of the CQT. The innocent subject has no trait knowledge about the culprit and tends to attribute the crime to the culprit's traits, embodied in the comparison questions. These attain importance if the subject shares them to any degree – if they are self-referent. The deceptive subject, the culprit, tends to attribute the crime to external or situational causes, and is less receptive to the dispositional information embodied in the comparison questions.

Such correspondent inferences promote the transition from the relevant question crime action – as indicative of the culprit's dispositions – to the comparison question culprit trait characteristic. For the polygraph examinee the transition is transparent and plausible.

Another objection concerns the doubt that the examiner consistently has the manipulative skill to influence the value of the comparison questions for the innocent subject, or establish the rapport necessary to do so. In reality, such influences don't depend on examiner skill, or even the presence of the examiner.

ACTIVATING RELATIONAL SCHEMAS

Relational schemas, which represent how one would be evaluated by a significant other, influence self-evaluative reactions when they are activated (Baldwin and Holmes, 1987). Unobtrusive presentation of the *name* of a critical significant other was used to prime a specific internalized relationship. This led subjects to report more negative self-evaluations and mood, under conditions of heightened self-awareness, or subliminal (implicit) priming of the critical significant other's name (Baldwin, 1994), or picture (Baldwin *et al.*, 1990, aptly entitled "Priming Relationship Schemas: My Advisor and the Pope Are Watching Me from the Back of My Mind"). The congruence with the polygraph circumstances is multiple. The examinee is acutely self-aware, "internally mirrored" by the polygraph. In the eyes of the polygraph subject, the examiner is a highly significant other, who is overtly critical of the culprit's characteristics, and those shared by the examinee. Furthermore, the examiner may easily "recruit" critical significant others of the subject, without knowing who they are, just by asking "If you ever did something like this, what would people you care about think?"

This combination of influences makes the examinee's self-evaluations with regard to the comparison questions more negative, with its concomitant physiological responses.

Gilbert *et al.* (1993) tested the hypothesis that merely comprehending a proposition includes an initial belief in that information. They exposed subjects to false information about a criminal defendant or a college student, with treatment groups under cognitive load or time pressure. Both load and time pressure caused subjects to believe false information and use it in making consequential decisions about the target – preventing them from "unbelieving" false information automatically believed during comprehension. Such emotion-induced changes during cognitive task performance were investigated by Simpson *et al.* (2001) in a study of brain activity, who found that the dynamic interplay between emotion and cognitive task performance is reflected in the activity of a network of neural sites. This cognitive handicap promotes the uncritical acceptance of the value of the comparison questions, as presented by an examiner. The polygraph subject is under very high stress throughout the test situation, more than equivalent to the cognitive load or time pressure used by Gilbert *et al.*

SHAME

Shame is intimately related to self-evaluation in respect to relational schemas. Scheff and Retzinger (2000) outline a social psychology of the basic emotions in social relationships. In their theory, shame and pride are the emotional building blocks of interpersonal relations. Much of their thought derives from Goffman's essay (1967) on "facework," which identified the underlying process in saving face, the avoidance of shame and embarrassment. They define shame as a class name for a large family of emotions which includes not only embarrassment, humiliation and disgrace, but also "discretionary" shame, such as modesty, shyness, and conscience. The common feature is seeing oneself negatively in the eyes of the other(s). They term shame "the master emotion" because they view it as having many more social and psychological functions than other emotions.

Shame is a central component of conscience, signaling moral transgression even without thoughts or words. Shame is our moral gyroscope. Shame also arises when there is a real or imagined threat to our bonds. Since an infant's life is completely dependent on the bond with the caregivers, this emotion is as primitive and intense as fear, and cannot be emphasized too strongly. Typically in psychology and psychoanalysis, shame is defined as a product of the individual's failure to live up to one's own ideal or duty. But these, for the most part, are usually a reflection of the ideals and duties of one's society of significant others. The perception that one's behavior has been inadequate or deviant, produces a disparity between behavior and ideals and duties, but also with shared group ideals and duties, jeopardizing basic social bonds.

According to Scheff and Retzinger shame plays a key role in regulating – mainly repressing and hiding – the overt expression, and indeed, even the awareness of other emotions. There is a powerful, though usually unspoken, rule in Western societies that feelings are a private matter, engendering a general prohibition against displaying one's feelings too quickly, not just embarrassment and shame, but all emotions. Anger, fear, guilt, grief, love, and embarrassment, for example, are not likely to be expressed outwardly to the degree that one is ashamed of them. They can be repressed almost completely, to the point that only unusual circumstances will allow them to come to awareness. Shame is a continuing presence or threat in most human contact, but people virtually never refer to it, and seldom seem to be aware of it.

In the polygraph setting shame is an inevitable spontaneous experience for examinee, arising, as Goffman (1959) indicated, out of disparities – real, anticipated, or just imagined – in the amount of deference received and given, no matter how slight the disparity. It permeates all of the question topics discussed in the pre-test interview, relevant and comparison. Examinees are keenly motivated to deny transgressions, maintain a positively toned bond with the examiner, and prevent leakage of emotional expression. Examiners are familiar with the involuntary and unaware nonverbal expressions of shame emitted by examinees, especially concerning comparison question issues, for which examinees are unprepared and unrehearsed.

For examinees guilty of the investigated crime the relevant questions are the major source of shame, exposure of: transgressions, disparity between behavior and ideals and duties, and justification for decreased deference on the part of the examiner, the investigator and significant others. For examinees innocent of the investigated crime the comparison questions are the focus of shame components.

SELF DISCREPANCY

According to self-discrepancy theory (Higgins, 1987, 1989), individuals possess distinct self-beliefs. When discrepancies among different types of self-beliefs are

culprit in the pre-test interview, and the accessibility of its self-relevant features in the comparison questions for the examinee.

CONSTRUCT ACCESSIBILITY

Higgins and Bargh (1992) described the judgmental assimilation bias as the tendency to use social constructs activated by exposure or priming to interpret ambiguous behaviors of the target person, over alternative, equally applicable, constructs. This priming effect has been demonstrated for a wide range of time spans. Two competing constructs, relevant for subsequent social task, were primed: one in 4 of 20 priming trials, the other on the 20th priming trial. After a short (15 s) delay of target behavior, the more recently primed construct was found to be used for encoding target behavior. After a longer post-priming delay (2 min), the more frequently primed construct was used for encoding (Higgins *et al.*, 1985). Priming effects on categorization can change the subjective meaning of the target's behavior over time, indicated by changes in the subjects' own attitudes toward the target person 2 weeks later (Higgins and Bargh, 1992). In the pre-test interview, the examiner primes the constructs of the culprit category (dishonesty, transgression, deception), reinforcing the accessibility of those features in the comparison questions for the examinee.

Similarly, with sufficient delay (3 min), the subjects' chronically accessible but unprimed social constructs are more likely to be used to interpret social behavior than an equally applicable construct recently primed by the situational context (Bargh *et al.*, 1988). Long-term, chronic construct accessibility exerts an influence on the encoding of construct-relevant input even when the construct is not currently active (Bargh *et al.*, 1986). Stimulus properties relevant to one's chronically accessible constructs receive preferential treatment in the initial automatic analysis of the environment (Bargh and Pratto, 1986). When a person possesses a chronically accessible construct that is primed, the two independent, long- and short-term, sources of accessibility have been found to combine additively to increase the likelihood of the construct's use (Bargh *et al.*, 1986). When the primed construct is not chronically accessible to the person, the effect of the primed construct persists (Bargh *et al.*, 1988).

Moreover, people might try to actively suppress thoughts about the possibility that they have undesirable personality traits, but this response to threat ultimately causes thoughts about the unwanted traits to become chronically accessible. As a result, those trait concepts will be used to interpret others' behavior. Newman *et al.* (1997) found that people who both avoid thinking about having threatening personality traits and deny possessing them also readily infer those traits from others' behavior, and when unfavorable traits were attributed to subjects, who were asked or predisposed to not think about the traits, they subsequently projected them onto someone else.

The discussion of the culprit's general characteristics in the pre-test interview is interpreted by the examinee in the light of his or her own particular chronically accessible social constructs, which he or she verbally expresses in some form. These are utilized in the discussion and wording of the comparison questions, reinforcing their personal relevance and accessibility.

The pre-test interview discussion of the culprit's dispositions to transgress, as well as those of the examinee, is sufficient to activate the examinee's negative self-schemata, promote unconscious cognitive processing of stereotypes and trait concepts, and encourage the tendency to use presented, primed, or chronically accessible social constructs activated to interpret the examinee's behaviors. These processes act as attractants, coherently organizing the accessed memory features according to personal relevance in relation to the comparison questions, which therefore need not be highly specific in order to compete effectively for the subject's attention.

The orienting response (OR) model, presented at the beginning of this chapter, attempts to map out how memory, emotion, and self-reference combine to form significance, thereby modulating the investment of attention. In the CQT, the examinee's pattern of resemblance to the culprit derives from the similarity relations obtained by the comparison between the culprit's behaviors and the behaviors of the examinee, stored in memory. The relevant questions refer to the specific crime act of the culprit, whereas the comparison questions refer to the culprit's general dispositions to transgress. The accessed memories determine the relative magnitude of the emotion evoked by each question – thus their relevance – and the attention allocated to each. This is expressed physiologically in the polygraph record: the deceptive examinee responds more to the relevant questions than to the comparison questions, whereas the truthful examinee experiences and exhibits the opposite response pattern.

The cognitive dynamics reviewed following the presentation of the OR model illustrate their congruent effects within the basic paradigm. The relation of emotion to memory, especially considering the encoding and reactivation of autobiographical episodes, which also reinstate sensorymotor, temporal, and spatial contexts, clarifies the acquisition and access of significance in memory. The accumulation of life experience in autobiographical memory, as well as its reactivation in explicit and implicit remembering, in response to external and internal life events, provides a rich foundation for constructs, of the self, significant others, stereotypes, and traits. These areas of study have typically been considered in isolation from each other and from the study of attention, but participate in the same process, utilizing the same substrates, and contributing to the outcomes described in the OR model. Together, these cognitive dynamics indicate how the comparison questions can effectively compete with relevant questions in the CQT.

Reconsidering the GKT in light of the processes involved in the CQT, it is easy to recognize the contribution of self-referent factors to the cognitive processes involved, enabling differential physiological response. The judgmental features arising from evaluation apprehension and self-discrepancy theory, implicit in the test situation, as well as the multiple reinstated contexts, are diagnostically specific features of the relevant alternative item for deceptive, but not for truthful, examinees.

The model described here appropriately reflects the complexity of human experience in the polygraph setting. However, since various interacting constituents contribute to the relatively unitary autonomic response system, the empirical validation of its components, individually and in combination, will be correspondingly complex. In light of the preceding discussion, some attention will be given to topics pertinent to polygraph testing.

CONFIRMATORY EXAMINATIONS

In the CQT, all tested examinees deny commission of the crime and the possession of negative behavioral attributes indicated by the crime. However, there are circumstances in which examinees assert an experience or act, rather than denying it, such as when they claim to be a witness or victim of a theft or assault, or have confessed to a crime, they may be suspected of false complaint or statement regarding their, or another's, actions.

The foregoing analysis of the CQT highlights the predicament where a truthful subject may be faced with the question sets: "Were you struck in the face by John?" "Yes." Or "Was your money taken from you by John?" "Yes." In terms of the OR model, the truthful subject virtually relives the episode and identifies him or herself in such relevant questions to a greater degree than in the comparison question "Before 1993 did you ever lie to hurt someone?," producing a correspondingly greater OR, and leading to an erroneous test outcome. Conversely, the deceptive subject – the false accuser – **does not** identify him or herself in the relevant questions, having no episode to relive, but does in the comparison questions, again leading to an erroneous conclusion. Reversal of the CQT criterion in such cases could be argued, theoretically.

On the whole, polygraph examiners recognize the existence of some problem, and tend to note that examinees in this type of situation may have been subject to some degree of "trauma," when they actually mean a state of extreme emotion and arousal. Typically, examiners attempt to avoid reviving the traumatic event by rephrasing the relevant questions to stress the "deception" feature rather than the event itself, for instance, "Are you lying that you were struck by John last week?" or, "Did you lie to the police that John took your money last week?" However, this solution is, literally, partial, since the self-referent features in this type of relevant question are in conflict: for the deceptive examinee the initial part of the question "Are you lying that you were punched by John last week?" is self-referent, while the latter part is not; and for the truthful examinee the opposite is true.

Another approach to this problem has been the "confirmatory" or "declaration" test, used when the examinee alleges to be a victim ("I was punched by John last week.") or witness to an event, or asserts some specific act ("I *did* give John $500 last week.") whose omission is illegal. In this type of CQT polygraph examination, the subject, under the guidance of the examiner, writes and signs a short and specific statement regarding his assertion, followed by an examination where a relevant question could be "Did you lie in the declaration you wrote here?" and a comparison question could be "Before 1993 did you ever cheat someone?" In this test, both the innocent and guilty subjects are able to conduct the self-referent feature-matching function in the expected manner, consistent with the CQT phenomenon.

THE DIRECTED LIE TEST FORMAT AND THE OR MODEL

The directed lie test (DLT) format (Fuse, 1982; Honts and Raskin, 1988; also see Raskin and Honts, Chapter 1 this volume) attempts to circumvent the objections regarding traditional types of comparison questions, which assume that the innocent subject is lying to them ("probable lie" – PL questions). During the pre-test interview, subjects are told to lie to the DL questions. An example of a DL question is "In your entire life, have you made even one mistake?" Subjects are instructed to answer "No," which is a lie for everyone. They are also instructed to think about a particular time when they made a mistake as they are answering the question. The examiner emphasizes DL questions by indicating that it is important to determine if the person's reactions to the relevant questions are the same or different from their lie to the DL questions. Horowitz *et al.* (1997) expected all individuals to focus their concern on the question(s) that poses the greatest threat to their passing the test. It is assumed that guilty persons will believe that DL questions will reveal their lie pattern, which will allow the examiner to determine that their answers to R questions are deceptive. Conversely, it is assumed that innocent persons will be concerned that they exhibit clear lie patterns to the DL question that will demonstrate their truthfulness on the R questions. Thus, innocent persons are expected to be concerned about the appropriateness of their physiological reactions to the DL questions. The directed lie test format has been shown to be accurate in laboratory experiments and in real-life field settings (see Raskin and Honts, Chapter 1 this volume).

The OR model of polygraph testing offers a supplementary explanation for the demonstrated effectiveness of the directed lie test format. Let us consider the comparison question types used by Horowitz *et al.* (1997): the personal directed lies (i.e., "Have you ever told a lie?, Have you ever broken a rule or regulation?, Have you ever made a mistake?"); and the conventional CQT probable lie comparison questions (i.e., "Did you ever take something that did not belong to you?, Did you ever do anything that was dishonest or illegal?, Did you ever lie to get out of trouble?"). The DL questions differ from the PL questions to some degree in the apparent gravity of the action concerned. However, as postulated in the OR model, the features of both DL and PL questions:

1. are categories of behavioral traits which describe the crime as well as the culprit;
2. enable similarity to, and retrieval of, a wide range of significant events because of their indistinctiveness; and
3. are crime-distinct, exclusive of the investigated crime.

Furthermore, their diagnostic features are:

4. continuous traits (error, dishonesty, immorality, damaging, harmful, etc.), rather than discrete ones, which include the crime (relevant issues) at the high end of the scale, but are not specific only to the crime. At the low end of the scale, the same traits characterize universal misconduct of all persons (i.e., regrettable behavior, a white lie, negligence, etc.), not related to the crime;
5. discussed with reference to the examinee, establishing self-reference as a diagnostic feature.

Finally, they:

6. share the universally negative motivational features of transgressions (shame, disapproval, responsibility, punishment), which also stem from the relevant questions.

In the directed lie test format no covert or overt attempt is made to perform a context shift to the culprit category. However, unintentionally and unknowingly, a multitude of contexts and representations, reviewed above, are conjured up automatically. Indeed, Bargh (1997) indicates that removing conscious aspects serves to increase, rather than decrease the generality of automatic evaluation and activation of self-relevant traits.

Both DL and PL questions are autobiographical, and utilize summary behaviors in their phasing, which would be expected to activate specific episodes or summary memories of misconduct in autobiographical memory. The evoked memories are likely to be representations of stressful experiences, which enhance memory of the arousing experience (Cahill and McGaugh, 1998). These memories vary in specific content from subject to subject, reflecting on the unique personal history of each, but overall they are the inevitable result of a procedure in which subjects retrieve particular ideographic events, personally relevant attributes, traits, self-guides, significant others, constructs, etc.

DL and PL questions regarding misconduct refer to violations of ought standards that result in punishment, and in general situations reflect the presence of negative outcomes (Higgins, 1989). As Strauman (1992) found, both types of questions can cue ought self-guides evoking autobiographical memories with negative emotional tone, as a result of experienced actual:ought discrepancies. Long-term, chronic construct accessibility exerts an influence on the encoding of construct-relevant input even when the construct is dormant (Bargh *et al.*, 1986). Stimulus properties relevant to one's chronically accessible constructs receive preferential treatment in the initial automatic analysis of the environment (Bargh and Pratto, 1986). This may also prime a specific internalized relationship with a significant other who is perceived as being critical or judgmental (Baldwin and Holmes, 1987). Similarly, the mere presence of misconduct features can activate a negative stereotype without the perceiver's intending it or being aware of the trait concept or stereotypic influence on perceptual interpretation or judgment (Chen and Bargh, 1997).

The correspondence between the CQT and the DLT in terms of the OR model and relevant psychological processes suggests that, despite the apparent difference in induction procedures, they converge in their underlying dynamics.

STANDARDIZATION AND CQT

Ben-Shakhar and Furedy (1990, also see Ben-Shakhar, Chapter 4 this volume) have criticized the CQT on the basis of being non-standard – the examiner is required to generate and present comparison questions which are personally relevant for the subject. However, because this is expected to vary from subject to subject, this task, if conducted successfully (discussed above), results in a non-standard procedure, different from subject to subject.

Andersen and Glassman (1996) addressed similar concerns regarding research on significant-other representations. The basic issue is to find a way to incorporate into the research design the particular idiographic understanding

standard deviation in direction of deception, relative to subjects innocent of both thefts, increasing the probability of a false positive outcome for the specific test issue. The use of outside issue questions did not indicate the presence of an outside issue.

The theme of differentiating among several event episodes of the same type in memory, with some common and some distinct features of event, context, and emotion, is an unexplored field, as yet, in any method.

FUTURE RESEARCH AND DEVELOPMENT

This chapter has endeavored to present findings from accepted psychological and psychophysiological research and theory as a foundation for the assumption at the root of the comparison questions test – there is a scientific basis for the expectation that truthful subjects will attend and respond to comparison questions to a greater degree than relevant questions. While it is hoped that the existence of this foundation has been made clear, the fact that the experimental contexts of the research and theory do not involve real-life circumstances of "lie detection" makes this exposition speculative to a degree. Empirical investigation is needed within a polygraph context to evaluate whether the assumptions presented here are valid. Fortunately, these issues complement and overlap current areas of interest in psychological research. Comparison questions present a counterintuitive challenge in this regard. Their apparent ability to compete with specific relevant questions calls for deeper understanding of the natural contexts in which they occur, their characterization, and effects.

There is a need to reveal the implicit and explicit assumptions that lead subjects to deny universal transgressions; "I've never told a lie." Several processes involved in establishing effective comparison question have been considered, including characterization of the culprit, negative self-view schema, actual/ought self-discrepancy, activation of accessible constructs and relational schemas. These may be equivalent aspects of a single self-evaluative dynamic, or they may differ in the degree to which they are effective.

The types of memories accessed by comparison questions – summaries of generic events and/or specific episodes – are of importance. It is not known if they evoke equivalent subjective experiences of reliving the event, physiological responses, or to what degree they share retrieved features – reactivation of sensory, motor, spatial, temporal, and emotional brain regions.

Comparison questions present the subject with broad, indistinct context features of his or her past misbehavior (e.g., Did you ever betray a trust?). By nature, each individual possesses a store of memories unique to that individual and unknown to the examiner, who assumes that the subject will access according to the question context. Every polygraph examiner has ample anecdotal experience that this is so (e.g., I cheated on my girlfriend when I was in high school). However, memories with just minimal context relevance may be reactivated if they are emotional and arousing, and thereby highly accessible. The interaction between emotional intensity and situated context features has not been systematically investigated.

Relevant questions also require investigation and exploration of their limits. The discussion of the CQT criteria in this chapter has considered the classic circumstance, where the truthful subject has no experience of the specific crime action, and therefore no episodic memory, self-reference, etc. In real-life settings, the suspect may, in fact, have experience of the event context, even though he or she may be truthful in denying the offence. He or she may have exchanged violent words with the complainant, but did not assault him or her; the suspect may have attacked the complainant recently, but didn't damage his or her car; the suspect may have been the victim of burglary, but didn't exaggerate about the amount of jewelry stolen. These types of instances are routinely examined using the CQT criteria with apparent accuracy. Their analogs can also be found in many experimental protocols in studies of episodic memory. Both indicate the innate capability to differentiate the presence or absence of a specific detail within a context that is known to exist. Yet, within the framework presented here, when the relevant detail is situated within an emotionally arousing context, retrieval of the context assumed evoking an OR for truthful and deceptive subjects, which is uninformative to the examiner because the context is assumed for subjects of both types. Retrieval of the relevant detail, and its indicative OR, depends on its presence or absence in subject memory. However, there is no way to know for certain whether a given response represents the summation of relevant detail and the arousing context, or the context alone. The question "When you argued with Janet in the entrance, did you slap her?" is likely to elicit an OR because of the emotionally laden argument, whether or not the subject struck Janet. Experienced examiners may attempt to balance this context by including it in the comparison question "Before the argument with Janet, did you ever raise your hand in violence?", or attempt to avoid the context, or discount it as inconsequential, asking, "Did you slap Janet last week?"

Limits regarding uncertain situations (e.g., a police officer may have struggled with a suspect who resisted arrest, and may, or may not, have kicked him as alleged, or may be unaware of foot–suspect contact in the fracas) and source memory (e.g., a suspect may now know that his partner falsifies receipts, but may, or may not, have known this before the investigation) need to be delineated and implemented in relevant questions. The effects of memory, emotion, self-reference, attention, context, etc. require a more refined understanding of their relations to ensure discrimination in such commonplace circumstances.

The chief topic in need of study is the understanding of the relationship of relevant/comparison effects in truthful and deceptive subjects. These have been characterized here in terms of attention, memory, emotion, self-reference, autonomic response, and other concepts. The relationship has been expressed in two general ideas, which are not entirely consistent. One is that the specificity of the relevant question leads to a more self-referent result for the deceptive subject than the comparison question, and visa versa for the truthful subject. The other idea is that these degrees of self-reference engender self-relevance, or subjective significance, differentially for the deceptive and truthful subjects. Theory and research increasingly indicate that affect – emotion, motivation – is a guiding vector for attention, cognition, and memory. The intricacies of the reference–relevance relation terms of comparison and relevant questions for polygraph subjects, and perhaps all persons in general, have yet to be fully understood. They need to be comprehended, not only by speculating from other contexts, but directly. The limits of conditions in which the CQT criteria are valid should be sought after, as should the circumstances that necessitate amendment of the criteria, as hypothesized above regarding confounding issues, confirmatory examinations, etc.

The overarching premise of the self and the relative significance of its components have been offered as the basis of the CQT criterion, determining the relationship between attributions embodied in the test questions for truthful and deceptive subjects. The impact upon the experience of the self, of a specific offense, or its absence, relative to other, lesser or greater, transgressions, requires further exploration. Possible contexts for such investigation are: the self as a cognitive schema; negative self-schemata; evaluation apprehension; the self-reference effect in memory; primed and chronically accessible social constructs; affect and judgments of self-descriptiveness from episodic and summary, generic memories; self-discrepancy; relational schemas; stereotypes and trait concepts and their automatic activation; thought suppression; correspondent inferences; the actor–observer difference; situated conceptualization; and self-referential mental activity and emotional processing as an organized mode of default brain function. Studies of specific and summary attributes in these contexts could serve to illuminate the validity and limitations of the CQT assumptions, and advance its procedures.

As discussed above, the essence of episodic memory lies in the subjective feeling that in the present instance one is re-experiencing something that has happened before in one's life (Wheeler *et al.*, 1997). Awareness of this re-experience may occur as the event is represented in the episodic buffer, a component of working memory – a limited capacity system that provides temporary storage of information held in a multimodal code, which is capable of binding information into a unitary episodic representation, from the subsidiary systems, and from long-term memory (Baddeley, 2000). This information derives from the reactivation of various brain regions originally involved in encoding the event features, along with features representing the situated context, sensory experience, time, location, and emotion. This correspondence between episodic memory and the reactivation of specific brain regions originally involved in encoding the event has been utilized to look for possible differences in correct and erroneous recognition of previously experienced events. Schacter *et al.* (1996) used positron emission tomography to compare brain regions involved in veridical recognition of printed words that were heard several minutes earlier and erroneous recognition of printed words that had not been heard earlier. Veridical and illusory recognition were each associated with increases in blood flow in a region previously implicated in episodic memory; veridical recognition was distinguished by additional increases in blood flow in a left temporoparietal region previously implicated in the retention of auditory sensory information. This is consistent with the findings of Nyberg *et al.* (1996, 2000), which showed that retrieval of item-specific event information reactivates sensory regions that were active during encoding, as well as brain regions involving location and time information at initial encoding. Similarly, Fabiani *et al.* (2000), using evoked response potentials, found that studied words leave sensory signatures of study experiences that are absent for false memories. Such findings may be relevant for those of Rosenfeld (see chapter 10), which revealed a characteristic distribution of evoked response potentials during deception.

In a similar manner, a corresponding approach may eventually be used in "detection of deception," by evaluating whether or not a criminal suspect possesses the characteristics of episodic memory for the crime that must be present for the culprit. These are event features, along with features representing the situated context, sensory experience, time, location, and emotion. They are indicated by the reactivation of specific brain regions originally involved in encoding the actual event, whereas the innocent suspect would not indicate activity of those characteristics when tested for episodic memory of committing the crime. Accordingly, assertions of victims could be evaluated in the same way, with opposite criteria: the actual victim would exhibit appropriate characteristics of episodic memory, while the simulator would not. The construct of deception, as in the GKT and CQT, is unnecessary. In due course, advances in imaging resolution, analysis, and interpretation of brain activity, accompanied by dwindling size and costs of instrumentation, are expected to make such approaches increasingly precise and practicable.

The areas of study reviewed above touch upon the plausibility of the assumptions in the comparison question technique of polygraph testing. A variety of findings and phenomena, studied and observed within diverse theoretical frameworks, in addition to the OR model, provide considerable support for the assumption that comparison questions indeed can effectively compete with relevant questions for allocation of attention in the CQT. These frameworks offer hypotheses that can be tested in settings including and excluding deception, promoting progress in the understanding of the psychological processes in detection of deception and resolution of its controversial aspects.

Polygraph testing is an instance of a basically reliable and robust procedure that was developed in the field by its practitioners, lacking the theoretical and empirical benefits of scientific method. The model offered here is simply a reorganization of what many polygraph examiners and psychologists know already, with reference to this particular context. Remarkably, the cognitive and physiological dynamics do not deal with lying *per se*, but rather with the examinee's ability to process the significance of the information about him or herself, in the test contexts. Similarly, Ekman (1985) was able to infer deceptive communication by detecting microexpressions, fleeting facial and body gestures of subjects, indicating emotions (fear, disdain, sadness, glee) inconsistent with the verbal content expressed. The contradictory emotional leakage was observed, indicating lying – not the lie itself.

This model of orienting response is offered as a conceptual framework within which polygraph issues may be redefined theoretically and operationally, and examined empirically. Once based on a theoretical framework, research observations may amend, elaborate, and refine the processes involved, with consequent improvements in cognitive management and physiological assessment procedures in the GKT and CQT. This approach is open to refutation and substitution by a more appropriate and valid system of concepts, and frees the CQT, to a certain extent, from overall validity as the sole instrument of evaluation. The theoretical approach encourages clear and consistent communication among polygraph examiners, trainers and trainees, as well as meaningful scientific dialog in the academy and legislature.

REFERENCES

Andersen, S. M. and Baum, A. (1994) Transference in interpersonal relations: Inferences and affect based on significant-other representations. *Journal of Personality*, 62, 459–498.

Andersen, S. M. and Glassman, N. S. (1996) Responding to significant others when they are not there. Effects on interpersonal inference, motivation, and affect. In E. T. Higgins and R. M. Sorrentino (eds), *Handbook of Motivation and Cognition: Foundations of Social Behavior* (Vol. 3). New York: Guilford Press.

Andersen, S. M., Glassman, N. S., Chen, S. and Cole, S. W. (1995) Transference in social perception: The role of chronic accessibility in significant-other representations. *Journal of Personality and Social Psychology*, 69, 41–57.

Backster, C. (1963) *Standardized Polygraph Notepack and Technique Guide.* USA: Cleve Backster.

Baddeley, A. D. (2000) The episodic buffer: a new component of working memory? *Trends in Cognitive Sciences*, 4 (11), 417–423.

Baddeley, A. D. and Hitch, G. (1974) Working memory. In: G. A. Bower (ed.) *The Psychology of Learning and Motivation*, vol. 8, pp. 47–89. New York: Academic Press.

Baddeley, A., Bueno, O., Cahill, L., Fuster, J. M., Izquierdo, I., McGaugh, J. L., Morris, R. G., Nadel, L., Routtenberg, A., Xavier, G. and Da Cunha, C. (2000) The brain decade in debate: I. Neurobiology of learning and memory. *Brazilian Journal of Medical Biological Research*, 33 (9), 993–1002.

Baldwin, M. W. (1994) Primed relational schemas as a source of self-evaluative reactions. *Journal of Social and Clinical Psychology*, 13 (4), 380–403.

Baldwin, M. W. and Holmes, J. G. (1987) Salient private audiences and awareness of the self. *Journal of Personality and Social Psychology*, 32 (6), 1087–1098.

Bargh, J. A. (1990) Auto-motives: Preconscious determinants of social interaction. In E. T. Higgins and R. M. Sorrentino (eds), *Handbook of Motivation and Emotion*, Vol. 2. New York: Guilford Press.

Bargh, J. A. (1997) The automaticity of everyday life. In: R. S. Wyer, Jr (ed.) *The Automaticity of Everyday Life: Advances in Social Cognition*, vol. X. Mahwah, NJ: Lawrence Erlbaum Associates.

Bargh, J. A., Bond, R. N., Lombardi, W. L. and Tota, M. E. (1986). The additive nature of chronic and temporary sources of construct accessibility. *Journal of Personality and Social Psychology*, 22, 293–311.

Bargh, J. A., Lombardi, W. J. and Higgins, E. T. (1988) Automaticity of chronically accessible constructs in person X situation effects on person perceptions: It's just a matter of time. *Journal of Personality and Social Psychology*, 55 (4), 599–605.

Bargh, J. A. and Pratto, F. (1986) Individual construct accessibility and perceptual selection. *Journal of Experimental and Social Psychology*, 22, 293–311.

Barsalou, L.W. (2001) *Situated Conceptualization*. Presented at the 3rd International Conference on Memory (ICOM), Valencia, Spain, July 16–21, 2001.

Barsalou, L. W. and Sewell, D. R. (1984) *Constructing Representations of Categories From Different Points of View*. Emory Cognition Project Report #2.

Ben-Shakhar, G. and Furedy, J. J. (1990) *Theories and Applications in the Detection of Deception.* New York: Springer-Verlag.

Ben-Shakhar, G., Gati, I. and Salamon, N. (1995) Generalization of the orienting response to significant stimuli: the roles of common and distinctive stimulus components. *Psychophysiology*, 32, 36–42.

Ben Shakhar, G., Gati, I., Frost, R. and Kresh, Y. (1996) Is an apple a fruit? Semantic relatedness as reflected by psychophysiological responsivity. *Psychophysiology*, 33 (6), 671–679.

Ben-Shakhar, G. and Lieblich, I. (1982) Similarity of auditory stimuli and generalization of skin conductance response (SCR) habituation. *Physiological Psychology*, 10, 331–335.

Berlyne, D. E. (1961) Conflict and the orientation response. *Journal of Experimental Psychology*, 26, 476–483.

Bernstein, A. S. (1969) To what does the orienting response respond? *Psychophysiology*, 6, 338–351.

Bernstein, A. S. (1979) The orienting response and novelty and significance detector: reply to O'Gorman. *Psychophysiology*, 16, 263–273.

Bower, G. H. and Gilligan, S. G. (1979) Remembering information related to one's self. *Journal of Research in Personality*, 13, 420–432.

Cahill, L., Haier, R., Fallon, J., Alkire, M., Tang, C., Keator, D., Wu, J. and McGaugh, J. L. (1996) Amygdala activity at encoding correlated with long-term, free recall of emotional information. *Proceedings of the National Academy of Sciences*, 93, 8016–8021.

Cahill, L. and McGaugh, J. L. (1998) Mechanisms of emotional arousal and lasting declarative memory. *Trends in Neurosciences*, 21, 294–299.

Callicott, J. H., Mattay, V. S., Bertolino, A., Finn, K., Coppola, R., Frank, J. A., Goldberg, T. E. and Weinberger, D. R. (1999) Physiological characteristics of capacity constraints in working memory as revealed by functional MRI. *Cerebral Cortex*, 9 (1), 20–26.

Cantor, N. and Kihlstrom, J. F. (1986) *Personality and Social Intelligence*. Englewood Cliffs, NJ: Prentice-Hall.

Chen, M. and Bargh, J. A. (1997) Nonconscious behavioral confirmation processes: The self-fulfilling consequences of automatic stereotype activation. *Journal of Experimental Social Psychology*, 33, 541–560.

Christianson, S.-A. (1992) Remembering emotional events: potential mechanisms. In: S.-A. Christianson (ed.) *The Handbook of Emotion and Memory: Research and Theory*. Hillsdale, NJ: Lawrence Erlbaum Associates.

Connoly, J. G. and Frith, C. D. (1978a) Effects of stimulus variability on the amplitude and habituation of the electrodermal orienting response. *Psychophysiology*, 15, 550–555.

Connoly, J. G. and Frith, C. D. (1978b) Effects of varying stimulus context on habituation and sensitization of the OR. *Physiology and Behavior*, 21, 511–514.

Critchley, H. D., Elliott, R., Mathias, C. J. and Dolan, R. J. (2000) Neural activity relating to generation and representation of galvanic skin conductance responses: a functional magnetic resonance imaging study. *Journal of Neuroscience*, 20 (8), 3033–3040.

Damasio, A. R., Tranel, D. and Damasio, H. (1991) Somatic markers and the guidance of behavior: Theory and preliminary testing. In: H. S. Levin, H. M. Eisenberg and A. L. Benton (eds) *Frontal Lobe Function and Dysfunction*, pp. 217–229. New York: Oxford University Press.

Dawson, M.E. (1980) Physiological detection of deception: Measurement of responses to questions and answers during countermeasures maneuvers. *Psychophysiology,* 17, 8–17.

Department of Defense Polygraph Institute Research Division Staff (1995) A comparison of psychophysiological detection of deception accuracy rates obtained using the counter-intelligence scope polygraph and the test for espionage and sabotage question formats. *Polygraph*, 26 (2), 79–106.

Diener, E. and Fujita, F. (1995) Resources, personal strivings, and subjective well-being: A nomothetic and idiographic approach. *Journal of Personality and Social Psychology*, 68 (5), 926–935.

Dolan, R. J., Lane, R., Chua, P. and Fletcher, P. (2000) Dissociable temporal lobe activations during emotional episodic memory retrieval. *Neuroimage*, 11 (3), 203–209.

Düzel, E., Yonelinas, A. P., Mangun, G. R., Heinze, H. J. and Tulving, E. (1997) Event-related brain potential correlates of two states of conscious awareness in memory. *Proceedings of the National Academy of Sciences, U.S.A.*, 94, 5973–5978.

Ekman, P. (1985) *Telling Lies*. New York: W.W. Norton and Co.

Elaad, E. (1990) Detection of guilty knowledge in real life criminal investigations. *Journal of Applied Psychology*, 75, 521–529.

Elaad, E. and Ben-Shakhar, G. (1989) Effects of motivation and verbal response type on psychophysiological detection of information. *Psychophysiology*, 26, 442–451.

Elaad, E., Ginton, A. and Jungman, N. (1988) Respiration line length and GSR amplitude as detection measures in criminal guilty knowledge tests. Paper presented at the NATO ASI Conference on Credibility Assessment, Maratea, Italy.

Fabiani, M., Stadler, M. A. and Wessels, P. M. (2000) True but not false memories produce a sensory signature in human lateralized brain potentials. *Journal of Cognitive Neuroscience*, 12, 941–949.

Furedy, J. J. and Heselgrave, R. J. (1989) The forensic use of the polygraph: A psychophysiological analysis of current trends and future prospects. In: P. K. Ackles, J. R. Jennings and M. G. H. Coles (eds) *Advances in Psychophysiology*, vol. 4. Greenwich, CT: JAI Press.

Fuse, L. S. (1982) *Directed Lie Control Testing Technique*. Unpublished manuscript.

Gati, I. and Ben-Shakhar, G. (1990) Novelty and significance in orientation and habituation: a feature matching approach. *Journal of Experimental Psychology: General*, 119 (3), 251–263.

Gilbert, D. T., Tafarodi, R. W., and Malone, P. S. (1993) You can't not believe everything you read. *Journal of Personality and Social Psychology*, 65 (2), 221–233.

Goffman, E. (1959) *The Presentation of Self in Everyday Life.* Garden City, New York: Doubleday.

Goffman, E. (1967) *Interaction Ritual*. New York: Anchor.

Gusnard, D. A., Akbudak, E., Shulman, G. L. and Raichle, M. E. (2001) Medial prefrontal cortex and self-referential mental activity: Relation to a default mode of brain function. *Proceedings of the National Academy of Sciences*, 98 (7), 4259–4264.

Gustafson, L. A. and Orne, M. T. (1965) The effects of verbal responses on the laboratory detection of deception. *Psychophysiology,* 2, 10–13.

Hamann, S., Cahill, L., McGaugh, J. L. and Squire, L. (1997) Intact enhancement of declarative memory by emotional arousal in amnesia. *Learning and Memory*, 4, 301–309.

Heil, P., Ahlmeyer, S., Simons, D. and English, K. (1999) *The Impact of Polygraphy on Admissions of Crossover Offending Behavior in Adult Sexual Offenders*. Research presented at the 18th Annual ASTA Research and Treatment Conference in Lake Buena Vista, Florida, 1999.

Higgins, E. T. (1987) Self-discrepancy: A theory relating self and affect. *Psychological Review*, 94, 319–340.

Higgins, E. T. (1989) Continuities and discontinuities in self-regulatory and self-evaluative processes: a developmental theory relating self and affect. *Journal of Personality*, 57 (2), 407–444.

Higgins, E. T. and Bargh, J. A. (1992) Unconscious sources of subjectivity and suffering: Is consciousness the solution? In: L. L. Martin and A. Tesser (eds) *The Construction of Social Judgments*. Hillsdale, NJ: Lawrence Erlbaum Associates.

Higgins, E. T., Bargh, J. A. and Lombardi, W. (1985) Nature of priming effects on categorization. *Journal of Experimental Psychology: Learning, Memory and Cognition*, 11, 59–69.

Honts, C. H., Amato, S. and Gordon, A. (2000) *Validity of Outside-Issue Questions in the Control Question Test* (DoDPI97-P-00012). Department of Defense Polygraph Institute, Fort Jackson, SC 29207.

Honts, C. R. and Raskin, D. C. (1988) A field study of the validity of the directed lie control question. *Journal of Police Science and Administration*, 16, 56–61.

Horowitz, S. W., Kircher, J. C., Honts, C. R. and Raskin, D. C. (1997). The role of comparison questions in physiological detection of deception. *Psychophysiology*, 34, 108–115.

Houck, R. L. and Mefford, R. B. (1969). Generalization of GSR habituation to mild intramodal stimuli. *Psychophysiology*, 6, 202–206.

Isenberg, N., Silbersweig, D., Engelien, A., Emmerich, S., Malavade, K., Beattie, B., Leon A. C. and Stern, E. (1999) Linguistic threat activates the human amygdala. *Proceedings of the National Academy of Sciences, U.S.A.*, 96, 10456–10459.

Jones, E. E. and Gerard, H. B. (1967) *Foundations of Social Psychology*. New York: John Wiley.

Jones, E. E. and Nisbet, R. E. (1972) The actor and the observer: Divergent perceptions of the causes of behavior. In: E. E. Jones, D. E. Kanouse, H. H. Kelleym, T. E. Nisbett, S. Valins and B. Weiner (eds) *Attribution: Perceiving the Causes of Behavior*, pp. 79–94. Morristown, NJ: General Learning Press.

Kahneman, D. (1973) *Attention and Effort*. Englewood Cliffs, NJ: Prentice-Hall.

Kihlstrom, J. F. and Cantor, N. (1984) Mental representations of the self. In: L. Berkowitz (ed.) *Advances in Experimental and Social Psychology*, vol. 17, pp. 1–47. New York: Academic Press.

Kircher, J. C., Horowitz, S. W. and Raskin, D. C. (1988) Meta-analysis of mock-crime studies of the control question polygraph technique. *Law and Human Behavior*, 12, 79–90.

Kircher, T. T., Senior, C., Phillips, M. L., Benson, P. J., Bullmore, E. T., Brammer, M., Simmons, A., Williams, S. C., Bartels, M. and David, A. S. (2000) Towards a functional neuro-anatomy of self processing: effects of faces and words. *Brain Research: Cognitive Brain Research*, 10 (1–2), 133–144.

Klein, S. B. and Loftus, J. (1993) The mental representation of trait and autobiographical knowledge about the self. In: T. K. Srull and S. Wyer (eds) *Advances in Social Cognition*, vol. 5. Hillsdale, NJ: Lawrence Erlbaum Associates.

Klein, S. B., Loftus, J. and Sherman, J. W. (1993) The role of summary and specific behavioral memories in trait judgments about the self. *Personality and Social Psychology Bulletin*, 19 (3), 305–311.

Klein, S. B., Sherman, J. W. and Loftus, J. (1996) The role of episodic and semantic memory in the development of trait self-knowledge. *Social Cognition*, 14 (4), 277–291.

Krause, J. B., Taylor, J. G., Schmidt, D., Hautzel, H., Mottaghy, F. M. and Muller-Gartner, H. W. (2000) Imaging and neural modeling in episodic and working memory processes. *Neural Networks*, 13 (8–9), 847–859.

Kreitler, H. and Kreitler, S. (1976) *Cognitive Orientation and Behavior*. New York: Springer.

Kugelmass, S., Lieblich, I. and Bergman, Z. (1967) The role of "lying" in psychophysiological detection. *Psychophysiology,* 3, 312–315.

Kuiper, N. A. (1981) Convergent evidence for the self as a prototype: The "inverted-U RT effect" for self and other judgments. *Personality and Social Psychology Bulletin*, 7, 438–443.

Lang, P. J., Bradley, M. M. and Cuthbert, B. N. (1997) Motivated attention: affect, activation, and action. In: P. J. Lang, R. F. Simons and M. T. Balaban (eds) *Attention and Orienting: Sensory and Motivational Processes*. Mahwah, NJ: Lawrence Erlbaum Associates.

Lang, P. J., Davis, M. and Öhman, A. (2000) Fear and anxiety: animal models and human cognitive psychophysiology. *Journal of Affective Disorders*, 61 (3), 137–159.

LeDoux, J. (1996) *The Emotional Brain*. New York: Simon and Schuster.

LePage, M., Ghaffar, O., Nyberg, L. and Tulving, E. (2000) Prefrontal cortex and episodic memory retrieval mode. *Proceedings of the National Academy of Sciences, U.S.A.*, 97 (1), 506–511.

Lykken, D. T. (1959) The GSR in the detection of guilt. *Journal of applied Psychology*, 45 (6), 385–388.

Lykken, D. T. (1974) Psychology and the lie detector industry. *American Psychologist*, October, 725–739.

Lykken, D. T. (1979) The detection of deception. *Psychological Bulletin*, 86, 47–53.

Lykken, D. T. (1981) *A Tremor in the Blood: Uses and Abuses of the Lie Detector*. New York: McGraw-Hill.

Lykken, D. T. (1998) *A Tremor in the Blood: Uses and Abuses of the Lie Detector*. New York: Plenum Press.

Lynn, R. (1966) *Attention, Arousal, and the Orientation Reaction*. Oxford: Pergamon.

Maguire, E. A. and Mummery, C. J. (1999) Differential modulation of a common memory retrieval network revealed by positron emission tomography. *Hippocampus*, 9 (1), 54–61.

Malle, F. B. and Horowitz, L. M. (1995) The puzzle of negative self-views: An explanation using the schema concept. *Journal of Personality and Social Psychology*, 68 (3), 470–484.

Maltzman, I. (1979) Orienting reflexes and significance: A reply to O'Gorman. *Psychophysiology*, 16, 274–282.

Maltzman, I. and Langdon, B. (1982) Novelty and significance as determiners of the GSR index of the orienting reflex. *Physiological Psychology*, 10, 229 234.

Maltzman, I. and Raskin, D. C. (1965) Effects of individual differences in the orienting response on conditioning and complex processes. *Journal of Experimental Research in Personality*, 1, 1–16.

Markus, H. (1977) Self-schemata and processing information about the self. *Journal of Personality and Social Psychology*, 35, 63–78.

Newman, L. S., Duff, K. J. and Baumeister, R. F. (1997) A new look at defensive projection: thought suppression, accessibility, and biased person perception. *Journal of Personality and Social Psychology*, 72 (5), 980–1001.

Nilsson, L. G., Nyberg, L., Klingberg, T., Aberg, C., Persson, J. and Roland, P. E. (2000) Activity in motor areas while remembering action events. *Neuroreport*, 11 (10), 2199–2201.

Nyberg, L. and Tulving, E. (1996) Classifying human long-term memory: Evidence from converging dissociations. *European Journal of Cognitive Psychology*, 8 (2), 163–183.

Nyberg, L., Mcintosh, A. R., Cabeza, R., Habib, R., Houle, S. and Tulving, E. (1996) General and specific brain regions involved in encoding and retrieval of events: What, where, and when. *Proceedings of the National Academy of Sciences, U.S.A.*, 93, 11280–11285.

Nyberg L., Habib R., McIntosh A. R. and Tulving E. (2000) Reactivation of encoding-related brain activity during memory retrieval. *Proceedings of the National Academy of Sciences, U.S.A.*, 97 (20), 11120–11124.

O'Gorman, J. G. (1979) The orienting reflex: novelty or significance detector? *Psychophysiology*, 16, 253–262.

Öhman, A. (1979) The orienting response, attention and learning: An information processing perspective. In: H. D. Kimmel, E. H. Van Olst and J. F. Orlebeke (eds) *The Orienting Reflex in Humans*, pp. 443–471. Hillsdale, NJ: Lawrence Erlbaum Associates.

Öhman, A. (1986) Face the beast and fear the face: animal and social fears as prototypes for evolutionary analyses of emotion. *Psychophysiology*, 23, 123–145.

Patrick, C. J. and Iacono, W. G. (1989) Psychopathy, threat, and polygraph test accuracy. *Journal of Applied Psychology*, 74, 347–355.

Paus, T. (2000) Functional anatomy of arousal and attention systems in the human brain. *Progress in Brain Research*, 126, 65–77.

Pavlov, I. P. (1927) *Conditional Reflex*. Oxford: Charmadon Press.

Phelps, E. A., O'Connor, K. J., Gatenby, J. C., Grillon, C., Gore, J. C. and Davis, M. (2001) Activation of the human amygdala to a cognitive representation of fear. *Nature Neuroscience*, 4 (4), 437–441.

Posner, M. I. and Dehaene, S. (1994) Attentional networks. *Neuroscience*, 17 (2), 75–79.

Raskin, D.C. (1973) Attention and arousal. In: W. F. Prokasy and D. C. Raskin (eds) *Electrodermal Activity in Psychological Research*. London: Academic Press.

Raskin, D. C. (1979) Orienting and defensive reflexes in the detection of deception. In: H. D. Kimmel, E. H. Van Olst and J. F. Orlebeke (eds) *The Orienting Response in Humans*. Hillsdale, NJ: Lawrence Erlbaum Associates.

Raskin, D.C. and Kircher, J.C. (1989) Comments on Furedy and Heslegrave: Misconceptions, misdescriptions, and misdirections. In: P. K. Ackles, J. R. Jennings and M. G. H. Coles (Eds) *Advances in Psychophysiology*, vol. 4. Greenwich, CT: JAI Press.

Raskin, D. C., Kircher, J. C., Honts, C. R. and Horowitz, S. W. (1988) A study of the validity of polygraph examinations in criminal investigation (Grant No. 85-IJ-CX-0040). Salt Lake City: University of Utah, Department of Psychology.

Raskin, D. C. and Podlesny, J. A. (1979) Truth and deception: A reply to Lykken. *Psychological Bulletin*, 86, 54–59.

Reid, J. E. and Inbau, F. E. (1977) *Truth and Deception – The Polygraph Technique*, 3rd edn. Baltimore: The Williams and Wilkins Co.

Rogers, T. B., Kuiper, N. A. and Kirker, W. S. (1977) Self-reference and the encoding of personal information. *Journal of Personality and Social Psychology*, 35, 677–688.

Rogers, T. B., Rogers, P. J. and Kuiper, N. A. (1979) Evidence for the self as a cognitive prototype: The "false alarms effect". *Personality and Social Psychology Bulletin*, 5, 53–56.

Rolls, E. T. (2000) Memory systems in the brain. *Annual Review of Psychology*, 51, 599–630.

Rosenberg, M. J. (1965) When dissonance fails: on eliminating evaluation apprehension from attitude measurement. *Journal of Personality and Social Psychology*, 1, 28–42.

Rosenberg, M. J. (1980) Experimenter expectancy, evaluation apprehension, and the diffusion of methodological angst. *The Behavioral and Brain Sciences*, 3, 472–474.

Ross, L. and Nisbett, R. E. (1991) *The Person and the Situation: Perspectives of Social Psychology.* New York: McGraw-Hill.

Safer, M. A., Christianson, S.-A., Autry, M. W. and Osterlund, K. (1998) Tunnel memory for traumatic events. *Applied Cognitive Psychology*, 12, 99–117.

Saxe, L. (1983) *Scientific Validity of Polygraph Testing: A Research Review and Evaluation.* A technical memorandum, Washington DC.: U.S. Congress, Office of Technology Assessment, OTA-TM-H 15, November 1983.

Schacter, D. L. and Tulving, E. (1994) What are the memory systems of 1994? In: D. Schacter and E. Tulving (eds) *Memory Systems*, 1–38. Cambridge, MA: MIT Press.

Schacter, D. L., Reiman, E., Curran, T., Yun, L. S., Bandy, D., McDermott, K. B. and Roediger, H. L. (1996) Neuroanatomical correlates of veridical and illusory recognition memory: evidence from positron emission tomography. *Neuron*, 17, 267–274.

Scheff, T. and Retzinger, S. (2000) Shame as the master emotion of everyday life. *Journal of Mundane Behavior*, 1 (3), 303–324.

Singer, J. A. and Moffitt, K. H. (1992) An experimental investigation of specificity and generality in memory narratives. *Imagination, Cognition and Personality*, 11 (3), 233–257.

Simpson, J. R., Snyder, A. Z., Gusnard, D. A. and Raichle, M. E. (2001) Emotion-induced changes in human medial prefrontal cortex: I. During cognitive task performance. *Proceedings of the National Academy of Sciences, U.S.A.*, 98 (2), 683–687.

Sokolov, E. N. (1963) *Perception and the Conditioned Reflex.* New York: McMillan.

Sokolov, E. N. (1966) Orienting reflex as information regulator. In: E. Rosch and B. Lloyds (eds) *Cognition and Categorization*, pp. 79–98. Hillsdale, NJ: Lawrence Erlbaum Associates.

Stern, J. A. (1972) Physiological response measures during classical conditioning. In: N. S. Greenfield and R. A. Sternbach (eds) *Handbook of Psychophysiology*. New York: Holt, Rinehart and Winston.

Strauman, T .J. (1989) Self-discrepancies in clinical depression and social phobia: cognitive structures that underlie emotional disorders? *Journal of Abnormal Psychology*, 98 (1),14–22

Strauman, T. J. (1992) Self-guides, autobiographical memory, and anxiety and dysphoria: toward a cognitive model of vulnerability to emotional distress. *Journal of Abnormal Psychology*, 101 (1), 87–95.

Strauman, T. J. and Higgins, E. T. (1987) Automatic activation of self-discrepancies and emotional syndromes: when cognitive structures influence affect. *Journal of Personality and Social Psychology*, 53 (6), 1004–1014.

Symons, C. S. and Johnson, B. T. (1997) The self-reference effect in memory: A meta-analysis. *Psychology Bulletin*, 212 (3), 371–394.

Tversky, A. (1977) Features of similarity. *Psychological Review*, 44 (4), 327–352.

Tversky, A. and Hutchinson, J. W. (1986) Nearest neighbor analysis of psychological spaces. *Psychological Review*, 93, 3–22.

Watt, D. F. (1999) At the intersection of emotion and consciousness: affective neuroscience and extended reticular thalamic activating system (ERTAS) theories of consciousness. In: S. Hameroff, A. W. Kaszniak and D. J. Chalmers (eds) *Toward a Science of Consciousness III: The Third Tucson Discussions and Debates*. Complex Adaptive Systems Series: Cambridge, MA: MIT Press.

Wheeler, M. A., Stuss, D. T. and Tulving, E. (1997) Toward a theory of episodic memory: the frontal lobes and autonoetic consciousness. *Psychology Bulletin*, 121 (3), 331–354.

Williams, L. M., Brammer, M. J., Skerrett, D., Lagopolous, J., Rennie, C., Kozek, K., Olivieri, G., Peduto, T. and Gordon, E. (2000) The neural correlates of orienting: an integration of fMRI and skin conductance orienting. *Neuroreport*, 11 (13), 3011–3015.

Yeh, W. and Barsalou, L. W. (2001) The situated nature of concepts (submitted for publication).

CHAPTER 6

THE PRE-TEST INTERVIEW: A PRELIMINARY FRAMEWORK

Dennis C. Mitchell

This chapter considers the pre-test interview, that portion of the polygraph examination that involves all communications between the examiner and examinee prior to the formal testing phase of the examination. The pre-test interview is often regarded as an integral aspect of polygraph examinations (e.g., Mullenix and Reid, 1980), yet it has received very little empirical attention. One possible reason for the paucity of research on the pre-test interview is the absence of a suitable framework for identifying and investigating relevant pre-test variables. The main goal of the present chapter is to provide a preliminary framework for organizing pre-test research.

The chapter will focus on the pre-test interview in examinations involving the control question technique (CQT). There are two major reasons for this. First, the CQT is the technique that is most commonly employed in criminal investigations, where there is a specific incident under investigation. Second, the validity of the CQT relies upon a powerful yet socially intricate aspect of the pre-test interview, namely the elicitation of suitable denials of comparison transgressions. By itself, this pivotal aspect of the CQT pre-test interview warrants a greater understanding of relevant psychological principles.

SOME CONCEPTIONS OF THE CQT PRE-TEST INTERVIEW

The pre-test interview encompasses those activities that occur after the examiner first enters the examination room and before the examiner begins the testing phase of the examination. The interview varies in length from about 30 min to more than an hour. During the pre-test interview, the examiner introduces him/herself to the examinee, takes care of various administrative and legal matters (e.g., advising about rights, obtaining consent, . . . etc.), estimates whether the examinee is psychologically and otherwise fit to take the polygraph test, reviews and clarifies the case facts with the examinee, develops questions about comparison transgressions ("comparison questions"), describes the rationale behind the polygraph examination and the instruments that record physiological responses, and reviews all questions that will be asked during the testing phase (Daily, 1974; Mullenix and Reid, 1980; Wygant, 1980). One may also consider the "acquaintance test" ("stimulation test" or polygraph demonstration) as part of the pre-test interview, but only if it precedes all test questions during the testing phase.

Polygraph professionals have identified a few major psychological objectives of the CQT pre-test interview (e.g., Barland and Raskin, 1973; Daily, 1974; Iacono and Patrick, 1987; Mullenix and Reid, 1980; Office of Technology Assessment (OTA), 1983; Wygant, 1980). By far the most cited pre-test objective is to convince the examinee that the polygraph is highly effective, if not infallible, at detecting deception. To accomplish this objective, the examiner provides a personalized and (hopefully) convincing description of the rationale and procedures of the exam, as well as provides a demonstration of lie detection (acquaintance test). A second frequently cited objective of the pre-test interview is to develop comparison questions that would be particularly disconcerting to otherwise innocent examinees. To accomplish this objective, the examiner must choose the comparison questions very carefully, convince the examinee that honesty regarding the comparison questions is very important, yet prevent the examinee from admitting the comparison transgressions. A third frequently cited objective of the pre-test interview is to provoke and observe various behaviors indicative of the examinee's deception or honesty regarding the crime in question (see Mullenix and Reid, 1980; Reid and Inbau, 1977). To accomplish this objective, the examiner might observe how the examinee responds to various inquiries, such as whether the examinee committed the crime, whether the examinee believes that he/she will pass the exam, how the examinee feels about the hypothetical offender or the polygraph test itself, whether the examinee can identify other suspects, whether the examinee had contemplated the crime (regardless of committing it), and whether the examinee told others that he/she was taking a polygraph examination (Mullenix and Reid, 1980).

The third pre-test objective falls within the purview of the so-called "clinical approach" to lie detection, in which the examiner judges deception according to both behavioral and psychophysiological observations. Unfortunately, but understandably, the clinical approach has been regarded as a potential compromise of methods aimed at the psychophysiological detection of deception (Lykken, 1981). While this may be true, I believe that the clinical approach should not be disregarded by psychophysiologists. It is entirely possible that behavior-provoking questions and diagnostic observations during the pre-test interview and/or testing phase of the examination have a systematic influence on psychophysiological outcomes. I will return to this issue later in this chapter.

The first two objectives described above are actually in the service of one overarching goal of the pre-test interview – to maximize the likelihood that examinees experience the expected **focus of concern** (see also "anticlimax dampening", Baxter, 1974; or "psychological set", Barland and Raskin, 1973). Theoretically, in order for the CQT examination to be effective, examinees must develop the expected focus of concern for the comparison questions vs. questions about the crime under investigation ("relevant questions"). Guilty examinees must maintain greater concern for the relevant questions than the comparison questions. In contrast, innocent examinees must become more concerned with the comparison questions than the relevant questions (for discussions, see Barland and Raskin, 1973; Reid and Inbau, 1977). If these patterns of concern were to occur naturally and consistently in both guilty and innocent subjects, without regard to the efforts of the examiner, then the pre-test interview might matter very little. It is most likely, however, that the pattern of concern is not natural, at least with regard to the innocent examinees (for discussions, see Furedy, 1993; Lykken, 1981). On the contrary, the desired focus of concern must be developed in these examinees through a careful and complex intervention – a kind of "behavioral engineering" (Lykken, 1981:116) that involves techniques of persuasion and compliance, as well as other mechanisms of cognitive and emotional influence. This, I would contend, is the real work and the real goal of the pre-test interview.

Is there any evidence that examiners typically accomplish this overarching goal? The research bearing on this question is a bit sparse. First, there is some evidence that examinees experience the expected focus of concern in polygraph examinations (Bradley and Janisse, 1981; Horowitz *et al.*, 1997; Palmatier, 1991). Unfortunately, these studies did not attempt to determine the extent to which focus of concern was "natural" vs. the product of various interventions by the examiner. Second, there is some evidence that focus of concern is related to physiological responding during the testing phase of the examination (Bradley and Janisse, 1981; Kircher and Raskin, 1986); however, these findings were either weak (Bradley and Janisse, 1981) or inconsistent for guilty and innocent subjects (Kircher and Raskin, 1986). Thus, in general, there is currently no compelling evidence that pre-test procedures have the predicted influence on the examinee's focus of concern or that such an influence is ultimately manifested as characteristic physiological responding on the polygraph examination. The lack of evidence should not imply that the pre-test interview is ineffective, but that it has not been researched adequately.

PRELIMINARY FRAMEWORK FOR RESEARCH ON THE CQT PRE-TEST INTERVIEW

The present framework assumes that the major goal of the pre-test interview is to maximize the likelihood that examinees experience the expected focus of concern during the testing phase of the examination. Accordingly, research on the pre-test interview should focus on pre-test variables that could have a non-trivial influence on examinees' focus of concern. The present chapter organizes a preliminary set of pre-test variables according to their mechanism of influence on examinees – through the examinee's attitudes, behavior, thoughts, or feelings. I summarize some relevant psychological research and concepts related to these variables, and I propose some potential applications to pre-test research.

MANAGING EXAMINEE ATTITUDES

In casual conversation, some polygraph professionals describe the pre-test interview as an elaborate sales pitch to the examinee. In this respect, the examiner attempts to persuade the examinee to develop particular attitudes in the polygraph examination. This persuasion may be directed toward two main objectives. First, as previously mentioned, the examiner must persuade the examinee that the polygraph test is highly, if not perfectly, effective in detecting deception. Second, the examiner must persuade the examinee that the comparison questions are, for the sake of the polygraph test, just as important as the relevant questions.

Persuasion

Theoretically, the likelihood of fulfilling the pre-test persuasion objectives could be maximized by managing relevant persuasion variables. In the present section, I will review several well-documented persuasion variables that could have a bearing on pre-test persuasion objectives. Before I turn to the specifics, however, the reader should know several things about how persuasion is conceptualized in social psychology.

First, in social psychological research, persuasion is studied under the rubric of attitude change. An **attitude** is a person's general evaluation of a person (e.g., the examiner), object (e.g., the polygraph), or issue (e.g., lying). Generally speaking, a change in attitude means that the person's evaluation has become more positive ("The polygraph will vindicate me"), more negative ("The polygraph will expose me"), or more neutral ("I no longer fear the polygraph"). Attitudes can vary in other ways, including clarity ("I'm not sure whether lying is always bad") and emotional and rational content ("I feel more calm about the polygraph now, and I know some facts about it"); however, these aspects are much less frequently examined in research (see McGuire, 1985).

Second, psychologists often categorize persuasion variables according to characteristics of the **message**, or persuasive communication; **source**, or agent of persuasion; and **recipient**, or target of persuasion (Petty and Wegener, 1998).

In the context of the pre-test interview, the source is generally the examiner, the recipient is the examinee, and the message may be a verbal statement (e.g., the description of the "fight–flight–freeze" response), a demonstration (e.g., the acquaintance test), or any other transmission of information.

Third, the dominant theoretical model in persuasion research is the 'elaboration likelihood model' (Petty and Cacioppo, 1986; for a similar model, see Chaiken, 1987). This model holds that the way in which a message influences a recipient depends upon the recipient's motivation and ability to evaluate the message in a careful way. Generally speaking, if the recipient is both strongly motivated and able to evaluate the message carefully ("high elaboration likelihood"), the message will be more persuasive if it has more compelling facts associated with it. On the other hand, if the recipient is less strongly motivated or unable to evaluate the message carefully ("low elaboration likelihood"), the message may be more persuasive if superficial aspects of the message (e.g., the length of the message) or other peripheral factors (e.g., the attractiveness of the source) are influential. Elaboration likelihood is important to consider because it identifies *when* certain persuasion variables may have their predicted effects on persuasion.

Source characteristics

Much of the research on persuasion source has centered on three source characteristics: **credibility**, which combines competence and trustworthiness; **likeableness**, which combines physical attraction, similarity to the recipient, and other likeable characteristics; and **power**, which combines the ability to monitor the recipient's attitudes with the ability to reward or punish the recipient (Kelman, 1958; see also Petty and Wegener, 1998). For each of these characteristics, there is some qualified support for influence on persuasion. For example, messages tend to be more persuasive when the recipient perceives the source of the message as trustworthy (e.g., Eagly *et al.*, 1978; Fine, 1957; McGinnies and Ward, 1980) or as an expert in the topic of the message (e.g., Kelman and Hovland, 1953; McGinnies and Ward, 1980); however, these effects may be limited to low elaboration likelihood, that is, when the recipient cannot or does not process the message carefully (Kiesler and Mathog, 1968; Petty *et al.*, 1981; Priester and Petty, 1995; Rhine and Severance, 1970; Wood and Kallgren, 1988). Likewise, some studies have shown that sources are more persuasive when they are perceived as more attractive (e.g., Horai *et al.*, 1974; Snyder and Rothbart, 1971); however, the influence of attractiveness on persuasion may be very weak (for reviews, see Chaiken, 1979; Simons et al., 1970) and may depend upon low elaboration likelihood (e.g., Chaiken, 1980; Petty *et al.*, 1983). Finally, some studies have shown that powerful sources are more "persuasive" than weak sources (e.g., Festinger and Thibaut, 1951; Kelman, 1958); however, it is unclear whether persuasion in the context of a powerful other represents attitude change or merely behavioral compliance (see Kelman, 1958).

In the context of a polygraph examination, it is unclear whether examiner credibility, attractiveness, or power would influence the examinee's perception of either the effectiveness of the polygraph or the importance of the comparison questions. One might speculate that examiners who appear to be well-practiced with and knowledgeable about their instrumentation and who otherwise exhibit various signs of expertise may be more successful with pre-test persuasion. Likewise, Reid and Inbau (1977:14, note 18) have suggested that examiners should wear a suit and otherwise "look the part of a respected professional or business person." Perhaps by bolstering credibility and attractiveness, such attire and a well-groomed appearance may increase the examiner's social influence (see Cialdini and Trost, 1998). Unfortunately, we don't know whether the appearance and general behavior of the examiner really matters. Also, it is likely that such influences depend upon low elaboration likelihood in the pre-test interview – that is, the examinee's inability or unwillingness to understand fully the polygraph procedures and rationale, as they are explained by the examiner. Whether in the pre-test interview elaboration likelihood is usually low, usually high, or quite variable, and whether it depends upon the true innocence/guilt of the examinee is all unknown.

Recipient characteristics

On the other side of a persuasive communication is the recipient of the message. As with source characteristics, various recipient characteristics have been researched in numerous studies on persuasion. Two general clusters of recipient characteristics are worth noting here. The first personality cluster includes two characteristics that increase elaboration likelihood – namely, **general intelligence**, or a person's ability to process information carefully, and **need for cognition**, or a person's preference for processing information carefully (Cacioppo and Petty, 1982). Consistent with the elaboration likelihood model, recipients who are higher in general intelligence (Rhodes and Wood, 1992) or higher in need for cognition (Cacioppo *et al.*, 1983) are more resistant to persuasion, at least when messages are weak in quality (Cacioppo *et al.*, 1983; McGuire, 1968). The second personality cluster concerns characteristics associated with self-evaluation – namely, **self-esteem**, or the extent to which a person regards him/herself positively, and **self-monitoring**, or the extent to which a person adjusts his/her apparent personality to fit different social contexts (Snyder, 1974). While the research is far from conclusive, it appears that when the message is factually or logically weak, recipients with lower self-esteem are more vulnerable to persuasion (Rhodes and Wood, 1992; Skolnick and Heslin, 1971). Similarly, when the message appeals to one's social image, recipients who are high in self-monitoring may be more vulnerable to persuasion (Debono, 1987; Lavine and Snyder, 1996).

As with source (examiner) characteristics, it is unclear whether any of the recipient (examinee) characteristics reviewed above would have a significant influence on persuasion in polygraph examinations. Perhaps, examinees who are more intellectual and have higher self-esteem may require a more thorough description of the comparison questions and a more careful demonstration of polygraph methods, whereas persons who are less intellectual or have lower self-esteem may benefit from less intellectualized approaches. To complicate matters, it is entirely possible that the typical guilty examinee differs from the typical innocent examinee with respect to various persuasion-relevant characteristics (e.g., self-esteem); accordingly, guilty and innocent examinees might come to accept (or reject) the effectiveness of the polygraph and the importance of the comparison questions in different ways. Again, however, this is a question for future research.

Message characteristics

Message characteristics can be organized into substantive aspects, which concern the logical or factual quality of the message, and superficial aspects, which concern things such as how quickly the message is presented. Ironically, persuasion researchers have focused upon superficial aspects of messages, almost to the exclusion of substantive aspects (see Petty and Wegener, 1998). With regard to superficial aspects of messages, several researchers have shown that persuasion increases with the **length** (e.g., Wood *et al.*, 1985), **quantity** (e.g., Petty and Cacioppo, 1984), and **repetition** of arguments (Krugman, 1972) – at least, up to a certain point (Cacioppo and Petty, 1979). Similarly, persuasion increases when messages are delivered at a higher **verbalization speed** (Apple *et al.*, 1979; Miller *et al.*, 1976) or with a more **powerful speaking style** (Erikson *et al.*, 1978), which includes fewer speech disfluencies (e.g., "uh") and disqualifiers (e.g., "I think"). Importantly, according to the elaboration likelihood model, such superficial aspects of messages would only exert an influence on persuasion when recipients are either unwilling or unable to process the message carefully (Petty and Wegener, 1998), thereby diminishing the impact of substantive aspects of the message.

During the pre-test interview, the examiner delivers messages concerning the effectiveness of the polygraph examination and the importance of the comparison questions. At present, it is unclear whether the typical examinee perceives these persuasion messages as factually/logically solid or weak. Also, we don't know the extent to which various superficial aspects of the messages (e.g., speed of delivery, length of message, . . . etc.) influence persuasion during the pre-test interview. Without understanding the influence of these variables, I am hesitant to suggest that examiners develop an approach that is persuasion-intensive, for an overly polished presentation may set examinees on the defensive. In lieu of adequate research on the topic, I would suggest that examiners exercise some degree of moderation with respect to the "sales pitch."

Suggestions for research on pre-test persuasion

At this point, the reader should understand that there is a wealth of existing research in social psychology on various persuasion variables. A researcher could spend his/her entire career exploring pre-test persuasion. To motivate such an undertaking, a sample of some preliminary research topics on pre-test persuasion is given below.

A program of research on pre-test persuasion should begin by addressing a few fundamental questions about persuasion in the pre-test interview – namely, when faced with messages of polygraph effectiveness and comparison question importance, (1) how carefully does the typical examinee understand these messages (i.e., is elaboration likelihood high or low), (2) how factually/logically strong are these messages in the mind of the typical examinee, and (3) to what extent does the typical innocent subject differ from the typical guilty subject in terms of understanding and evaluating the messages? The answer to these questions may determine how the two persuasion objectives are fulfilled in the pre-test interview. For example, if elaboration likelihood is typically high for both innocent and guilty subjects, then research should focus upon maximizing the perceived quality of messages of polygraph effectiveness and comparison question importance. On the other hand, if elaboration likelihood is typically low for both innocent and guilty subjects, then research might be directed toward maximizing the influence of various peripheral factors (e.g., message speed, examiner credibility, . . . etc.) on pre-test persuasion. Finally, if elaboration likelihood or perceived message quality differs for the typical innocent vs. typical guilty subject (with perhaps the guilty subject scoring lower on both), then research might be directed toward maximizing perceived message quality *and* the influence of peripheral factors.

Once the above questions have been addressed, it may be worthwhile to examine the influence of perceived examiner credibility, likeableness, and power on the examiner's ability to carry out the two persuasion objectives. Likewise, it may be worthwhile to examine the relationship between pre-test persuasion and examinee intelligence, need for cognition, self-monitoring, and self-esteem. Finally, researchers might investigate the influence of various superficial aspects of messages (e.g., length and speed) on persuasion in the pre-test interview. Importantly, for each of these suggested studies, researchers should determine the extent to which the persuasion variable under investigation has a different influence on guilty vs. innocent examinees.

Once the basic questions above have been addressed, researchers will have a better foundation for exploring more advanced topics in pre-test persuasion. Consider the acquaintance test, variously known as the "card test," "numbers test," "stimulation test," or "accuracy demonstration." In a typical acquaintance test, the examinee chooses a number (e.g., 4), which the examiner attempts to identify amid a series of numbers (e.g., 1–7) with an encapsulated polygraph test. The polygraph records responses while the examinee denies each of the numbers in the series, including the chosen number, for which a denial is considered a lie. The examiner then shows or explains that the polygraph detected the lie. Importantly, there is some research that supports the idea that the acquaintance test improves psychophysiological detection of deception (e.g., Bradley and Janisse, 1981); however, there is no research that has examined how the acquaintance test influences the examinee's perception of polygraph effectiveness, or whether this perception differs for the typical innocent vs. typical guilty examinee. Furthermore, the research has not examined substantive departures from the pick-a-number, game-like approach to the acquaintance test. From the examinee's perspective, there may be more compelling demonstrations of polygraph effectiveness.[1]

MANAGING EXAMINEE BEHAVIOR

During the pre-test interview, the examiner exercises some degree of control over the examinee's behavior. One can identify two major objectives of such behavioral control. First, the examiner must induce the examinee to deny a set of comparison transgressions that are likely to elicit considerable concern in the examinee. Theoretically, if the examinee admits to too many comparison transgressions, and the comparison questions have to be qualified around significant admissions, then the examinee may not feel enough concern for the comparison questions during the testing phase of the examination. Second, the examiner should induce the examinee to cooperate with the testing procedures and forgo attempts at countermeasures. If the examiner is successful in the latter regard, then the polygraph examination may be influenced by fewer artifacts. Together, the two major objectives of behavioral influence fall within the purview of a second research area within social psychology, i.e., compliance.

Compliance

Compliance refers to the act of yielding to another's wishes or demands. Compliance is different from persuasion in that compliance occasions changes in observable behavior, whereas persuasion operates on a person's attitudes or evaluations. Often, the goal of compliance is commitment to a solicitation or request, such as a request by one's boss to work late. In contrast, the goal of

[1] Consider just one possible alternative to the conventional acquaintance test. Polygraph professionals who videotape their examinations could secure permission from several confirmed guilty examinees and several confirmed innocent examinees to use their videos as demonstration material. Imagine that the videos show the examinee's face, above which is the caption "ACCUSED OF –" and below which is a brightly colored electrodermal amplitude (EDA) channel. For simplicity, the video clip could show the examinee's denial of an illustrative relevant question, below which the projected channel displays the difference in baseline-adjusted EDA for the relevant question vs. comparison question. Immediately following each clip, another caption would appear – either "GUILTY" or "INNOCENT." This admittedly sensational demonstration might be particularly compelling in that it would show (1) how easily the polygraph identifies guilty *and* innocent examinees, (2) the power of the polygraph in real-life criminal situations, (3) peers with whom the examinee may identify, and (4) multiple instances of correct identification. Also, such a video would provide more uniformity to the administration and results of the acquaintance test. To be most effective, the developers of the video should review the literature on observational learning (e.g., Bandura, 1986) and consult experts on persuasive media.

persuasion is often a change in values, such as a more favorable attitude toward working late. While persuasion and compliance are conceptually distinguishable, much of the research that applies to one concept also applies to the other. To avoid redundancy, the present section focuses upon social psychological influences that are directed more toward behavior than attitudes. These influences can be organized into more general influences and more specific tactics.

General influences

There are at least five general influences on compliance that are relevant for the topic of pre-test interviews. First, there are the **personal characteristics** of the agent of compliance (in our case, the examiner) and the target of compliance (in our case, the examinee). Some research suggests that the same personal characteristics that make a person more persuasive (e.g., attractiveness) can make that person a more powerful agent of compliance (for a review, see Cialdini and Trost, 1998). Furthermore, those characteristics that make a person more vulnerable to persuasion (e.g., lower intelligence) may increase the likelihood that the person complies with other persons' requests. Because I have reviewed such characteristics in the section on persuasion, I will curtail their consideration here.

Second, **social norms** can exert powerful or subtle influences on compliance. Social norms are unstated rules, standards, and expectations about acceptable or desirable behavior in certain social situations (Cialdini and Trost, 1998). For example, there is a norm of persistent conversation in the context of dinner with a friend, business associate, or neighbor. Likewise, there are norms for all kinds of social situations, including interactions with friends, colleagues, teachers, coaches, supervisors, law enforcement officers, counselors, clergy members, . . . etc. Unfortunately, it is not entirely clear how social norms influence behavior in polygraph examinations. On the one hand, many examinees have never experienced a polygraph examination, and thus they may have fuzzy expectations regarding appropriate behavior in a polygraph examination. On the other hand, many examinees may be able to apply social norms for other situations to the polygraph examination. For example, perhaps the examinee has a fairly well-developed social norm for law enforcement interrogations, and this norm is activated when the examinee enters the polygraph examination room. In the course of the pre-test interview, when it is clear that the tenor of the interview is less interrogatory and more psychological and physiological, the examinee may access a social norm for counseling, medical diagnosis, or some other social situation. In turn, the activation of such norms in the mind may lead the examinee to comply more with the examiner's expectations.

Third, compliance in social situations is no doubt influenced by **impression**

management. Also called self-presentation (Baumeister, 1982), impression management (Schlenker, 1980) refers to a person's attempt to present oneself to others in a particular way, usually to get something (e.g., a job, sex, political endorsement) from them (Baumeister, 1998). There are many forms of impression management (see Jones and Pittman, 1982), which include "selling" others one's moral goodness or ideology (exemplification), one's neediness and deservingness (supplication), and one's power to harm others (intimidation). In terms of the polygraph examination, impression management may have a profound influence on the compliance of the examinee. If the examinee perceives that the polygraph examiner has some degree of control over the outcome of the examination, then the examinee has a motive to make a favorable impression on the examiner. Such a favorable impression might come in the form of near-perfect compliance with all explicit directions provided by the examiner (e.g., remain still during the testing phase), as well implicit suggestions (e.g., do not attempt countermeasures, deny significant transgressions).

Fourth, compliance may result from **operant conditioning**. According to the principles of operant conditioning (Skinner, 1938, 1953), a particular behavior (e.g., lying) is more likely to be repeated when it has been favorably productive in the past (e.g., avoiding punishment) and less likely to be repeated when it has been ineffective (e.g., not avoiding punishment) or counterproductive (e.g., detection of the lie and more punishment). For example, during the course of the pre-test interview, if the examiner welcomes or praises the examinee's morally good disclosures (e.g., he/she had a stable job) and discounts or discourages the examinee's morally bad disclosures (e.g., he/she was often late to work), such reinforcement might encourage the examinee to deny comparison transgressions later in the interview. Similarly, if prior to the testing phase of the examination, the examinee somehow experienced unproductive or counterproductive (i.e., detected) attempts at countermeasures or movement artifacts,[2] then this learning experience might discourage him/her from such activities during the testing phase.

Finally, compliance may be inspired by **fear or uncertainty**. Clearly, if noncompliance with a request or demand (e.g., agreeing to work through lunch) presents a significant risk (e.g., perhaps losing a promotion), then the typical person will be more inclined to comply. There is considerable research that demonstrates the effectiveness of general threats or jeopardized opportunities on both persuasion (Boster and Mongeau, 1984) and compliance (Cialdini and Trost, 1998). In the context of the pre-test interview, fear may have a more powerful influence on compliance if the feared consequence is made more salient. For example, the examinee may be less likely to admit significant comparison transgressions if the examiner implies that such admissions would make

[2] I think that it is worthwhile to consider a video demonstration of detected artifacts. To be most effective, the video would display several uncontrived examples of examiners detecting movement artifacts in typical examinees, many of whom acknowledge the artifacts and a few of whom deny them, but all of whom are identified as guilty. Again, the success of the video might depend upon a number of subtle factors; therefore, I would recommend that it was developed in consultation with experts on persuasive media.

the examinee appear guilty. Similarly, the examinee may be less likely to produce countermeasures or other artifacts if he/she is lead to believe that such activities are detectable and indicative of guilt. Note that this kind of threat differs from operant conditioning (see above) in that the person must imagine negative consequences, rather than experience them.

Specific tactics

Salespersons, lobbyists, fund-raisers, con artists, and other "commercial compliance professionals" (Cialdini and Trost, 1998) have developed various tactics for producing compliance in potential customers or targets. Social psychologists have observed, cataloged, and researched a number of these professional compliance tactics. A comprehensive review of popular compliance tactics is beyond the scope of this chapter (see Cialdini, 1993; Cialdini and Trost, 1998). Instead, the present section will describe a few compliance strategies that may be applicable to the objective of obtaining denials of comparison transgressions.

There are a few compliance tactics that involve multiple requests of the target person. In the "foot-in-door" strategy (Freedman and Frasier, 1966), a salesperson persuades a consumer to commit to a small favor (e.g., simply listening to the description of a few products), after which the salesperson asks for a more substantial, but related favor (e.g., a 30-day product trial, with a money-back guarantee). By capitalizing upon the target's initial commitment, the foot-in-door strategy reliably increases the likelihood of compliance with subsequent requests (for a meta-analytic review, see Beaman *et al.*, 1983). In the "low-ball" procedure (Cialdini *et al.*, 1978), a requester obtains a commitment from a person (e.g., willingness to buy a particular automobile) before clarifying all of the costs of such a commitment (e.g., the fact that floor mats and other seemingly standard things are "extras"). By capitalizing upon the person's commitment to the purchase (Cialdini and Trost, 1998) and/or salesperson (see Burger and Petty, 1981), the low-ball procedure produces compliance in a number of circumstances (Brownstein and Katzev, 1985; Joule, 1987). Finally, in the "door-in-the-face" technique (Cialdini *et al.*, 1975), a salesperson asks the target to commit to an unreasonable request (e.g., one hour a week for the next year). When the request is denied, the requester counters with a more reasonable request (e.g., two hours of one's time this week). By capitalizing upon the norm of reciprocal concessions (see Cialdini *et al.*, 1975), or "meeting a person half-way", the door-in-the-face technique significantly increases the likelihood that a person will comply with the more reasonable request (for a review, see Cialdini and Trost, 1998).

Each of the above multiple-request techniques can be adapted for use by the polygraph examiner. In the context of the pre-test interview, the examiner "requests" that the examinee deny significant comparison transgressions (e.g., that the examinee has never lied about anything important). To increase compliance with this main request, the examiner may make a strategic initial request of the examinee. Following the foot-in-door strategy, the examiner might increase compliance by first securing an easier denial (e.g., that the examinee is the kind of person who never tells the truth). Following the low-ball procedure, the examiner might increase compliance by presenting the second denial as a mere rewording of an easier denial (e.g., that the examinee lies about important things), to which the person has already committed. Following the door-in-the-face technique, the examiner might increase compliance with the second denial by first asking the examinee to make an outrageous denial (e.g., that the examinee has never lied about anything in his/her life) and when the examinee hedges on this denial, asking him/her to commit to the more reasonable target denial.

There are a couple of compliance strategies that involve indirect guidance toward the desired behavior. Perhaps the most popular of these strategies is the "leading question" technique, in which an interviewer asks a question in such a way that the desired answer is indicated (e.g., "You were at the scene of the crime, weren't you?") or any appropriate answer supports a significant assumption in the question (e.g., "How many times have you stolen office supplies from your employer?"). Such leading questions have been shown to be quite effective in influencing responses (e.g., Gudjonsson, 1984; Loftus, 1980), as well as memory for events (e.g., Loftus and Palmer, 1974). Also, consider the compliant models strategy, in which a requester provides evidence that similar people have complied with the request in the past (bartenders "salt" their tip jars, door-to-door salespersons show a list of neighbors who have purchased the product, . . . etc.). Because people often look to similar others for appropriate behavior (Festinger, 1954), the compliant models strategy generally encourages compliance (for a discussion, see Cialdini and Trost, 1998).

The two compliance strategies described above can be applied to compliance in the pre-test interview. For example, the examiner can encourage the denial of comparison transgressions by asking leading questions such as "You've never lied about anything important, have you?" or "In terms of morality, would you say you score 9 out of 10 or 10 out of 10? And this means that you are not the kind of person who has ever stolen anything, right?" Clearly, such leading questions strongly favor the denial of transgressions. Similarly, the examiner can encourage the denial of comparison transgressions by showing the examinee how similar examinees have denied these comparison transgressions during their examinations. The examinee could be shown a series of video clips in which various examinees denied the same comparison transgressions, or he/she could be shown a list of "examinees" who made the same denials, or perhaps the examiner could casually mention or imply that most examinees who are similar to the current examinee deny the transgressions.

One final compliance strategy is worthy of mention here. Often, sales persons are taught to mirror and match the target person in terms of his/her underlying mood (e.g., excited or depressed), body orientation (e.g., stiff or relaxed, upright or slumped, cross-armed or open-armed, . . . etc.), and verbal style (e.g., formal or colloquial, for a discussion, see Cialdini and Trost, 1998). Mirroring and matching is effective in increasing compliance because it makes the salesperson appear similar to the target person, and similar persons are generally better liked, respected, and trusted. Mirroring and matching in the pre-test interview may have similar consequences. If the examinee perceives the examiner as a similar person, the examinee may like and trust the examiner and subsequently comply with the examiner's implicit requests to deny the comparison transgressions and avoid countermeasures and artifacts. Indeed, mirroring and matching may represent one aspect of the kind of examiner–examinee rapport that many examiners feel is integral to the success of the pre-test interview (e.g., Daily, 1974; Wygant, 1980).

Suggestions for research on pre-test compliance

I have provided a list of possible general influences on pre-test compliance – persuasion-relevant examiner and examinee characteristics, social norms that prescribe acceptable behavior, impression management concerns, operant conditioning of behavior, and fear/uncertainty associated with non-compliance. Each of these general influences may have an impact on the two pre-test compliance objectives – denying comparison transgressions and avoiding countermeasures/artifacts. Furthermore, as with pre-test persuasion, it is possible that the influence of these pre-test compliance factors depends upon the examinee's true guilt/innocence. In the absence of any relevant supporting research, however, one can only speculate about the role of these general factors in pre-test compliance.

As with the research on persuasion, the research on compliance is replete with potential applications to the pre-test interview. Indeed, many polygraph examiners may employ routinely the kind of compliance techniques that I have described above. Whether and under what circumstances these compliance techniques work is presently unclear. In the present section, I will outline some possibilities for pre-test compliance research.

I have argued that there are two compliance objectives in the pre-test interview – namely, inducing the examinee to deny significant comparison transgressions and to avoid countermeasures and other artifactual influences on the polygraph examination. I have presented a series of general factors (e.g., social norms) that may have a bearing on these compliance objectives, as well as a set of specific strategies (e.g., leading questions) that may increase the likelihood that the examinee denies the comparison transgressions. Again, each of these factors and strategies may be worthy of empirical attention. For example, one could examine how persuasion-relevant characteristics of the examiner (e.g., perceived credibility) and examinee (e.g., intelligence) influence the extent of admissions of comparison transgressions and the number of apparently intentional and unintentional artifacts. One could examine the influence of social norms on pre-test compliance by measuring the examinee's perception of the rules, standards, and expectations of the polygraph examination. Impression management can be studied by varying the examiner's apparent control over the outcome of the examination and assessing the examinee's impression management tactics (e.g., rates of smiling and nodding). Operant conditioning, threats associated with non-compliance, and specific compliance tactics (e.g., leading questions) can be studied by manipulating the extent to which the examiner makes use of these things during the pre-test interview.

While research on the above-mentioned compliance variables would be useful, such hypothesis-testing research might overlook some very important compliance techniques that have been developed by experienced polygraph examiners. Robert Cialdini (e.g., Cialdini and Trost, 1998), the leading expert on social compliance research, has argued that the best approach to studying compliance is not through experimental methods (at least not initially), but by systematically observing the behavior of commercial compliance professionals on the job. According to Cialdini and Trost (1998), compliance professionals who use successful compliance strategies will succeed in their jobs and pass on their successful compliance strategies to trainees. Over successive generations of professionals and a wide variety of compliance contexts, "the strongest and most adaptable procedures for generating compliance will rise, persist, and accumulate" (Cialdini and Trost, 1998:169–170).

By systematically observing compliance professionals, Cialdini (1993) was able to identify a variety of compliance techniques (e.g., the low-ball procedure), as well as some fundamental principles of compliance (e.g., the norm of reciprocity). Perhaps, the same method of systematic observation could be applied to the study of compliance strategies used by the nth generation of polygraph examiners. In such an approach, researchers would observe pre-test interviews given by a large, representative sample of polygraph examiners. The researchers would identify and tally various compliance techniques used by the examiners. Only after completing a catalog of pre-test compliance techniques would researchers attempt to experimentally manipulate these techniques and assess their influence on the compliance objectives.

In addition to investigating ways to improve compliance in the polygraph examination, researchers should examine the consequences of compliance failure on polygraph outcome. For example, researchers should investigate the extent to which pre-test admissions of comparison transgressions influence the accuracy of polygraph examinations. From a theoretical standpoint, an examinee's admissions could have an influence on the effectiveness of the polygraph. Logically, each admission of a comparison transgression reduces the "scope of denial" – that is, the range of comparison questions that can be denied with an answer to comparison questions. In the extreme, a person who admits to everything has nothing to deny. Psychologically, the admission of comparison transgressions might produce a state of "catharsis," or emotional relief (Pennebaker *et al.*, 1987), which could desensitize the examinee to the comparison questions (see Wolpe, 1961); or, such admissions might weaken responding by making it easier to suppress thoughts associated with the undisclosed transgressions and improving one's perception of mental control (see Wegner and Wenzlaff, 1996). On the other hand, if such comparison admissions are praised or otherwise well-received by the examiner, the guilty examinee might experience greater ambivalence regarding other significant denials. At this point, one may only speculate about the influence of pre-test admissions on polygraph outcome.

Another advanced research topic concerns the influence of pre-test denials on the examinee's likelihood to confess to the crime in question. According to the principles of operant conditioning, if the examinee is conditioned to deny significant comparison transgressions, this conditioning could generalize to the crime itself, making the examinee less likely to confess to the crime. Similarly, other things that discourage the admission of comparison transgressions (e.g., the examiner's suggestion that the examinee is a good person or not the sort of person who would commit the crime) might also serve to discourage confession of the crime. Perhaps, however, the typical examiner has developed such strong compliance-related skills that he/she can lead the same examinee from steadfast denial of comparison transgressions to docile confession of the crime itself with relative ease; and in such a case, there may be little relationship between the extent of pre-test denials and subsequent confession of the crime. Again, however, this is a question for future research.

MANAGING EXAMINEE THOUGHTS AND FEELINGS

Again, the overarching goal of the pre-test interview is to maximize the likelihood that an examinee experiences the appropriate focus of concern during the testing phase of the examination. The pre-test interview affords the examiner an opportunity to influence thoughts and feelings that have a bearing upon the examinee's focus of concern. Accordingly, I suggest that a major objective of the pre-test interview is to promote thoughts and feelings in the examinee that would help to identify the examinee as guilty or innocent on the polygraph test. In this chapter, I will refer to this general activity as "priming."

Priming

When psychologists speak of priming, they may imply the more restricted definition of enhancing the subsequent processing of a stimulus with prior exposure to that stimulus (Anderson, 1995; Smith, 1998). On the other hand, psychologists might imply a more liberal definition of priming – namely, facilitating certain thoughts or feelings through prior exposure to some kind of stimulus (see Forgas, 1995; Higgins, 1996; Sedikides and Skowronski, 1991). In this chapter, I mean to imply the latter definition. In this sense, priming differs from persuasion and compliance because the target of influence is the stream of consciousness or its unconscious tributaries – short-term thoughts, feelings, attention, biases, or tendencies. In the pre-test interview, the targets of priming are the fleeting thoughts and momentary feelings of concern that relevant and comparison questions elicit during the testing phase of the examination. Theoretically, the more influence that an examiner has over these thoughts and feelings, the more influence he/she has over the outcome of the polygraph examination.

So how can the examiner influence these thoughts and feelings? In this preliminary framework, it is worthwhile to consider three means of such influence – facilitating memory of pre-test content, amplifying feelings of guilt or shame, and making deception more difficult.

Facilitation memory of pre-test content

During the pre-test interview, the examiner discusses several ideas and images that can influence the examinee's thoughts during the testing phase of the examination. In particular, the examiner discusses ideas and images related to (1) the crime in question, (2) the comparison transgressions, and (3) the examinee's physiological responses to lying. The relative quality, quantity, and timeliness of such ideas and images may have a significant effect on the examinee's thoughts and feelings during the testing phase of the examination. What do I mean by quality, quantity, and timeliness of ideas and images? Cognitive psychologists have identified a number of ways to facilitate specific memories (e.g., thoughts of committing a crime). A comprehensive review of memory facilitation is beyond the scope of this chapter (for an introductory review, see Weiten, 1995); however, it is worthwhile to consider a few of the more popular concepts here.

First, memory for a particular item (e.g., the name William Marston) is influenced directly by the **frequency** and **distribution** of times that a person thinks about that item. In general, an item is remembered better when the item has been thought about more times, when these thoughts have been distributed across significant intervals of time, and when these thoughts have occurred recently (see Anderson, 1995). Applying these concepts to the pre-test interview, the examiner might facilitate recall of comparison transgressions during the testing phase by discussing the comparison transgressions more frequently across the pre-test interview, separating each mention of the comparison transgressions by a longer period of time, and reviewing more thoroughly the comparison questions later in the interview.[3]

Second, memory for an item can be improved with **visual imagery**. Both rigorous scientific studies (e.g., Bower and Winzenz, 1970) and popular accounts in memory books (e.g., Lorayne and Lucas, 1974) illustrate substantial improvements in memory when the to-be-remembered material is connected to visual imagery in a meaningful, creative, or even bizarre way (e.g., remembering the name Marston by imagining a polygraph examination over a stolen 'ton' of 'Mars' rocks). In the pre-test interview, the examiner may use visual imagery to make various ideas more memorable. For example, the examiner might produce one or more vivid, imaginable examples of the "fight–flight–freeze" response and imaginable examples of one's autonomic response to lying. Likewise, to help the examinee remember the supposed importance of the comparison questions, the examiner might describe an imaginable scenario in which an examinee "fails" the comparison questions and is treated as a person who could have committed the crime.

Third, memory can be enhanced through **self-reference**. Quite simply, when to-be-remembered material is linked to the self in some way, the material is more likely to be remembered (see Bellezza and Hoyt, 1992). In the pre-test interview, the examiner may make extensive use of the self-reference principle. For example, the examiner may solicit examples of the fight–flight–freeze response and autonomic responses to lying from the examinee's personal experiences. Also, by mentioning a wide variety of hypothetical transgressions (e.g., stealing from one's brother, mother, employer, spouse, classmate, neighbor, friend, fellow team member, . . . etc.) and by drawing the examinee's attention to his/her motives and behavior in these hypothetical transgressions, the examiner may make the comparison transgressions more memorable via their salient connection to the self.

Finally, memory for an item can be improved by increasing the person's **level of processing** or **mental elaboration** of the item. In general, a person tends to remember an item better when the item is thought about ("processed") at a more meaningful level (e.g., thinking about William Marston's role in the development of the polygraph), rather than a more superficial level (e.g., thinking about how to pronounce "Marston") (see Craik and Lockhart, 1972). Similarly, a person tends to remember an item better when he/she embellishes (or

[3] For an even greater impact of the distributed practice, the examiner might contact the examinee's counsel a couple of days before the interview takes place and instruct the examinee to recall various personal transgressions.

"elaborates" upon) this item with additional thoughts (e.g., thinking about William Marston's connection to Wonder Woman) (see Anderson and Reder, 1979). On the opposite side of the processing/elaboration continuum, when a person does not pay *attention* to the to-be-recalled material (for instance, when a student daydreams in class), the presentation of the material may have little or no effect on memory (Broadbent, 1958; Treisman and Geffen, 1967). In the pre-test interview, the examiner can improve the processing/elaboration of various materials by making sure that the examinee is paying attention to this material and by having the examinee reconstruct or embellish this material. For example, immediately after the examiner has discussed the nature of the fight–flight–freeze response, the examiner might ask the examinee to describe this response in his/her own words and provide a new example. In this way, the examiner can evaluate the examinee's level of processing and elaboration. The examiner could take a similar approach with the discussion of comparison transgressions – namely, ask the examinee to describe the importance of these questions in his/her own words, as well as provide examples of comparison questions.

In the foregoing discussion, I have not provided examples of enhancing memory for the crime in question. I did this for two reasons. First, the innocent subject could not benefit from the enhancement of such material. On the contrary, the more vividly the examiner describes the crime under investigation, the more likely the innocent examinee will develop a fabricated mental image of the crime, which could be disturbing during the testing phase of the examination. Second, the guilty examinee's memory for the crime in question may be quite strong *before* the pre-test interview. Most likely, the guilty examinee has thought about the crime several times over many days or weeks, including recently; he/she has a vivid mental picture of the commission of the crime; he/she has thought about the self in relation to the crime; and, in the process of rationalizing the crime or preparing for encounters with law enforcement, he/she may have elaborated extensively upon the thought of the crime. For these reasons, I suggest that the examiner does not attempt to prime the examinee's memory for the crime in question.

Amplifying feelings of guilt or shame

In this chapter, I have suggested that the success of the polygraph examination depends upon the guilty or innocent examinee developing the appropriate focus of concern (toward the relevant questions or comparison questions, respectively). Unfortunately, an innocent examinee's concern for relevant questions may dominate because the questions are obviously important, they deal with very negative material, and despite the examinee's innocence he/she might still imagine possible "failure" on these questions. In other words, an

their feelings. Levenson (1994) attributed these findings to the effort involved in "braking" the machinery of emotional expression. In a series of very interesting studies by Wegner and colleagues (e.g., Wegner *et al.*, 1987, 1990, 1993; Wegner and Erber, 1992), subjects were asked to suppress particular thoughts (for instance, for the next three minutes, try to not think about a white bear. Go ahead, try it!). In these studies, Wegner and colleagues found that persons have a very difficult time suppressing thoughts; that emotional thoughts are particularly difficult to suppress; that attempts at suppression often backfire (leading to greater preoccupation with the unwanted thoughts), especially when the suppressed thought is a secret or the person is otherwise mentally taxed; and that attempted thought suppression occasions elevated autonomic activity (see Wegner, 1994; Wegner and Bargh, 1998). In summary, to the extent that deception requires effortful suppression of overt emotions (e.g., facial expressions) as well as exciting thoughts, deception may manifest itself as autonomic indices of such suppression.

One should bear in mind that polygraph examinees have to be particularly concerned about emotional suppression. Not only do they have to monitor and control their covert facial and bodily expressions, but they also have to monitor and control their overt autonomic reactions. This dual focus of controlling internal and external emotion may be quite difficult for the examinee to manage and is particularly subject to error (emotional leakage). By monitoring and controlling overt emotional expression, the examinee may mobilize resources (attentional and otherwise) that undermine attempts at physiological relaxation.

Assuming that deception requires effort, perhaps deception is more easily detected when the effort to deceive is greater. How can one increase the effort associated with deception? One possibility is to make the person attend to more emotional outlets (physiological and otherwise) during attempted deception. Within the polygraph examination, if an examinee attempts to monitor and control facial expressions, gaze behavior, vocal quality, breathing, heart rate, sweating, and other outlets for emotion, then the examinee will have to recruit considerable attentional resources, which may produce significant increases in autonomic activity during deception. To promote this kind of **multiple-outlet monitoring**, the examiner should draw the examinee's attention to the various emotional outlets, convince the examinee that these outlets may betray one's deception during the polygraph test, and counsel the examinee to avoid monitoring or controlling these outlets if he/she is actually innocent.

Again, the idea is that by making deception more difficult for the examinee, the truly innocent examinee should manifest a greater physiological response to the comparison questions, which will decrease the likelihood that this examinee is identified incorrectly as guilty. On the contrary, making deception more difficult should not make truly guilty examinees appear innocent, for these examinees will expend considerable deception effort while responding to the relevant questions.

Suggestions for research on pre-test priming

As with the research on pre-test persuasion and compliance, there is considerable opportunity for substantive research on pre-test priming. Again, one can identify both fundamental and more advanced research questions on this topic. I summarize just some of the possibilities below.

With regard to memory facilitation, one fundamental question that needs to be answered is what is the proper balance of content (crime vs. comparison questions vs. nature/detection of lying) in the pre-test interview? Perhaps it is best to have nearly equal quantity, quality, timeliness, and memorability of the various pre-test topics. On the other hand, perhaps a greater focus on the comparison transgressions and less focus on the crime itself would reduce the frequency of false positives. Or, perhaps the optimal balance of content depends upon other factors (e.g., the criminal history of the examinee). Assuming that an optimal balance of content is identifiable, then researchers should explore specific strategies that examiners may use to ensure that this balance is achieved during examinations. Certainly, researchers might develop various techniques for improving the examinee's processing and elaboration of the topics. I have mentioned a few possibilities earlier (e.g., having the examinee restate why the comparison questions are important).

With regard to amplifying feelings of guilt or shame, researchers should explore how such amplification might be accomplished in the pre-test interview and what ultimate effect it has on polygraph outcome. I have suggested that drawing the examinee's attention to aspects of his/her "ought self" or "ideal self" should make the examinee more aware of his/her failures with respect to the comparison transgressions or the crime under investigation. This negative self-awareness may occasion additional autonomic activity in response to the troubling truth of the examinee's failures. Another possible strategy for amplifying guilt in the polygraph involves bolstering the examinee's social commitment to the examiner. If the examinee feels a greater obligation to help the examiner with the polygraph test, then this felt obligation may amplify the examinee's feelings of guilt when he/she cheats on the test. Assuming that this is true (and again, this is merely speculative), then researchers might explore ways to increase the examinee's sense of social commitment to the examiner. Finally, researchers should determine whether examinees who have a low level of socialization or alternatively a "guilt complex" (see Reid and Inbau, 1977) are responsive to guilt/shame amplification.

With regard to making deception more difficult, there are many possibilities for substantive research. First, it would be worthwhile to manipulate the number of emotion outlets that an examinee has to control and to determine whether this has a direct influence on autonomic responsivity. Second, researchers might evaluate various ways of increasing the examinee's attempts to monitor and control various emotion outlets. For example, perhaps a convincing pre-test review (and re-review) of the various emotion outlets of deception might inspire examinees to monitor and control these outlets when they deceive. On the other hand, perhaps the examinee will monitor and control only those emotion outlets that the examiner also apparently monitors. If the examiner seems to ignore facial and vocal cues to deception, the examinee might not care to monitor these outlets. Consistent with this line of reasoning, one might hypothesize that the so-called clinical approach to polygraph examinations – which involves the examiner monitoring various bodily and verbal cues to deception, as well as polygraph tracings – may improve the psychophysiological detection of deception. As with all of the suggestions in this chapter, however, this is merely informed speculation deserving empirical attention.

Before concluding this section, I would like to highlight one more possible research topic related to deception effort. Consider an examinee's inclination to confess to the crime under investigation. When this inclination is substantial, the examinee may have a harder time suppressing relevant thoughts and controlling his/her feelings. In other words, it is possible that the more an examinee feels internal pressure to confess, the more effort he/she must devote to deception; and the more effort the examinee devotes to deception, the more his/her deception will be betrayed by physiological responses. If these speculations are correct, then researchers might discover that the same variables that promote an examinee's confession (see Gudjonsson, 1992; Inbau *et al.*, 1986; Kassin, 1997) also promote the psychophysiological detection of deception.

AN ANALYTIC MODEL FOR PRE-TEST RESEARCH

At this point, I hope that the reader understands that there are many possibilities for important and interesting research on the pre-test interview. Researchers can investigate numerous factors that promote pre-test persuasion (concerning polygraph effectiveness of comparison question importance), compliance (concerning the denial of comparison transgressions and the avoidance of countermeasures/artifacts), and priming (concerning the examinee's momentary thoughts and feelings during the testing phase of the examination), as well as factors that moderate these pre test activities (e.g., the examinee's elaboration likelihood, true guilt or innocence, level of socialization, . . . etc.). Furthermore, researchers can investigate how pre-test persuasion, compliance, and priming ultimately influence the psychophysiological detection of deception. Given the sheer breadth of potential pre-test topics, it would be unwise to recommend a general methodology for pre-test research. Some pre-test topics might be explored adequately with systematic observation of experienced examiners (e.g., compliance techniques), whereas others might benefit from experimental research (e.g., the psychophysiological effects of monitoring multiple channels of emotion). Still, I think that it is worthwhile to consider a general analytic approach with which researchers can examine the role of various pre-test variables in the psychophysiological detection of deception.

"Mediator analysis" (Baron and Kenny, 1986) is a method of assessing the extent to which an independent variable (e.g., a particular photograph) influences a dependent variable (e.g., heart rate) through one or more mediator variables (e.g., the subject's familiarity with the photograph). In social psychological research, researchers use mediator analysis to examine how different social contexts or stimuli affect aspects of people's behavior through various internal processes (or mediators), such as thoughts, feelings, or traits. As a theoretical tool, mediator analysis is quite powerful because it provides a model of *how* an independent variable influences a dependent variable (i.e., through a mediator variable).

In the context of research on the CQT pre-test interview, mediator analysis is particularly appropriate. According to the theory underlying the CQT, innocent and guilty examinees are identified accurately with the polygraph when (and only when) these examinees exhibit the expected focus of concern – that is, when guilty subjects are more concerned with the relevant questions and innocent subjects are more concerned with the comparison questions (Reid and Inbau, 1977). Consistent with this idea, any pre-test variable that improves or undermines the effectiveness of the CQT may do so by improving or undermining the expected focus of concern in the examinees. In mediational language, a given pre-test variable (independent variable) may influence the accuracy of the polygraph examination (dependent variable) indirectly by influencing the examinee's focus of concern. This mediational model is depicted in Figure 6.1.

The mediator analysis portrayed in Figure 6.1 symbolizes a considerable amount of information. First, there is the relationship between the independent variable (balance of pre-test content) and the mediator variable (focus of concern). Second, there is the relationship between the mediator and the dependent variable (polygraph accuracy). Third, there is the direct relationship between the independent variable and the dependent variable (denoted by the path of the dashed arrow). Finally, there is the indirect relationship between the independent and dependent variables, through the mediator

Figure 6.1

Theoretical model in which the examinee's focus of concern (toward relevant or comparison questions) mediates the influence of any CQT pre-test variable on the accuracy of the polygraph examination.

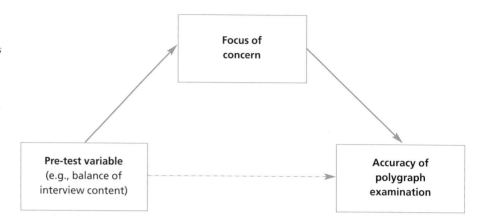

Figure 6.1

Theoretical model in which the examinee's focus of concern (toward relevant or comparison questions) mediates the influence of any CQT pre-test variable on the accuracy of the polygraph examination.

(denoted by the path of the two solid arrows). Importantly, for focus of concern to be considered a viable mediator between any pre-test variable and polygraph outcome, the indirect relationship must be significant.

Why not simply examine the relationship between pre-test variables and polygraph accuracy? There are a few advantages to using mediator analysis in pre-test research. First and foremost, mediator analysis allows the researcher to examine the theoretical mechanism through which CQT pre-test variables are supposed to have an influence on polygraph outcome. Evidence that focus of concern significantly mediates the relationship between several pre-test variables and polygraph outcome would be a very powerful statement of support for the theory that supposedly underlies the CQT. Second, a modestly influential pre-test variable might not have a noticeable indirect effect on polygraph outcome, but may have a noticeable direct effect on focus of concern. In such a case, the variable should not be dismissed as trivial. Across hundreds of cases, the variable may demonstrate a reliable impact on polygraph outcome. Third, the mediational model that I have described would enable researchers to evaluate the validity of the polygraph examinations and/or scoring methods. If there is a weak relationship between focus of concern and polygraph outcome for a particular study, then the validity of the study is questionable. In such a context, the presence or absence of pre-test variable effects might be misleading. Fourth, the mediator analysis would in no way prohibit the researcher from examining the direct relationship between a pre-test variable and polygraph outcome. The mediator analysis simply provides more information about how the pre-test variable is related to polygraph outcome.

Of course, the mediator analysis that I suggest is not problem-free. In particular, the validity of such an analysis would rest upon the validity of one's measure of focus of concern. Pre-test researchers who wish to pursue a mediator analysis could adopt a self-report measure of focus of concern, as other researchers have done in the past (e.g., Bradley and Janisse, 1981; Mitchell, 1999). Unfortunately, self-report measures may not fully capture the nature and extent of concern that examinees "feel" (perhaps partly unconsciously) for the relevant and comparison questions. Thus, one challenge for pre-test researchers is the identification or development of complementary measures of focus of concern. Some potential candidates may include facial electromyography, dichotic listening effects, and subliminal preference.

CONCLUSION

In this chapter, I have provided a preliminary framework for organizing pre-test research and theory. I have argued that the role of the examiner in the pre-test interview is to manage the examinee's attitudes, behavior, thoughts, and feelings in such a way that promotes the appropriate focus of concern in examinees. Consistent with the conceptualization, I have provided a compendium of potentially important pre-test variables that may affect polygraph outcome through their influence on the examinee's focus of concern. My goal was to inspire research, reflection, and professional dialog on various aspects of the pre-test interview. To this end, I have made a number of bold assertions and have engaged in liberal speculation throughout the chapter. My hope is that my assertions and speculations will be replaced gradually with solid research findings, useful theories, and informed ideas about how to make the best use of the pre-test interview.

REFERENCES

Anderson, J. R. (1995) *Cognitive Psychology and Its Implications*, 4th edn. New York: W. H. Freeman and Co.

Anderson, J. R. and Reder, L. M. (1979) An elaborative processing explanation of depth of processing. In: L. S. Cermack and F. I. M. Craik (eds) *Levels of Processing in Human Memory*. Hillsdale, NJ: Lawrence Erlbaum Associates.

Apple, W., Streeter, L. A. and Krauss, R. M. (1979) Effects of pitch and speech rate on personal attributions. *Journal of Personality and Social Psychology*, 37, 715–727.

Bandura, A. (1986) *Social Foundations of Thought and Action. A Social Cognitive Theory.* Englewood Cliffs, NJ: Prentice-Hall.

Barland, G. H. and Raskin, D. C. (1973) Detection of deception. In: W. F. Prokasy and D. C. Raskin (eds) *Electrodermal Activity in Psychological Research*, pp. 418–471. New York: Academic Press.

Baron, R. M. and Kenny, D. A. (1986) The moderator-mediator variable distinction in social psychological research: Conceptual strategic, and statistical considerations. *Journal of Personality and Social Psychology*, 51, 1173–1181.

Baumeister, R. F. (1982) A self-presentational view of social phenomena. *Psychology Bulletin*, 91, 3–26.

Baumeister, R. F. (1998) The self. In: D. T. Gilbert, S. T. Fiske and G. Lindzey (eds) *The Handbook of Social Psychology*, 4th edn, vol. I, pp. 680–740. New York: McGraw-Hill.

Baxter, C. (1974) Anticlimax dampening concept. *Polygraph*, 3, 48–50.

Beaman, A. L., Cole, C. M., Preston, M., Klentz, B. and Steblay, N. M. (1983) Fifteen years of the foot-in-door research: A meta-analysis. *Personality and Social Psychology Bulletin*, 9, 181–196.

Bellezza, F. S. and Hoyt, S. K. (1992) The self-reference effect and mental cueing. *Social Cognition*, 10, 51–78.

Boster, F. J. and Mongeau, P. (1984) Fear-arousing persuasive messages. In: R. N. Bostrom (ed.) *Communication Yearbook*, vol. 8, pp. 330–375. Beverly Hills, CA: Sage.

Bower, G. H. and Winzenz, D. (1970) Comparison of associative learning strategies. *Psychonomic Science,* 20, 119–120.

Bradley, M. T. and Janisse, M. P. (1981) Accuracy demonstrations, threat, and the detection of deception: Cardiovascular, electrodermal, and pupillary measures. *Psychophysiology*, 18, 307–315.

Broadbent, D. E. (1958) *Perception and Communication*. New York: Pergamon.

Brownstein, R. and Katzev, R. (1985) The relative effectiveness of three compliance techniques in eliciting donations to cultural organizations. *Journal of Applied Social Psychology*, 15, 564–574.

Burger, J. M. and Petty, R. E. (1981) The low-ball compliance technique: Task or person commitment? *Journal of Personality and Social Psychology*, 40, 492–500.

Cacioppo, J. T. and Petty, R. E. (1979) Effects of message repetition and position on cognitive responses, recall, and persuasion. *Journal of Personality and Social Psychology*, 37, 97–109.

Cacioppo, J. T. and Petty, R. E. (1982) The need for cognition. *Journal of Personality and Social Psychology*, 42, 116–131.

Cacioppo, J. T., Petty, R. E. and Morris, K. J. (1983) Effects of need for cognition on message evaluation, recall, and persuasion. *Journal of Personality and Social Psychology*, 45, 805–818.

Chaiken, S. (1979) Communicator physical attractiveness and persuasion. *Journal of Personality and Social Psychology*, 37, 1387–1397.

Chaiken, S. (1980) euristic versus systematic information processing in the use of source versus message cues in persuasion. *Journal of Personality and Social Psychology*, 39, 752–766.

Chaiken, S. (1987) The heuristic model of persuasion. In: M. P. Zanna, J. M. Olsen and C. P. Herman (eds) *Social Influence: The Ontario Symposium*, vol. 5, pp. 3–39. Hillsdale, NJ: Erlbaum.

Cialdini, R. B. (1993) *Influence: Science and Practice*, 3rd edn. New York: HarperCollins.

Cialdini, R. B., Cacioppo, J. T., Bassett, R. and Miller, J. A. (1978) Low-ball procedure for producing compliance: Commitment, then cost. *Journal of Personality and Social Psychology*, 36, 463–476.

Cialdini, R. B. and Trost, M. R. (1998) Social influence: Social norms, conformity, and compliance. In: D. T. Gilbert, S. T. Fiske and G. Lindzey (eds) *The Handbook of Social Psychology*, 4th edn, vol. II, pp. 151–192. New York: McGraw-Hill.

Cialdini, R. B., Vincent, J. E., Lewis, S. K., Catalan, J., Wheeler, D. and Darby, B. L. (1975) Reciprocal concessions procedure for inducing compliance: The door-in-the-face technique. *Journal of Applied Social Psychology*, 31, 206–215.

Craik, F. I. M. and Lockhart, R. S. (1972) Levels of processing: A framework for memory research. *Journal of Verbal Learning and Verbal Behavior*, 11, 671–684.

Daily, B. J. (1974) Pre-test interview. *Polygraph*, 3, 338–342.

Debono, K. G. (1987) Investigating the social-adjustive and value-expressive functions of attitudes: Implications for persuasive processes. *Journal of Personality and Social Psychology*, 52, 279–287.

de Rivera, J. (1977) *A Structural Theory of the Emotions*. New York: International Universities Press.

Eagly, A. H., Wood, W. and Chaiken, S. (1978) Causal inferences about communicators and their effects on opinion change. *Journal of Personality and Social Psychology*, 36, 424–435.

Erickson, B., Lind, E. A. and Johnson, B. C. (1978) Speech style and impression formation in a court setting: The effects of "powerful" and "powerless" speech. *Journal of Experimental and Social Psychology*, 14, 266–279.

Festinger, L. (1954) A theory of social comparison processes. *Human Relations*, 7, 117–140.

Festinger, L. and Thibaut, J. (1951) Interpersonal communication in small groups. *Journal of Abnormal Social Psychology*, 46, 92–100.

Fine, B. J. (1957) Conclusion-drawing, communicator credibility, and anxiety as factors in opinion change. *Journal of Abnormal Social Psychology*, 54, 369–374.

Forgas, J. P. (1995) Strange couples: Mood effects on judgments and memory about prototypical and atypical relationships. *Psychology Bulletin*, 117, 39–66.

Freedman, J. L. and Fraser, S. C. (1966) Compliance without pressure: The foot-in-door technique. *Journal of Personality and Social Psychology*, 1, 145–155.

Furedy, L. S. (1993) The "control" question "test" (CQT) polygrapher's dilemma: Logico-ethical considerations for psychophysiological practitioners and researchers. *International Journal of Psychophysiology*, 15, 263–267.

Gross, J. J. and Levenson, R. W. (1993) Emotional suppression: Physiology, self report, and expressive behavior. *Journal of Personality and Social Psychology*, 64, 970–986.

Gudjonsson, G. (1984) A new scale of interrogative suggestibility. *Personality and Individual Differences*, 5, 303–314.

Gudjonsson, G. (1992) *The Psychology of Interrogations, Confessions and Testimony.* New York: John Wiley.

Gustafson, L. A. and Orne, M. T. (1963) Effects of heightened motivation on the detection of deception. *Journal of Applied Psychology*, 47, 408–411.

Higgins, E. T. (1987) Self-discrepancy: A theory relating self and affect. *Psychology Review*, 94, 319–340.

Higgins, E. T. (1989) Self-discrepancy theory: What patterns of self-beliefs cause people to suffer? *Advances in Experimental and Social Psychology*, 22, 93–136.

Higgins, E. T. (1996) Knowledge activation: Accessibility, applicability, and salience. In: E. T. Higgins and A. W. Kruglaski (eds) *Social Psychology: Handbook of Basic Principles*, pp. 133–168. New York: Guilford Press.

Higgins, E. T., Roney, C. J. R. Crowe, E. and Hymes, C. (1994) Ideal versus ought predilections for approach for avoidance: Distinct self-regulatory systems. *Journal of Personality and Social Psychology*, 66, 276–286.

Horai, J., Naccari, N. and Fatoullah, E. (1974) The effects of expertise and physical attractiveness upon opinion agreement and liking. *Sociometry*, 37, 601–606.

Horowitz, S. W., Kircher, J. C., Honts, C. R. and Raskin, D. C. (1997) The role of comparison questions in physiological detection of deception. *Psychophysiology*, 34, 108–115.

Iacono, W. G. and Patrick, C. J. (1987) What psychologists should know about lie detection. In: I. B. Weiner and A. K. Hess (eds) *Handbook of Forensic Psychology*, pp. 460–489. New York: John Wiley.

Inbau, F. E., Reid, J. E. and Buckley, J. P. (1986) *Criminal Interrogation and Confessions*, 3rd edn. Baltimore, MD: Williams and Wilkins.

Jones, E. E. and Pittman, T. S. (1982)Toward a general theory of strategic self-presentation. In: J. Suls (ed.) *Psychological Perspectives on the Self*, vol. 1, pp. 231–262. Hillsdale, NJ: Lawrence Erlbaum Associates.

Joule, R. V. (1987) Tobacco deprivation: The foot-in-door technique versus the low-ball technique. *European Journal of Social Psychology*, 17, 361–365.

Kassin, S. (1997) The psychology of confession evidence. *American Psychology*, 52, 221–233.

Kelman, H. C. (1958) Compliance, identification, and internalization: Three processes of attitude change. *Journal of Conflict Resolution*, 2, 51–60.

Kelman, H. C. and Hovland, C. I. (1953) "Reinstatement" of the communicator in delayed measurement of opinion change. *Journal of Abnormal Social Psychology*, 48, 327–335.

Kiesler, S. B. and Mathog, R. (1968) The distraction hypothesis in attitude change. *Psychological Reports*, 23, 1123–1133.

Kircher, J. C. and Raskin, D. C. (1986) Visceral perception in the detection of deception [Abstract]. *Psychophysiology*, 23, 446.

Krugman, H. E. (1972) Why three exposures may be enough. *Journal of Advertising Research*, 12, 11–14.

Lavine, H. and Snyder, M. (1996) Cognitive processing and the functional matching effect in persuasion: The mediating role of subjective perceptions of message quality. *Journal of Experimental and Social Psychology*, 32, 580–604.

Levinson, R. W. (1994) Emotional control: Variations and consequences. In: P. Ekman and R. J. Davidson (eds) *The Nature of Emotion: Fundamental Questions*, pp. 273–279. New York: Oxford University Press.

Lewis, M. (1993) Self-conscious emotions: embarrassment, pride, shame, and guilt. In: M. Lewis and J. M. Haviland (eds) *Handbook of Emotions*, pp. 563–573. New York: Guilford Press.

Loftus, E. F. (1980) *Eyewitness Testimony.* Cambridge, MA: Harvard University Press.

Loftus, E. F. and Palmer, J. C. (1974) Reconstruction of automobile destruction: An example of the interaction between language and memory. *Journal of Verbal Learning and Verbal Behavior*, 13, 585–589.

Lorayne, H. and Lucas, J. (1974) *The Memory Book.* New York: Ballantine.

Lykken, D. T. (1981) *A Tremor in the Blood: Uses and Abuses of the Lie Detector.* New York: McGraw-Hill.

McGinnies, E. and Ward, C. D. (1980) Better liked than right: Trustworthiness and expertise as factors in credibility. *Personality and Social Psychology Bulletin*, 6, 467–472.

McGuire, W. J. (1968) Personality and attitude change: An information-processing theory. In: A. G. Greenwald, T. C. Brock and T. M. Ostrom (eds) *Psychological Foundations of Attitudes*, pp. 171–196. New York: Academic Press.

McGuire, W. J. (1985) Attitudes and attitude change. In: G. Lindzey and E. Aronson (eds) *The Handbook of Social Psychology,* 3rd edn, vol. II, pp. 233–346. New York: Random House.

Miller, N., Maruyama, G., Beaber, R. J. and Valone, K. (1976) Speed of speech and persuasion. *Journal of Personality and Social Psychology*, 34, 615–624.

Protection Act of 1988 substantially restricted the use of the polygraph in the private sector in the US. Polygraphy has expanded on many fronts, and into new applications. US government counterintelligence polygraph screening examinations outnumber the government forensic polygraphs many times over, with new screening programs taking shape in the US Federal Bureau of Investigation and the Department of Energy. Multiple-issue polygraph testing is also becoming a standard condition of parole and probation for convicted sex offenders in many jurisdictions. Polygraph screening of police applicants has remained stable, or increased in most states. Moreover, polygraphy is no longer the peculiar practice of North Americans. There are significant numbers of polygraph practitioners in Latin America, Asia, Middle East, Africa, Russia, and other regions, though all to a lesser degree than in North America. Part of this expansion overseas may be attributable simply to the aura and allure of American technology. It may also be an outgrowth of the worldwide sensitivity to human rights issues, where polygraph has come to replace other, more controversial means of securing information from individuals. Or, it may only be a symbol of the new world economy, where many tools and techniques transmigrate across borders. Regardless of the reasons, polygraph screening is now entrenched in government, law enforcement, and industrial security around the globe.

The polygraph used in a screening examination differs in three important ways from the more familiar specific issue of criminal testing. First, screening examinations are multiple-issue examinations, covering several different topics that can have varying degrees of overlap with one another. The screening examiner is ordinarily not tasked with only correctly classifying a deceptive person, as is the case in specific issue examinations, but also with localizing the deception to the correct topic(s) for each deceptive examinee.

Second, the typical screening test questions are much more general in scope than specific issue test questions ("In the last five years have you stolen anything of value from an employer," versus "On the night of 17 August did you break into Bob's Appliance Store?"). The polygraph screening questions require more memory searching by the examinee in order to comply with the demands of the test questions. It can be reasonably expected that it would be clearer in an examinee's mind whether he had participated in a particular noteworthy event, such as a burglary, than in a more ambiguous class of behaviors during an extended period of time. Doubt in an examinee's mind can sometimes give rise to bodily responses in itself, introducing the problem of discerning those physiological responses attributable to deception from those of mere uncertainty.

Third, the body of research on screening examinations is but a fraction of that for specific issue testing. There are far more unanswered questions about the various polygraph screening techniques, especially as they are employed in the field.

According to Meesig and Horvath (1995), 99% of large and 90% of small law enforcement agencies in the US require a polygraph screening examination as a condition of employment for applicants to sworn positions. In addition, several US federal agencies use the polygraph to screen applicants for sensitive positions, and some have periodic polygraph testing of employees who hold top security clearances. The Department of Defense Polygraph Institute (1998) reports that these examinations total many thousands each year. One might ask the question: why have political leaders and policy-makers made polygraph screening an important part of hiring decisions and security clearance processing without first requiring validity research?

The purpose of this chapter is explore what polygraph screening is, what it brings to the typical applicant and employee screening system, and how it has come to play its current role in law enforcement and government. Information presented here has multiple interpretations, permitting all sides of the debate to emphasize and extrapolate those details that support their politics. The writer acknowledges that, having been a practitioner, subject, and researcher of the polygraph screening process, his views have been influenced by the combination of data and personal experience. It is hoped that the information here has been presented in a balanced way, and that all questions have been subject to the same level of criticism and analysis.

HISTORY

The instrumental collection of physiological data for lie detection was first applied to the problem of identifying criminal suspects (Lombroso, 1895), an area still in prominent use today. Published reports of the polygraph being used in a screening capacity first appeared in the 1930s (Keeler, 1931; O'Leary, 1934). A small handful of polygraph examiners were beginning to conduct routine testing of bank employees in the Chicago area to resolve shortages. Many thieves were reportedly found, but typically more thefts were uncovered during polygraph testing than had been previously known. In his monograph, Keeler (1931) wrote that, out of 12 banks there were "none that didn't have three or more embezzlers within the bank." At that time Keeler was just beginning to make a reputation for himself and his device, thanks to his resolution of several sensational cases and the enthusiasm of news reporters, and the legend of the "lie detector" was born.

By the early 1940s polygraph screening was being suggested as a means of detecting subversives and saboteurs who might strike against US armament production as World War II loomed. Bledsoe (1941), a polygraph practitioner, proposed a four-point polygraph program to detect the enemies within, which included applicant screening and periodic employee testing. There is no indication that Bledsoe's suggestions were put into practice by the US government. However, by August 1945 the US government experimented with the use of polygraph screening of German POWs for the purpose of identifying good candidates to train for a police force to be installed in post-World War II Germany (Linehan, 1978). That effort, with Keeler as the chief polygraph examiner, entailed the testing of 274 pre-screened POWs, with the aim of identifying those with undesirable affiliations, sympathies, or intentions. Many Nazi members and sympathizers were uncovered during the project. Also discovered were criminal activities, plans to commit sabotage, and a witness to war crime atrocities against Jews. For unreported reasons, the US Army abandoned the police training program, and the polygraph screening of German POWs came to a close.

On 17 February 1946 the Manhattan District of the Corps of Engineers, producers of the atomic bomb, began using the polygraph services of Leonarde Keeler and a team of six experienced polygraph examiners to test employees for the Oak Ridge facility (Linehan, 1990; *New York Times*, 14 March 1946). Linehan reported that 690 employees at the Final Product Building were in the first group of those tested. Initially, there were five employees who objected to the testing, but all except one withdrew the objection when they were advised that testing would not cover their personal lives. The polygraph screening projected netted serious admissions, including the stealing of product material and concealing from authorities the spillage of product material. There were also confessions of tool thefts and disclosure of classified information to unauthorized persons. It was noted that, once the polygraph program had commenced, previously stolen tools and miscellaneous supplies were being brought back to the facility in such quantity that the inventory figures were unable to account for them all. The polygraph screening program was discontinued in April 1953 by the Washington office of the Atomic Energy Commission, in part because it was seen as providing "only a marginal increase in security." The polygraph was discontinued for screening purposes at the Oak Ridge plant. On a related note, in 1984 it was reported that the Oak Ridge facility could not account for 1,710 pounds of bomb-grade uranium from its inventory for the previous 30-year period (*Indianapolis Star*, 24 January 1984).

In the US, the use of the polygraph to screen applicants and employees has had periods of growth and decline. At present the US government has about two dozen agencies with a polygraph program, and screening polygraph examinations easily outnumber forensic polygraph examinations by the government. Most US state law enforcement agencies have a cadre of polygraph examiners who conduct polygraph screening, and there are hundreds of other municipal entities also with this capability. Other countries having significant screening programs in government, law enforcement or private sector include Mexico,

Israel, Canada, South Africa, Bulgaria, and Canada. Recently, polygraph screening training and instrumentation were provided by the US to help Russia maintain control over its nuclear inventory. According to Barland (1999), a total of 69 countries now have a polygraph capability, though the percentage engaged in polygraph screening is not known. Also in the last ten years, commercial manufacturers of polygraphs have appeared in Russia and China.

HOW POLYGRAPH SCREENING IS CONDUCTED

The screening polygraph examination has the same principal components as the single-issue polygraph examination. It begins with a pre-test interview, in which basic background is gathered, and the test issues are discussed with the examinee. In some settings, a rights advisement is part of the pre-test interview. During the pre-test interview the examiner will solicit information from the examinee on the relevant issues, so that the test questions can be individually tailored. The final wording of each test question is then reviewed with the examinee, and if he or she has no further comments, the testing phase begins. Testing involves the presentation of the test questions during physiological recording from two to five times in two or three individual tests. Analysis of the data is conducted using global, numerical or automated assessment systems.

Part of virtually all polygraph sessions, but separate from the testing process itself, is the post-test stage. During the post-test the examinee is afforded the opportunity to receive and discuss the test results. If analysis of the physiological data indicates that the examinee has not withheld information on the relevant issues, he or she is debriefed and released. If the results are not clearly indicative of non-deception, additional measures are taken to resolve the issues. These measures can include the arranging of another polygraph session, an extensive interview, or a simple repeat of the testing with reworded questions.

Some multiple-issue polygraph screening testing formats are more sensitive to detecting deception than detecting truthfulness. In order to guard against false negatives, scoring or decision rules are often tipped in favor of detecting deception, with an attendant cost in false positives. To compensate for this tendency, during the post-screening phase of the polygraph session the examiner will take additional steps to eliminate alternate explanations for the physiological responding. The examiner will typically first try to elicit an explanation from the examinee for the polygraph reactions. Often examinees provide additional information during the post-screening discussion, sometimes confessing to having withheld information, other times expressing passing concerns about the topic.

Generally, following the screening post-test discussion, polygraph examiners will subject the test issue associated with physiological responding to a single-issue test format, the type for which there is a substantial body of validation research. This two-step screening process (multiple-issue to single-issue test format) is consistent with Meehl and Rosen's "successive hurdles" approach (1955), which serves to lessen the adverse effects of imperfect validity and unbalanced base rates. It also bears no small resemblance to medical diagnostic screening strategies, where tests with high sensitivity are given to the population of interest, followed by testing those with positive results with the more expensive tests that have better specificity. The present writer risks the suggestion that, once field research data on polygraph screening are finally available, one will probably find the false positive inclination of the polygraph screening examination is not as high as the laboratory data investigating individual screening formats would suggest. This is primarily because the methods are so dissimilar. This arguable prediction awaits verification.

ROLE OF THE POLYGRAPH IN THE HIRING PROCESS

In the 1970s and 1980s applicant screening with the polygraph had gained popularity among employers in the US. In some situations, the polygraph examiner's role included vetoing potential candidates who had performed poorly during polygraph testing. For a host of reasons, including abuses in the field, the US Congress enacted the 1988 Employee Polygraph Protection Act (EPPA), which prohibited polygraph screening of applicants and employees except under some clearly specified circumstances. Government and law enforcement polygraph testing were excluded from the provisions of the bill.

It is fairly uncommon for polygraphy as practiced today to be the final arbiter for employment, contrary to common portrayals (see Lykken, 1998, Chapter 15). Analogous to the selection of graduate students by universities, where the chosen are a small subset of the number of applicants, no single screening tool, regardless of validity, is relied upon solely. Users of the screening polygraph tool understand that this technology does not predict future behavior, assess attitudes, or determine suitability. Instead, polygraph screening provides but one source of information regarding a candidate's previous behavior for hiring officers to evaluate. It is to be weighed against the assessment of the candidate's resumé, background investigations, personal interview, psychological testing, or other available techniques, which may also suffer imperfect validity. For employers who use the polygraph, it typically provides more adjudicable information than other means. In the "best practices" model, the polygraph decisions are used to direct post-test questioning, prompt background investigators to focus on certain issues, or shape the allocation of investigative resources from some individuals to others. Its contribution in this capacity aids, but does not supercede a hiring officer in his or her responsibility to make critical decisions in the complex and imprecise science of applicant selection.

WHY THE POLYGRAPH IS USED

The value of the screening polygraph depends on the end user, and not all consumers of polygraph screening services see the costs and benefits the same. Meesig and Horvath (1995) explored those reasons in their survey of law enforcement agencies in the US. Some agencies reportedly believe it has the effect of causing a proportion of unsuitable applicants to self-select out of the process, thereby permitting agencies to better husband processing resources. Others find that polygraph screening is able to deliver information that is simply not available from other sources. For example, a pattern of physical violence by a police candidate may not be detectable by other means. Still other polygraph screening users have concluded that applicants will be more honest in the application process if they are aware that they will also be assessed by polygraph. One might note the apparent focus on the utility of polygraph screening, rather than validity. The Meesig and Horvath data show a presumption of validity among users. Validity of the polygraph screening examination will be taken up later in this chapter.

One significant finding of the Meesig and Horvath study of police agencies is that users of polygraph screening are more inclined than non-users to employ a larger array of screening methods. In other words, the field use of polygraph screening in the law enforcement sector is more likely to be part of an overall multi-faceted screening process than a stand-alone method. There are two conclusions that might be drawn from these data. First, polygraph screening is not a redundant process, that it contributes unique information. Second, polygraph screening examination results are not used exclusively to make hiring decisions, but rather the hiring officials are considering other information. Its relative usefulness can be gauged from the data collected by Meesig and Horvath, and presented below (Table 7.1).

Of equal interest are the reasons why former users of polygraph screening abandoned it. Meesig and Horvath found that the most common reason was a lack of confidence in the test (29 responses out of 100 former users). However, the ranking of reasons was strikingly different for the large and small agencies. Table 7.2 is taken from Meesig and Horvath's data, and reveals the dissimilar views toward polygraph screening.

Careful scientific inquiry to uncover the reasons government or private companies use polygraph screening has not been published, nor could any be located among the unpublished reports and government documents in the library of the US Department of Defense Polygraph Institute. The differences in

Table 7.1

Large and small user's evaluations of pre-employment polygraph screening regarding its importance in the selection process. (From Meesig and Horvath, 1995)

	Agency size		
	Large (*n* = 386)	Small (*n* = 199)	Combined (*n* = 585)
Number of responses	380	191	571
Range	10–100	5–100	5–100
Mean	84	75	81
Median	90	80	90

Range: 1 = very little importance to 100 = extreme importance.

Table 7.2

Top three ranked reasons given by former users of polygraph screening for discontinuing its use. (Respondents allowed to provide more than one reason.) (Data from Meesig and Horvath, 1995).

Large agencies (*n* = 44)			Small agencies (*n* = 56)	
Rank	Reason	*n*	Reason	*n*
1	Prohibitive legislation	17	Lack confidence in test	20
2	Too controversial	12	Cost too high	19
3	Lack positive results	9	Lack positive results	18
	Lack confidence in test	9		
	Lack qualified examiners	9		
	Too much resentment	9		

selection criteria and employment duties between the law enforcement, commercial and government sectors may influence the perceived costs and benefits by these users, and it would be premature to generalize the Meesig and Horvath data beyond US law enforcement. Given the size and apparent importance of government screening programs in the US and other countries, uncovering rationales for maintaining the programs would be an informative and useful line of study.

(IN)FAMOUS POLYGRAPH SCREENING CASES

In 1994, CIA Directorate of Operations officer Aldrich Hazen Ames was arrested for selling highly classified information to Russia and the former Soviet Union. Immediately questions began to surface regarding the government's use of the polygraph to uncover treasonous activities in the CIA and elsewhere. According to various writers, Ames had managed to beat the CIA's polygraph, even without help from his Russian handlers (Lykken, 1998; *New York Times*, 24 February 1994, 19 February 1995, 17 September 1996; *Washington Post*, 27 April 1997). From most accounts, it appeared that Ames had managed to escape detection in at least two polygraph screening examinations between the time he began his espionage career and his arrest. This reported failure of polygraph screening buttressed the critics' argument that the polygraph is not an effective tool in this application, and undercut the proponents' claims as to what the polygraph can do.

Whether Ames passed his polygraph testing is seen by some as a crucial issue, since the government polygraph screening programs base their existence on detection of just these types of crimes. In balance, however, what is not known from the public record is how many traitors were uncovered or deterred by the screening polygraph. That is, if the accounts about Ames were true, we only know of one false negative, and as significant to US intelligence as it was, it is, in the final analysis, a single data point. If all, most, or few spies were deterred by or defeated polygraph screening, that would be a factor on which the government could assess the usefulness of the screening tool.

Searching for a test to catch all spies is a fool's errand, analogous in the psychological testing world to developing the perfect IQ test. Neither are achievable. As it happens in the real world, perfection is not the only criterion for using a particular instrument, or no psychological testing tool, including polygraph testing, would be available anywhere. A more relevant question regarding the Ames case is whether his was an anomaly or a representative example of government screening effectiveness.

The polemics surrounding the Ames fiasco have obscured one significant fact. According to very reliable sources, Ames did indeed, register his deception on his polygraph charts. House Intelligence Committee Chairman Representative Dan Glickman announced that the FBI concluded that polygraph tests administered by the CIA in 1986 and 1991 to Ames detected deception in two of his answers (*New York Times*, 10 August 1994). Similarly, then-CIA Director James Woolsey acknowledged that the CIA had failed to follow up on Ames' failure on two polygraph test questions (*New York Times*, 8 March 1994). This information is not provided here to support or refute any statements regarding polygraph screening efficacy, as no single case has that power: it is merely to set the record straight. Two other noteworthy successes for the routine polygraph examination of government employees in recent memory include the Nicholson spy case (*Newsweek*, 2 December 1996), and the Scranage spy case (*Washington Post*, 13 July 1985). Allegedly, others exist (List, 1997; *Tri Valley Herald*, 11 September 1999), but most are not known to the public because of the security classification of the cases. The problem remains that in the shadowy world of intelligence and counterintelligence, obtaining information on how well polygraph screening detects espionage acts and plans is not available for scientific scrutiny outside of government circles, if anywhere.

COUNTERMEASURES

There is sufficient evidence to suggest that an average person who receives countermeasure training from a sophisticated trainer can reduce the likelihood of the detection of their deception dramatically with some strategies (Honts, 1987), though not with all strategies (Timm, 1991). In the past, countermeasure instruction at a level where success was probable might have only been available from foreign governments or a few unscrupulous profit-motivated individuals who had sufficient knowledge of the decision rules used in polygraphy. As Lykken points out, "No good social purpose can be served by inventing ways of beating the lie detector or deceiving polygraphers" (1998:277). Now at least one former polygraph examiner sells a countermeasure instruction book, and more than one scientist critical of polygraphy has gone on record as having provided countermeasure advice to individuals undergoing counterintelligence screening and criminal investigations. In these recent cases, the expressed motivation of the countermeasure instructors was to help defend the innocent against the abuses of the polygraph, and they have gone to considerable effort to carry this message to the public. Details of how they had gone about independently establishing innocence are not found, and such advice from scientists raises non-trivial ethical questions. However, a review of their countermeasure advice is consistent with the lab findings of Honts (1987), and the instructions in the counterculture press (Kalashnikov, 1984; Williams, 1996). Examinees are taught to induce reactions during the presentation of comparison questions[1] while appearing to be cooperative with the examiner, and to refuse to disclose information if the examiner detects the deception or the countermeasure. The proportions of innocent or guilty examinees that elect to practice this strategy are not known. Lykken (1998) and Williams (1996) anecdotally report high success with individuals they have instructed, but there is evidence of increasing awareness among US federal examiners of the methods being taught to defeat them (London and Krapohl, 1999).

The countermeasurer plotting against a screening examination may encounter an additional challenge not found in other types of polygraph testing. For single-issue criminal testing in the field, there is a handful of techniques used, virtually all of which rely on a form of the probable-lie comparison question. Multiple-issue screening formats come in several varieties, and use very different decision rules. Traditional comparison questions might be used by some polygraph testing agencies, but in others they employ concealed comparison questions (those that would appear relevant to an examinee), directed lies, or no comparison questions at all. A combination of these techniques is also used by some agencies. A countermeasure appropriate against one type of screening format may doom an examinee when used on another format. The

[1] Historically, the expression "control question" has been used to denote the probable-lie question commonly used in field practice. In 1999 the American Polygraph Association voted to abandon this terminology in favor of "comparison question," which appears in all published works beginning in 2000. The new terminology is already taught at the US DoD Polygraph Institute, and other polygraph schools.

selection of an anti-polygraph strategy becomes problematic for the would-be countermeasurer unless the test format were known in advance. Lacking this inside knowledge, the examinee would have to learn to identify all likely test formats, predict the decision criteria, and then successfully employ the correct ensemble of countermeasures without being detected. Such a goal is certainly attainable for some individuals, but it would entail substantially more counter-measure training than if the objective were to defeat a known testing technique.

VALIDITY

Though polygraph screening is widely practiced, investigations into its validity have fallen far behind those of criminal testing. The published analog studies suggest that screening examinations work much better than chance (Barland, 1981; Barland *et al.*, 1989; Correa and Adams, 1981; DoDPI, 1995, 1998; Honts and Amato, 1999; Kircher *et al.*, 1998; Reed, 1994), with an average accuracy of about 70% to 80% in the correct classification of truthful and deceptive examinees (Table 7.3). Field research underwritten by the US government, using the Relevant/Irrelevant method in a single session that excluded confir-matory testing, found similar accuracy (Brownlie, 1999). Accuracy is somewhat higher overall when inconclusive outcomes are set apart, and this is the recom-mended method of computation according to the American Society for Testing and Materials in their *Annual Book of ASTM Standards* (1999).

Once the deceptive examinee has been identified, it becomes important to the field practitioner to determine to which of the issues the examinee has been untruthful so that follow-up testing, questioning, or investigative resources can be correctly directed. In the listed research, identification of individual questions to which a deceptive examinee had lied has a range of accuracy much wider than that of the accuracy of classifying examinees as deceptive and non-deceptive. This may be simply a function of the amount of data used to make the decisions; decisions by the examinee include all question presentations on all charts, whereas assessment of the veracity to a given question is restricted to only the presentation of that question and perhaps its comparison question(s). Not surprisingly, the research shows correct classification of veracity by question varies widely, from chance to perfection.

How much practical significance the findings regarding the correct classifi-cation of individual questions have is unclear. In field practice, an indication of deception anywhere in the testing could trigger closer scrutiny of the examinee, with a presumed increased likelihood of uncovering the specific deception. Also, the two-step approach outlined earlier in this chapter is helpful in separat-ing true positives from false positives. Like most questions regarding the validity of polygraph screening, conjecture fills the void awaiting sound research. Those

		Deceptive examinees				Nondeceptive examinees				All
	Format	Correct	Error	Inc	n	Correct	Error	Inc	n	Avg w/o Inc
Analog studies										
Barland (1981)	CIST[1]	50.0%	23.3%	26.7%	30	76.9%	15.3%	7.7%	26	75.8%
Correa and										
Adams (1981)	RI	100.0%	0.0%	0.0%	20	100.0%	0.0%	0.0%	20	100.0%
Honts and Amato (1999)	RI[2]	75.0%	25.0%	0.0%	20	80.0%	20.0%	0.0%	20	77.5%
	RI[3]	66.7%	33.3%	0.0%	20	63.2%	36.8%	0.0%	20	65.0%
Kircher *et al.* (1998)	RI[4]	88.5%	11.5%	0.0%	96	–	–	–	–	88.5%
DoDPI (1995)	TES	77.3%	18.2%	4.5%	22	88.5%	11.5%	0.0%	52	84.7%
	CSP-DLC	36.0%	48.0%	16.0%	25	86.4%	5.1%	8.5%	59	68.6%
	CSP-PLC	50.0%	45.8%	4.2%	24	88.7%	6.5%	4.8%	62	72.7%
DoDPI Research Staff										
(1995)	TES	83.3%	16.7%	0.0%	30	96.2%	1.9%	1.9%	52	90.7%
Barland, *et al.* (1989)	Unreported	30.8%	60.4%	8.8%	91	93.8%	2.7%	3.6%	112	65.5%
	ZCT >1 Issue	66.6%	5.1%	28.2%	39	54.5%	18.2%	27.2%	11	83.9%
	ZCT 1 Issue	81.6%	7.9%	10.5%	38	41.7%	8.3%	50.0%	12	87.3%
	ZCT >1 Issue	75.0%	17.5%	7.5%	80	90.0%	10.0%	0.0%	20	85.5%
Field studies										
Brownlie (1999)	RI	66.4%	25.0%	8.6%	232	76.4%	11.6%	12.0%	501	79.7%

CIST = Counterintelligence Screening Test
CSP = Counterintelligence Scope Polygraph
DLC = Directed Lie Comparison Question
Inc = Inconclusive

PLC = Probable Lie Comparison Question
RI = Relevant/Irrelevant Test
TES = Test for Espionage and Sabotage
ZCT = Zone Comparison Test

1. In this study three different scoring procedures were used. Only the procedure matching that currently in common practice is reported here, though another performed better.
2. Results of the automated condition.
3. Results of the human condition.
4. Deceptive subjects only in this study.

Table 7.3

Studies on the validity of the screening polygraph examination.

who would use these tools are obligated to assess validity, and to demonstrate that utility is not the only concern.

PROBLEMS OF PREVALENCE: THE BASE RATE DILEMMA

The base rate problem is an issue frequently cited by some as a chief reason the polygraph should not be used in large-scale screening applications, such as in the hiring processes of some government agencies. They point out that at very low base rates of deception, most of the individuals identified as deceptive are actually truthful (Ben-Shakhar *et al.*, 1982; Gastwirth, 1987; Lykken, 1998; Murphy, 1987). The following illustrates the argument:

Suppose that the validity of the screening polygraph examination were 80% in the discrimination between truthful and deceptive examinees, with inconclusive outcomes excluded here for the sake of simplicity. Also assume that the base rate of the behavior of interest is low; for example, the rate that foreign agents apply for positions in government which would give them access to national secrets. Since the incidence of foreign attempts to penetrate a government's applicant screening procedures is unknowable, let us accept for ease of computation that the rate is ten foreign agents among 1,000 applicants. If the polygraph were used to test 1,000 applicants, and the polygraph had a demonstrated validity of 80%, a total of 792 truthful (non-spy) applicants would clear the process. Out of the ten spies, eight would be caught, but these spies would be among 198 non-spies who also failed the polygraph examination. If the polygraph had not been used, the error rate would have been 1%, since only the spies would have been errors. With the polygraph, the error rate is 20%, and 99% of those errors were misclassified truthful examinees. Therefore, contend the critics, the polygraph is a poor tool for this task, since it actually lowers accuracy of hiring decisions drastically. This statistical relationship was noted in the classic paper on clinical assessments by Meehl and Rosen (1955), that techniques having moderate validity result in an increase in incorrect decisions over the non-use of the techniques when base rates are extreme.

The base rate argument is compelling. Unless polygraph screening were 100% accurate, a level not even the most ardent proponents suggest, then truthful examinees would always outnumber the deceptive examinees among those called deceptive by the polygraph when base rates are very low. The central question is, how relevant is the argument?

Martin and Terris (1991) re-examined the base rate argument, and had strong reservations when it was applied to the assessment of personnel selection tools. First, it assumes that all applicants would have been hired if the polygraph had not intervened. In most settings, the applicant pool for large organizations typically exceeds the number of positions available. Extending the example above, let's assume that there were 500 positions available for the 1,000 applicants. Therefore, any tool that reduces the proportion of spies to non-spies from the applicant pool increases the odds that a given truthful non-spy would be hired. If eight out of the ten spies were eliminated by the polygraph examination, this would improve the chances collectively for the non-spy group. This relationship holds true so long as the number of available positions is less than the number of applicants. Therefore, any screening tool that discriminates between truthfulness and deception at better than chance works in the favor of the truthful applicant and the employer.

Martin and Terris point out that so long as the screening tool is valid, arguing the false positive rate has no meaning.

> It is simply inappropriate to state that, despite the validity of a selection instrument, the false positive rate may be too high. If the screening procedure is valid, the proportion of false-positive decision errors will increase if the procedure is not used for the selection (p. 486, emphasis in the original).

The significance of the base rate problem changes, however, when one leaves the applicant setting to the use of this tool with employees. Unlike applicants, the employees already occupy the job, and assuming that determinations of deceptions lead to adverse employment actions, the cost of a false positive is significantly higher than for those who are merely seeking to have the job.

One conclusion that might be drawn from Table 7.3 is that, even in the laboratory where the consequences to the examinee of failure are relatively minor, false positives are manifest in most studies. If the laboratory data generalize, they would suggest that very large agencies that use polygraph screening should be virtually awash in examinees called deceptive, both correctly and in error. Such a logical conclusion, however, leads to the second problem with the base rate argument: the evidence.

The largest pool of available polygraph screening data to investigate the consequences of base rates comes from the US Department of Defense (DoD), which conducts thousands of polygraph screening examinations each year on low base rate counterintelligence issues. In the years 1993 through 1998, the DoD administered 61,618 counterintelligence screening polygraph examinations (DoD Polygraph Institute, 1993, 1994, 1995, 1996, 1997, 1998). Of the 61,618 examinations, there were 144 cases where the polygraph decisions were of deceptiveness, and the examinees provided no admissions. Taking the extreme but unlikely position that all of these 144 cases were false positive outcomes and not just non-confessing deceptive examinees, the false positive rate would be 0.0023. A false positive rate of less than 1% is difficult to reconcile with critics' projections, and there is not a shred of real-world evidence to suggest that the base rate hypothesis is made manifest in polygraph screening. As the great scientist Thomas Huxley lamented: "The great tragedy of science – the slaying of a beautiful hypothesis by an ugly fact." So it is, too, for the base rate hypothesis.

If the laboratory studies indicate that errors should be higher, how is it that the data show, at least for false positives, the numbers are not there? In the field there are mechanisms available to mitigate the error rate that are not generally included in laboratory studies. The use of multiple sessions is one such method, whereby examinees found deceptive in one session are afforded another opportunity to be tested. Another factor controlling DoD polygraph errors is the multiple levels of quality control for each examination conducted in the field, reducing the effects of examiner variability. Examiners may also be considering base rate information when opinions are formed. A final important factor is the quality of examiner training that produced these results. Admittedly, these factors may not be uniformly present across the profession, and those not following the US federal model may have different accuracies. However, these and other administrative procedures may serve to reduce false positive errors among US federal examiners from where these statistics were reported.

The fatal shortcoming of the base rate argument is that it in no way addresses the cost of errors. Implicit in the argument is that the cost of a false positive is equal to or greater than the cost of a false negative. While this notion resonates with some, it should be remembered that the cost of an error is dictated by the consequences of the error, not by a fixed proportion of errors of the screening method. As Timm (1991) points out:

> Most people would probably support using different preemployment selection criteria
> for screening soldiers for a position in a nuclear missile silo, where false negatives
> might destroy humanity, as opposed to screening inventors, where false positives might
> result in the loss of many valuable contributions.

Arguments regarding the rates of errors are incomplete when they do not include an analysis of the cost of errors. Some may declare that a cost of 100 false positives is reasonable to catch one spy, while others will just as ardently contend that not a single false positive can be tolerated. Proponents and critics of polygraph screening will reliably point toward a particular end of this spectrum consistent with personal ideology or interests. Consumers of polygraph screening decisions must set a balance that considers the costs attendant to the tool. The level of tolerance for false positives to minimize false negatives, or the reverse, is a value judgment, and not a statistical one. The base rate argument as currently framed gives rise to more confusion than clarity, and contributes very little by itself to the debate.

SUMMARY

Like all tools, the polygraph in itself is neither inherently good nor evil. Sterling examples of both are found in its history, and it is the application of the polygraph and its decisions that dictate its value. Notwithstanding the polygraph's status as a strong performer among personnel screening techniques, it also holds a great potential for abuse when in the hands of the untrained, incompetent, or the unethical. There are promising signs of improved standards and oversight among government programs, but outside of that sphere standards are uneven or absent. Not all jurisdictions have licensing laws that mandate minimum training and performance standards. Only two organizations of size outside of government have any meaningful standards across the profession: the American Polygraph Association and the American Society for Testing and Materials. Neither, however, have legal authority to regulate the practices in the field. Consequently, abuses and errors occur more often than would if the field were regulated by legislation, licensure, and oversight.

There has long existed a profound love–hate relationship for the polygraph in all sectors that utilize it for personnel screening. Users wish to have all that the polygraph delivers without actually using the polygraph. The US government shares this schizophrenic view of polygraphy. While expanding its own use of polygraph screening, it has made polygraph screening one of the most scrutinized of its many functions, with external evaluations taking place in one agency or another almost continually. Government seems always to be seeking a way to avoid polygraph screening, and perhaps would do so, if another tool could be found to perform the same tasks. Alternate technologies have been explored and funded, with no immediate successor on the horizon. Other traditional methods, such as background investigations and reference checks, have been suggested as substitutes, but these have been repeatedly found inadequate alone or in combination for vetting personnel for positions of high trust. Typical of the many investigations into US government use of the polygraph is the report of the US Joint Security Commission (1994), which, after an exhaustive review of the evidence, reported to the Secretary of Defense and the Director of Central Intelligence:

> Despite the controversy, after carefully weighing the pros and cons, the Commission concludes that with appropriate standardization, increased oversight, and training to prevent abuses, the polygraph program should be retained. In the CIA and the NSA, the polygraph has evolved to become the single most important aspect of their employment and personnel security programs. Eliminating its use in these agencies would limit the effectiveness of security, personnel, and medical officers in forming their adjudicative judgments.

Such is the state of polygraph screening; highly valued, hotly contested, and hardly researched. While the former two aspects are unlikely to change, there appears to be little to justify the status of research in this area. The twin goals of future research should be to validate the existing polygraph screening methodologies, and search for the next generation of deception detection technology. Until the time a true "lie detector" is found, the polygraph will likely remain the most useful, and controversial, tool in the personnel screening inventory.

REFERENCES

Annual Book of ASTM Standards (1999) Standard E-1954-98. Standard practice for conduct of research in psychophysiological detection of deception (polygraph), vol 14.02.

Barland, G. H. (1981) Unpublished manuscript.

Barland, G. H. (1988) The polygraph test in the US and elsewhere. In: A. Gale (ed.) *The Polygraph Test; Lies, Truth and Science*, pp. 73–95. Beverly Hills, CA: Sage.

Barland, G. H. (1999) *American Polygraph Association Newsletter*, 32 (3), 16–17.

Barland G. H., Honts, C. R. and Barger, S. D. (1989) *Studies of the Accuracy of Security Screening Polygraph Examinations*. Ft. McClellan, AL: Department of Defense Polygraph Institute.

Ben-Shakhar, G., Lieblich, I. and Bar-Hillel, M. (1982) *Journal of Applied Psychology*, 67, 701–713.

Bledsoe, A. H. (1941) *Police and Peace Officers' Journal*, February, 12.

Brownlie, C. J. (1999) Paper presented at the 34th Annual Seminar of the American Polygraph Association.

Correa, E. J. and Adams, H. E. (1981) *Polygraph*, 10 (3), 143–155.

Department of Defense Polygraph Institute (1993) *Department of Defense Polygraph Program Annual Polygraph Report to Congress*. Ft. McClellan, AL.

Department of Defense Polygraph Institute (1994) *Department of Defense Polygraph Program Annual Polygraph Report to Congress*. Ft. McClellan, AL.

Department of Defense Polygraph Institute (1995) *Psychophysiological Detection of Deception Accuracy Rates Obtained Using the Test for Espionage and Sabotage*, DODPI94-R-0009. Ft. McClellan, AL.

Department of Defense Polygraph Institute (1995) *A Comparison of Psychophysiological Detection of Deception Rates Obtained Using the Counterintelligence Scope Polygraph and the Test for Espionage and Sabotage Question Formats*, DoDPI94-R-0008. Ft. McClellan, AL.

Department of Defense Polygraph Institute (1995) *Department of Defense Polygraph Program Annual Polygraph Report to Congress*. Ft. McClellan, AL.

Department of Defense Polygraph Institute Research Division Staff (1995) *Psychophysiological Detection of Deception Accuracy Rates Obtained Using the Test for Espionage and Sabotage*. Ft. McClellan, AL.

Department of Defense Polygraph Institute (1996) *Department of Defense Polygraph Program Annual Polygraph Report to Congress*. Ft. McClellan, AL.

Department of Defense Polygraph Institute (1997) *Department of Defense Polygraph Program Annual Polygraph Report to Congress*. Ft. McClellan, AL.

Department of Defense Polygraph Institute (1998) *Department of Defense Polygraph Program Annual Polygraph Report to Congress*. Ft. McClellan, AL.

Furedy, J. (1999) Personal communication with author, 17 May 1999.

Gastwirth, J. L. (1987) *Statistical Science*, 2 (3), 213–238.

Honts, C. R. (1987) *Journal of Police Science and Administration*, 15 (3), 204–209.

Honts, C. R. and Amato, S. (1999) *The Automated Polygraph Examination*. Final report to the Central Intelligence Agency. Contract No: 110224-1998-MO.

Joint Security Commission (1994) *Redefining Security*: A report to the Secretary of Defense and Director of Central Intelligence, 28 February 1994.

Indianapolis Star (1984) Department wants FBI to check news service, 24 January 1984.

Kalashnikov, V. (1984) *Beat the Box: The Insider's Guide to Outwitting the Lie Detector*. Deep Cover Press.

Keeler, L. (1931) Lie detector applications. In: Donald C. Dilworth's (ed.) *Silent Witness*. Gaithersburg, MD: International Association of Chiefs of Police.

Kircher, J. C., Woltz, D. J., Bell, B. G. and Bernhardt, P. C. (1998) *Effects of Audiovisual Presentations of Test Questions During Relevant–Irrelevant Polygraph Examinations and New Measures*. Final report to the Central Intelligence Agency.

Linehan, J. G. (1978) *Polygraph*, 7 (3), 233–239.

Linehan, J. G. (1990) *Polygraph*, 19 (2), 131–138.

List, B. E. (1997) *The Utility of Polygraph in Counterintelligence: A Viable Screening and Investigative Tool*. Unpublished manuscript.

Lombroso, C. (1895) *L'Homme Criminel* , 2nd edn. Paris: Felix Alcan.

London, P. S. and Krapohl, D. J. (1999) *Polygraph*, 28 (2), 143–148.

Lykken, D. T. (1981) *A Tremor in the Blood, Uses and Abuses of the Lie Detector*. New York: McGraw-Hill.

Lykken, D. T. (1998) *A Tremor in the Blood, Uses and Abuses of the Lie Detector*. New York: Plenum Trade.

Martin, S. L. and Terris, W. (1991) *Journal of Applied Psychology*, 76 (3), 484–487.

Meehl, P. E. and Rosen, A. (1955) *Psychological Bulletin*, 52 (3), 194–216.

Meesig, R. and Horvath, F. (1995) *Polygraph*, 24 (2), 57–136.

Murphy, K. R. (1987) *Journal of Applied Psychology*, 72 (4), 611–614.

Newsweek (1996) The spy who sold out. Evan Thomas and Gregory L. Vistica, 2 December 1996.

New York Times (1946) Lie detector testing in atom bomb plant. Staff writer, 14 March 1946.

New York Times (1952) Morse denounces lie detector use. Staff writer, 18 January 1952.

New York Times (1994) Essay: Holy Moley. William Safire, 24 February 1994.

New York Times (1994) Spies, lies, averted eyes. Ronald Kessler, 8 March 1994.

New York Times (1994) Polygraph detected lies by Ames, FBI finds. Tim Weiner, 10 August 1994.

New York Times (1995) Lie detectors lie (tell the C.I.A.). Jeff Stein, 19 February 1995.

New York Times (1995) The CIA security blanket. Staff writer, 17 September 1995.

Office of Technology Assessment (1983) *Scientific Validity of Polygraph Testing: A Research Review and Evaluation – A Technical Memorandum*. Washington, D.C.: U.S. Congress, OTA-TM-H-15.

O'Leary, N. (1934) *The Literary Digest*, 118 (14), 22.

Reed, S. (1994) *Psychophysiology*, 31(Suppl. 1), S80, Abstract.

Timm, H. W. (1991) *Journal of Forensic Sciences*, 36 (5), 1521–1535.

Tri Valley Herald (1999) Polygraph specialist joins test debate; Method's reliability remains an issue. Suzanne Pardington, 11 September 1999.

Washington Post (1985) Routine polygraph opened Ghanaian Espionage Probe; CIA employee aroused suspicions. Joe Pichirallo and John Mintz, 13 July 1985.

Washington Post (1997) To tell the truth: the feds rely too heavily on polygraphs. Jeff Stein, 27 April 1997.

Williams, D. (1996) *How to Sting the Polygraph*. Chickasha, Oklahoma: Sting Publications.

CHAPTER 8

POST-CONVICTION SEX OFFENDER TESTING AND THE AMERICAN POLYGRAPH ASSOCIATION

Captain John "Jack" E. Consigli

In the United States today, post-conviction sex offender polygraph testing has become synonymous with community protection from paroled sex offenders. In a survey conducted by Gordon R. Simmons, a Spokane Washington Police Detective, he discovered that 35 states in 1998 were using polygraph testing for monitoring convicted sex offenders. Although in most states mentioned in the survey it was not a statewide program, it was obvious that post-conviction sex offender testing is firmly routed in our country's law enforcement efforts toward community safety.

A BRIEF HISTORY

Post-conviction sex offender polygraph testing had its beginnings in the late 1960s. The idea was conceived by judges, independent and unknown to each other. In 1966, because of high recidivism and insufficient resources for adequate parole supervision, Judge Clarence E. Partee of Illinois utilized polygraphy as an aid in making decisions on probation application.

In 1969, Judge John C. Tuttle developed a similar plan in Washington. Probationers were periodically polygraphed to determine if they were violating the terms of their probation. About the same time, Judge John Cooper of Spokane, Washington, offered polygraph testing to convicted shoplifters as an option to incarceration. Just the threat of the polygraph elicited over 1,400 undetected shoplifting incidents from 60 defendants.

In 1973, Judge John Beaty initiated the first polygraph surveillance program in Oregon. The success of periodic polygraph testing was rapidly being recognized in areas of reducing prison populations and incarceration expenses, assisting supervision by recognizing parolees more predisposed to re-offense, identification and apprehension of re-offenders, community protection, deterrent effect on re-offense, and helping the aversive treatment process by deterring offenders from gratifying their sexual needs in an aberrant manner (Abrams and Abrams, 1993).

In 1973, Dr Stan Abrams, a clinical psychologist and forensic psychophysiologist, initiated the use of the polygraph examination in the state of Oregon on a group of convicted child molesters, who, because of their past record, never would have been placed on probation. These individuals were given the option of being sentenced to prison or probation with periodic polygraph testing (Abrams and Ogard, 1986).

It was soon realized that the polygraph alone was not the complete cure for convicted sex offenders. Sex therapists and parole officers with special training were also needed to monitor the behavior of this segment of our population.

Jackson County, Oregon was one of the first areas of the country to realize that a coalition was essential and made provisions for regular communication among all specialists involved. In the late 1970s, Oregon developed one of the nation's first team approaches to controlling paroled sex offenders. The Jackson County Sex Offender Treatment Program (JCSOTP) is a coalition of parole officers, therapists' and polygraph examiners. This coalition has become a model that most of the nation has adopted: it has become known as the Containment Approach. The elements of this program include:

- Court ordered treatment.
- Long-term, intensive probation supervision.
- Pre-sentence investigations and psychological evaluations.
- Behavioral treatment, with a strong confrontation component.
- Immediate sanctions for program failure or non-compliance.
- Monitoring behavior and treatment through polygraph testing.

RESEARCH

Charles Edson (1991) and Schwartz and Cellini (1995) published papers on the reasons why the examiner should work in partnership with the treatment providers and probation or parole officers. Several recidivism studies were conducted. Dr Stan Abrams and Dr Ernest Ogard reported 71% of a small test group of sex offenders did not re-offend while under polygraph monitoring. In 1991, Charles Edson, a parole officer and sex offender specialist for Medford (Oregon) Department of Correction reported a 95% success rate over a nine-year period. His study consisted of 173 parole/probation cases.

Other studies have been conducted on the benefit to clinicians of the polygraph (Edson, 1991; Emerick and Dutton, 1993) disclosures prior to actual examinations (Blasingame, 1998), granting immunity to facilitate disclosures (Schwartz and Cellini, 1995), polygraph as a method for increasing accountability (Association for the Treatment of Sexual Abuser or ATSA, 1993). Kim English, Research Director for the Colorado Department of Corrections, with a grant from the Center for Sex Offender Management, completed a study in

1999 on "Integration of Polygraph Testing with Adult Sex Offenders." She found the disclosure process (confessions, admissions) as facilitated by the polygraph to be phenomenal.

Other studies have been conducted on the importance of competent examiners by Abrams (1991), Horvath (1977), and Raskin *et al.* (1976). In a paper written by clinical psychologist William G. Allengaugh II, entitled "The Utility of Clinical Polygraph Examination with Convicted Sex Offenders," he also describes the polygraph as an excellent tool for assessing risk. He further stated that "the polygraph is better than Minnesota Multiphasic Personality Inventory for that purpose."

Those of us who conduct post-conviction sex offender testing know that it has been the missing link in preventing recidivism. Intensive parole and group therapy alone do not generate the concerns of detection like the polygraph. Most sex offenders have long histories of victims and concealment. Most are very adept at lying to therapists and parole officers.

With the polygraph, just the knowledge of a pending examination has a profound effect, eliciting numerous disclosures of parole violations. The ability of the examiner to elicit admissions from paroled sex offenders serves a dual purpose. First, by breaking through denial, it aids the therapist in rehabilitation. Second, it alerts both the therapist and parole officers as to where the parolee is in his or her cycle of abuse or re-offense.

THE CYCLE OF ABUSE

The reason the polygraph works so well in curbing further victimization by sex offenders is that sexual abuse is a premeditated offense. The sex offender goes through a cycle, or series of steps prior to offending or re-offending. The examiner, using maintenance/monitoring examinations can help identify where the parolee is in the Cycle of Abuse (Salter, 1995).

The deviant cycle is generally triggered by:

1. an affective stage, such as rage, anxiety, depression or boredom;
2. a chronically disordered sexual arousal pattern, in which the offender is sexually attracted to children or violence; or
3. an antisocial attitude, in which the offender is willing to use anyone or anything for sexual gratification and the fulfilment of his need to have power and control over others.

In all cases, the next step for the offender is to place himself in a situation in which he can gain access to potential victims.

A Seemingly Unimportant Decision (SUD) is an internal lie or an attempt by offenders to convince themselves that the action being taken to place them in a position where they have access to and power over potential victims has nothing to do with sexual aggression. Vocations or avocations, adult relationships, physical proximity and emotional proximity are all ways by which child molesters gain access.

High-Risk Factors would follow in the Cycle of Abuse. They can be broken down into two categories: generic elements and idiosyncratic elements. For a child molester, generic high-risk situations are those that allow offenders access to children – public places such as malls, parks and arcades are generic high-risk situations, as is involvement in the community such as Boy Scouts, Big Brother/Sisters, church youth groups and sports teams. Idiosyncratic elements might include photography, alcohol and drugs, pornography, or specialized hobbies.

Target Selection would be next in the Cycle. This appears to involve two elements – choosing a victim that appeals to the offender, and picking someone the offender believes he can safely victimize.

Planning and Deviant Fantasy usually tends to follow covert behavior and precedes overt behavior. Planning is an integral part of the deviant cycle, although it may occur at different stages of the cycle for offenders who admit they are going to commit an offense, or offenders who lie to themselves about it.

Grooming or Force: the next step in the process is engaging the intended victim and either manipulating or coercing him/her into sexual activity. Those offenders who use coercion against children or adults frequently use more force than necessary to accomplish a specific sexual goal. Grooming appears nearly universal, either in place of or in addition to coercion as a technique for gaining sexual access to children. The establishment of affection and trust occupies a central role in the child molester's interaction with children.

Offense: after all of the preceding parts of the Cycle are complete, the perpe-trator commits the sexual offense. The type of offense is often not static, but changes over time. Sexual offending is frequently a progressive disorder, and offenses grow more intrusive as time goes on.

Maintaining secrecy: to avoid the legal and social consequences of their behavior, sex offenders must keep the child from disclosing the abuse. They maintain secrecy in a variety of ways – threats, promises, bribes – but most commonly by exploiting the child's caring. The manipulation of trust is such a powerful device that offenders frequently see no need to threaten. Remorse or fear usually follows for the offender, then deviant thinking patterns begin the Cycle of Abuse all over again.

The best protection against sexual abuse is understanding this Cycle of Abuse. Knowing where an offender is in the Cycle is critical to therapy and community safety. This is where the well-trained examiner exemplifies the value of the polygraph. By identifying where in the Cycle that offender is, we prevent re-offense. We make known to the therapist where his patient really is in the relapse prevention plan and we "red flag" potential re-offenders to their parole officers. Sexual abuse is not an accident: it doesn't just happen. It is not usually an impulsive act, but a process that requires planning and premeditation. It cannot be cured, but it can be controlled by competent therapists, parole officers and polygraph examiners.

TYPES OF POST-CONVICTION SEX OFFENDER POLYGRAPH (PCSOT) EXAMINATIONS

A critical point in understanding the PCSOT is that the polygraph is a diagnostic tool. The polygraph examinations utility is its ability to obtain information as a separate issue from forming diagnostic opinions that are scientifically valid, reliable and defensible. Eric Holden's definition of a utility examination is clear: "The value of the entire setting, instrument, interviews/interrogation techniques, etc., is to resolve issues, obtain statements and elicit admissions" (Holden, 2000).

There are three types of polygraph tests being conducted in conjunction with sex offender therapy and maintenance: Instant Offense Disclosure Test, Sexual History Disclosure Test, and the Maintenance/Monitoring Test.

The Instant Offense Disclosure Test is used primarily for therapy. It is designed to break through denial of the offense for which the examinee was incarcerated or is on parole. Most sex offender therapists believe that rehabilitation begins only when the sex offender is out of denial. Usually a zone comparison test is used for this purpose. This test is considered one of the most reliable testing formats in the polygraph and is the workhorse of the polygraph profession. For an excellent review of research on validity and reliability of polygraph testing formats, refer to *The Accuracy and Utility of Polygraph Testing* or Norman Ansley's *White Pages* (1983).

Comparison questions are time-barred prior to date of offense. Lie comparisons are the dominant choice among practitioners. It is important to point out that the examinee has already been punished for the crime which you are testing. There is no fear of detection or of punishment, the theoretical underpinning of the polygraph science. Confession results in praise. It is an examination for utility purposes only.

The Sexual History Disclosure Test is again a utility-based examination, designed to break through denial. Instead of concentrating on the offense for which the individual was incarcerated or paroled, it covers all sexual deviancy in the offender's life prior to that conviction. Again, I must point out there is no fear of detection, no fear of punishment, and the effect of confession is praise. There is no fear of punishment because the offender is told only to give a gender and a number to past victims, to protect the offender's Fifth Amendment rights against incrimination. This examination is usually administered while the offender is incarcerated and in therapy. The purpose again is to break through denial and begin rehabilitation. It is usually a zone comparison test on truthfulness to answers given in a full disclosure questionnaire, which the offender works for weeks prior to his examination.

The last type of polygraph examination used most widely in post-conviction sex offender testing is the Maintenance/Monitoring Test. This test is designed to help therapists determine where the offender is in the Cycle of Abuse, by determining whether or not he or she is conforming to a relapse prevention plan. It alerts parole officers to possible violations of parole or actual re-offense. It is this writer's opinion that the Maintenance/Monitoring Test is the most accurate of the three examinations because there is fear of detection and fear of punishment, but much more research is needed to establish its validity and reliability over utility. It is important to note that there are strong concerns among examiners conducting Maintenance/Monitoring Examinations as to the effect of habituation, i.e., testing examinees biannually year after year. It has been recommended that an examiner should not test the same examinee more than three or four times consecutively. Examiners should be rotated periodically.

The Maintenance/Monitoring Testing of paroled sex offenders has created the greatest controversy among polygraph examiners specializing in sex offender testing. This controversy, coupled with a lack of standardization to control this new field resulted in associations being formed to regulate testing. The two most recognized associations specializing in this testing are the National Association of Polygraph Specialists in Sex Offender Testing/Monitoring (NAPS), founded by Jim Morris of Tennessee and Robert Lundell of Oregon, and the Joint Polygraph Committee on Offender Testing (JPCOT) of Texas. This committee's membership includes representation from:

- The Council on Sex Offender Treatment (CSOT).
- The Interagency Advisory Council (IAC) of the CSOT.
- The Texas Polygraph Examiners Board (TPEB).
- The Texas Association of Polygraph Examiners (TAPE).
- The Texas Association of Law Enforcement Polygraph Investigators (TALEPI).
- The Texas Association for Sex Offender Treatment (TASOT).

Both associations recognize the uniqueness of this specialized testing and have made noble efforts to standardize examiner qualifications and testing practices. I am convinced that sex offender testing has had the opportunity to evolve without court intervention because of the hard work and effort of these organizations and others.

The only major difference between the two schools of thought is in comparison question construction. JPCOT teaches time-barred non-current exclusive "lie" comparison questions. NAPS prescribes to the theory of non-exclusive lie and sex comparison questions.

NON-CURRENT EXCLUSIVE/NON-EXCLUSIVE COMPARISON QUESTIONS (MATTE, 1996)

NON-CURRENT EXCLUSIVE COMPARISON QUESTION

This comparison question, also known as the Backster Comparison Question, is formulated to be in the same category of offense or matter as the relevant question or issue. However, this comparison question is separated from the relevant issue with the use of a time bar, thus it is considered an earlier in life or Non-current Exclusive Comparison Question. The comparison question excludes the period in which the crime was committed, usually by at least two years or more.

NON-EXCLUSIVE COMPARISON QUESTION

This comparison question, also known as the Reid Comparison Question, is formulated to be in the same category as the relevant question or issue. However, this comparison question is not separated in time from the relevant issue, nor does it exclude the crime or matter contained in the relevant question. This is an inclusive comparison question but has been named by its employers as a non-exclusive comparison question.

Most research to date has focused on substantiating the validity of Non-Current Exclusive Comparison Question techniques. Some research has been conducted to validate the Non-Exclusive Comparison question technique. In addition to the work of the inventor, John Reid, Dr Frank Horvath of the University of Michigan has published a study entitled "The Utility of Comparison Questions and the Effects of Two Comparison Question Types in Field Polygraph Techniques" (1989). Most recently, at the request of this writer as Chairman of the APA's Research and Development Committee, Dr Tuvya T. Amsel of Israel further substantiated the validity of this technique in a published study, "Exclusive or Non-Exclusive Control/Comparison Question – A Comparative Field Study." Although much more research is needed, it is this examiner's opinion that the Non-Exclusive Lie Comparison Question is most suitable for Maintenance/Monitoring Testing.

THE MASSACHUSETTS EXPERIENCE

As the Officer-in-Charge of the Massachusetts State Police Polygraph Section, I began work with the Department of Parole on a maintenance/monitoring polygraph program for Massachusetts in 1991. In 1996, we started testing some of the state's worst paroled sex offenders in a pilot program, located at the Framingham Parole Office in Massachusetts.

Our program consists of intensive parole by the Massachusetts Parole Department, group therapy from therapists recognized by the Department of Parole, and maintenance monitoring polygraph examinations biannually.

To date, there has not been a single new victimization committed by the 84 offenders in this pilot test program. Our work has led to our Governor signing into law the toughest sex offender legislation in the country. Now, in Massachusetts, anyone convicted of a designated sex offense, whether or not that individual does a day of jail time, he or she is placed on community supervision for life, to include mandatory polygraph testing for up to 15 years.

I use non-exclusive lie comparisons that are pertinent to the parolee. Truthfulness to all questions is emphasized. I advise the examinee that not only will I ask questions about parole violations and re-offense, but I will also be asking general questions about their honesty to ensure that the trust their parole officer or therapist has in them has not been betrayed or violated.

In Massachusetts, as in most states, significant physiological change indicative of deception on questions concerning parole issues does not result in parole revocation, but would warrant increased supervision or therapy. All examinees read and sign a waiver form prior to testing. Miranda Warnings are included on the form. Admissions and/or confessions may result in parole revocation or other sanctions (i.e., increased supervision, electronic monitoring, drug/alcohol screening, increased therapy).

Approximately 30 of the parolees have been re-incarcerated for parole violations detected by polygraph testing and admitted to in subsequent interrogation. As previously stated, no new victimizations have occurred since the program's inception. Parole violations (use of alcohol or drugs, curfew, use of pornography, unsupervised contact with children) are being detected when they occur. The Non-Exclusive Lie Comparison Questions are effective and not overpowering.

With emphasis to the examinees that their truthfulness to all questions is imperative, coupled with subsequent interrogation on indications of deception to both comparisons, as well as relevant, the entire examination is pertinent to the examinee and withstands the threat of habituation from repeated testing.

To the examinees, the examination loses the appearance of a zone comparison test. The use of non-exclusive comparisons also creates an added dilemma for examinees predisposed to attempt countermeasure. Without time bars, even the examinees who read up on countermeasures cannot distinguish a comparison question from a relevant question.

In my opinion (and I am talking specifically about Maintenance/Monitoring Testing), a time-barred control question has a greater probability of being over-powering. It is no secret that most sex offenders have many undetected victims. Any question delving into a period of time other than the maintenance period could trigger fears of detection of other victims. These questions could now take on a life of their own and become overpowering to the examinees with past undetected victims. This would result in examiner errors in determinations of truthfulness to maintenance issue questions.

APA INVOLVEMENT

In 1997, Dr James Earle from Colorado was elected to the APA Board of Directors and established a committee to begin work on post-conviction sex offender testing standards. The committee met for the first time in San Francisco, California in January 1998. The committee discussed examiner training and the expressed differences between the two leading organizations involved: the National Association of Polygraph Specialists in Sex Offender Testing/Monitoring (NAPS) and the Joint Polygraph Committee on Offender Testing (JPCOT). Both organizations recognized the need for national, as opposed to regional, control over this new field of polygraphy due to its unexpected growth.

In 1998, the following Post-Conviction Sex Offender Testing Standards, encompassing American Society for Testing and Materials recommended standards, were ratified by the Board of Directors:

3.10 Post Conviction Polygraph Standards for Sex Offender Testing

3.10.1 The practice of post conviction sex offender testing is a specialized subdiscipline in polygraphy, unique in its application. Practitioners are required to satisfy the provisions set forth in the Standards of Practice for investigative examinations, in addition to those standards below.

3.10.2. Minimum Training
3.10.2.1 A minimum of 40 hours of post conviction specialized instruction, beyond the basic polygraph examiner training course requirements, shall be requisite to those who practice sexual offender testing.

3.10.3 Written examination

3.10.3.1 A Final written examination, approved by the American Polygraph Association (APA) or its designated representative, shall be given subsequent to the approved training. The student must pass this written examination to receive a diploma for the training. The written examination shall be properly controlled and protected to prevent exposure of the test questions or answers to any unauthorized persons.

3.10.4 Instructors Knowledge of the Written Examination Content.

3.10.4.1. The instructors of the approved course shall be informed of the topics areas, along with a pool of possible test questions, for the final written examination. However, those questions specifically selected for any given final examination shall not be made known to the instructors before the administration of the test to the students.

3.10.5 Quality Control Requirements.

3.10.5.1 All polygraph examinations of sexual offenders submitted for quality control shall be recorded in their entirety. Though video recording is preferred medium, audio recording is sufficient to meet this standard.

3.10.6 Testing Facilities.

3.10.6.1 Testing facilities shall support recording equipment, either audio visual or audio.

3.10.7 In-Test Specifications

3.10.7.1 All recorded physiological data shall be retained as part of the examination file as long as required by regulation or law, but for a minimum of one year.

3.10.7.2 Each single-issue examination shall employ a technique and format that has been validated through research.

3.10.7.3 Reasonable departures from validated formats are permissible, to the extent that an independent examiner/reviewer would concur that the employed method was not significantly dissimilar from the format validated in research. Any deviations from validated formats shall be fully explained and justified by the examiner in writing where this test is subjected to an independent quality control.

At the July 1999 Dallas, Texas APA Board Meeting, a Post-Conviction Sex Offender Testing Specialist Sub Directory Membership Classification was ratified. This recognized those members who had attended the APA recommended course of instruction and had passed the certification examination. At the January 2000 Board Meeting in Albuquerque, New Mexico, the following PCSOT standard was adopted:

The distinct roles of polygraph examiners, treatment providers and parole officers cannot be combined without compromising the efficacy of the process. Therefore, it shall be considered unethical for any member of the treatment team to serve as both polygraph examiner and parole officer or treatment provider of the same sex offender.

Standards of practice will evolve to coincide with the needs of this emerging discipline of polygraph.

AMERICAN POLYGRAPH ASSOCIATION PHILOSOPHY

Excerpts from APA President Donald A. Weinstien's address to the Michigan Association of Polygraph Examiners, 31 October 1999:

The leadership of the American Polygraph Association has recognized that the values and mores of certain groups in our society may necessitate specialized approaches in performing polygraph examinations. Sex offenders as a group have unique psychological characteristics which typically have allowed them to prey on defenseless members of society for long periods of time. The diagnosed sex offender is not like the average polygraph examinee, not in the way he thinks, not in his values, not his defense mechanisms, not in the way he deals with stress. We simply can no longer presume that everyone is alike, that chronic sex offenders are just like other offenders, especially with the safety of our communities at stake.

Some have expressed concern about the paucity of research to support the specialized techniques being endorsed for field use. There is much yet to do in this area, and it will take many years to fill the void. The interim, there is advantage in learning from decades of experience of the specialists in psychology who work in this field (and who, similarly, receive specialized training), and from polygraph examiners who have collaborated with them.

The Board and I have taken the position that the quality of education provided by the APA will be second to none. The APA will furnish the tools our examiners need to meet the needs of society.

I do not presume to have all of the answers in dealing with every segment of society that lands on our front porch. Sexual criminals have been with us since the beginning, and no method yet has controlled every offender. The polygraph is only a tool, yet one of the most powerful tools available in the area of credibility assessment. In the face of growing skepticism in the media and the public, it is often overlooked that our discipline uncovers hidden crimes, absolves the innocently accused, helps protect the vulnerable, and serves the cause of justice. It does so several times a day, every day, without fanfare, usually without acknowledgment, in a charged political atmosphere. Polygraphy has survived for nearly 80 years in a difficult environment because the

properly trained practitioners can do what no one else can: verify an examinee's statements. This capability entails a tremendous responsibility, and requires the best skills,
instrumentation and training one can obtain. It is for this reason that I believe we have
taken the proper course of action in making sure that there exists a standard of
training and performance associated with this testing.

I think the above excerpts aptly reflect the position of the entire APA Board of
Directors on post-conviction sex offender testing.

Post-conviction sex offender testing is a new application of the polygraph.
There are no validity studies specific to this application. However, the utility use
of polygraph testing to elicit admissions and break through denial in sex
offenders has demonstrated its necessity.

When used by competent examiners, the polygraph is the single most
important breakthrough for community protection from paroled sex offenders.
There are, however, serious concerns regarding examiners and their competence. Stories have emerged of examiners conducting far too many examinations daily, entering into bidding wars with competing examiners, or advising
examinees not to make admissions in order to increase their client base. Individuals are opening practices without formal training or with questionable back-
grounds, and non-validated testing formats being used. There is a lack of quality
review and no preservation by audio or video of the examination procedures.

The need for a regulatory device is crucial. The Federal Government was not
interested in national regulation of polygraphy; most states were not even interested in the licensing of polygraph examiners in general. This is why the
American Polygraph Association's Board of Directors took the first steps toward
regulation of post-conviction sex offender testing. It would be a significant loss
to community safety if this dynamic new tool was turned into the next national
anti-polygraph legislation.

We have now developed standards of practice, a curriculum for training, recognized competent instructors, and have developed a membership classification for the examiners receiving advanced training and passing a certifying
examination. However, much more work is needed. The APA will continue to
do its part to ensure this testing remains strong and viable.

On 31 July 1999, the APA adopted the following position statement on post-
conviction sex offender testing:

> It is the position of the APA that any examiner who conducts Post Conviction Sex
> Offender Testing must receive the requisite specialized training and demonstrate com-
> petency through written examination. Training must be ongoing and a continuous
> process. All examiners who conduct PCSO testing must move immediately to obtain
> the requisite training and continue to pursue training in this specialized area.

Professionalism is contagious. Our members are complying with our requests. As I have said, the first APA course and certification examination was administered in April 1999. We now have 342 certified examiners in PCSOT. Their competence and integrity is being recognized nationally.

The US Department of Justice's Center for Sex Offender Management has recognized the use of the polygraph and the APA in the management of sex offenders. Under community supervision, in their Community Management of the Sex Offender Executive Summary Order, Draft 11-99, they state:

> The use of the polygraph with sex offenders has shown promising results and is now considered by many to be an essential component in the effective management of sex offenders. The Safer Society currently reports that 35 percent of all treatment programs are utilizing the polygraph as a supervision tool.

One of the most significant challenges associated with using the polygraph as a sex offender supervision tool is that not all states have licensing laws or procedures for post-conviction sex offender testing. When supervising agents or treatment providers identify a polygraph examiner with whom to work, they should inquire about the training that the examiner has received, and more specifically, if the training has been endorsed by the American Polygraph Association. The APA has developed standards for post-conviction polygraph testing of sex offenders and offers a 40-hour block of instruction for polygraph examiners who are interested in working with sex offenders.

In selecting a polygraph examiner who has been trained and certified by the APA to test sex offenders, a treatment provider and a supervision agent must also ensure that the examiner has undergone a comprehensive internship, has conducted a certain number of post-conviction polygraph examinations with sex offenders, and that he or she applies standardized and accepted polygraph examination scoring techniques.

States without licensing are also now developing sex offender testing standards through their own Departments of Parole or Probation and are incorporating APA standards into their own.

Most importantly, recidivism rates of paroled sex offenders monitored by polygraphy is on a decline.

It has been an honor and a privilege to have been a part of this noble effort and to have worked with the dedicated members of this committee. I hope that this overview of post-conviction sex offender testing conveys the need for standardization. The compliance by our membership has exceeded all expectations. National compliance to APA standards by all practicing examiners is needed to ensure our continued success in this effort to protect our children.

REFERENCES

Abrams, S. (1991) Polygraph: A new beginning. *Polygraph*, 20 (3), 204–213.

Abrams, S. and Abrams, J. B. (1993) *Polygraph Testing of the Pedophile.* Oregon: Ryan Gwinner Press.

Abrams, S. and Ogard, E. (1986) Polygraph surveillance of probationers. *Polygraph*, 15, 174–182.

Ansley, N. (1983) *A Review of the Scientific Literature on the Validity, Reliability, and Utility of Polygraph Technqiues* (3rd edn). Fort Meade, MD: National Security Agency.

ATSA (1993) *Sexual Abuse: A Journal of Research and Treatment.* Beaverton, OR: Association for the Treatment of Sexual Abusers.

Blasingame, G. D. (1998) Suggested clinical use of polygraphy in community-based sexual offender treatment programs. *Sexual Abuse: A Journal of Research and Treatment* 10, 37–45.

Edson, C. (1991) *Sex Offender Treatment*. Medford, OR: Department of Corrections.

Emerick, R. and Dutton, W. (1993) The effect of polygraphy on the self-report of adolescent sex offenders: Implications for risk assessment. *Annals of Sex Research* 6, 83–103.

Holden, E. J. (2000) Special issue: Post-conviction sex offender testing. *Polygraph* 29 (1). American Polygraph Association.

Horvath, F. S. (1977) The effect of selected variables on interpretation of polygraph records. *Journal of Applied Psychology* 62, 127–136.

Horvath, F. (1989) The utility of comparison questions and the effects of two comparison question types in field polygraph techniques. *Journal of Police Science and Administration,* 16 (2), 198–209.

Matte, J. (1996) *Forensic Psychophysiology Using the Polygraph*. JAM Publications.

Raskin, D. C., Barland, G. H. and Podlesny, J. A. (1976) Validity and reliability of detection of deception. *Polygraph*, 6 (1), 1–39.

Salter, A. C. (1995) *Transforming Trauma. A Guide to Understanding and Treating Adult Survivors of Child Sexual Abuse*. California: Sage Publications.

Schwartz and Cellini (1995) *The Sex Offender: Corrections, Treatment and Legal Practice*. Kingston, NJ: Civic Research Institute.

Tuvya, T. A. (1999) Exclusive or nonexclusive comparison questions: A comparative field study. *Polygraph*, 28 (4), 273–283.

CHAPTER 9

COUNTERMEASURES

Charles R. Honts and Susan L. Amato

INTRODUCTION

Polygraph countermeasures are anything that a subject might do in an effort to defeat or distort a polygraph examination. Much has been written on the topic of polygraph countermeasures (see reviews by Barland, 1984; Gudjonsson, 1983; Honts, 1987; Lykken, 1998; Office of Technology Assessment, 1983), but relatively little research has been published on the topic. This chapter addresses what is presently known about polygraph countermeasures. Every effort has been made to separate speculation from scientific fact.

For ease of presentation we will follow Honts (1987) and divide countermeasures into two large families, General State (GS) countermeasures and Specific Point (SP) countermeasures. GS countermeasures are intended to alter the general physiological and/or psychological state of the subject for the entire period of the examination. GS countermeasures are not focused on any specific portion of the polygraph examination. The most commonly noted type of GS countermeasure is the use of drugs. SP countermeasures are intended to alter the psychological and/or physiological state of the subject at specific points during the examination. The purpose of SP countermeasures is to either produce a large physiological response that would normally not occur, or would be small, or to inhibit a physiological response that would be large without the intervention of the countermeasure.

REQUIREMENTS FOR A SUCCESSFUL COUNTERMEASURE

The requirements for a successful countermeasure vary with the polygraph technique being employed. With the test most commonly used in forensic practice, the Comparison (control) Question Test (CQT), a countermeasure user faces a formidable problem. The Comparison Question Test requires differential responding between two types of critical stimuli, relevant and comparison questions. Relevant questions are direct accusatory questions that address the matter under investigation. Comparison questions are designed to evoke physiological responses from innocent subjects. They are designed so that they are either assumed lies (probable lie comparison tests) or known lies (directed lie comparison tests). To be successful, a deceptive countermeasure user must produce larger responses to the comparison questions than to the relevant questions. This must be done in the face of relevant questions to which the subject is lying. Moreover, the countermeasures must be implemented in a manner that is not observable to the polygraph examiner either by visual inspection of the subject (sometimes by closed circuit television and/or videotape), or from an analysis of the physiological data.

With the Concealed Knowledge Test (CKT), the potential countermeasure user has more options than with the Comparison Question Tests. In a CKT key items are created from case information. Key items must be memorable pieces of information from the crime that are known to investigators and to the perpetrator of the crime, but not to the general public. Key items are randomly sequenced with at least five foil items that are not accurate details of the crime. The most common way of scoring a CKT is to use the system first described by Lykken (1959). In the Lykken scoring system only the electrodermal response is scored and then only for amplitude. The first item in a series is never scored. The remaining items are rank-ordered from largest to smallest. The largest item is assigned a score of 2, the second-largest item a score of 1, and all the remaining items a score of 0. All of the values for the keys are then summed. If the sum is greater than or equal to the number of keys plus 1, the subject is reported to be knowledgeable.

To be successful against a CKT, a countermeasure user must change their reactivity so that on most of the question series two foils produce larger electrodermal responses than do the key items. Theoretically, countermeasures that affect the general state of the subject could be effective against the CKT. Any countermeasures that inhibited all responding to CKT items could be effective. Similarly any countermeasure that produced maximal responding to all items might also be effective. However, such GS manipulations might cause an examiner to be suspicious, simply because of the dramatic and unusual nature of the subject's general response patterns.

A potentially more successful approach to countermeasure against a CKT might be to attempt to dramatically increase responding to two of the foil items of each series. If the responses to one or two of the foils could be augmented to the point of a larger response than the key, then the test could be beaten.

The third major technique in use within the polygraph profession is the Relevant–Irrelevant test (RI). The RI asks a series of relevant questions interspersed with irrelevant (neutral) questions. Since there are no studies in the published scientific literature demonstrating the validity of the RI test even under ideal conditions (e.g., Horowitz *et al.*, 1997; Horvath, 1988; also see the unpublished study by Barland *et al.*, 1989), it doesn't make much sense to consider countermeasures used against the RI. How do you go about beating an invalid test? Other than in the section on spontaneous countermeasures, the RI will not receive additional mention in this chapter.

SPONTANEOUS COUNTERMEASURE ATTEMPTS

Spontaneous countermeasures are attempts at influencing exam outcome that are conducted without apparent forethought or planning. Although there are some anecdotal reports of spontaneous countermeasure use in the field (e.g., London and Krapohl, 1999; Raskin, 1990), to our knowledge there are no systematic field studies of spontaneous countermeasure use. However, this topic has been examined in laboratory settings. Honts *et al.* (1988) found that although 65% of their guilty subjects reported the use of spontaneous countermeasures, such countermeasures were ineffective. The Honts *et al.* subjects reported using a variety of countermeasures that ranged from vague mental efforts to "control their physiology," to the application of specific point countermeasures such as pressing toes to the floor. Honts *et al.* report that none of the deceptive subjects who used spontaneous countermeasures were able to produce a truthful outcome, nor were inconclusive rates increased. Honts *et al.* also reported that none of the innocent participants made any attempt to utilize countermeasures during their examinations.

Otter *et al.* (1999) replicated the Honts *et al.* (1988) analysis with the RI test in the context of a mock-screening study. With guilty subjects, Otter *et al.* found similar results to Honts *et al.* In the Otter *et al.* study, 77.5% of the guilty subjects attempted one or more spontaneous countermeasures. Statistical analyses revealed no effects for the use of spontaneous countermeasures by deceptive subjects. However, Otter *et al.* also found that 30% of their innocent subjects used one or more spontaneous countermeasures in an effort to help themselves pass the test. Again, statistical analyses failed to reveal any effects of spontaneous countermeasure use.

Honts *et al.* (1999) recently collected spontaneous countermeasure data from a large study of the effect of outside issues on the CQT. Their results extend and amplify those found by Otter *et al.* (1999). In a sample of 192 subjects (96 innocent) Honts *et al.* (1999) found that 82.3% of their guilty subjects and 42.7% of their innocent subjects attempted one or more spontaneous countermeasure. The Honts *et al.* (1999) statistical analyses replicated the earlier findings by failing to reveal any significant effects of spontaneous countermeasures.

In summary, three laboratory studies have examined the effects of sponta-

comparison questions and also informed subjects about the scoring of the CQT. It was make clear to subjects that if they were to pass the test, then they would have to produce larger responses to the comparison than to the relevant questions. Subjects were also given an extensive list of maneuvers they might attempt in an effort to create responses to the comparison questions. The final third (information plus practice) of the subjects in the Rovner *et al.* (1979) study received the "beat the polygraph" information and were then given the chance to practice their chosen countermeasures during a two-chart mock polygraph test conducted by a confederate.

One result of the Rovner study was very clear – information had no effect on the accuracy of the CQT with either innocent or guilty subjects. There was identical accuracy for CQTs with both innocent and guilty subjects who had, and had not, been exposed to the information manipulation. There were effects with the information plus practice manipulation. Information plus practice increased both the false negative and the false positive rates. However, statistical analyses of the numerical scores revealed no significant effects with guilty subjects across the three conditions, but did indicate that numerical scores for innocent subjects in the information plus practice condition were lower than for the other two conditions. Unfortunately, the effects of information plus practice condition are difficult to interpret because they are confounded. Subjects in the information plus practice condition were given two polygraph tests where they could practice their countermeasures while attached to an instrument. Then they were immediately given their actual polygraph examination. Thus, the first question repetition of the actual polygraph examination was in fact the third repetition for the information plus practice subjects. The fact that actual testing immediately followed the practice manipulation raises the possibility that habituation was the active agent rather than practice. Until additional research is conducted to separate the effects of countermeasure practice from those of habituation, the nature of the information plus practice effect in the Rovner *et al.* study will remain ambiguous.

The Rovner *et al.* study provides the only systematic study of the effect of information on the CQT. It has been widely and recently speculated that the dissemination of such information is harmful to the validity of the CQT (Wygant, 1999). However, the Rovner *et al.* study suggests that such concerns are unfounded.

Research on spontaneous countermeasure and on information strongly suggest that they are not serious problems for polygraph validity. However, research that has involved systematic training in countermeasure has sometimes produced different results. Dawson (1980) reported that method actors who used mental imagery as a countermeasure were ineffective in altering polygraph outcomes. However, one possible criticism of the Dawson study is that his subjects were not informed about the nature of the CQT. Thus, they may not have applied their mental imagery countermeasure in an effective manner. Similarly, Kubis (1962) reported no effects for the use of modified yoga (disassociation) on the CKT. However, more recent studies have found significant effects of training in countermeasures.

Honts and his colleagues have reported a systematic series of mock-crime laboratory studies examining the effects of countermeasure training on the CQT. In all of these studies subjects who enacted a mock crime were given hands-on training in the use of one or more countermeasures. Countermeasure subjects were fully informed about the nature of the test they were going to be given and about how it would be scored. They were specifically told how and when to employ their countermeasures. Subjects were then coached in using the countermeasure unobtrusively during a mock presentation of a question list, similar to, but not identical with, the questions they would be given in their actual examination. However, unlike the subjects in the Rovner (1986) study, subjects in the Honts studies were never attached to an instrument during their training. Honts *et al.* (1985) reported two studies of the effects of the physical countermeasures of biting the tongue and/or pressing the toes to the floor during the comparison questions. Although they produced minimal findings in their first experiment, there were significant effects in their second experiment, with 47% of the countermeasure-trained subjects producing false negative outcomes. In a constructive replication of the second Honts *et al.* (1985) experiment, that used a stronger motivational context, Honts *et al.* (1987) reported a 70% false negative rate following training to press the toes and bite the tongue during the comparison questions.

The next study in the Honts countermeasure series (Honts *et al.*, 1994) attempted to determine the underlying nature of the countermeasure effects. There were four countermeasure conditions in Honts *et al.* (1994). Three of those countermeasure conditions replicated physical countermeasure conditions from previous studies. Subjects were instructed to either bite their tongue, press their toes to the floor, or to do both during the comparison questions. Subjects in the fourth countermeasure condition received the same information but were instructed to pick a number larger than 200 and to then count backwards by sevens during the comparison questions. Honts *et al.* (1994) were interested in determining the relative contribution of psychological and physiological reflex factors to the effectiveness of countermeasures. Honts *et al.* (1994) reported that the mental countermeasure produced a significant effect, but that the effect of the mental countermeasure was not as strong as the effects associated with the physical countermeasures. Those results suggest that both psychological and physiological reflex factors contribute to the effectiveness of the countermeasures examined by Honts and his colleagues.

Elaad and Ben-Shakhar (1991) examined the effects of mental dissociation on the CKT. They instructed their subjects to count sheep throughout the polygraph examination. They reported a reduction in the differentiation between key and foil items, but the effect was small. This is not surprising since the manipulation represented a less than optimal strategy for a countermeasure user. Had subjects been instructed to count only on the foil items, their effects might have been much larger.

Honts *et al.* (1996) applied the same techniques and training used by Honts *et al.* (1994) against the CQT, to the CKT. Countermeasure subjects in Honts *et al.* (1996) were instructed to use their countermeasure on two foil items of the test. Honts *et al.* (1996) reported significant effects of both the physical and mental countermeasure, reducing correct detection rates to 10% and 40% respectively.

Honts and Kircher (1995) reported additional analyses of the Honts *et al.* (1996) data by examining the countermeasure detection methods described by Lykken (1960), who reported a countermeasure study of CKT. Lykken's subjects were informed about the nature of the CKT and were told that to beat the CKT they would have to produce responses to the foil items. They were attached to an instrument and were allowed to practice making voluntary physiological responses. Lykken reported a scoring system to detect countermeasures that involved creating a distribution of ranks. Lykken (1960) reported that scoring system to be highly effective and the countermeasures to be highly ineffective against the CKT. Ben-Shakhar and Furedy (1990) make the following statement about the Lykken (1960) scoring system, " . . . the GKT [CKT] can be made immune to such manipulations by adopting sophisticated scoring techniques" (p. 74). Honts and Kircher (1995) demonstrated that nothing could be further from the truth. Not only did the Lykken (1960) scoring system not detect the countermeasures employed in the Honts *et al.* (1996) study, it did a very poor job of detecting the non-countermeasure using knowledgeable subjects. Further examination of the Lykken (1960) manuscript suggests why his distribution analysis gave the illusion of validity; it appears that few of the subjects in Lykken (1960) actually used a countermeasure in an effort to beat the test.

Ben-Shakhar and Dolev (1996) report a study of the effects of a mental countermeasure on the CKT. They informed their countermeasure subjects about the nature of the CKT and told them that to pass the test they would have to produce responses to the foil items. Countermeasure subjects were told to recall an emotional situation from the past during some of the foil items. Some countermeasure subjects were given a practice test and were given feedback on their ability to generate physiological responses by using the countermeasure. Ben-Shakhar and Dolev report that both countermeasure conditions were effective in reducing detection and that the addition of practice did not increase the effectiveness of the countermeasure. However, the effect sizes for countermeasures in this study were much smaller than those reported by Honts *et al.* (1996).

MISINFORMATION

Another possible problem for knowledge-based tests is the influence of misinformation on memory. The effects of misinformation, or information concerning a crime that is incorrect, have been shown to influence an eyewitness's recollection of crime-relevant details in numerous investigations (e.g., Loftus and Hoffman, 1989). Amato and Honts (1999) examined the effects of misinformation on guilty suspects' CKT performance. In their study, guilty suspects were provided with misinformation concerning details of their crime prior to a CKT. Half of the CKT series (three items) represented items that suspects had not received misinformation on, and the remaining three items stemmed from crime-relevant details where suspects were given misinformation. The CKT items associated with the misinformation contained the key (the correct crime-relevant information) and five foils, one of which represented the misinformation provided to the suspects following the crime commission. To determine the effects of misinformation on CKT performance, skin resistance amplitude data were scored using the procedures described by Lykken (1959). Regardless of the success of the misinformation manipulation (i.e., whether or not the guilty suspects demonstrated the misinformation effect on a multiple choice memory test), a majority (54.2%, or 52 of 92 suspects) of guilty suspects were incorrectly classified as truthful utilizing Lykken's scoring procedures. In sum, Amato and Honts (1999) found that the mere *introduction* of misinformation rather than the *effect* of misinformation led to lowered Lykken scores, hence a higher rate of false negative errors on the CKT. A rather rich empirical basis exists examining memory-related factors' influence on the CKT. For example, Waid *et al.* (1981) reported a relationship between memory for CKT items and frequency of detection, with better memory for test items associated with a higher probability of detection. Bradley and Rettinger (1992) investigated whether innocent suspects with crime-relevant information could be found innocent on the CKT. Their findings indicated that although the innocent (but knowledgeable) suspects had CKT scores less indicative of guilt when compared to a guilty suspect group, 50% were misclassified as guilty. Given the findings from the Amato and Honts (1999) investigation into the effects of misinformation on the CKT, memory-related problems and possible countermeasure efforts need further empirical attention, especially within other testing formats. One can hypothesize, however, that memory-related countermeasures would have a much greater impact on knowledge-based tests, such as the CKT, than other testing formats.

POSSIBLE SOLUTIONS TO THE PROBLEMS OF COUNTERMEASURES

There seem to be two possible approaches to solving the problems of counter-measures against detection of deception tests. One approach would be to use counter-countermeasures. That is, the examiner would engage in strategies designed to prevent the subject from using countermeasures in the first place. If you were concerned that the subject was going to press their toes to the floor, the subject's feet could be elevated. If you were concerned that the subject was going to bite their tongue, then you could require that the mouth be held open during the examination. However, it seems likely that as soon as a counter-countermeasure was used, another countermeasure could be developed. The list of preventative measures necessary to thwart all possible countermeasures could and would grow quickly to the absurd. Moreover, it is not clear that there are effective counter-countermeasures that could be used against mental counter-measures.

The second possible approach to the problem would be to develop counter-measure detectors. Research has consistently shown that polygraph examiners are very poor at detecting the use of trained countermeasures, either from observing the subject during the examination or from an examination of the resulting data (Honts and Hodes, 1983; Honts *et al.*, 1985, 1987, 1994).

The use of special instrumental sensors might offer a partial solution. The Stoelting Instrument Company offers a movement detection device with their current Computerized Polygraph System. Unfortunately, we know of no published scientific data exploring the efficacy of this device in detecting the types of countermeasures that have been shown to be effective by Honts and his colleagues. Moreover, such a device would likely be ineffective against mental countermeasures. Honts *et al.* (1987) reported using electromyographic (EMG) recordings to detect countermeasures. They reported some success, but there are serious limitations to this technology. EMG recordings are very specific to the muscle over which the electrodes are placed. The Honts *et al.* studies used optimal placements of the electrodes because they knew beforehand which muscle groups were going to be used by the trained countermeasure subjects. In a field setting, once a trained countermeasure subject knew where the elec-trodes had been placed, they could simply tense muscles that were not being monitored. Again, the number of sensors necessary to cover all of the muscles that might be tensed as a countermeasure rises quickly to the absurd.

A more promising strategy was reported by Honts *et al.* (1994). They used sta-tistical analyses of the physiological data to see if the responses produced by innocent subjects could be discriminated from the physiological responses produced by guilty countermeasure subjects. They reported some success. This increased the detection rate with countermeasure subjects to 78%, a rate comparable with the 75% detection rate of guilty control subjects in that study. Honts *et al.* (1994) note that their subject sample size was small. This means that it is likely that the discriminant analysis they performed overfit their data and overestimated the accuracy rates. Honts *et al.* (1994) call for additional research on this promising approach to the countermeasure problem, but to date no additional research has been published. Possible reasons for this lack of research are explored in the next section.

THE FUTURE OF SCIENTIFIC RESEARCH ON COUNTER-MEASURES?

Currently the prospects for scientific advancements in the area of countermeasure research are bleak in the United States. Research on polygraph countermeasures is resource intensive and expensive to conduct. Such research generally is beyond the resources of academic researchers unless they receive external support. Research funding for detection of deception research in the United States has been centered at the Department of Defense Polygraph Institute (DoDPI). The DoDPI has a policy that all countermeasure research will be classified. As a result, very little research on countermeasures has been conducted in an open environment in the United States since the beginning of the 1990s.[1]

If research is being conducted in the classified environment, then it is of no benefit to the scientific community, nor to the polygraph profession at large. This is a deplorable situation that stifles scientific advancement and limits progress in the profession. Unfortunately, the prospects for any change in DoDPI policy on this matter are minimal. Until a more enlightened attitude is evidenced by DoDPI it is likely that little progress will be made in this area by American scientists. Researchers in other countries are strongly encouraged to continue this important line of research.

[1] The Honts *et al.* (1996) study is an exception. That study was supported by a Minority Access to Research Careers (MARC) grant that was not associated with the US Department of Defense.

REFERENCES

Amato, S. L. and Honts, C. R. (1999) *Misinformation Decreases the Detection of Guilty Knowledge* (submitted for publication).

Barland, G. H. (1984) *Polygraph Countermeasures: The State of the Art in 1984*. Unpublished manuscript.

Barland, G. H., Honts, C. R. and Barger, S. D. (1989) *Studies of the Accuracy of Security Screening Polygraph Examinations*. Fort McClellan, Alabama: Department of Defense Polygraph Institute.

Ben-Shakhar, G. and Dolev, K. (1996) Psychophysiological detection through the guilty knowledge test: Effects of mental countermeasures. *Journal of Applied Psychology*, 81, 273–281.

Ben-Shakhar, G. and Furedy, J. J. (1990) *Theories and Applications in the Detection of Deception: A Psychophysiological and International Perspective*. New York: Springer-Verlag.

Bradley, M. T. and Ainsworth, D. (1984) Alcohol and the psychophysiological detection of deception. *Psychophysiology*, 21, 63–71.

Bradley, M. T. and Rettinger, J. (1992) Awareness of crime-relevant information and the guilty knowledge test. *Journal of Applied Psychology*, 77, 55–59.

Dawson, M. E. (1980) Physiological detection of deception: Measurement of responses to questions and answers during countermeasure maneuvers. *Psychophysiology*, 17, 8–17.

Elaad, E. and Ben-Shakhar, G. (1991) Effects of mental countermeasures on psychophysiological detection in the guilty knowledge test. *International Journal of Psychophysiology*, 11, 99–108.

Gatchel, R. J., Smith, J. E. and Kaplan, N. M. (1984) *The Effect of Propranolol on Polygraphic Detection of Deception*. Unpublished manuscript, Department of Psychiatry, University of Texas Health Science Center.

Gudjonsson, G. H. (1983) Lie detection: Techniques and countermeasures. In: S. M. A. Lloyd-Bostock and B. R. Clifford (eds) *Evaluating Witness Evidence*, pp. 137–155. New York: Wiley.

Honts, C. R. (1987) Interpreting research on countermeasures and the physiological detection of deception. *Journal of Police Science and Administration*, 15, 204–209.

Honts, C. R., Amato, S. and Gordon, A. (1999) *Effects of an Outside Issue on the Validity of the Comparison Question Test*. Manuscript in preparation.

Honts, C. R., Devitt, M. K., Winbush, M. and Kircher, J. C. (1996) Mental and physical countermeasures reduce the accuracy of the concealed knowledge test. *Psychophysiology*, 33, 84–92.

Honts, C. R. and Hodes, R. L. (1983) The detection of physical countermeasures. *Polygraph*, 12, 7–17.

Honts, C. R., Hodes, R. L. and Raskin, D. C. (1985) Effects of physical countermeasures on the physiological detection of deception. *Journal of Applied Psychology*, 70, 177–187.

Honts, C. R. and Kircher, J. C. (1995) *Legends of the Concealed Knowledge Test: Lykken's Distributional Scoring System Fails to Detect Countermeasures*. Paper presented at the meetings of the Society for Psychophysiological Research, Toronto, Canada, October 1995.

Honts, C. R., Raskin, D. C. and Kircher, J. C. (1987) Effects of physical countermeasures and their electromyographic detection during polygraph tests for deception. *Journal of Psychophysiology*, 1, 241–247.

Honts, C. R., Raskin, D. C. and Kircher, J. C. (1994) Mental and physical countermeasures reduce the accuracy of polygraph tests. *Journal of Applied Psychology*, 79, 252–259.

Honts, C. R., Raskin, D. C., Kircher, J. C. and Hodes, R. L. (1988) Effects of spontaneous countermeasures on the physiological detection of deception. *Journal of Police Science and Administration*, 16, 91–94.

Horowitz, S. W., Kircher, J. C., Honts, C. R. and Raskin, D. C. (1997) The role of comparison questions in physiological detection of deception. *Psychophysiology*, 34, 108–115.

Horvath, F. (1988) The utility of control questions and the effects of two control question types in field polygraph techniques. *Journal of Police Science and Administration*, 16, 198–209.

Iacono, W. G., Boisvenu, G. A. and Fleming, J. A. (1984) Effects of diazepam and methylphenidate on the electrodermal detection of guilty knowledge. *Journal of Applied Psychology*, 69, 289–299.

Iacono, W. G., Cerri, A. M., Patrick, C. J. and Fleming, J. A. E. (1992) Use of antianxiety drugs as countermeasures in the detection of guilty knowledge. *Journal of Applied Psychology*, 77, 60–64.

Kubis, J. F. (1962) *Studies in Lie Detection: Computer Feasibility Considerations (Technical Report 62-205)*. U. S. Air Force Systems Command, Contract No. AF 30 (602)-2770, Project No. 5534. New York: Fordham University.

Loftus, E. F. and Hoffman, H. G. (1989). Misinformation and memory: The creation of new memories. *Journal of Experimental Psychology: General,* 118, 100–104.

London, P. S. and Krapohl, D. J. (1999) A case study in PDD countermeasures. *Polygraph*, 28, 143–148.

Lykken, D. T. (1959) The GSR in the detection of guilt. *Journal of Applied Psychology*, 43, 385–388.

Lykken, D. T. (1960) The validity of the guilty knowledge technique: The effects of faking. *Journal of Applied Psychology*, 44, 258–262.

Lykken, D. T. (1998) *A Tremor in the Blood: Uses and Abuses of the Lie Detector*, New York: Plenum.

Office of Technology Assessment (1983) *Scientific Validity of Polygraph Testing: A Research Review and Evaluation – A Technical Memorandum.* Washington, DC: U.S. Congress, OTA-TM-H-15.

Orne, M. T. (1983) Statement before the National Advisory Panel to the Office of Technology Assessment, Washington, DC.

O'Toole, D., Yuille, J. C., Patrick, C. J. and Iacono, W. G. (1994) Alcohol and the physiological detection of deception: Arousal and memory influences. *Psychophysiology*, 31, 253–263.

Otter, K. D., Amato, S. and Honts, C. R. (1999) *Spontaneous Countermeasures During Polygraph Examinations: An Apparent Exercise in Futility*. Paper presented at the Annual Meeting of the Rocky Mountain Psychological Association, Fort Collins Colorado, April 1999.

Raskin, D. C. (1990) Hofmann, hypnosis, and the polygraph. *Utah Bar Journal*, 3(9), 7–10.

Rovner, L. I. (1986) The accuracy of physiological detection of deception for subjects with prior knowledge. *Polygraph*, 15, 1–39.

Rovner, L. I., Raskin, D. C. and Kircher, J. C. (1979) Effects of information and practice on detection of deception. *Psychophysiology*, 16, 197–198.

Waid, W. M., Orne, E. C. and Orne, M. T. (1981) Selective memory for social information, alertness and physiological arousal in the detection of deception. *Journal of Applied Psychology*, 66, 224–232.

Waid, W. M., Orne, E. C., Cook, M. R. and Orne, M. T. (1981) Meprobamate reduces accuracy of physiological detection of deception. *Science*, 212, 71–73.

Wygant, J. R. (1999) *Scientific American* helps liars beat tests. *Polygraph News and Views*, 7(6), 1.

CHAPTER 10

EVENT-RELATED POTENTIALS IN THE DETECTION OF DECEPTION, MALINGERING, AND FALSE MEMORIES

J. Peter Rosenfeld[1]

[1]I am profoundly grateful to the following colleagues, without whose creative participation and ideas this work would not have been possible: Joel Ellwanger, Antoinette Reinhart Miller, Archana Rao, and Matt Soskins.

P300 AND EVENT-RELATED POTENTIALS

An event-related potential (ERP) is a series of peaks and troughs which appears in the electroencephalogram (EEG) in response to occurrence of a discrete event, such as presentation of a stimulus or psychological reaction to a stimulus. The former ERP is called *exogenous* (or an evoked potential), whereas the latter is called an *endogenous* ERP. ERPs are typically recorded from human scalps with standard EEG electrodes and amplifiers. Because the ERP is superimposed on the ongoing EEG, it is often difficult to see an ERP in a single sample. Typically, an eliciting event is repeatedly presented and the resulting ERPs (aligned at the time point of the eliciting event) are averaged to yield the subject's average ERP, in which activity not timelocked to the eliciting event averages out (i.e., to zero), and what remains is the timelocked wave series (see Figure 10.1).

An endogenous ERP which has been extensively studied is the P300 (P3) wave. It is seen in response to rare, meaningful stimuli (often called "oddball"

Figure 10.1

Average ERP responses at scalp sites Fz, Cz, Pz, and EOG, to a subject's name presented with probability = .12, darker curve, and to other names, presented with probability (p) = .88. Note (arrow in Pz waves, lower left) the prominent P300 response in the ERP in response to the rarer, more meaningful stimulus, but absent in the other waveform (positive is down, negative is up in all ERP figures). EOG is electro-oculogram, recording of eye movements whose flatness indicates freedom from eye movement artifacts.

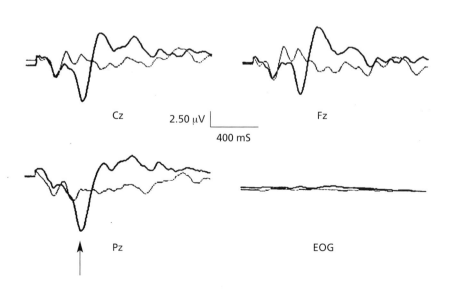

Cz

2.50 μV

400 mS

Fz

Pz

EOG

stimuli; Donchin and Coles, 1988; Johnson, 1988). For example, if a subject is viewing a Bernoulli (random) series of names, one every three seconds, and occasionally one of these is the subject's name, a P3 wave is evoked in response to this rarely presented, recognized, meaningful (autobiographical) stimulus (see Figure 10.1). P3 is a positive-going wave with a scalp amplitude distribution in which it is largest parietally (at Pz) and smallest frontally (Fz), taking intermediate values centrally (Cz). (Fz, Cz, and Pz are scalp sites along the midline of the head.) Its peak has a typical latency of 300–1,000 msec from stimulus onset, and this latency varies with stimulus processing time, which is often determined by stimulus complexity. The size or amplitude of P3 at a given recording site is inversely proportional to the rareness of presentation; in practice, probabilities $\leq .3$ are typically used. The meaningfulness of the stimulus is also influential in determining P3 size.

EARLY STUDIES OF P3 IN DECEPTION DETECTION

[2] Other ERP components have been utilized also, as reviewed by Rosenfeld (1995).

The first published studies to utilize some of these attributes of P3 in detection of deception[2] were those of Rosenfeld and colleagues in the 1980s (e.g., Rosenfeld *et al.*, 1988). In these studies we utilized a guilty knowledge or concealed information test (CIT) paradigm with college student subjects, as follows. We instructed each subject to go to a private room to select an item from a box containing several small items such as a transistor radio, a camera, a wallet, a watch, and so on. The subject was instructed to remove the chosen item and pretend he/she was stealing it. The subject then had EEG electrodes attached and was seated before a display screen. On this screen, every few seconds, the name of an item would appear and elicit an ERP. One of the nine item names repeatedly presented at random was the name of the subject's chosen ("stolen") item. Separate ERP averages were collected by a computer for each of the nine presented items. Visual inspection of the ERPs allowed us to identify one, and only one, average ERP in each subject, which contained a distinct P3 component. Invariably it was the ERP in response to the chosen item. In these studies we also had an "innocent" control group whose members also looked at nine, repeatedly presented items, but none of these was the chosen item. In none of the ten control subjects was a P3 detectable by visual inspection. An analysis of variance (ANOVA) on the group mean P3s showed a significantly larger P3 in the "guilty" than in the "innocent" group (p < .001). No individual diagnostics were done.

Group statistics have no use in the field, and in our follow-up studies of P3 in deception detection (e.g., Johnson and Rosenfeld, 1992), we tried to remedy the lack of individual diagnostics in the 1988 paper. We also used a somewhat different paradigm, one with features of a screening control question test

(CQT), although it still had some CIT-like elements. Specifically, each subject was shown a list of 14 antisocial or illegal acts not untypical of the college student population from which subjects were drawn: "Use false ID," "Cheat on test," "Plagiarize a paper," and so on. As subjects viewed these two- or three-word phrases, their detailed meanings were spelled out on a standard audiotape, e.g., "'USE FALSE ID' means that sometime in the past five years, you used a document to show you were legally old enough to buy alcoholic beverages, when in fact you were not old enough and the document you used was false." From our first use of this paradigm (Rosenfeld et al., 1991), we knew that about 50% of our subject population would be guilty of "USE FALSE ID." The subjects were then wired for EEG recording as they heard and read the stimulus list, and we led them to believe that we were recording their physiology (we were not) as they experienced the stimulus list. This allowed us to execute the subsequent accusation phase of the study in which we told them that, based on the previous "recording" phase, we suspected that they committed act A, but possibly also B, C, or D. Act B or C was always "USE FALSE ID," our relevant question (as in a CQT). Other acts on the list were always acts which we (but not the subjects) knew to have a low probability in the population. We designated B or C (whichever was unused as the relevant question) as the control question. We then seated subjects in the EEG recording chair, activated the computer and recording equipment, and randomly presented nine phrases (from the study list), one at a time, each repeated twelve times. We recorded the ERPs and collected average ERPs for each phrase. Two groups were formed naturally: a guilty group which had used false identification, and an innocent group which had not done so. We determined ground truth (who was really innocent and who guilty) by monitoring a checklist of acts with a concealed, closed circuit TV camera. The checklist was completed by the subject after the ERP recording session, in a room which subjects believed afforded privacy. They were falsely told there would be one final brain wave test after we forced them to re-activate their memories by checking "Yes" or "No" to the items on the list of acts. Finally there was a final bogus recording session. Within each subject, the P3 amplitude (from one scalp site, Pz) to the relevant question was compared to that of the control question, of which all subjects were innocent. To make these comparisons, we utilized various methods, most notably a bootstrap method (detailed later). There were no false positives in the innocent subjects and we correctly diagnosed 77% of the guilty subjects. In an earlier study (Rosenfeld et al., 1991), we obtained similar results, but in that study there was a confound: the TV monitoring and checklist activity were done prior to the real ERP test sessions, allowing the interpretation that enhanced P3s to the relevant question were related to the fact that the relevant stimuli were made meaningful by their having uniquely been checked "Yes," rather than having been acts of which subjects were uniquely guilty. By running the ERP test prior to establishing ground truth, as in our later study, this confound was avoided.

These studies (certain details of which are here omitted for brevity) were designed to be analogs of the specialized version of the CQT used in employee screening. Thus, the questions were general, "Did you do it"-type questions, and key comparisons were between responses to relevants and controls. On the other hand, the control questions were not developed on the basis of an interview, as they frequently are in field CQTs (which is a practice often criticized; e.g., Ben-Shakhar and Furedy, 1990). Our controls were false accusations, and so we were essentially comparing responses to real, correct information with responses to erroneous alternatives. This is a CIT-like element which avoids the typical criticism of the CQT (Ben-Shakhar and Furedy, 1990; Furedy, 1986).

It should also be noted that in addition to these studies just reviewed, there have been other reports of results with P3-based CITs, e.g., Farwell and Donchin (1991) and Allen *et al.* (1992). All this work was reviewed in Rosenfeld (1995) by way of criticizing an earlier review by Bashore and Rapp (1993).

THE SIMULATED MALINGERING PARADIGM

In the mid-1990s, we temporarily turned attention away from criminal and screening models, and began to utilize P3 to detect models of malingerers feigning cognitive deficit subsequent to mild head injury. As much of this work has just been reviewed (Rosenfeld and Ellwanger, 1999), the present review will be brief.

The paradigms we have developed to detect malingered cognitive deficit are closely linked to data from the neuropsychological literature bearing on behavioral signs of malingering (Nies and Sweet, 1994). For one example, there are a small number of malingerers who claim to suffer loss of long-term memories, such as autobiographical memories. It has been a straightforward matter to utilize P3 diagnostically in such situations. Ellwanger *et al.* (1996) tested simulating malingerers stating (under instruction) that they could not recognize their birthdates presented in a Bernoulli series with other dates. This paradigm was very similar to the CIT described previously (Rosenfeld *et al.*, 1988). There were distinct P3 responses uniquely to the rare ($p = .12$) birthday stimuli, but not to the frequent ($p = .88$) other dates in the simulators. Using a bootstrap test, 90% of the individual simulators were correctly detected.

The bootstrap test is utilized to demonstrate that the average P3 to the birthdate is larger than the average P3 to the other dates, despite the fact that the simulating malingerer is manipulated to verbally "mistakenly" misidentify about 50% of all stimuli. The idea is that if the brain signals that it recognizes the autobiographical stimulus (via the P3), the behavioral claim of non-recognition becomes difficult to sustain. One might expect that a simple t-test comparing the average P3 response of the birthdate with that of the response to other dates would be appropriate. The problem with this standard approach is that one would have to determine the average P3 within each compared category by first calculating the P3 response in each single sweep. Single ERP sweeps, as noted above, are very noisy, and we have shown previously (Rosenfeld *et al.*, 1991) that t-tests based on single sweeps are relatively insensitive. The more accurate bootstrap approach works as follows.

Single sweeps are digitally filtered to pass low frequencies; 3 dB point: 4.23 Hz. P3 amplitude recorded at site Pz is used. The main question is whether, within each (lying or feigning) participant, the P3 amplitude is greater in response to a Birthday-oddball than to a frequent other date (Novel item). For each participant, a computer program draws at random *with replacement* a set of N1 (the total number of accepted Birthday-oddball sweeps for that participant) waveforms from the Birthday-oddball set of waveforms, and then averages this sample, and calculates P3 amplitude from this single (bootstrapped) average ERP. The program then draws randomly *with replacement* a set of N2 (the total number of accepted Novel-frequent sweeps for that participant) waveforms from the Novel-frequent set of waveforms, then calculates first an ERP average and then P3 amplitude from that average. The calculated Novel-frequent mean P3 is subtracted from the comparable Birthday-oddball value, and a difference value is obtained to place in a bootstrapped distribution which contains 100 values after 100 iterations of the process described above. In order to state with 95% confidence that Birthday-oddball and Novel-frequent P3s are indeed different, it is required that the value of zero or negative (see below) difference value not appear within 1.65 standard deviations from the mean of the bootstrapped distribution (see review by Wasserman and Bockenholt, 1989). A significantly larger amplitude in response to the Birthday-oddball items than that to the Novel-frequent items is then considered to be an indication of intact ability to recognize such autobiographical information. If this measure contradicts indications from the behavioral responses of the individual (which may give the impression of impairment) then the contradiction provides evidence for deceptive malingering of amnesia with respect to these memory items (Ellwanger *et al.*, 1996; Rosenfeld *et al.*, 1998). Note that the bootstrap approach is based on averages and avoids the problem of having to work with noisy single sweeps.

These bootstrap tests are always one-tailed. The difference values in the distribution are obtained by subtracting Novel from Birthday amplitudes, and a distribution containing only negative values would mean that Novel-frequent > Birthday-oddball in amplitude. (This outcome is the opposite of that signifying deception.) If zero is in the interval (lower end of the distribution is negative), the hypothesis that a larger P3 was elicited by the Birthday-oddball item in that participant is also rejected.

Many malingerers are too clever to deny recognition of basic autobiographical information. For such subjects, one needs a different approach. Thus, the other paradigm we have used to diagnose simulated cognitive deficit with P3 is a matching-to-sample procedure which is based on a similar, commercially available instrument lacking psychophysiological recording. This is basically an entrapment procedure in which an extremely simple test is given. Most normals and non-litigating head injury patients score > 90% correct on this simple test. It was thus suggested by some neuropsychologists that those test-takers scoring < 90% be classified as malingerers. The problem, as we reviewed in Rosenfeld and Ellwanger (1999), is that occasional head injury patients who are not litigating and who are likely doing their best on this test will honestly score well under 90% correct. We thus decided it would be helpful to enhance the simple behavioral test with P3 recording, as follows.

In this P3-based test, a sample three-digit number is presented, then followed a few seconds later with a probe number which either perfectly matches or mismatches (in all three-digit positions) the sample. Each trial consists of one sample followed by one probe. If the probability of a match trial is reduced below .2, a P3 will be evoked by a matching probe, but not by the other probes (mismatches). Using the bootstrap technique described above (in which we compare, within each subject, the P3 amplitude of the response to match with that of the mismatch), we correctly diagnosed up to 70% of the malingering simulators. In a more recently developed version of this approach, each sample was followed by nine probes, one of which was a perfect match. In this version of the procedure, 87% of subjects were correctly diagnosed (Rosenfeld and Ellwanger, 1999; Rosenfeld *et al.*, 1999).

There are various control procedures we have utilized to address problems with the methods just reviewed. For example, if a malingerer is performing at or below 50% correct but his P3 to a match significantly exceeds the P3 to mismatches, then his claim of cognitive deficit is hard to make. However, if he is a clever malingerer, he could reason that he should perform above chance but below 90% correct, e.g., he should perform at about 75% correct. Thus, if his P3 to a match is greater than the P3 to the mismatch, his attorney could argue that 75% is still well below normal, yet does afford some match–mismatch discrimination which could account for the P3 difference. To deal with this problem in one way, we manipulated simulators to score at a dishonest 75% correct and found that their P3s to matches were larger than P3s to matches in a truth-telling group (Rosenfeld *et al.*, 1998). (We had theoretical reasons to expect this, as reviewed in Rosenfeld and Ellwanger, in 1999.) The point is that an attempt to foil the procedure by undershooting a target hit rate will result in a recognizably enhanced P3.

We also created a version of the match-to-sample test which was difficult (Ellwanger *et al.*, 1999). That is, on average, normal, truth-telling subjects doing their best score at a legitimate 75% correct level. (What we did was to use seven- and nine-digit strings with mismatches off in only one digit position.) We did this so as to model honest patients with true deficit secondary to head injury, i.e., patients who might score only 75% on the easy (three-digit) version of the test. In these cases, the match P3 was obliterated. There were good conceptual reasons to expect this effect also (Johnson, 1988, 1993; Rosenfeld and Ellwanger, 1999). The point is that a genuine 75% hit rate is characterized by an absent P3, whereas a malingered 75% rate is characterized by an enhanced P3, relative to a normal subject telling the truth.

Finally, in connection with control procedures for autobiographical oddball paradigms, we ran a study (Ellwanger *et al.*, 1999) in which we tested subjects using the experimenter's name as the oddball stimulus. Some subjects legitimately forgot it; others remembered, but were manipulated to simulate forgetting. The real forgetters showed no P3s, the simulators showed large P3s. We conclude that P3 amplitude is a reliable sign of recognition or the lack thereof despite deceptive verbal behavior.

P3 PROFILE AS A NOVEL DEPENDENT INDEX

To this point, I have considered the amplitude of P3 as an index of recognition in various paradigms. The amplitude has been typically measured in these studies, at one scalp site, Pz, where P3 is usually maximum. I also stated above that P3 amplitude is typically largest parietally (Pz) and the smallest frontally (Fz). However there are many ways that such a distribution may be achieved (see Figure 10.2). Moreover, there are circumstances which can alter even the basic pattern of Pz > Cz > Fz. Johnson (1988, 1993) has given elegant theoretical accounts of the significance of varying scalp profiles in which he emphasizes that each particular profile represents a unique pattern of activation of P3 neurogenerating neurons associated with a particular psychological state or task. Thus, if two tasks or conditions, within or between subjects, produce differing amplitude distributions (or profiles), one may infer that differentially located groups of P3-neurogenerating neurons are involved by the two conditions. Although there are other explanations for differing profiles (e.g., Donchin *et al.*, 1997), all are consistent in assuming that differing profiles in two states mean that the brain is working differently in the two states. The profiles are actually scaled scalp distributions, the scaling being necessary to guarantee that the scaled amplitude profiles are orthogonal to simple amplitude differences (McCarthy and Wood, 1985; Johnson, 1988, 1993). The typical familiar statistical method of showing that two group profiles differ at the same three sites is to do a 2 (groups) × 3 (sites) ANOVA on the scaled amplitudes and show a significant group-by-site interaction.

Figure 10.2

Hypothetical plot o
P3 amplitude at 3
sites under 5 differ
conditions. In all c
Pz (site 3) > Cz (si
Fz (site 3), yet not c
curves are parallel.

Erratum

The Publisher apologises for the error on page 272 where an incorrect figure has been printed for Figure 10. 2. The correct Figure 10.2 is shown below:

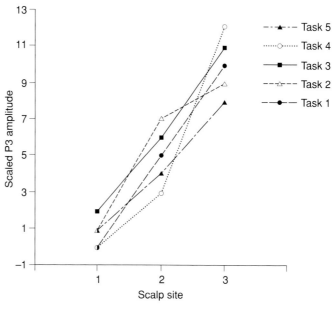

Site 1 = Fz, Site 2 = Cz, Site 3 = Pz

possible stimulus–responses combinations: Match stimulus and Match response (Mat–Mat); Mismatch stimulus and Mismatch response (Mis–Mis). For the L-subjects there were two additional possible combinations, Mat–Mis and Mis–Mat on dishonest trials. One major finding was that a comparison of T and L subjects' scaled P3 amplitudes as a function of site (Fz, Pz, Cz) and stimulus type (regardless of response) yielded a significant group-by-site interaction, meaning that the P3 profiles of the truth group differed from those of the liar group. This is seen in Figure 10.3 where both the Mat and especially the Mis profiles of the liar group (called "malinger" in the figure) show a quadratic component, whereas the T-profiles appear more linear (or, as we jest in the lab , "liars are crooked").

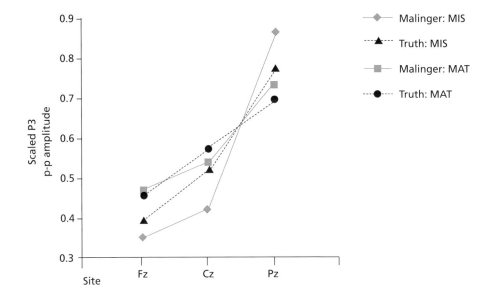

Figure 10.3

Scaled P3 amplitude distributions for truth and liar (called "MALINGER" in figure) groups associated with the four stimulus–response combinations shown.

The other major finding of this study is seen in Figure 10.4. There, the four scaled P3 profiles associated with all four stimulus–response combinations in the liar group are shown. What is noteworthy is that within just the liars, regardless of the stimulus type, the profiles superimpose, suggesting a deception-specific profile. In the truthtellers, the two corresponding profiles clearly differ, as they should, since the brain probably does process matches differently than mismatches and thus the associated neurogenerator sets recruited by the two kinds of processing should be different. However, engaging in deception appears to swamp out these effects, as just noted. (All the results just presented were statistically confirmed.) As we will see, however, in other experiments, this swamping out does not happen.

As the results just described were being collected, we were prompted to re-analyze profile data from some older published studies in which we had the profile data set but analyzed it only for simple amplitude and latency effects at one site only. One study utilized the autobiographical oddball paradigm with subjects' birthdates as oddballs. The other study utilized the original match-to-sample paradigm with one test probe per sample. In each study, there were two

Figure 10.4

Computer calculated, scaled P300 amplitudes as a function of site within liar group during four types of stimulus–response combination: match-truthful (MAT-MAT) match-deceptive (MAT-MIS), mismatch-truthful (MIS-MIS), and mismatch-deceptive (MIS-MAT). Note the superimposability of deceptive responses, regardless of stimulus

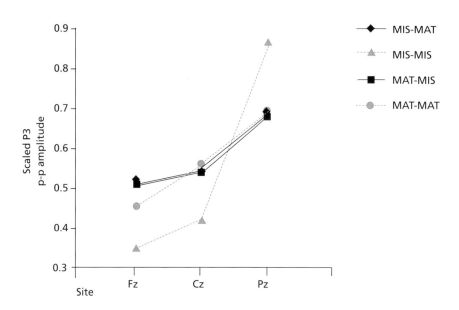

Figure 10.5

Scaled P3 condition mean amplitudes at three sites from two experiments, the "Birthday" (autobiographical) study and the "FCP" (match-to-sample or forced choice procedure) study for liar ("malinger") and truth-telling conditions in both studies. Only responses to oddballs and matches are shown.

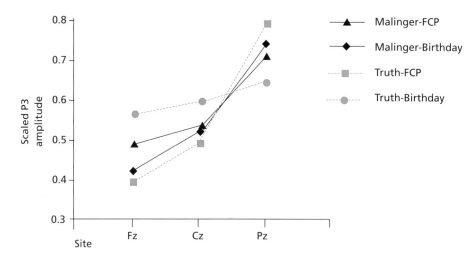

conditions: a truth-telling condition and a lie condition in which subjects were instructed to lie on about 50% of the trials. It is well worth noting that these studies were done two years apart by two experimenters on two sets of subjects. The key results (from Rosenfeld *et al.*, 1998) are seen in Figure 10.5.

What are shown are scaled P3 profiles from Fz, Cz, Pz for the liars and truth tellers in both experiments. If one looks only at the truth conditions, there is a clear interaction (statistically confirmed) between the autobiographical and match-to-sample studies. This was quite expectable since the two paradigms have obvious differences, requiring differential cognitive processes which should activate differentially located sets of neurogenerator neurons, a situation resulting (see above) in differing scalp profiles. In contrast, the profiles from the two paradigms in the lie conditions yielded no significant interaction and are indeed virtually superimposed between Cz and Pz. Again, there seemed to be a deception-specific profile which seems to swamp out other influences which can express their effects in truth-tellers. This is comparable to the situation in Figure10.4, discussed above.

In another study (Miller, 1999a) using an autobiographical paradigm, two groups of subjects, truthtellers (T) and liars (L), were run in two blocks each. In the first, the autobiographical oddball stimulus was the subject's phone number, and all subjects were instructed to respond truthfully. In the second block, where the oddball was the birthdate, the T-subjects responded truthfully, whereas the L-group lied on 50% of the trials. Figure 10.6 below (from Miller, 1999a) shows that only liars ("malingerers" in the figure) have a P3 profile which differs from the others (all truth-telling blocks), an effect which was statistically supported.

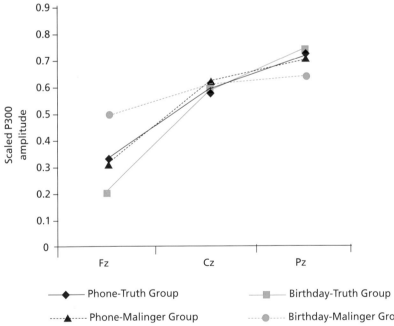

Figure 10.6

Scaled group mean P3 amplitude as a function of site in two trial blocks: the first ("Phone") where both liars (called "malinger") and truth-telling subjects told the truth, and the second ("Birthday") where liars lied and truth-tellers continued to tell the truth. Only responses to autobiographical oddballs are shown. (From Miller, 1999a.)

When the lie and truth response trials are separately plotted for the L-group as in Figure 10.7, however (from Miller 1999a), no interaction appears nor is found statistically. Again, it appeared that the deceptive mind-set carries over in truth-telling trials, swamping out the effect of the specific behavioral response.

Figure 10.7

Scaled mean P3 amplitudes in the liar group, second ("Birthday") block on trials in which they told the truth ("yes") and on trials in which they lied ("no"). Only responses to oddballs are shown. (From Miller, 1999a.)

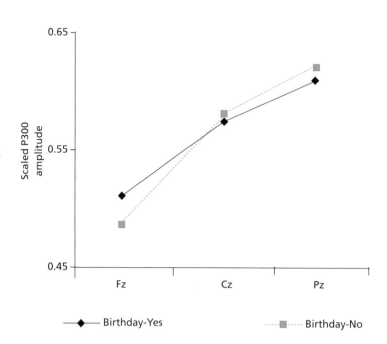

These kinds of datasets generate hope that a specific lie response (a deception-specific profile) can be found. Unfortunately, things are not so simple. Another study (Miller, 1999b) used exactly the same methods as the one just described, with the following differences:

1. There were two groups, both of which told the truth in Block 1 but lied in Block 2. These two groups were selected to be either high or low in psychopathic attributes.
2. Seven scalp sites were used (F3, F4, Fz, Cz, P3, P4, Pz) instead of the usual midline three used in other studies heretofore described.
3. A different experimenter ran the subjects.

The profile results, to the extent that they are comparable, were opposite to what was obtained in Miller (1999a). Figure 10.8, which is somewhat comparable with Figure 10.6, shows no interactions (and none were statistically detected); the subjects' profiles did not differ between deceptive and truth-telling blocks (regardless of high or low psychopathy, a variable which had no effects on scaled P3 profile in these studies, as the figure shows).

On the other hand, Figure 10.9 shows a statistically confirmed interaction between deceptive versus honest response trials and scalp site. Here, for the first time it has been noted in this review, within one block, deceptive profiles differed from truthful profiles in the same subjects. (Again, psychopathy level had no effect.) Why then were there no interactions in Figure 10.8? Perhaps

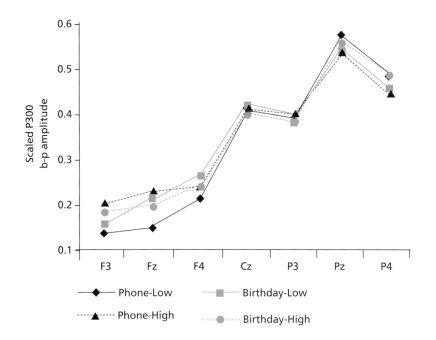

Figure 10.8

Scaled group mean P3 profiles for first block ("Phone") and second block ("Birthday") in response to autobiographical oddball stimuli in "Low" and "High" psychopathy groups, both lying, as a function of scalp site. No interactions with site are apparent. (From Miller, 1999b.)

because the truth trials diluted the effect of deception. Why this occurred in Miller (1999b) but not Miller (1999a) is not clear, but probably relates to the differences between the two studies listed above. The point is that profile effects are likely influenced by many cognitive and emotional variables in addition to deception, and any putative profile-based specific lie responses found in the future may not generalize beyond the paradigm utilized. (More evidence on this point will be presented shortly. We wish to first note here parenthetically that using specialized bootstrap tests on amplitudes only at Pz, as in our earlier studies, 100% of the low psychopathy individuals were detected (12/12) and 92% (12/13) of the high psychopathy individuals were detected during deception blocks. There was no difference, statistically, between these proportions.)

There are other inconsistencies across our studies which temper expectations of finding a generalized specific lie response. For one thing, it can be seen in this review that liars in some figures have upward concavities in profiles, whereas in other figures the concavities are downward. Associated with these effects, is another inconsistency. In the scaled profiles of Rosenfeld *et al.* (1998) (autobiographical study, Figure 10.5) the scaled truth condition Fz oddball value was greater than the comparable value in the liar group. In contrast, in Figure 10.6 above, the liar group's lie block profile shows an enhanced Fz value in comparison with the truthful profiles. In the match-to-sample paradigm of Rosenfeld *et al.* (1998, Figure 10.5) the same pattern is seen. These contrasts (all based on standard base-to-peak measurement of P3[3]) could be related to

[3] In many of our earliest studies, we used a peak-to-peak method of P300 determination. We still think it best for diagnostic bootstrap tests of simple amplitude at one site. However, in profile work, for both theoretical and empirical reasons, we use the standard base-to-peak index, although in one of our earliest studies (cited here as Rosenfeld *et al.*, 1999) we used both methods, and Figure 10.4 here is based on peak-to-peak values. The comparisons made across studies in this paper, with the exception of Rosenfeld *et al.* (1999), all used the base-to-peak method.

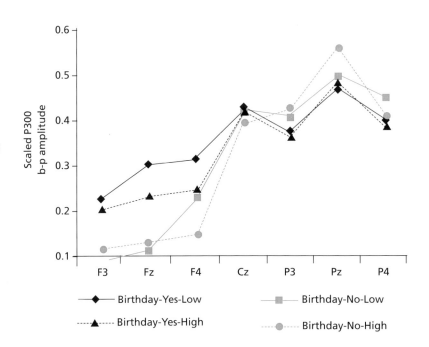

Figure 10.9

Data as in Figure 10.7, Birthday block only, but sorted by response type (honest = "yes" and dishonest = "no"). The dishonest and honest response curves are not parallel for both high and low psychopathy groups. (From Miller, 1999b.)

paradigm and experimenter differences, to slight changes in instructions to subjects, to between versus within group comparisons, and so on. They reinforce the point that deceptive profile effects will probably not be straightforward, but will be complex, interacting with other paradigm-elicited cognitive and emotional variables, and thus will require much tuning before they can be made field-ready. However it must be emphasized that in several studies to date, we do consistently find differences between liar and truth-teller profiles. This suggests that once paradigms are standardized, the basic method may be utilized in the field. The next study to be described (the last in this section) also failed to find swamping effects (Figure 10.10) and like Miller (1999b, Figure 10.6) illustrates that only liars when they lie produce an aberrant profile. The study was also undertaken for more theoretical reasons, however.

The aim of Rosenfeld *et al.* (submitted) was mostly theoretical. For practical detection of deception, it does not matter why the truth-teller profile is different from that of the liar. This difference *may* relate to a specific deception signature in the P3 profile, but it need not have to be so. It may well be that the previously described truth-teller profiles differ from associated liar profiles for the simple reason that our deception instructions place a greater task demand on the liar, who must try to track a random appearing, target lie rate of 50% and thus decide on (or just prior to) each trial whether or not to lie. In contrast, the truth-tellers have none of this work to do, they simply tell the truth. This probably accounts for our typical finding that simple unscaled P3 amplitude is typically greater in the truth-teller than in the liar. Doing multiple tasks along

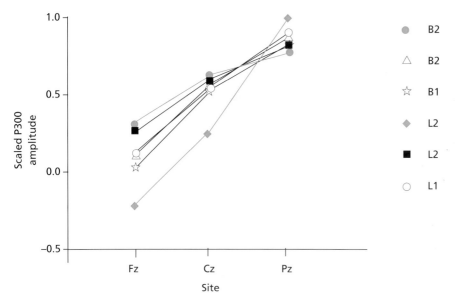

Figure 10.10
Scaled P3 amplitude as a function of site in control (B1, B2) and liar groups (L1, L2) in response to autobiographical oddball stimuli. The numbers indicate first (B1, L1) or second (B2, L2) blocks. The filled symbols are for dishonest responses in the liar group (L2) or honest responses repeated backwards in the control group (B2). Unfilled symbols are for both groups on honest, forwards-repeating trials. It is seen that only liars, when they lie, produce an aberrant profile (filled diamonds).

with an oddball-P3 task typically reduces P3 amplitude (Kramer *et al.*, 1987). Of course the scaled P3 profile is independent of simple amplitude effects; that is the point of scaling, so truth-teller/liar scaled profile differences are not necessarily related to simple amplitude effects.

In Rosenfeld *et al.* (submitted), we tried to create a control task in which no deception would be occurring, but in which control subjects would have task demands approximating those of liar subjects. Again we used a paradigm similar to that in Miller (1999a,b) with two blocks of trials: a truth-telling block for all subjects, followed by a second block in which liars were told to lie on about half the trials to both rare autobiographical and frequent non-autobiographical stimuli. The control group, on the second block, was instructed to respond truthfully, but to then repeat aloud backwards about half the stimuli (a random half). To equalize the speaking aloud demand, the liars were told to repeat aloud all stimuli normally (forwards) after giving the "Yes" or "No" response (birthdate or not). Figure 10.10 shows scaled profile results for oddball (autobiographical) stimuli in both blocks, for both groups, and for both response types (yes/no) in each of the groups. What is dramatically apparent is the fact that all profiles seem alike except that of liars on the second block during lie trials, and this visual impression was statistically confirmed. This result supports the existence of a specific lie response, at least in this paradigm, and suggests in two ways that the difference between the lie profile and the other profiles is *not* simply a matter of difference in task demand.

1. The truth-telling, control group was designed to have equivalent task demands but had a different profile than that of the liars;
2. Within the liar group in the second block, there is a different profile associated with lie and truth trials.

It is clear that within the liar group, task demand must be constant from trial to trial. One could argue that the difference between results with the control group and those of the liar group was due to the difference in cognitive processing elicited by the two tasks (backwards repetition versus deception). This is not consistent, however, with the similarity (Figure 10.10) of forwards and backwards response profiles in the control group on the second (test) block. In any case, however, the second point just noted provides incontrovertable evidence that task demand is not the source of the difference between liars lying and liars telling the truth all within their second block.

This dramatic difference between the profiles of the liars lying versus liars on truth-telling trials is quite consistent with the results of Miller (1999b). In that study also, there is no swamping on truth trials of effects of the liar mindset on lie trials within the second (test) block. These results suggest a specific lie response at least within the paradigm. However, as noted above, we do not routinely obtain this result. The swamping by deception effects across experiments and paradigms (Rosenfeld et al., 1998) noted above, is not the same process, it must be recalled, as the (lack of) swamping across trials within a time block. The latter did occur in Miller (1999a), a comparable autobiographical oddball paradigm (unlike Rosenfeld et al., 1999, Figure 10.4, which used a nine-probe, match-to-sample paradigm). We don't know what the within block response type effect was in the also comparable autobiographical paradigm of Rosenfeld et al. (1998), because at that time we lacked the software to obtain it. Thus there are three studies in which the liar groups are comparable: Miller (1999a), Rosenfeld et al. (submitted) and Miller (1999b). Of these three, the latter two show distinct (lie versus truth-telling) response type distributions supporting the notion of specific lie profiles within a paradigm.

It must be emphasized that most of the studies reviewed in this section utilized just three scalp sites, an electrode density which is low by today's standards where 20–30 leads are common and 64–256 electrode studies are becoming less unusual. I am of the view that as our electrode density increases (we are presently recording from 30 channels), greater profile specificities will be seen. In this connection, it should be recalled that in Miller (1999a) which did not find response specificities, only three sites were utilized, but in Miller (1999b) which used seven electrodes, the response specificities were obtained. It will be recalled that these two studies were otherwise very similar, paradigmatically.

One issue we have not yet addressed with regard to profile analysis is the matter of intraindividual diagnostics. The bootstrapping methods described above are obviously not appropriate for profile comparisons, as they involve amplitude comparisons at one site. At the time of writing of this chapter, we are in the process of developing such methods for multi-site profiles. Since we do not now know which will work, and which will not, we will refrain from presenting our as yet untried diagnostic algorithms.

FALSE MEMORY STUDIES

False memory refers to honestly believed recall of events which did not happen (Miller, 1999c). This is clearly a highly topical subject in the United States, where it has involved claims made by psychiatric outpatients of childhood abuse (Loftus, 1997; Loftus and Pickrel, 1995). The claims have been typically stimulated by apparent retrieval of memories in the course of psychotherapy. Some of these claims turn out to be true, but many have been later recanted as in error. When the claims turn out to be false, great and irreparable damage can be done to those wrongly accused. When the claim is malingered (i.e., the claimant knows full well of the innocence of the accused) damage to accusees is criminal. It is also likely that some honestly believed memories are never recanted although they are false. In this case, there is no remedy for falsely accused innocents. In any of these situations, it would be well to have an objective method of discriminating real and false memories of whatever subtype.

Honestly believed false memories have been modeled in the laboratory utilizing a method developed by Deese (1959) and Roediger and McDermott (1995). In this paradigm, a subject studies a list of words (*OLD* words) which are all associated with a word (*LURE*) which is *not* presented in the study session. For example, a subject might study words such as stars, bed, dream, pajamas, darkness and so on, all associates of the word *night* which is not presented for study. In a test session following the study session, the subject is tested on *OLD* words, *LURE* words, and *NEW* words, which are words which were not presented in the study session and which are not associatively related to *OLD* words (as the *LURE* words are). The subject's task is to signal "OLD" if he/she recognizes the word. Otherwise, the response is to be "NEW." There is much evidence (reviewed by Miller, 1999c) that subjects will genuinely believe that they recognize 50–80% of the *LURE*s, as they do for 99% of the *OLD*s. (Recognized *LURE*s are here referred to as *LURES-OLD*. Correctly rejected *LURE*s are called *LURES-NEW*.)

Miller (1999c) utilized a variant of this paradigm in our lab in which the probability of *LURE*s and *OLD*s in the test session was .15 each, leaving the probability of *NEW* words at .7. Miller recorded ERPs during word presentation in the test session and expected that rare *OLD* and *LURE* words would evoke the P3. We further expected that the P3 scaled profiles would differ between *OLD* and *LURE* trials as it seemed that the brain would process these two stimulus types in a different manner, and thus we would have a physiological means of distinguishing real and false memories.

We were disappointed: Figure 10.11 shows that *OLD* and *LURE-OLD* scaled profiles at seven scalp locations seem to superimpose, and indeed no word-type-by-site interaction was found. (Figure 10.11 shows peak-to-peak values. However, no word-type-by-site interaction was found with base-peak values, either.) Similarly, P3s evoked by *NEW* and *LURE-NEW* had overlapping distributions.

Figure 10.11

Mean scaled P300 amplitudes in response to Old, Lure-Old, Lure-New, and New words. (From Miller, 1999c.)

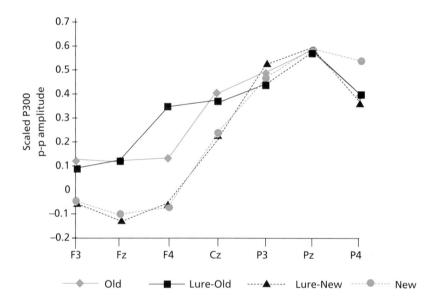

When we combined *OLD* and *LURE-OLD* distributions, and also combined *NEW* and *LURE-NEW* profiles, we did obtain a significant response type ("OLD" or "NEW") by site interaction, meaning that the cognitive process leading to the differing responses involve differing neurogenerator sets. However, we were still left without a way of distinguishing real and false memories – until we looked at the P3 latencies (times from stimulus presentation to P3 peak). Figure 10.12 (from Miller, 1999c) shows, remarkably, that the *LURE-OLD* latency is dramatically less than the *OLD* latency (P < .03). This result had important implications, and so the experiment was entirely replicated by another experimenter on another group of subjects. The results also largely replicated, in particular, the latency results (p < .006). The possible reason for this effect (and the fact that the *LURE-OLD* latency is the shortest seen in Figure 10.12) is well described by Miller (1999c), and space limitations prevent re-stating Miller's hypothesis

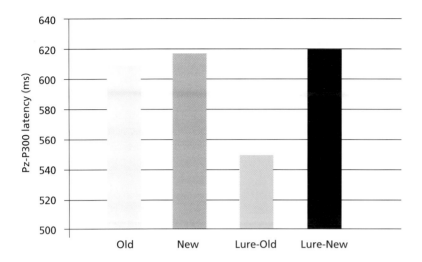

Figure 10.12
Mean P300 latencies at
site Pz in response to
words as in Figure 10.11.
(From Miller 1999c.)

here. The significance of the results on latency is that they suggest that P3 latency is a correlate of the brain's *unconscious* recognition of false memory, even as the subjects genuinely and strongly believe in their memory illusions. There is the further implication that we may, in P3 latency, have after all a potentially practical means of distinguishing real and false memory.

The main obstacle in the way of realizing this goal is the difficulty of doing a diagnostic analysis of P3 latency within an individual. This is because of the variability of latency over trials. The bootstrapping technique used within individuals as described above for use with P3 amplitude has been tried also with latency in these false memory studies and has a sensitivity just greater than .5, which is unacceptable. The problem is that calculating a P3 latency in a bootstrapped ERP average will frequently involve a P3 wave which is very broad, due to the smearing of P3 waves of differing latencies over trials. Alternatively, there will be two or three peaks in the bootstrapped average ERP in the time window in which we search for P3. Our current algorithm for selecting latency cannot accurately determine P3 latency in these cases. It simply looks for the maximum positive peak in a window usually extending from 300 to 1,500 ms. If there is a broad peak or multiple peaks, two findings often seen in this false memory paradigm, the algorithm may select a non-representative latency. We are currently working on new algorithms for latency diagnostics within individuals.

SUMMARY

Based on several studies, I believe that the P3 component of the ERP, which is clearly related to cognitive processes, has great potential in detection of deception. Its amplitude, profile, and latency have all been seen to correlate with deception-related phenomena. As of this writing, however, there is a great deal of work to be done in paradigm development and selection, which will depend on the needs of potential users, and in tuning of intraindividual analysis methods, particularly for profile and latency.

REFERENCES

Allen, J., Iacono, W. G. and Danielson, K. D. (1992) The identification of concealed memories using the event-related potential and implicit behavioral measures: A methodology for prediction in the face of individual differences. *Psychophysiology,* 29, 504–522.

Bashore, T. T. and Rapp, P. E. (1993) Are there alternatives to traditional polygraph procedures? *Psychological Bulletin,* 113, 3–22.

Ben-Shakhar, G. and Furedy, J. J. (1990) *Theories and Applications in the Detection of Deception.* New York: Springer-Verlag.

Deese, J. (1959) On the prediction of occurrence of particular verbal intrusions in immediate recall. *Journal of Experimental Psychology,* 58 (1), 17–22.

Donchin, E. and Coles, M. (1988) Is the P300 component a manifestation of context updating? *Behavioral Brain Sciences,* 11, 357–374.

Donchin, E., Spencer, K. and Dien, J. (1997) The varieties of deviant experience: ERP mainfestation of deviance processors. In: G. J. M. Van Boxtel and K. B. E. Bocken (eds) *Brain and Behavior: Past, Present, and Future,* p. 116. Tilburg Univeristy Press.

Ellwanger, J., Rosenfeld, J. P., Sweet, J. J. and Bhatt, M. (1996) Detecting simulated amnesia for autobiographical and recently learned information using the P300 event-related potential. *International Journal of Psychophysiology,* 23, 9–23.

Ellwanger, J., Rosenfeld, J. P., Hannkin, L. B. and Sweet, J. J. (1999) P300 as an index of recognition in a standard and difficult match-to-sample test: A model of Amnesia in normal adults. *The Clinical Neuropsychologist,* 13, 100–108.

Fabiani, M., Gratton, G., Karis, D. and Donchin, E. (1987) The definition, identification, and reliability of measurement of the P3 component of the event related brain potential. In: P. K. Ackles, J. R. Jennings and M. G. H. Coles (eds) *Advances in Psychophysiology,* vol. 2. Greenwich: JAI Press.

Farwell, L. A. and Donchin, E. (1991) The truth will out: Interrogative polygraphy ("lie detection") with event-related potentials. *Psychophysiology,* 28, 531–547.

Furedy, J. L. (1986) Lie detection as psychophysiological differentiation. In: G. Coles, M. Donchin and S. Porges (eds) *Psychophysiology: System, Processes, and Applications,* pp. 683–701. New York: Guilford Press.

Johnson, M. M. and Rosenfeld, J. P. (1992) Oddball-evoked P300-based method of deception detection in the laboratory II: Utilization of non-selective activation of relevant knowledge. *International Journal of Psychophysiology,* 12, 289–306.

Johnson, R., Jr. (1988) The amplitude of the P300 component of the event-related potential. In P. K. Ackles, J. R. Jennings and M. G. H. Coles (eds) *Advances in Psychophysiology,* vol. 2, pp. 69–138. Greenwich, Ct: JAI Press.

Johnson, R. (1993) On the neural generators of the P300 component of the event-related potential. *Psychophysiology,* 30, 90–97.

Loftus, E. F. (1997) Memory for a past that never was. *Current Directions in Psychological Science,* 6, 60–64.

Loftus, E. and Pickrell, J. E. (1995) The information of false memories. *Psychiatric Annals,* 25, 720–725.

Lykken, D. T. (1981) *A Tremor in the Blood.* New York: McGraw-Hill.

McCarthy, G. and Wood, C. (1985) Scalp distributions of event-related potentials: an ambiguity associated with analysis of variance models. *Electroencephalopathy and Clinical Neurophysiology,* 62, 203–208.

Miller, A. R. (1999a) *P300 Amplitude and Topography in Pseudomemory Phenomena.* Unpublished doctoral dissertation, Northwestern University, Evanston, IL., 11–59.

Miller, A. R. (1999b) *P300 Amplitude and Topography in Pseudomemory Phenomena.* Unpublished doctoral dissertation, Northwestern University, Evanston, IL., 60–122.

Miller, A. R. (1999c) *P300 Amplitude and Topography in Pseudomemory Phenomena.* Unpublished doctoral dissertation, Northwestern University, Evanston, IL., 123–144.

Nies, K. and Sweet, J. (1994) Neuropsychological assessment and malingering: A critical review of past and present strategies. *Archives of Clinical Neuropsychology,* 9, 501–552.

Roediger, H. L. and McDermott, K. B. (1995) Creating false memories: remembering words not presented in lists. *Journal of Experimental Psychology: Learning, Memory, and Cognition,* 21 (4), 803–814.

Rosenfeld, J. P. (1995) Alternative views of Bashore and Rapp's (1993) alternatives to traditional polygraphy: A critique. *Psychological Bulletin,* 117, 159–166.

Rosenfeld, J. P., Angell, A., Johnson, M. and Qian, J. (1991) An ERP-based, control-question lie detector analog: Algorithms for discriminating effects within individuals' average waveforms. *Psychophysiology,* 38, 319–335.

Rosenfeld, J.P ., Cantwell, B., Nasman, V.T., Wojdac, V., Ivanov, S. and Mazzeri, L. (1988) A modified, event-related potential-based guilty knowledge test. *International Journal of Neuroscience,* 24, 157–161.

Rosenfeld, J. P. and Ellwanger, J. W. (1999) Cognitive psychophysiology in detection of malingered cognitive deficit. In: J. J. Sweet (ed.) *Forensic Neuropsychology: Fundamentals and Practice*. Lisse, Netherlands: Swets and Zerlanger Publishers.

Rosenfeld, J. P., Ellwanger, J. W., Nolan, K., Wu, S. and Bermann, R. (1999) P300 scalp amplitude distribution as an index of deception in a simulated cognitive deficit model. *International Journal of Psychophysiology,* 33 (1), 3–20.

Rosenfeld, J. P., Reinhart, A. M., Bhatt, M., Ellwanger, J., Gora, K., Sekera, M. and Sweet, J. (1998) P300 correlates of simulated malingered amnesia in a matching-to-sample task: topographic analyses of deceptive vs. truthtelling responses. *International Journal of Psychophysiology,* 28 (3), 233–249.

Rosenfeld, J. P., Sweet, J. J., Chuang, J., Ellwanger, J. and Song, L. (1996) Detection of simulated malingering using forced choice recognition enhanced with event-related potential recording. *The Clinical Neuropsychologist,* 10 (2), 163–173.

Rosenfeld, J. P., Rao, A., Soskins, M. and Miller, A. (submitted) *Scaled P300 Scalp Distribution Correlates of Deception in an Autobiographical Oddball Paradigm.*

Wasserman, S. and Bockenholt, U. (1989) Bootstrapping: Applications to psychophysiology. *Psychophysiology,* 26, 208–221.

CHAPTER 11

COMPUTER METHODS FOR THE PSYCHOPHYSIOLOGICAL DETECTION OF DECEPTION

John C. Kircher and David C. Raskin

INTRODUCTION

The validity of any diagnostic technique that relies on human evaluations of test data is adversely affected by bias, drift, inexperience, and incompetence (Nunnally, 1978). In the psychophysiological detection of deception (PDD), those problems are compounded by the complexity of the physiological responses and the lack of generally accepted methods for evaluating them (Office of Technology Assessment [OTA], 1983). One polygraph interpreter might consider a particular change in a physiological tracing to be highly diagnostic, whereas another interpreter might view the same change as an artifact of the recording system.

A study by Raskin and Barland (1976) addressed the general question of interrater agreement among practicing field polygraph examiners. They numerically evaluated 419 sets of polygraph recordings made by 43 police and private polygraph examiners and compared their decisions to those by the original examiners. The overall rate of agreement in classifying subjects as truthful, deceptive, or inconclusive was only 58%. Most of the disagreements were cases in which one interpreter reached a definite decision and the other considered the test inconclusive. Nevertheless, disagreements among polygraph examiners are common, and they limit the validity and utility of the polygraph in field settings.

Methods for interpreting physiological recordings from comparison question polygraph tests may be broadly classified as global, numerical, or computer methods. Global approaches are the most subjective, computer approaches are most objective, and numerical methods fall between the two extremes. Polygraph examiners who use global methods form an overall impression of the strength and consistency of the examinee's physiological reactions to comparison and relevant questions. To decide if the subject was deceptive, the polygraph examiner combines information obtained from the polygraph charts with informal evaluations of the case facts and the subject's statements and demeanor during the polygraph test (Reid and Inbau, 1977).

Polygraph examiners who use numerical methods also assess the relative strength of physiological reactions to comparison and relevant questions, but they do so in a systematic manner according to an established set of rules (e.g., Bell *et al.*, 1999; Swinford, 1999). Although several methods of numerical evaluation are currently used by field polygraph examiners, each method specifies scoring windows, exclusionary criteria, and the types of physiological changes that qualify as reactions. In addition, the physiological recordings constitute the only source of information that is formally used to reach a decision.

Raskin (1976) compared the decisions made by professional polygraph examiners who used either global or numerical methods for scoring polygraph charts. He provided each of 25 polygraph examiners with the charts from 16 field polygraph examinations. The 16 suspects had been either cleared of wrongdoing by the confession of another person (four innocent suspects) or incriminated by their own confession some time after they had taken their polygraph test (12 guilty suspects). Eighteen of the polygraph examiners used global methods to evaluate the polygraph charts, and the remaining seven examiners used numerical methods.

The mean accuracy of decisions made by the interpreters who used global methods (M = 87.4%) was significantly lower than the accuracy achieved by the seven numerical evaluators (M = 98.9%). The difference between global and numerical methods was greatest for innocent suspects. The percentage of false positive errors for the global evaluations (26.4%) was over seven times greater than the percentage of false positive errors for the numerical evaluations (3.6%). The results of the Raskin (1976) study suggest that systematic, rule-bound approaches to chart interpretation are superior to less formal, global methods.

Computer analysis was the next step in the evolution of methods for interpreting polygraph charts. The remainder of the present chapter discusses the current status of computer methods for PDD. The chapter is divided into six sections. The first section discusses advantages in using a computer to collect and analyze polygraph charts, and the next section traces major historical events that led to the development of the computerized polygraph systems. The third section reviews the hardware and software components of a computerized polygraph system, and the fourth section summarizes research on the reliability and validity of computerized polygraph systems. The chapter concludes with a discussion of areas in need of additional development and our views about the proper role of computer techniques in field applications.

ADVANTAGES OF A COMPUTERIZED POLYGRAPH SYSTEM

RELIABILITY

Unlike global or numerical methods, a computer analysis of polygraph charts is completely reliable. Given the same set of recordings, a computer will score the charts in exactly the same manner. The same cannot be said of different polygraph interpreters or even the same interpreter on different occasions. The results of the Raskin and Barland (1976) study suggest that there is a high probability that field polygraph interpreters will disagree about the outcome of a polygraph examination. Although the subsequent study by Raskin (1976) indicated that numerical methods are superior to global methods, several different approaches to numerical evaluation are used by field polygraph examiners that can lead to disagreements. Even among numerical evaluators who use the same scoring rules, agreement is not perfect. Senter *et al.* (2000) found that the interrater agreement among polygraph interpreters who used Utah rules of numerical scoring ranged from .75 to .94 (M = .84), whereas polygraph interpreters who used scoring rules taught by the US Department of Defense Polygraph Institute ranged from .66 to .89 (M = .73).

Reliability does not guarantee that the decisions will be valid. Polygraph examiners may agree that a suspect was deceptive on the test, but the decision may be wrong. On the other hand, polygraph outcomes must be reliable in order to be valid. According to psychological test theory, the true correlation between decisions and the actual deceptive status of the examinee (validity) cannot exceed the square root of the reliability of the decisions (Nunnally, 1978). Since the evaluations performed by a computer are perfectly reliable, the theoretical limit to the accuracy of its decisions depends only on the reliability of the subject's responses to test questions.

Computer measurements of physiological reactions are also more precise than those made by expert human interpreters. Whereas numerical evaluators assign scores on an ordinal scale, the computer provides exact measurements of the magnitude of physiological reactions. Because computer measures are more reliable and precise than those made by human interpreters, computer measures generally contain more diagnostic variance than do numerical scores assigned by expert human interpreters (Kircher and Raskin, 1988).

PROCESSING POWER AND SPEED

Computers may be programmed to measure aspects of the physiological recordings that would be difficult or practically impossible to obtain by any other means.

For example, it would be possible to measure the area under a response curve by hand, but it would be difficult, time-consuming, and subject to computational error. The variance in heart period associated with respiration (vagal tone) may be assessed by filtering frequencies from interbeat intervals that lie outside the frequency range of normal respiration, but the application of digital filters is computationally intensive. The computer provides ready access to a host of signal conditioning and signal processing methods. However, arbitrary data transformations can distort measurements of underlying physiological processes and create more problems than they solve (Porges *et al.*, 1996).

MULTIVARIATE STATISTICAL ANALYSIS

Computers facilitate the use of powerful statistical techniques for extracting diagnostic information from the physiological recordings and for optimizing the discrimination between truthful and deceptive individuals. Ellson *et al.* (1952) first suggested the use of discriminant analysis as a means of combining measurements from the various channels of the polygraph, which is the method we have used (Kircher and Raskin, 1988). Discriminant analysis weighs multiple physiological measures differentially and then sums the measures to produce a single discriminant score. The discriminant score places the individual on a truthful–deceptive continuum, and the weights are mathematically optimal for separating groups of known truthful and known deceptive subjects on that continuum. Conceptually, the discriminant score for a subject is similar to the total numerical score assigned by a polygraph interpreter. Cutrow *et al.* (1972) described another method for pooling measurements from different channels. Cutrow *et al.* weighed physiological measures according to their level of diagnosticity, but the weights were suboptimal because they did not take into account the covariance among the physiological measures.

More recently, Devitt and Honts (1993) and Olsen *et al.* (1997) recommended the use of logistic regression. Logistic regression is similar to discriminant analysis in that it weighs and combines physiological measures into a single score that is optimal for separating known groups of truthful and deceptive individuals. However, discriminant analysis and logistic regression use different statistical methods for deriving variable weights, and the assumptions that underlie the use of logistic regression are less restrictive than those that underlie discriminant analysis. Devitt and Honts (1993) also explored a computationally intensive, neural network approach to classification. However, they found that when the neural network was cross-validated on a new sample of cases, its accuracy of classifications was significantly lower than that obtained for the discriminant function or logistic regression model.

RECORDING QUALITY

Traditional analog instruments require polygraph examiners to set the channel gains and offsets manually. Unexpectedly strong physiological reactions may cause the recording pen to hit the pen stop and cause a loss of data. A computerized polygraph can prevent the loss of data by controlling the level of amplification of polygraph signals and offsets to ensure that the signal will not exceed its ability to measure change. Conversely, if the examiner sets the gain on a traditional analog instrument too low, relatively weak reactions may not be visible on the recorded chart. A computerized system allows the user to adjust the amplification of signals on the computer screen. Such adjustments have no effect on the computer analysis, and they facilitate manual scoring of the polygraph charts.

DECISION AIDS

To facilitate human evaluations of polygraph charts, a computerized system may superimpose its measurements on the physiological recordings. For example, a Utah rule of numerical evaluation requires the evaluator to measure the amplitude of the SC response to comparison and relevant questions. A nonzero numerical score is assigned when one reaction is twice as large as the other. When the chart is displayed on the screen for numerical evaluation, the computer can display its measurements of SC amplitude and show precisely where on the tracing it made those measurements. The computer measurements are convenient for numerical evaluation and instructive. They show how the SC response should be measured if the rules of numerical scoring are properly followed.

HISTORICAL DEVELOPMENTS

1960–1975

In 1962, Kubis discussed the possibility of developing computer algorithms to score polygraph charts, and concluded "the use of a computer as a decision machine in the lie detection process cannot be considered feasible at this time." A decade later, Kubis (1973) revisited the question and drew a different conclusion. He wrote, "It is theoretically conceivable that the objectively measured responses – ultimately done under computer control – can be optimally weighted by a computer into an objective decision reflecting the guilt or innocence of a subject." Historically, the Kubis (1973) study is important because it marks the first application of discriminant analysis for combining multiple objective measurements from the polygraph charts to make statistical judgments concerning truthfulness or deception. However, because he analyzed physiological data from relevant–irrelevant polygraph tests, the results from his study provide little information about computer methods for the types of comparison question tests that are commonly used in criminal investigations.

1975–1980

Podlesny and Raskin (1978) were the first investigators to use the computer to digitize and quantify polygraph signals for statistical analysis. They administered comparison question tests and concealed information tests, both of which are commonly used for criminal investigations. Their use of the computer was limited to the quantification of cardiovascular measures. They programmed the computer to measure the time between successive R waves in the electrocardiogram (EKG) and converted the interbeat intervals to heart rate. A new measure of heart rate was obtained for each heart beat. Since heart rates varied across subjects, they computed a weighted average of the heart rates that occurred during a given second and reported heart rate on a second-by-second basis. The algorithm to transform interbeat intervals to second-by-second heart rate provided the same number of heart rate measurements for each test question and each subject and made it possible to analyze them statistically.

Podlesny and Raskin (1978) also developed computer algorithms for charting second-by-second changes in the cardiograph, finger blood volume, finger pulse amplitude, and an experimental measure known as the cardio activity monitor (CAM). Cardiovascular measures are characterized by relatively rapid pulses caused by the beating heart and relatively slow baseline changes associated with changes in blood pressure and blood volume. At the moment the heart beats, pulse pressure is dropping in the peripheral measure. When the pulse reaches the periphery, the pressure rises rapidly, peaks, and then begins to recover. The pressure continues to drop until the next pulse arrives and the cycle is repeated. Podlesny and Raskin used this information to develop an algorithm for isolating low (diastolic) and high (systolic) points in a cardiovascular signal. They used the interval between two successive R waves in the EKG to define a search space for locating the diastolic and systolic points for the cardiac cycle. Each diastolic or systolic point was represented in computer memory by its level and time of occurrence. From the levels and times, they derived separate second-by-second response curves for diastolic and systolic points. The resulting characterization of a cardiovascular response was analyzed with repeated measures analysis of variance (ANOVA). ANOVA allowed the investigators to test for statistically significant differences between guilty and innocent subjects in their physiological reactions to relevant and comparison questions.

The Podlesny and Raskin (1978) study is also significant because it was the first study of the comparison-question polygraph technique that used a realistic mock crime scenario. Prior to Podlesny and Raskin, laboratory researchers commonly recruited college students and used a card test to study the detection of deception. Podlesny and Raskin recruited participants from the general community and assigned them at random to guilty and innocent treatment conditions. Participants reported to a room where they played a tape recording that gave them instructions. Guilty participants were instructed to go to a different floor of the building, wait for a secretary to leave her office unattended, search her desk for a ring, take the ring, and report to a room to await the polygraph examiner. They were told to avoid leaving fingerprints and to prepare an alibi in case they were caught. Innocent participants did not take the ring, but they were informed about the theft. Participants had no face-to-face contact with anyone involved in the experiment prior to carrying out their instructions. They were then given a polygraph examination by an experimenter who was unaware of the participant's guilt or innocence. In the field, all polygraph subjects, whether they are guilty or innocent, are highly motivated to pass the test. In the Podlesny and Raskin experiment, all participants were offered a monetary bonus to convince the polygraph examiner of their innocence.

1980–1985

In 1978 we began a line of research designed to assess the feasibility of using a computer to collect and store polygraph charts, quantify physiological reactions to test questions, and assess the probability that the subject was deceptive on the test. Three years later, we reported results of our initial attempt to conduct computer analyses of polygraph charts from 48 subjects who had participated in a mock crime experiment (Kircher and Raskin, 1981). The following year, we described results from a mock crime experiment that compared computer decisions to those made by an expert human interpreter (Kircher and Raskin, 1982). The results of the latter study were published several years later (Kircher and Raskin, 1988).

Although the computer methods described in these early papers built on the work of Podlesny and Raskin (1978), we measured physiological differences between truthful and deceptive individuals differently. Rather than using ANOVA to test hypotheses about differences in response curves, we adopted a psychometric approach. The question was no longer whether diagnostic information was available in the polygraph charts – that question had already been answered by Raskin and co-workers (Barland and Raskin, 1975; Podlesny and Raskin, 1978; Raskin and Hare, 1978; Rovner, 1986) – the question was how best to extract and use the information to discriminate between truthful and deceptive individuals.

We began by writing a computer program to digitize and store skin conductance (SC), cardiovascular, and respiration recordings. We then developed an algorithm to extract features from the SC and cardiovascular signals (Kircher, 1982). The features were characteristics of a response curve such as its amplitude, duration, and response latency. To assess the diagnostic validity of a feature, we correlated changes in the feature with the guilt/innocence criterion. The magnitude of the correlation indicated the extent to which the particular feature discriminated between guilty and innocent subjects. In addition to assessing the diagnostic validity of various response parameters, we assessed the internal consistency or reliability of the measures over repeated presentations of the relevant questions. The coefficients of reliability and validity guided our selection of measures for a discriminant function.

Initial attempts to extract diagnostic information from SC and cardiovascular signals were generally fruitful. In contrast, our initial attempts to measure respiration reactions with the computer were less successful. Analysis of numerical evaluations by polygraph experts had indicated that deception was associated with suppressed respiratory activity (e.g., Raskin and Hare, 1978; Rovner, 1986). Polygraph examiners who use the Utah method of numerical evaluation score decreases in the amplitude of respirations, increases in the baseline, and increases in the time between successive respirations (Bell *et al.*, 1999). To measure these changes with the computer, we generated three separate response curves that tracked changes in the amplitude of respirations, baseline increases, and cycle times. From each response curve, we extracted features such as amplitude and the area under the curve, and we assessed their psychometric properties. The results of these analyses were disappointing. Internal consistency (reliability) and correlations with the guilt/innocence criterion (validity) were generally less than .30. Attempts to develop a combination of optimally weighted features from the derived respiration response curves were equally disappointing. In contrast, correlations between the criterion and human numerical evaluations of the same respiration recordings exceeded .55 (Kircher and Raskin, 1988).

Timm (1982) published a paper that described a simple alternative to deriving separate response curves and forming a composite index of suppressed respiratory activity. Timm used a planimeter to measure the length of the respiration tracing for a fixed period following question onset. The length of the tracing decreases with reductions in the amplitude and frequency of respirations following question onset.

Following Timm's lead, we wrote a program to calculate the length of the respiration tracing. The obtained correlation between the length measure and the criterion was comparable to the value obtained for the expert numerical evaluator, and the internal consistency was similar to that of many of the SC measures. We have since introduced the sum of absolute deviations between successive samples of the respiration tracing (respiration excursion) as our standard measure of respiration suppression. Respiration excursion is highly correlated with line length ($r > .95$). The advantage in using excursion is that it avoids the need to specify an arbitrary metric for distance on the X-axis.

The computer made 11 measurements of each SC, cardiograph, and peripheral vasomotor reaction in addition to the length of the respiration tracing (Kircher and Raskin, 1982, 1988). A subset of variables was then selected from the available pool of physiological measures to form a discriminant function. The variables were selected for the discriminant function based on their psychometric properties, common use by psychophysiologists, and prior knowledge of response features known to be diagnostic for numerical evaluation.

The discriminant function provided a discriminant score for each guilty and innocent participant in the experiment. The distributions of discriminant scores for guilty and innocent subjects were used in combination with Bayes' Theorem to develop a probability-generating model. The model could then be used to compute the probability of truthfulness (or deception) for a person whose deceptive status was unknown.

Our research demonstrated that it was possible to program a computer to sample and store polygraph charts, extract diagnostic information from the charts, and calculate the probability that the individual was deceptive on the test (Kircher and Raskin, 1981, 1982, 1988). The algorithm was based on knowledge of theories and methods of psychophysiology and well-established psychometric principles. The algorithm was based on laboratory and field experience in the administration and scoring of polygraph tests. The probability output by the algorithm was not a decision: rather, it was a continuous measure of certainty about the subject's truthfulness or deception that is easily understood by consumers of polygraph test results.

Szucko and Kleinmuntz (1981) collected polygraph charts from 30 college students, half of whom had committed a mock theft. They made ten measurements of changes in the physiological recordings by hand and used multiple regression to form a linear combination of the measurements to predict group membership. Multiple regression and discriminant analysis are mathematically equivalent techniques when there are only two groups. The statistical predictions were compared to dichotomous decisions by six global evaluators. The authors concluded that the regression equation was better able to discriminate between the truthful and deceptive subjects than were the polygraph interpreters.

Contrary to the conclusions by Szucko and Kleinmuntz, after adjusting for the small ratio of subjects-to-variables, the level of discrimination achieved by

1990–2000

In 1991, we introduced the Computerized Polygraph System (CPS), which is manufactured and marketed by Stoelting Company (Wood Dale, IL). CPS replaced the traditional analog field polygraph with circuitry for recording skin conductance, respiration, cardiograph, finger plethysmograph, and body movement. The electronics are housed in a small box (about 10 × 20 × 5 cm) that attaches to the computer. Physiological sensors from the subject attach to the CPS unit. The CPS unit digitizes the signals and transmits the recordings to the computer over a serial communications port. The computer displays the physiological recordings in real time on the computer screen and stores the charts with question lists and biographical information on the hard disk of the computer.

The early 1990s saw the introduction of two other computerized polygraph systems. One was developed by Axciton Systems, Inc. (Houston, TX), and the other is marketed by Lafayette Instrument Company (Lafayette, IN). These systems support many of the features introduced by CAPS and CPS. The Axciton and Lafayette systems output the probability of deception rather than a categorical decision and report the strength of response in the form of bar graphs. The Lafayette system also supports predefined question lists, antici-pated answers by the subject, templates for developing new question lists, and an editor with the same capabilities as CPS for removing movement artifacts from the physiological recordings.

The original scoring algorithm for the Axciton and Lafayette systems was known as Polyscore (Olsen *et al.*, 1997). Polyscore was developed at the Applied Physics Laboratory at Johns Hopkins University. Blackwell (1999) reported that outcomes produced by Polyscore (version 3.3) were more accurate than those obtained from experienced field examiners. However, insufficient detail was provided about the procedures used to develop the database of confirmed criminal cases to know if the results provide reasonable estimates of the validity of the Polyscore program. Recently, AXCON (Axciton Systems, Houston, TX), Chart Analysis (Axciton Systems, Houston, TX), and Identifi (Olympia, WA) polygraph scoring algorithms have been introduced to process charts produced by the Axciton polygraph (Dollins *et al.*, 2000).

COMPONENTS OF A COMPUTERIZED POLYGRAPH SYSTEM

The present section describes the essential components of a computerized polygraph system. We begin with a discussion of the hardware that converts the physiological reactions by subjects to digital form and supplies the physiological signals to the computer for additional processing and analysis. We then describe the algorithms we developed to process and analyze the physiological recordings.

HARDWARE

The hardware for a computerized polygraph system consists of the sensors that attach to the subject, electronic circuits for transducing signals from the subject to a continuously varying voltage, an analog-to-digital converter, and circuits to control signal gains and offsets. The CPS records skin conductance, cardiograph, two channels of respiration, peripheral vasomotor activity, and body movement.

Physiological channels

Of the various physiological responses recorded by the polygraph, the electrodermal response is the most diagnostic (Raskin *et al.*, 1988). Traditional analog polygraphs typically record skin resistance (SR) from large metal plates placed on the fingertips. These plates develop bias potentials, are subject to movement artifacts, and relatively large voltages applied to the subject affect sweat gland activity. Skin resistance recordings often show rapid drops in the baselines that are a nuisance because the polygraph operator must constantly re-center the recording pen. To prevent this, some polygraph manufacturers include a high-pass filter on their analog instruments. The filter stabilizes the baseline but alters the shape and amplitude of the subject's SR responses to test questions.

By the early 1970s, academic psychophysiologists had abandoned the recording of SR in favor of SC. The advantages of SC are that large bias potentials can be avoided, the baseline is stable, so there is no need to filter the signal, and a low constant-voltage circuit is used that does not affect the activity of the sweat glands. In addition, research indicates that SC is linearly related to the number of active sweat glands at the recording site, whereas SR is not (Venables and Christie, 1980). A disadvantage in using the low voltage, SC circuit is that it requires the use of wet electrodes: that is, the polygraph examiner must apply a small amount of paste to the electrode before placing it on the skin. The dry metal plates used to record SR are more convenient because they do not require the use of a conductive electrode gel.

CPS uses a constant 0.5V circuit to record SC from wet Ag-AgCl electrodes, which meets standards for the measurement of electrodermal activity established by the Society for Psychophysiological Research (Fowles *et al.*, 1981). Cestaro (1998) manipulated resistance from 50K ohms (20 µS) to 2000 K ohms (0.5 µS) and confirmed that CPS reproduces SC accurately within that range. CPS has been used not only for polygraph examinations but also to investigate the SC and heart rate responses of war veterans with post-traumatic stress disorder (Rich *et al.*, 1998).

A recent laboratory study compared SC and SR responses during comparison question tests (Kircher *et al.*, 2000). Skin conductance was recorded with the standard constant-voltage circuit from wet electrodes. Since SR is the reciprocal of SC, each digitized SC sample was inverted to measure SR in ohms. Response amplitudes were then extracted from the SC and derived SR signals. They found that SC amplitude and SR amplitude correlated 0.99 and that the diagnostic validities of the two measures were virtually identical. For polygraph tests, there appears to be no particular disadvantage in measuring SR as long as it is properly recorded with a low constant-voltage circuit and wet electrodes. However, the Kircher *et al.* study did not compare SC to SR recorded with the high constant-current circuits and bare metal plates used by traditional analog polygraph instruments. The study also did not compare measures of SC or SR to the electrodermal signals generated by Axciton or Lafayette computerized polygraphs, which in addition to using bare metal plates and high current, appear to filter the signal.

CPS records respiration from two piezoelectric transducers mounted in elastic fabric sleeves. The transducers are secured with Velcro around the upper chest and abdomen. The transducers alternately stretch and relax with changes in the circumference of the chest and abdomen as the subject breathes. The piezoelectric elements convert the movements to electric currents that are routed to the polygraph unit and amplified.

CPS records cardiovascular responses from a blood pressure cuff that is wrapped around the upper arm and inflated to about 60 mmHg. A rubber tube from the cuff attaches to a pressure transducer in the polygraph unit to monitor variations in the pressure of cardiograph cuff. The cardiograph covaries with blood pressure (Geddes and Newberg, 1977; Podlesny and Kircher, 1999).

CPS records changes in peripheral vasomotor activity from a finger photoplethysmograph. The transducer contains an infra-red light-emitting diode and a pin diode that are placed against the skin on the tip of a finger. The pin diode converts the light reflected back from the finger to an electrical current that is high-pass filtered and amplified by the polygraph. The filter removes changes in the baseline and shows changes in the amplitude of the finger pulses. Physiological arousal is indicated by a phasic reduction in the amplitude of the pulses.

The movement sensor is an I-beam-shaped aluminum bar with an attached strain gauge that is placed under two legs of the subject chair. Changes in the weight distribution on the bar cause changes in resistance that are recorded by the polygraph. The movement sensor is used to detect attempts by subjects to use physical countermeasures to defeat the test. A truthful polygraph outcome is suspect when movements are uniquely associated with the presentation of comparison questions.

Analog-to-digital conversion

The analog-to-digital converter samples the analog physiological signals generated by the polygraph and converts the signal to a stream of numeric values. Analog-to-digital converters differ in their precision, which is measured in terms of bits of resolution, and the rate at which the analog signal is sampled. CPS uses a high-resolution 16-bit analog-to-digital converter and samples each of its six channels at 384 Hz. CPS computes the mean of each consecutive set of 48 samples to produce a storage rate of 8 Hz for the SC, respiration, and body movement channels. For the cardiograph and finger plethysmograph, means of eight consecutive samples are computed and the means are stored at 48 Hz. Higher storage rates are needed to accurately reproduce the cardiovascular signals because they contain higher frequency components than do the other measures.

Gains and offsets

There are large differences among individuals in basal levels of physiological activity (Stern *et al.*, 1980; Sternbach, 1966). Minor changes in the tension and placement of respiration and cardiovascular transducers on the subject also cause large variations in signal strength. A computerized polygraph system can adjust for variations in general signal strength with a digital-to-analog converter (DAC). The DAC converts a numeric value supplied by the computer to an analog voltage that is added to the signal from the subject and serves as an offset control. Digital-to-analog converters bring the signal within the range of the analog-to-digital converter without filtering or distorting the signal from the subject. Once the signal is within the range of the analog-to-digital converter, the computer can adjust the signal gain. The gain is adjusted to ensure that the variance in the signal voltage is neither too high nor too low to monitor changes in physiological activity during the test. If, during the test, the signal drifts toward the upper or lower end of the range of the analog-to-digital converter, the DAC resets the offset.

SOFTWARE

Data editing

Small movements by the subject during the polygraph examination can produce brief distortions in the physiological recordings. In some cases, a deep breath or large body movement may render all of the recordings for a particular question unusable. In other cases, the quality of the recording for an entire channel may be inadequate for computer or human evaluation. For example, it may be impossible to obtain adequate cardiograph recordings from an obese subject. A graphic data editor may be used to replace brief (1–3 s) distortions of a signal with interpolated values or to indicate that a particular reaction or set of reactions should not be scored by the computer.

Since the polygraph examiner decides whether and how to modify the polygraph data, the use of a data editor introduces a potential source of error in analyses subsequently performed by the computer. One polygraph examiner may decide to edit a portion of a recording, whereas another examiner may decide to let it go. To avoid reliance on human judgment, we developed computer algorithms in the early 1980s to detect and remove artifacts automatically, but we were not satisfied with the results. More recently, Olsen *et al.* (1997) reported that they treated a reaction as an outlier if it accounted for more than 89% of the total variability. Reactions marked as outliers were omitted from the computer analysis. Otherwise, they did no editing of the polygraph data. Although the Olsen *et al.* approach might be an effective alternative to manual editing of the polygraph charts, they provided no rationale or empirical justification for this approach.

Effects of automatic or manual data editing on the accuracy of computer decisions have not been investigated systematically. However, clear and proper instructions to the subject minimize the occurrence of movement artifacts. If a limb or transducer is repositioned prior to collecting the data for a chart, there is rarely a need to drop an entire channel. In our laboratory experiments, we typically edit only 1% to 2% of the data, and most of those edits have no effect on the computer measurements used to reach a decision.

Regardless of whether automatic or manual editing of the charts is performed, any report produced by the computer should clearly indicate if the charts have been modified, if the modifications affected the measurement of reactions that were used by the computer in its analysis, and if any data were eliminated from the computer analysis. It is also essential for the computer program to protect the original, unedited data, and allow ready access to the original charts even after they have been edited. CPS meets these requirements.

Feature extraction

From the series of digitized polygraph signals, response curves are generated for SC, cardiograph, and peripheral vasomotor activity. The SC response curve is defined by the series of stored samples. For the cardiograph, a trend line is created by summing the samples for one second and then interpolating between the sums. The trend line follows the diastolic points more closely than the systolic points because the pulse pressure is closer to the diastolic level throughout most of the cardiac cycle.

To measure decreases in the amplitude of finger pulses, a response curve is defined by differences between the systolic and diastolic levels for each post-stimulus second. The differences are expressed as proportions of the mean pre-stimulus amplitude. Physiological arousal in this measure is indicated by a reduction in pulse amplitudes due to peripheral vasoconstriction. Since the scoring algorithm treats increases rather than decreases in the response curve as indications of increased arousal, the vasomotor response curve is reflected by multiplying each post-stimulus pulse amplitude by −1 prior to feature extraction. In that way, a decrease in the amplitude of finger pulses is associated with a rise in the response curve.

The algorithm identifies the time and level of each point of inflection in the SC or cardiovascular response curve. Low points in the response curve are located where the slope changes from a negative value to a positive value, and high points are located where the slope changes from positive to negative. From the times and levels of inflection points, multiple features are extracted. For example, to measure peak amplitude, the computer measures all possible differences between each low point and every succeeding high point. Peak amplitude is the greatest observed difference. Number of responses is the number of changes from positive to negative slope. Response latency is the time from question onset to the time of the low point from which peak amplitude is measured (response onset). Half recovery time is the time of occurrence of the peak amplitude to the time at which the recovery limb reaches a level that is half the obtained amplitude. These features are commonly used in psychophysiological research to measure specific SC responses and general arousal.

Although the algorithm was originally designed to extract features from SC responses (Kircher, 1981), it has been used to extract features from respiration, cardiograph, finger pulse amplitude, finger blood volume, heart rate, systolic and diastolic blood pressure, and skin potential responses (Kircher et al., 2000; Kircher and Raskin, 1988; Podlesny and Kircher, 1999). In addition to the traditional SC features, the algorithm also measures onset and recovery rates, area under the response curve, duration of the response, line length or excursion (Timm, 1982), and burst frequency (Edelberg and Goldstein, 1983). The line length measure was developed to measure respiration suppression, but it can be used to measure arousal when the response is biphasic. Skin potential and heart rate responses during polygraph tests are usually biphasic (Kircher et al., 2000; Podlesny and Raskin, 1978; Raskin and Hare, 1978).

Feature standardization

The features extracted from SC, cardiovascular, and respiration responses are measured on different scales (e.g., ms, mm, μSiemens, mmHg). This makes it difficult to compare the different types of measurements. It is also difficult to compare measurements of the same type across individuals. Difficulties arise because there are substantial differences among individuals in tonic and phasic levels of physiological arousal (Sternbach, 1966). For one individual, a 1.0 µSiemens increase in SC is a dramatic reaction; for another individual, the same measured change may be average or even small.

We examined several methods for transforming the raw measurements to a common metric that controls for individual differences in tonic and phasic reactivity (log ratios, proportions, range adjustments, standard (z) scores). Examination of the psychometric properties of the measures produced by these transformations did not reveal any particular advantage in choosing one transformation over another. For ease of interpretation, we opted for within-subject standardization of the measurements obtained for an individual (Lacey, 1956). The transformation of raw scores to standard scores or z-scores is linear, and it produces a set of values with a mean of 0.0 and variance of 1.0.

The question sequence in our laboratory experiments typically contains three comparison questions and three relevant questions, and the question sequence is repeated three times. This provides 18 repeated measurements of each feature. The mean and standard deviation of the 18 measurements are used to transform the raw scores to z-scores. To obtain a z-score, the distance between the score and the mean is divided by the standard deviation. The resulting z-score is the distance between the raw score and the mean expressed in standard deviation units. If the mean of the 18 measurements is 100 and the standard deviation is 10, a raw score of 80 would be transformed to −2 because 80 is two standard deviations below the mean of 100.

Another method for standardizing raw scores is to compute separate standard deviations for comparison and relevant questions and to pool the two standard deviations (Olsen *et al.*, 1997; Podlesny and Kircher, 1999). In the Podlesny and Kircher study, we compared the two methods for calculating the standard deviation. The validity coefficients were slightly greater when a single standard deviation was calculated using all questions than when standard deviations were obtained separately for comparison and for relevant questions and were then pooled. However, the differences were small and non-significant.

For all physiological measures except respiration excursion, the largest measured response is associated with the strongest reaction. For respiration excursion, the smallest measured response is associated with the strongest reaction (respiration suppression). By reversing the signs of the z-scores for respiration, the z-scores for all physiological measures are interpreted in the same manner; large positive z-scores always indicate strong physiological reactions.

Indices of differential reactivity

An index of differential reactivity to comparison and relevant questions is computed from the z-scores for each physiological measure. A mean z-score is calculated for all relevant questions, and another mean z-score is calculated for all comparison questions. The mean z-score for relevant questions is then subtracted from the mean z-score for comparison questions. A positive difference indicates that the reactions on average were stronger to the comparison questions, and a negative difference indicates that the reactions to the relevant questions were stronger. The magnitude of the difference indicates the extent to which the subject responded differentially to the comparison and relevant questions. In general, positive differences between the z-scores are expected for truthful subjects, since they are expected to react more strongly to comparison questions than to relevant questions. Negative differences are expected for deceptive subjects since they are expected to react more strongly to relevant questions. This computer index of differential reactivity is analogous to the total numerical score assigned by a polygraph examiner to a particular channel of physiological activity.

Discriminant analysis

Although the computer can make many measurements of physiological responses, measurements from the same physiological response are typically highly correlated. For example, correlations among SC amplitude, area, and line length measures typically exceed 0.95. Such measures are all highly diagnostic of truth and deception. However, they do little to increase the accuracy of decisions because the information they provide about the criterion is redundant.

Several computer algorithms have been developed to select a subset of relatively independent variables for a regression equation, discriminant function, or logistic regression model that captures most of the reliable information available in a pool of potential predictor variables. These methods include forward, backward, stepwise, and all-possible-subsets regression. Forward, backward, and stepwise solutions are problematic because they rely exclusively on the statistical relationships observed in the available sample of cases (Hocking, 1983). They work very well when they classify the cases that were used to develop the prediction model (training set), but they do not work well when they are tested on a new sample of cases (validation sample). The failure of a model to generalize to an independent sample of cases is known as shrinkage (McNemar, 1969). The expected drop in accuracy from the training set to the validation sample depends on the ratio of subjects to variables. For any given number of subjects, the greater the number of variables from which the selected subset was obtained and the greater the number of variables in the model, the greater the expected drop in accuracy on cross-validation.

Our approach has been to use all-possible-subsets regression to select variables for a discriminant function. The all-possible-subsets algorithm begins by producing an ordered list of subsets, each of which contains a single predictor variable. The subsets are ordered according to the extent to which they accurately discriminate between the samples of truthful and deceptive subjects. The algorithm then produces an ordered list of subsets composed of two predictor variables, then three predictor variables, and so on.

The advantage of the all-possible-subsets approach is that statistical and extra-statistical criteria may be used to select a subset of predictor variables. For example, the statistically optimal subset for a particular sample of cases may consist of four variables about which little is known. Because little is known about the measures, their reliability is suspect. One or more of the four variables may happen to correlate strongly with the criterion in the particular sample of cases at hand, but the correlation(s) may be due to chance. The next best subset may account for only slightly less variance in the criterion, but it may contain four variables about which much is known. They may be measures that are commonly used by psychophysiologists to measure emotional states and processes in a variety of research settings, not only for the detection of deception. They may be characteristics of response curves that are used by numerical evaluators when they score polygraph charts and have been validated in numerous laboratory and field studies. The second best model may account for slightly less variance in the criterion for the particular sample at hand, but it may well be the theoretically meaningful and most dependable model for PDD.

The first discriminant function we developed contained seven measures of differential reactivity (Kircher and Raskin, 1981). After collecting additional laboratory (Kircher and Raskin, 1988) and field data (Raskin et al., 1988), the number of variables was reduced to five and then to three. Our current model includes only SC amplitude, the amplitude of increases in the baseline of the cardiograph, and a composite measure of thoracic and abdominal respiration excursion.

Probability of deception

The discriminant score for a subject is mapped onto two likelihood functions to calculate the probability that the subject was deceptive on the test. The two likelihood functions are partially overlapping normal curves, the parameters of which are estimated from the distributions of discriminant scores for known truthful and deceptive individuals. The likelihood function for known truthful subjects was used to calculate the conditional likelihood of the tested individual's discriminant score (X) given the individual was truthful, $P(X/T)$. The likelihood function for deceptive subjects is used to calculate the conditional likelihood of the tested individual's discriminant score given the subject was deceptive, $P(X/D)$. The two conditional likelihoods are combined by means of Bayes' Theorem to calculate the posterior probability that the subject was deceptive given the subject's discriminant score, $P(D/X)$. Given that $P(D)$ and $P(T)$ are the prior probabilities of deception and truthfulness respectively, Bayes' Theorem states:

$$P(D/X) = [\, P(D)P(X/D) \,] / [\, P(D)P(X/D) + P(T)P(X/T) \,]$$

The probability that the individual was truthful on the test, $P(T/X)$, is the complement of the probability of deception; i.e., $P(T/X) = 1 - P(D/X)$ (Kircher and Raskin, 1982, 1988). Similarly, the prior probability that the subject was truthful is the complement of the prior probability that the subject was deceptive, $P(T) = 1 - P(D)$. When the prior probabilities are equal, $P(D) = P(T) = 0.50$, they cancel out of Bayes' Theorem. Then, the probability that the subject was deceptive on the test depends only on the subject's discriminant score, and the discriminant score is based on measurements obtained from the polygraph charts.

Numerical evaluators use cutoffs of $+/-6$ to classify polygraph outcomes as truthful, deceptive, or inconclusive. A score of $+6$ or greater is considered a truthful outcome, a score of -6 or less is a deceptive outcome, and scores between the cutoffs are considered inconclusive. In contrast to the categorical decisions by the polygraph examiner, the probabilities output by the computer are continuous. To compare computer outcomes to the decisions by polygraph interpreters, cutoffs may be established for the probability of truthfulness, $P(T/X)$. Our research suggests that the optimal cutoffs are .70 and .30 for truthful and deceptive decisions respectively. They are optimal in the sense that they produce relatively few inconclusive outcomes and relatively high accuracy rates.

Other computerized polygraph systems

The Axciton and Lafayette computerized polygraphs also record electrodermal activity, two channels of respiration, and the cardiograph. The Lafayette offers an optional fifth channel that may be configured to record either the finger photoplethysmograph or body movement. The Axciton and Lafayette systems record respiration from pneumatic bellows secured about the chest and abdomen. The air pressure in the bellows changes as the subject breathes. A rubber tube attaches the bellows to the polygraph unit, and a pressure transducer converts the changes in air pressure to a voltage that varies with respiratory activity. All three systems also record cardiovascular responses from a blood pressure cuff and pressure transducer. Unless the Axciton and Lafayette systems use filters that can cause non-linearity in their respiration and cardiograph recordings, it does not appear that there are any substantive differences among the CPS, Axciton, and Lafayette systems in the obtained recordings of respiration and cardiovascular activity.

In contrast to the CPS, the Axciton and Lafayette systems measure electrodermal activity from bare metal plate electrodes and pass large electrical currents through the skin. In his tests of computerized polygraph systems, Cestaro (1998) found that the signals generated by Axciton and Lafayette computer systems did not accurately reproduce known changes in resistance. Not only were the output signals inaccurate, they were not even monotonically related to the inputs. A large or a small decrease in resistance could be associated with a large or a small change in the output of the system. Examination of the electrodermal recordings from these units suggests that the manufacturers use high pass filters to prevent the signal from drifting during the polygraph examination. The use of filters may explain the observed lack of correspondence between known inputs and the signals generated by these units. However, as noted above, drift can be minimized with a properly constructed circuit while maintaining a close linear relationship between the output of the system and the subject's physiological response.

At its introduction, the Axciton/Polyscore system was adopted by most US Government agencies with polygraph programs. In 1996, the Central Intelligence Agency, which had supported some of the research on Polyscore, requested a peer review of the Axciton/Polyscore system. The review committee consisted of two past presidents of the Society for Psychophysiological Research (SPR), an author of the present chapter (JCK), another member of SPR, and a statistician. The committee concluded that the entire research and development effort by the group at Johns Hopkins was seriously flawed and unscientific (Porges et al., 1996). They found that the criteria used to create the database of polygraph charts for model development were inadequate. The correspondence between the signals generated by the Axciton and subjects' physiological reactions to test questions was unknown. The methods for scoring the polygraph signals were unorthodox and capitalized on chance, and the developers of Polyscore had never assessed the validity of the Polyscore program for discriminating between truthful and deceptive subjects. The committee was also concerned that Polyscore had been marketed as a highly effective computer program for detecting deception and had gained widespread acceptance in the polygraph community when its accuracy had never been adequately tested.

RESEARCH ON THE RELIABILITY AND VALIDITY OF COMPUTER METHODS

Research on the reliability and validity of computer measurements and diagnoses may be conducted with data collected in the laboratory or field. There are many advantages to studying deception-related physiological responses in the laboratory (Podlesny and Raskin, 1977), the most important of which is that the participants' deceptive status is known with absolute certainty. Field research on polygraph techniques is difficult because knowledge of the suspect's actual deceptive status that is independent of the polygraph outcome is rarely available in real-life situations. Another advantage of laboratory research is the instrumentation. The number, variety, and quality of physiological recordings that can be obtained in the laboratory surpass what is generally available from portable field equipment.

The major disadvantage of laboratory research is the artificial nature of the mock crime. Participants know that they are involved in an experiment. The consequences of failing a polygraph test in a laboratory experiment differ significantly from the consequences of failing a polygraph test that is administered as part of an actual criminal investigation. Because of this, critics argue that the results from laboratory experiments tell us little about the accuracy of polygraph techniques in the field (e.g., Iacono and Lykken, 1997; Lykken, 1981).

We have argued that the results from laboratory experiments are useful to the extent that they adequately simulate the field context (Podlesny and Raskin, 1977; Raskin *et al.*, 1997). We have shown that the accuracy rates in laboratory experiments are similar to those obtained in field studies when commission of the mock crime evokes a strong emotional response and participants are offered meaningful incentives to pass the test (Kircher *et al.*, 1988). We have also compared physiological data from laboratory and field polygraph examinations (Kircher *et al.*, 1994). The results revealed that the response patterns exhibited by truthful and deceptive subjects in a realistic mock crime experiment are similar to those obtained from truthful and deceptive field suspects. The diagnostic validity of each of the physiological measures used in our discriminant function was similar across laboratory and field settings. The covariance among the physiological measures was also similar across settings. However, as compared to laboratory subjects, the differential reactivity scores for field suspects were generally shifted in the negative direction. In the field, truthful and deceptive suspects generally reacted more strongly to relevant questions than to comparison questions. For the computer model, the tendency for both groups to respond more strongly to relevant questions is easily accommodated by adjusting the constant in the discriminant function. Notwithstanding research that supports the use of realistic mock crime scenarios, conclusions based on findings from laboratory experiments should be viewed as tentative until the findings are replicated with field data (Podlesny and Raskin, 1977).

Table 11.1 summarizes results of laboratory and field studies that assessed the accuracy of decisions made by the CPS algorithm. All of the polygraph examinations included probable-lie comparison questions. Within a given laboratory experiment, the comparison and relevant questions were constant, and the relevant questions addressed a single issue. In each field study, the comparison and relevant questions varied over cases, and the relevant questions addressed different issues.

The number of charts available for computer analysis also varied across studies. In two experiments, five charts were collected from each subject (Bernhardt, 2000; Kircher and Raskin, 1988). The probability of truthfulness was assessed after the third chart. If the result was inconclusive, data from the last two charts were pooled with the data from the first three charts. The probability of truthfulness based on all five charts was then recomputed and used to classify the case. In the Podlesny and Kircher (1999) experiment, all decisions were based on four charts. In all remaining studies, the results in Table 11.1 were based on three charts. Finally, data for only confirmed deceptive answers by suspects were available in one field study (Raskin *et al.*, 1989). In that study, the accuracy was assessed for 51 individual relevant questions, not 51 different polygraph tests.

The percent correct decisions is the accuracy rate excluding inconclusive outcomes. The overall accuracy of CPS decisions was approximately 90% on both truthful and deceptive subjects. The similarity of accuracies for truthful

Table 11.1

Percent outcomes for laboratory and field studies of the CPS algorithm.

Study	Setting	Sample[a]	Truthful					Deceptive				
			n	Correct	Wrong	?[b]	Correct decisions	n	Correct	Wrong	?[b]	Correct decisions
Kircher and Raskin, 1988	Lab	S	50	90	4	6	96	50	90	4	6	96
Rovner, 1986	Lab	V	24	67	4	29	94	24	92	0	8	100
Gatchel et al., 1984	Lab	V	14	64	0	36	100	14	71	0	29	100
Podlesny and Kircher, 1999	Lab	V	60	75	10	15	88	60	63	15	22	81
Honts et al., 2000	Lab	V	48	79	13	8	86	48	69	21	10	77
Bernhardt, 2000	Lab	V	30	90	7	3	93	30	87	13	0	87
Raskin et al., 1988	Field	S	33	76	9	15	89	43	72	9	19	86
Raskin et al., 1989	Field	V	0	–	–	–	–	51	79	0	21	100
Dollins et al., 1999	Field	V	41	68	7	24	90	56	73	7	20	91

a S = Standardization sample. Variables and variable weights were optimal for the sample.
  V = Validation sample. Variables and variable weights were based on an independent sample.
b Inconclusive.

and deceptive subjects suggests that the CPS algorithm is unbiased. The mean accuracy rates from laboratory and field studies were also quite similar. These findings are consistent with the conclusion that properly constructed mock crime scenarios adequately reproduce patterns of physiological responses observed in the field.

Statistical theory predicts that the accuracy rates for standardization samples will be higher than those obtained from validation samples because the weights for variables in the discriminant function are optimal for the standardization sample. However, there was little difference between the accuracy rates for standardization and validation samples in these laboratory and field studies. The results indicate that the CPS algorithm is robust, probably because its decisions are based on measurements of only three features and they are all highly reliable.

Although the accuracy rates were stable across studies, the inconclusive rates varied from 3% to 32%. The lowest inconclusive rates were obtained in the Kircher and Raskin (1988) and Bernhardt (2000) experiments. These were the only studies in which as many as five charts of data were used to reach a decision. In both of those studies, the addition of the fourth and fifth charts reduced the inconclusive rate by more than half. Together, the results suggest that the rate of inconclusive outcomes for CPS is about 20% after three charts, but it drops to about 10% when the algorithm is provided with two additional charts.

COMPARISONS BETWEEN COMPUTER AND HUMAN EVALUATIONS

Independent numerical evaluations of the polygraph charts were performed by expert polygraph interpreters in eight of the nine studies listed in Table 11.1. Dollins *et al.* (2000) was the only exception. In all but one of those eight studies (Honts *et al.*, 2000), the overall accuracy of CPS decisions was greater than the accuracy achieved by human experts who had had no contact with the subjects. Statistical tests to determine if computer decisions were significantly more accurate than human evaluations were not performed in those studies because, in most cases, the accuracy of computer decisions was only a few percentage points higher than that of the numerical evaluators. However, seven of eight studies favoring the computer is statistically significant with a one-tailed sign test, $p < .05$, and it approaches significance with a two-tailed test, $p < .063$.

COMPARISONS AMONG SCORING ALGORITHMS

Dollins *et al.* (2000) compared the CPS, Polyscore, AXCON, Chart Analysis, and Identifi programs for scoring charts. Program developers were provided with polygraph charts from 103 confirmed cases. Cases were considered confirmed deceptive if the tested individual confessed or if the individual was inculpated by incontrovertible physical evidence. Cases were confirmed truthful if the tested individual was exculpated by the confession of another person. Three cases were dropped when the authors were unable to reconfirm the status of subjects because the original case files were lost. Three other cases were dropped because the quality of the polygraph charts was considered inadequate. Of the remaining 97 cases, 85 examinees were suspects, eight were witnesses, and four were victims. The authors noted that the sampling procedures might well have produced biased estimates of the accuracy on confirmed truthful and deceptive cases overall. However, the purpose of their study was not to estimate the diagnostic validity of any of the computer algorithms in absolute terms. Rather, the purpose of their study was to compare the outcomes from the various computer algorithms. However, even their assessments of relative accuracy were problematic.

All of the polygraph charts were collected with the Axciton polygraph, and all of the algorithms read the original Axciton data files except CPS. The developer of the Axciton polygraph wrote a program to produce ASCII text files for analysis by CPS. Three charts of data were provided for all but five of the 97 cases. Four charts were available for four cases, and two charts were available for one case. The results are summarized in Table 11.2.

The unweighted mean accuracy of decisions ranged from 85% to 91%. There were no significant differences among the five algorithms in overall decision accuracy. However, only CPS was unbiased. The authors found that the decisions by all algorithms except CPS were significantly less accurate for truthful subjects than for deceptive subjects. Although CPS produced 7% fewer correct decisions on deceptive subjects (91%) than did the other programs (M = 98%), decisions by CPS on truthful subjects (90%) were 15% more accurate (M = 75%).

The overall decision accuracy of CPS was slightly higher than that of the other algorithms, but it also produced the greatest number of inconclusive outcomes. As noted previously, an inconclusive rate as high as 22% after three charts is not atypical for CPS. Had more charts been available, the inconclusive

Table 11.2

Percent correct decisions and inconclusive outcomes for five computer programs evaluated by Dollins et al. (1999).

Computer program	Truthful (n = 41)		Deceptive (n = 56)		Mean	
	Correct decisions	Incon-clusive	Correct decisions	Incon-clusive	Correct decisions	Incon-clusive
CPS	90	24	91	20	91	22
Polyscore	79	20	98	11	88	15
AXCON	73	20	98	9	86	14
Chart Analysis	73	27	96	9	85	18
Identifi	73	27	98	11	86	18

rate would have been lower. Nevertheless, all of the programs were tested with the same number of charts, and CPS had the greatest number of inconclusive outcomes. Several factors may have contributed to the relatively high rate of inconclusive outcomes for CPS. The results were biased against CPS because all of the algorithms except CPS had been developed with data collected by Axciton polygraphs (Dollins *et al.*, 2000). As noted previously, the Axciton records electrodermal activity from polarizing bare metal plates, passes high current densities through individual sweat glands, uses high pass filtering, and produces recordings that are not even monotonically related to SC or SR (Cestaro, 1998). Consequently, SC responses are poorly represented by the signals generated by the Axciton polygraph. This problem was compounded by the fact that CPS weighs changes in SC more heavily than changes in any other channel. Since the problems in recording electrodermal activity occurred for both comparison and relevant questions, the expected effect is an increase in the number of inconclusive outcomes.

Another problem was that the CPS scoring algorithm assumes that event marks coincide with the onset of the test questions. The accuracy of CPS results suffered to the extent that indications of question onset were incorrect. In this sample of Axciton charts, there was little doubt that the event marks were only approximately correct. In some cases, it appeared that the event marks occurred one to two seconds after the actual presentation of the question. It is unclear if the problem with event timing originated when the data were collected with the Axciton or when the data were converted from native Axciton files to ASCII for analysis by CPS. If the problem occurred when the ASCII files were created for CPS, as suggested by Dollins *et al.* (2000), then CPS was uniquely disadvantaged by errors associated with question onsets. These problems introduced small errors in the measurement of all respiration responses, variable errors in some cardiograph measurements, and large errors in some SC measurements. Following conventional scientific practice, CPS automatically rejects SC responses that begin prior to question onset. The program assumes that a response that begins before the question is asked, or within 500 ms of question onset, is not a response to the question. CPS may have rejected *bona fide* electrodermal responses to test questions because the event marks were misplaced and occurred in the middle of the subject's response. Again, if the errors in the placement of question onsets occurred randomly, the effect would be to reduce the discrimination between truthful and deceptive subjects and increase the number of inconclusive outcomes.

COMPUTER ANALYSIS OF DIRECTED-LIE POLYGRAPH EXAMINATIONS

The results reported thus far were obtained from laboratory and field tests that used probable-lie questions. The directed-lie question has been proposed as an alternative to the probable-lie question (Fuse, 1982; Raskin et al., 1997). The effectiveness of the directed-lie technique has been evaluated in the laboratory (Horowitz *et al.*, 1997) and field (Honts and Raskin, 1988), and the findings of both studies supported the use of directed-lie questions.

We recently completed a laboratory study that compared CPS decisions from probable-lie and directed-lie polygraph examinations (Bell *et al.*, 2000). The results from the 60 participants who were given probable-lie tests were presented earlier in Table 11.2. Another 60 participants (30 guilty and 30 innocent) received directed-lie tests. The results from the directed-lie tests are presented in Table 11.3, along with the probable-lie results from the Bell *et al.* (2000) study.

Table 11.3

Percent outcomes of computer analysis of probable-lie and directed-lie tests.

	Truthful				Deceptive			
	Correct	Wrong	Incon-clusive	Correct decisions	Correct	Wrong	Incon-clusive	Correct decisions
Probable-lie test (*n* = 30 / group)	90	7	3	93	87	13	0	87
Directed-lie test (*n* = 30 / group)	83	13	3	86	67	17	17	80

Excluding inconclusives, the accuracy of CPS decisions was 7% higher for the probable-lie test than the directed-lie test, but the difference was not statistically significant. The overall inconclusive rate was unusually low for the probable-lie test (2%), and it was lower than the inconclusive rate for guilty subjects who were given directed-lie tests (17%). The computer results tended to favor the probable-lie test because it produced fewer errors and fewer inconclusive outcomes.

The point-biserial correlation (r_{pb}) between each physiological measure and the criterion are presented in Table 11.4 for probable-lie and directed-lie tests. Coefficient alpha reliabilities are also reported (r_{kk}). The reliability coefficient is an index of the similarity of differences between adjacent comparison and relevant questions across the first three repetitions of the question sequence.

The reliability coefficients are consistent with those reported previously for electrodermal, cardiograph, and respiration measures (Kircher and Raskin, 1988). The validity coefficients (r_{pb}) are also representative of those reported

Index of differential reactivity	Probable-lie tests ($n = 60$)		Directed-lie tests ($n = 60$)	
	r_{pb}	(r_{kk})	r_{pb}	(r_{kk})
Skin Conductance Amplitude	.73	(.80)	.63	(.80)
Cardiograph Baseline Increase	.45	(.56)	.36	(.60)
Respiration Excursion	.43	(.73)	−.02	(.60)

Table 11.4

Validity (r_{pb}) and reliability (r_{kk}) of indices of differential reactivity for probable-lie and directed-lie polygraph tests.

Note: The r_{pb} for all measures except respiration excursion for directed-lie tests were significant, p < .01.

previously, with one notable exception. Indices of differential respiration responses were uncorrelated with the guilt/innocence criterion for subjects who received directed-lie tests. All other measures were significantly correlated with the criterion. In addition, the validity coefficients for probable-lie and directed-lie tests did not differ, except for respiration excursion. The validity coefficient for respiration excursion was significantly greater for the probable-lie test than for the directed-lie test, z = 2.57, p < .02.

Examination of group means revealed that the difference between respiration responses to probable-lie and relevant questions was positive for innocent participants (M = .20) and negative for guilty participants (M = −.36). These findings for the probable-lie condition were consistent with predictions; innocent participants showed greater respiration suppression in response to probable-lie questions than to relevant questions, whereas guilty participants showed greater suppression to the relevant questions. The results from guilty participants who received directed-lie tests were also consistent with predictions. Guilty participants who received directed-lie tests showed greater respiration suppression to relevant questions than to directed-lie questions (M = −.38). However, innocent subjects also produced a negative difference between directed-lie and relevant questions (M = −.40), and the means for the guilty and innocent groups in the directed-lie condition did not differ. Interestingly, the negative difference between directed-lie and relevant questions for innocent participants was not due to suppression on the relevant questions; rather, it was a consequence of increased respiratory activity to directed lie questions.

The findings from the Bell *et al.* (2000) study are consistent with results reported previously by Horowitz *et al.* (1997). They suggest that the discriminant function, which was developed for probable-lie tests and shows considerable generalizability across probable-lie studies (see Table 11.1), is not optimal for directed-lie tests. More laboratory and field research is needed to develop and validate a computer model for the directed-lie technique.

316 HANDBOOK OF POLYGRAPH TESTING

COMPARISON OF DISCRIMINANT ANALYSIS AND LOGISTIC REGRESSION

As noted previously, CPS uses a discriminant function to weigh and combine physiological measures, whereas the Polyscore program by Olsen *et al.* (1997) uses logistic regression. We were unable to locate any reports of the methods used by the AXCON, Chart Analysis, and Identifi programs to make decisions.

Devitt and Honts (1993) compared polygraph outcomes produced by discriminant analysis and logistic regression and found that the logistic regression model was significantly superior to the discriminant function. We also compared discriminant analysis to logistic regression but found no difference between them (Kircher *et al.*, 1994). In the latter study, we extracted SC amplitude, cardiograph baseline increase, and the composite respiration excursion from polygraph charts from 100 subjects in a laboratory experiment and 63 suspects from a field study. We then developed a discriminant function from the three physiological measures and a logistic regression model from the same three physiological measures. The correlation between the probabilities of truthfulness derived from the discriminant function and the logistic regression exceeded .99. Predictably, there was little difference between the two statistical approaches in terms of correct decisions and inconclusive outcomes. The superiority of the logistic regression model noted by Devitt and Honts (1993) might have been due to the manner in which variables were selected for the discriminant and logistic regression models in her study. Devitt and Honts used the stepwise algorithm to select variables for the discriminant function and used the backward elimination algorithm to select variables for the logistic regression model. Therefore, the discriminant and logistic regression models may have contained different variables, and these differences may have contributed to the effects reported by Devitt and Honts.

AREAS FOR ADDITIONAL RESEARCH AND DEVELOPMENT

INSTRUMENTATION

The advent of computerized polygraphs in the early 1990s provided a unique opportunity to improve the quality of psychophysiological measurements for the detection of deception. Unfortunately, two of the three computerized polygraph systems actually took a step backward rather than forward. The traditional analog polygraphs recorded SR. Skin resistance was abandoned by the scientific community in favor of SC for reasons discussed above. Despite the limitations of SR recordings, there is a known relationship between SR and the activity of the eccrine sweat glands (Venables and Christie, 1980). The same cannot be said of the electrodermal signals generated by the Axciton and Lafayette computerized polygraphs (Cestaro, 1998). To facilitate comparisons of polygraph research and basic psychophysiological research on motivation and emotion and to increase the acceptance of polygraph research by the academic community, computerized polygraphs should use scientifically acceptable methods for recording physiological reactions during polygraph examinations.

NEW PHYSIOLOGICAL MEASURES

We have reached the point where little more diagnostic information can be extracted from the physiological measures recorded by traditional or computerized polygraphs. Although multiple diagnostic features can be extracted from the same physiological response curve, they tend to be highly intercorrelated. The features are often highly correlated with the criterion, but because they are largely redundant, a single well-chosen feature captures most of the diagnostic variance available from a given response curve. In contrast, features from entirely different response systems are relatively independent and do make unique contributions to statistical models for discriminating between truthful and deceptive subjects. These findings suggest that significant gains in computer accuracy are more likely to come from new types of physiological measures than from novel ways of quantifying traditional polygraph signals.

Much of our research has focused on new autonomic measures, such as vagal tone, skin potential, arterial blood pressure, and pupil diameter. Arterial blood pressure and pupil diameter are currently the most promising of the new autonomic measures. Podlesny and Kircher (1999) compared cardiograph recordings to continuous measures of blood pressure from a Finapres finger cuff (Datex-Ohmeda, Tewksbury, MA). They found that measures extracted from the Finapres were at least as diagnostic as those obtained from the cardiograph. In addition to possible improvements in decision accuracy, the Finapres has other advantages. The cardiograph restricts blood flow in the arm and causes discomfort if it is inflated for more than a few minutes. Use of the cardiograph requires that repetitions of the question sequence be interrupted to re-establish circulation in the arm below the cuff. In contrast, the Finapres can be operated for extended periods without discomfort and is less subject to movement artifact. The Finapres or similar device would allow for an increase in the number of test questions that may be presented without a rest period. An increase in the number of test questions could improve the reliability and validity of polygraph outcomes. It could even allow for an uninterrupted series of test questions. In an extended series of test questions, the responses of truthful and deceptive individuals to comparison and relevant questions might habituate at different rates (Ben-Shakhar *et al.*, 1975). If so, differences in the rates of habituation might contribute to a computer model for diagnosing truth and deception.

Kircher *et al.* (2000) reported the results of a recent pilot study that assessed the pupillary responses of 24 participants, half of whom were guilty of committing a mock theft of $20. Pupil diameter was measured at 60 Hz for eight seconds following the onset of each comparison and relevant question. The samples defined a response curve that increased with increases in pupil dilation. The computer was then programmed to measure the area under the curve for each test question. Following our standard practice, the computer measurements were converted to standard scores within the subject. An index of differential reactivity was then calculated for each subject by subtracting the mean standard score for relevant questions from the mean standard score for comparison questions. The pupillary difference score correlated .62 with the criterion, which was as high as the correlation between SC and the criterion in that study (r = .59). However, the sample size was small and the pupillary measure correlated .65 with SC. Consequently, the pupillary measure did not make a statistically significant contribution to a discriminant function that contained the standard SC, cardiograph, and respiration measures.

The recent successes with new physiological measures are encouraging. New measures not only may make independent contributions to computer-based statistical predictions of truth and deception, but they also provide opportunities to improve the psychometric properties of traditional physiological measures, for example, by increasing test length.

DIRECTED-LIE POLYGRAPH TESTS

There are considerable conceptual and methodological advantages to directed-lie tests (Horowitz *et al.*, 1997). However, respiration responses to directed-lie questions differ significantly from responses to traditional probable-lie questions (Bell *et al.*, 2000; Horowitz *et al.*, 1997). Although we have not shown significant differences between probable-lie and directed-lie tests in decision outcomes produced by CPS, it is clear that the CPS model is not optimal for directed-lie tests. Additional research on alternative computer models is needed to support the use of directed-lie questions.

DATABASE DEVELOPMENT

A computerized polygraph system creates electronic files of the polygraph charts. These files may be used to reconstruct the physiological recordings at

developed to the point that they should replace the human polygraph interpreter. At the current stage of development, computer analysis should serve as a form of quality control that either supports or casts doubt on traditional human evaluations of the charts. If the evaluation by the polygraph examiner agrees with the computer result, the examiner can have increased confidence in their interpretation of the charts. If the examiner's evaluation disagrees with the computer analysis, the reasons for the discrepancy should be identified. Measurements made by the computer may be reviewed and compared to the numerical evaluations. Polygraph examiners would then have the opportunity to reconsider their initial assessments in light of the computer measurements.

Computer analysis may also be instructive. Characteristics of physiological reactions that are measured by the CPS program are also used by the polygraph interpreter to assign numerical scores. The computer may highlight the specific regions of the physiological signal from which it takes its measurements when the charts are displayed on the screen for numerical evaluation. The computer shows the polygraph examiner precisely where to look for the effects of test questions on physiological responses. Computer measurements are especially helpful when there is some doubt about the magnitude of the difference between reactions to comparison and relevant questions.

The outcomes of field polygraph examinations often have significant consequences for the individual and society. Whether or not the polygraph examiner uses a computerized polygraph, the examiner, not the computer, ultimately decides if the subject was deceptive on the test. Polygraph examiners cannot accept the outcome of a computer analysis in good conscience unless they have some idea about how the system works. For example, it is necessary to know which characteristics of the physiological recordings are measured by the computer before one can decide if the computer analysis could have been affected by inadequate recordings, deep breaths, movements artifacts, or countermeasures. To be confident in the outcome produced by a computerized polygraph system, the examiner also should be aware of the scientific evidence that supports or challenges the use of a particular instrument or data analysis program. In most cases, claims of high validity by computerized polygraph manufacturers, software developers, and self-proclaimed polygraph authorities are unsubstantiated by credible scientific research (e.g., Porges *et al.*, 1996). At a minimum, users of computerized polygraph systems should expect that the signals generated by the computerized polygraph be at least monotonically related to levels of physiological arousal. Users should also expect that claims of high accuracy be supported by scientific studies. Scientific studies would include cases that are independent of the database used to develop the scoring algorithms and are representative of the population of criminal suspects.

REFERENCES

Barland, G. H. and Raskin, D. C. (1975) An evaluation of field techniques in the detection of deception. *Psychophysiology,* 12, 321–330.

Bell, B. G., Bernhardt, P. C., Kircher, J. C. and Packard, R. E. (2000) Effects of prior demonstrations of test accuracy on outcomes of probable-lie and directed-lie polygraph tests. *Psychophysiology,* 37, S27 (Abstract).

Bell, B. G., Raskin, D. C., Honts, C. R. and Kircher, J. C. (1999) The Utah numerical scoring system. *Polygraph,* 28, 1–9.

Ben-Shakhar, G. and Lieblich, I. (1984) On statistical detection of deception: Comment on Szucko and Kleinmuntz. *American Psychologist,* 39, 79–80.

Ben-Shakhar, G., Lieblich, I. and Kugelmas, S. (1975) Detection of information and GSR habituation: An attempt to derive detection efficiency from two habituation curves. *Psychophysiology,* 12, 283–288.

Bernhardt, P. C. (2000) *Effects of Prior Demonstrations of Polygraph Accuracy on Probable-Lie and Directed-Lie Polygraph Tests.* Unpublished doctoral dissertation, University of Utah.

Blackwell, J. (1999) Polyscore 3.3 and psychophysiological detection of deception examiner rates of accuracy when scoring examinations from actual criminal investigations. *Polygraph,* 28, 149–175.

Bradley, M. T. and Ainsworth, D. (1984) Alcohol and the psychophysiological detection of deception. *Psychophysiology,* 21, 63–71.

Cestaro, V. (1998) *Memorandum for Record: Laboratory Tests Performed on the Electrodermal Activity (EDA) Channels of Various Polygraph Instruments.* Report on Project DoDPI98-P-0003 to the US Department of Defense Polygraph Institute, Ft. McCellan, AL.

Cutrow, R. J., Parks, A., Lucas, N. and Thomas, K. (1972) The objective use of multiple physiological indices in the detection of deception. *Psychophysiology,* 9, 578–588.

Dawson, M. E. (1980). Physiological detection of deception: Measurement of responses to questions and answers during countermeasure maneuvers. *Psychophysiology,* 17, 8–17.

Devitt, M. K. and Honts, C. R. (1993) *Multivariate Classifiers Perform as Well as Experts in the Detection of Deception.* Paper presented at the Fifth Annual Convention of the American Psychological Society, Chicago, June 1993.

Dollins, A. B., Krapohl, D. J. and Dutton, D. W. (2000) A comparison of computer programs designed to evaluate psychophysiological detection of deception examinations: Bakeoff 1. *Polygraph.*

Ellson, D. G., Davis, R. C., Saltzman, I. J. and Burke, C. J. (1952) *A Report on Research on Detection of Deception.* Contract N6onr-18011 with Office of Naval Research. Bloomington: Department of Psychology, Indiana University.

Fowles, D. C., Christie, M. J., Edelberg, R., Grings,W. W., Lykken, D. T. and Venables, P. H. (1981) Publication recommendations for electrodermal measurements. *Psychophysiology,* 16, 66–70.

Fuse, L. S. (1982). *Directed-lie Control Test.* Unpublished manuscript.

Gatchel, R. J., Smith, J. E. and Kaplan, M. D. (1984) *The Effect of Propanolol on the Polygraphic Detection of Deception.* Unpublished manuscript, University of Texas Health Services Center at Dallas.

Geddes, L. A. and Newberg, D. C. (1977) Cuff pressure oscillations in the measurement of relative blood pressure. *Psychophysiology,* 14, 198–202.

Hocking, R. R. (1976) The analysis and selection of variables in linear regression. *Biometrics,* 32, 1–49.

Honts, C. R. and Amato, S. (1998) The automated polygraph examination: Validity in a mock-screening paradigm. Final report to the federal government. Department of Psychology, Boise State University.

Honts, C. R., Amato, S. and Gordon, A. (2000). Validity of outside-issue questions in the control question test. Final report on Grant No. N000 14-98-1-0725 to the Department of Defense Polygraph Institute. Department of Psychology, Boise State University.

Honts, C. R. and Raskin, D. C. (1988) A field study of the validity of the directed-lie control question. *Journal of Police Science and Administration,* 16, 56–61.

Horowitz, S. W., Kircher, J. C., Honts, C. R. and Raskin, D. C. (1997) The role of control questions in physiological detection of deception. *Psychophysiology,* 34, 108–115.

Iacono W. G. and Lykken, D. T. (1997) The scientific status of research on polygraph techniques: The case against polygraph tests. In D. L. Faigman, D. Kaye, M. J. Saks and J. Sanders (eds), *Scientific Evidence Reference Manual* (582–618). West Publishing Co.

Kircher, J. C. (1981) *Automated Electrodermal Response Quantification.* Paper presented at the Annual Meeting of the Society for Psychophysiological Research, Washington, DC, October 1981.

Kircher, J. C., Horowitz, S. W. and Raskin, D. C. (1988) Meta-analysis of mock crime studies of the control question polygraph technique. *Law and Human Behavior,* 12, 79–90.

Kircher, J. C., Packard, R. E., Bernhardt, P. C. and Bell, B. G. (2000) *A Comparison of Skin Conductance and Skin Resistance Measures for the Psychophysiological Detection of*

Deception. Report to the Department of Defense Polygraph Institute, Office of Naval Research. Salt Lake City, Utah: Department of Educational Psychology, the University of Utah.

Kircher, J. C. and Raskin, D. C. (1981) Computerized decision-making in the detection of deception. *Psychophysiology,* 18, 204–205, (Abstract).

Kircher, J. C. and Raskin, D. C. (1982) Cross-validation of a computerized diagnostic procedure for detecting deception. *Psychophysiology,* 19, 568 (Abstract).

Kircher, J. C. and Raskin, D. C. (1983) Clinical versus statistical lie detection revisited: Through a lens sharply. *Psychophysiology,* 20, 452, (Abstract).

Kircher, J. C. and Raskin, D. C. (1986) *Computer-Assisted Polygraph System.* Scientific Assessment Technologies, 2532 Chadwick Street, Salt Lake City, UT.

Kircher, J. C. and Raskin, D. C. (1988) Human versus computerized evaluations of polygraph data in a laboratory setting. *Journal of Applied Psychology,* 73, 291–302.

Kircher, J. C., Raskin, D. C., Honts, C. R. and Horowitz, S. W. (1994) Genereralizability of statistical classifiers for the detection of deception. *Psychophysiology,* 31, S73, (Abstract).

Kircher, J. C., Raskin, D. C., Honts, C. R. and Horowitz, S. W. (1995) Lens model analysis of decision making by field polygraph examiners. *Psychophysiology,* 32, S45, (Abstract).

Kubis, J. F. (1962) *Studies on Lie Detection: Computer Feasibility Considerations.* Contract AF30(602)-2270, Project 5534. Prepared for Rome Air Development Center, TR62-205. Distributed by Arlington, Virginia: Armed Services Technical Information Agency, AD-284902.

Kubis, J. F. (1973) Analysis of polygraph data, part 2. *Polygraph,* 2, 89–107.

Lacey, J. I. (1956) The evaluation of autonomic responses: Toward a general solution. *Annals of the New York Academy of Sciences,* 67, 123–163.

Lykken, D. T. (1981) *A Tremor in the Blood: Uses and Abuses of the Lie Detector.* New York: McGraw Hill.

McNemar, Q. (1969) *Psychological Statistics*, 4th edn. New York: John Wiley and Sons.

Nunnally, J. C. (1978) *Psychometric Theory*, 2nd edn. New York: McGraw-Hill.

Office of Technology Assessment (1983) *Scientific Validity of Polygraph Testing: A Research Review and Evaluation – A Technical Memorandum* (OTA-TM-H-15). Washington, DC: US Government Printing Office.

Olsen, D. E., Harris, J. C., Capps, M. H. and Ansley, N. (1997) Computerized polygraph scoring system. *Journal of Forensic Sciences,* 42, 61–70.

Podlesny, J. A. and Kircher, J. C. (1999) The Finapres (volume clamp) recording method in psychophysiological detection of deception examinations: Experimental comparison with the cardiograph method. *Forensic Science Communication,* 1(3), 1–17.

Podlesny, J. A. and Raskin, D. C. (1977) Physiological measures and the detection of deception. *Psychological Bulletin,* 84, 782–799.

Podlesny, J. A. and Raskin, D. C. (1978) Effectiveness of techniques and physiological measures in the detection of deception. *Psychophysiology,* 15, 344–359.

Porges, S. W., Johnson, R., Kircher, J. C. and Stern, J. A. (1996) Report of peer review of Johns Hopkins University/Applied Physics Laboratory to the Central Intelligence Agency.

Raskin, D. C. (1976) *Reliability of Chart Interpretation and Sources of Errors in Polygraph Examinations.* Report No. 76-3, Contract 75-NI-99-0001. US Department of Justice. Salt Lake City: University of Utah: Department of Psychology.

Raskin, D. C. and Barland, G. H. (1976) *An Evaluation of Polygraph Techniques Currently Practiced by Law Enforcement and Private Polygraph Examiners.* Report No. 76-2, Contract 75-NI-99-0001, U.S. Department of Justice. Salt Lake City, Utah: Department of Psychology, the University of Utah.

Raskin, D. C. and Hare, R. D. (1978) Psychopathology and the detection of deception in a prison population. *Psychophysiology,* 15, 126–136.

Raskin, D. C., Honts, C. R. and Kircher, J. C. (1997) Polygraph techniques: Theory, research, and applications from the perspective of scientists-practicioners. In: D. L. Faigman, D. Kaye, M. J. Saks and J. Sanders (eds) *Scientific Evidence Reference Manual,* pp. 551–582. West Publishing Co.

Raskin, D. C., Horowitz, S. W. and Kircher, J. C. (1989) *Computerized Analysis of Polygraph Outcomes in Criminal Investigation.* Report of research and results of phase II of Contract TSS 86-18 from the US Secret Service. Salt Lake City: University of Utah.

Raskin, D. C., Kircher, J. C., Honts, C. R. and Horowitz, S. W. (1988) *A Study of the Validity of Polygraph Examinations in Criminal Investigation.* Final report to the National Institute of Justice (Grant No. 85-IJ-CX-0040). Salt Lake City: University of Utah, Department of Psychology.

Reid, J. E. and Inbau, F. E. (1977) *Truth and Deception: The Polygraph ("Lie Detector") Technique.* Baltimore: Williams and Wilkins.

Rich, T., Smith, T. W., Kircher, J. C. and Martin, S. N. (1998) Emotional suppression and physiological response to trauma cues in PTSD. *Psychophysiology,* 34 (Abstract).

Rovner, L. I. (1986) The accuracy of physiological detection of deception for subjects with prior knowledge. *Polygraph,* 15, 1–39.

Senter, S. M., Dollins, A. B., and Krapohl, D. J. (2000) *Comparison of Utah and DoDPI Scoring Accuracy: Equating Veracity Decision Rule, Chart Rule, and Number of Channels Used.* Paper presented at the Annual Meeting of the Society for Psychophysiological Research, San Diego, CA.

Stern, R. M., Ray, W. J. and Davis, C. (1980) *Psychophysiological Recording.* New York: Oxford University Press.

Sternbach, R. A. (1966) *Principles of Psychophysiology.* New York: Academic Press.

Swinford, J. (1999) Manually scoring polygraph charts utilizing the seven-position numerical analysis scale at the Department of Defense Polygraph Institute. *Polygraph,* 28, 10–27.

Szucko, J. J. and Kleinmuntz, B. (1981) Statistical versus clinical lie detection. *American Psychologist,* 36, 488–496.

Timm, H. W. (1982) Effect of altered outcome expectancies stemming from placebo and feedback treatments on the validity of the guilty knowledge technique. *Journal of Applied Psychology,* 67, 391–400.

Venables, P. H. and Christie, M. J. (1980) Electrodermal activity. In: I. Martin and P. H. Venables (eds) *Techniques in Psychophysiology.* New York: John Wiley and Sons.

Wiggins, J. S. (1981) Clinical and statistical prediction: Where are we and where do we go from here? *Clinical Psychology Review,* 1, 3–18.

CHAPTER 12

LEGAL ASPECTS OF POLYGRAPH ADMISSIBILITY IN THE UNITED STATES

Charles W. Daniels

INTRODUCTION

There is no single category of evidence in the history of American law that has been subjected to stricter scrutiny by the courts, to greater resistance against admission and to such a widespread reluctance to accept scientific developments in the courtroom than has been the case with polygraph evidence. The cases in which it has been admitted are the exceptional ones, and the vast majority of reported opinions either deny its use with little analysis, or employ techniques of exclusion that are not used against other forms of evidence. Ironically, this hostile response by the courts occurs in a country which sees widespread use of the polygraph in other settings, particularly by the same government entities which routinely and vigorously oppose its use against them in court.

This chapter will review the historical development of the approaches of courts in the United States to the admission of results of polygraph examinations, will analyze the current realities, and will consider what the future might bring in this area.

THE *FRYE* "GENERAL ACCEPTANCE IN THE SCIENTIFIC COMMUNITY" TEST

The development of American polygraph law began with the seminal case of *Frye v. United States*.[1] The defendant Frye was convicted of murder in a Washington, DC, federal court and appealed his conviction on the ground that the trial court erroneously refused to admit defense evidence based on a crude precursor to the modern polygraph. The systolic blood pressure deception test used in *Frye* was based on a periodic sampling of readings from a simple blood pressure cuff during a dialogue with the defendant concerning the alleged crime. There was no scientifically sound method of measurement or comparison of the reactions to particular questions. The technique actually was based on a promising psychophysiological theory, but was so unscientific in its methodology as to be unreliable.

[1] *Frye v. United States*, 293 F.1013 (D.C. Cir.1923).

The fundamental evidentiary problem posed to the courts in *Frye* went far beyond the particular technique under review. Increasingly, courts were confronting new forms of evidence based on modern scientific studies, but which ordinary juries were unable to evaluate on the basis of their own everyday experience and common understanding. Judges were similarly handicapped in deciding whether to admit the evidence before the jury without the advice of qualified members of the scientific community. The rationale developed by the court of appeals in upholding the trial court's refusal to admit the novel evidence became widely known as the "*Frye* test." It applied not only to polygraph evidence, but to novel scientific evidence in general:

> Just when a scientific principle or discovery crosses the line between the experimental and demonstrable stages is difficult to define. Somewhere in this twilight zone the evidential force of the principle must be recognized, and while courts will go a long way in admitting expert testimony deduced from a well-recognized scientific principle or discovery, the thing from which the deduction is made must be sufficiently established to have gained general acceptance in the particular field in which it belongs.[2]

[2] *Id.* at 1014.

For the systolic blood pressure deception-testing technique under review, the *Frye* court concluded that it had not gained sufficient acceptance among physiological and psychological authorities to be admissible.

The *Frye* "general acceptance in the scientific community" test dominated the admissibility of scientific evidence in general, and polygraph evidence in particular, for the next 70 years. During that time, while other forms of novel scientific evidence were deemed to have developed the level of acceptability mandated by *Frye*, the advances in the study of psychophysiology as applied to polygraph testing were ignored by the courts. For other forms of evidence, *Frye* stood for a process of analysis of acceptability; for polygraph, it was used to support the conclusion that the evidence was always inadmissible as a matter of law (McCall, 1996).

There were two noteworthy exceptions to this overwhelmingly exclusionary reaction in the State and federal court systems in the United States. *State v. Dorsey*[3] and the subsequent promulgation of New Mexico evidence rule 11-707 opened the doors of the New Mexico State courts to the use of polygraph evidence from 1975 through the present. No other state admits the evidence without an agreement by the parties participating in the case, an approach that almost invariably results in exclusion.

[3] *State v. Dorsey*, 88 N.M.184, (N.M. 1975).

In 1989, the federal appeals court opinion in *United States v. Piccinonna*[4] promised to have greater impact. It provided the most thorough judicial study to that time of the scientific and legal issues and determined that "since the *Frye* decision, tremendous advances have been made in polygraph instrumentation

[4] *United States v. Piccinonna*, 885 F.2d 1529 (11th Cir. 1998).

and technique;" that "the FBI, the secret service, military intelligence and law enforcement agencies use the polygraph;"[5] that "in recent years polygraph testing has gained increasingly widespread acceptance as a useful and reliable scientific tool;" that there is "a lack of evidence that juries are unduly swayed;" and that "a *per se* rule disallowing polygraph evidence is no longer warranted."[6] That court therefore articulated standards for admissibility in the 11th federal judicial circuit, encompassing the federal trial courts located in the southeastern corner of the United States. Although the decision has never been overruled and theoretically is in force today,[7] no other jurisdiction has followed the *Piccinonna* precedent.

THE *DAUBERT* "SCIENTIFIC KNOWLEDGE" APPROACH

The most promising opinion to those who favored a fresh look at polygraph admissibility came several years after *Piccinonna*, when the Supreme Court of the United States expressly replaced the *Frye* test for determining admissibility of scientific evidence in another landmark case, *Daubert v. Merrell Dow Pharmaceuticals, Inc.*[8] *Daubert* concluded that the austere *Frye* approach of waiting for general acceptance in the community before recognizing scientific developments was too restrictive, given the more liberal approach to admissibility of the modern federal rules of evidence in general and, in particular, expert evidence rule 702. That rule allows expert testimony to be placed before the jury if it is based on "scientific knowledge" and if it will "assist the trier of fact," such as a jury, to determine a fact in issue. *Daubert* provided some general guidelines in determining whether the offered evidence is based on scientific knowledge; that is, whether it has been derived by the scientific method, rather than unsupported speculation. The fact that the scientific community may be divided or that a majority may not yet be in agreement about the conclusions to be drawn was not itself to be deemed an automatic bar to admission of the evidence.

The relevant factors suggested by the *Daubert* opinion included:

1. whether the theory or technique on which the testimony is based is capable of being tested;
2. whether the technique has a known rate of error in its application;
3. whether the theory or technique has been subjected to peer review and publication;
4. the level of acceptance in the relevant scientific community of the theory or technique; and
5. the extent to which there are standards to determine acceptable use of the technique.

[5] *Id.* at 1532.

[6] *Id.* at 1535.

[7] *United States v. Padilla*, 908 F. Supp. 923 (S.D. Fla. 1995); *Elortegui v. United States*, 743 F. Supp. 828 (S.D. Fla. 1990).

[8] *Daubert v. Merrell Dow Pharmaceuticals, Inc.*, 509 U.S. 579 (1993).

None of the factors suggested by the court was to be rigidly dispositive, and the inquiry was to be a flexible one, keeping in mind the competing needs of keeping untrustworthy pseudoscience from the jury and of keeping the courts open to emerging scientific developments.

Several federal courts addressing the implications of *Daubert* for the admissibility of polygraph evidence acknowledged that the rigid exclusionary stance of the *Frye* years was no longer justified and that a fresh *Daubert* analysis was required.[9] Several of the more thorough analyses of the *Daubert* factors in reported trial court opinions resulted in findings that the modern control question polygraph is scientific evidence which should be admitted under rule 702.[10] However, the majority of the post-*Daubert* opinions exhibited and often openly expressed great reluctance to change their exclusionary positions on polygraph evidence.[11]

Given the wealth of literature on the subject, an objective application of the *Daubert* factors to polygraph should be quite capable of being accomplished both by experts in the field and by the judges who must make the ultimate determination of admissibility. The reality was, however, that *Daubert* did not result in opening the doors of American courts to use of polygraph evidence.

The overwhelmingly dominant trend of the post-*Daubert* decisions has been to continue to exclude polygraph evidence, either on the basis of a stringently hostile *Daubert* analysis that is employed against no other form of proposed scientific evidence[12] or by the use of what amount to evidentiary blackballs that inevitably prevent the evidence from being considered under *Daubert* at all (Imwinkelreid and McCall, 1997). Some of the theories are either inexplicable in themselves or impossible to reconcile with each other. For example, in *United States v. Pulido*,[13] a federal appeals court excluded a defendant's polygraph evidence where the results were deemed peripheral to the "core issues," while the very next year, in *United States v. Sherlin*,[14] a federal appeals court in an adjacent circuit excluded another defendant's polygraph because his credibility "was maybe the central issue in this case."

One of the most common exclusionary techniques is the use of federal Rule 403 and its State court equivalents, which allow a trial judge to disregard other rules of admissibility and exclude evidence that is relatively weak or may cause confusion, consume too much time, or cause unnecessary prejudice to a party. Use of this approach can avoid a court's even having to hold a *Daubert* hearing or consider any of the scientific realities.[15] Despite the promise inherent in the *Daubert* opinion itself, the experience in the courts in subsequent years makes it clear that one or more of the recurring exclusionary positions in the ensuing section are likely to be faced by any proponent of the use of polygraph evidence.

[9] *United States v. Cordoba*, 104 F.3d 225 (9th Cir. 1997); *United States v. Pulido*, 69 F.3d 192 (7th Cir. 1995); *United States v. Posado*, 57 F.3d 428 (5th Cir. 1995).

[10] *United States v. Galbreth*, 908 F. Supp. 877 (D.N.M. 1995); *United States v. Crumby*, 895 F. Supp. 1354 (D. Ariz.1995); *Ulmer v. State Farm Fire and Casualty Co.*, 897 F. Supp. 299 (W.D. La. 1995).

[11] *See Cordoba, supra,* at 226 ("we have long expressed our hostility to the admission of unstipulated polygraph evidence") and *United States v. Call*, 129 F.3d 1402, 1408 (1997) ("our holding [that *Daubert* allows a possibility of admitting polygraph] does not suggest a newfound enthusiasm for polygraph evidence").

[12] See, *e.g., United States v. Cordoba*, 991 F. Supp. 1199 (C.D. Ca. 1998) (on remand for a *Daubert* hearing), and *United States v. Orians*, 9 F. Supp.2d 1168 (D. Ariz. 1998).

[13] *United States v. Pulido*, 69 F.3d 192 (7th Cir. 1995).

[14] *United States v. Sherlin* 67 F.3d 1208 (6th Cir. 1995).

[15] *United States v. Call*, 129 F.3d 1402 (10th Cir. 1997).

THE RECURRING EXCLUSIONARY ISSUES

1. WHETHER THE POLYGRAPH WOULD REPLACE THE FUNCTION OF THE JURY

Often clearly articulated and equally often implicit, there is a pervasive apprehension in the exclusionary opinions that the introduction of polygraph evidence would wreak some fundamental change in the American judicial system of determining truth. A fundamental premise of that system is that "the jury is the lie detector."[16] Polygraph testimony is viewed as something that should be excluded "because it usurps a critical function of the jury and because it is not helpful to the jury."[17]

The opinions fail to understand the nature of the evidence. The polygrapher is not dictating how the case should be decided or even whether the test subject is telling the truth from the witness stand. The testimony is simply that on a previous occasion out of court, the subject exhibited measurable psychophysiological responses shown by scientific study to be indicative of a likelihood of consciousness of truth or deception as to the particular answers to the relevant polygraph questions.

Juries traditionally have been encouraged to consider observations of external demeanor in court as guides to determining consciousness of truthfulness or deception by a witness, despite the known difficulties in making accurate judgments in that manner. Flight, evidence tampering, obstruction of justice and numerous other physical activities reflecting consciousness of guilt have routinely been admissible in all courts (Imwinkelried, 1996). Similarly, circumstantial evidence of subjective consciousness of innocence is admissible "as relevant to show defendant's lack of guilty knowledge" (McLaughlin, 1997). The polygraph simply provides another, and arguably more accurate, form of circumstantial evidence of consciousness of guilt.[18]

Despite the pervasive judicial apprehension of the impact of polygraph on juries, courts occasionally have evidenced a less exclusionary approach when polygraph evidence is to be considered by a trained judge in non-jury proceedings.[19]

2. WHETHER THE EVIDENCE WOULD OVERWHELM AND CONFUSE THE JURY

This concern is related to the first, but relates more to the fear that a lay jury is simply incapable of processing rationally the testimony of the polygraph expert, who would be surrounded by "an aura of near infallibility, akin to the ancient oracle of Delphi."[20] The United States Supreme Court appeared to have put this

[16] *United States v. Barnard*, 490 F.2d 907, 912 (9th Cir. 1973), cert. denied, 416 U.S. 959 (1974).

[17] *United States v. Call*, 129 F.3d 1402 (10th Cir. 1997).

[18] *See, United States v. Scheffer*, 523 U.S. 303, 332 (1997) (Stevens, J., dissenting). "No constitutional provision, law or rule requires the automatic exclusion of expert testimony simply because it concerns a credibility question." *United States v. Shay*, 57 F.3d 126, 131 (1st Cir. 1995).

[19] *United States v. Posado*, 57 F.3d 428 (5th Cir. 1995); *United States v. Holguin*, 946 F. Supp. 157 (D. Conn. 1996); *United States v. Chaney*, 1996 U.S. App. LEXIS 8657 (10th Cir.).

[20] *United States v. Alexander*, 526 F.2d 161, 168 (8th Cir. 1875).

[21] *Daubert v. Merrell Dow Pharmaceuticals, Inc.*, 509 U.S. 579, 595–96 (1993).

kind of argument to rest when it overruled *Frye* in *Daubert v. Merrell Dow Pharmaceuticals, Inc.*:[21]

> Respondent expresses apprehension that abandonment of "general acceptance" as the exclusive requirement for admission will result in a "free-for-all" in which befuddled juries are confounded by absurd and irrational pseudo-scientific assertions. In this regard Respondent seems to us to be overly pessimistic about the capabilities of the jury, and of the adversary system generally. Vigorous cross-examination, presentation of contrary evidence, and careful instruction on the burden of proof are the traditional and appropriate means of attacking shaky but admissible evidence.

That admonition in *Daubert* has not been heeded in the multitude of cases relying on undue jury influence in rejecting admissibility of polygraph. Those opinions never refer to any actual research or experience to support the view that the jury will be unduly swayed by polygraph testimony; instead, they merely rely on the unsupported statements to that effect in prior opinions.[22] The few opinions which refer to actual studies on the subject find no evidence to support the fear that the polygraph evidence will confuse or mislead the jury.[23]

[22] *See, e.g., United States v. Wright*, 1998 U.S. Dist. LEXIS 15127 (W.D. Tenn. 1998); *State v. Dean*, 103 Wis. 2d 228 (1981).

[23] *See, e.g., United States v. Scheffer, supra* at 337 (Stevens, J., dissenting); *United States v. Piccinonna*, 885 F.2d 1529, 1533 (11th Cir. 1989) (the "studies refute the proposition that jurors are likely to give disproportionate weight to polygraph evidence."); *United States v. Starzecpyzel*, 880 F. Supp. 1027, 1048–49 (S.D.N.Y. 1995); *United States v. Galbreth*, 908 F. Supp. 877, 895 (D.N.M. 1995).

The experience in the one American jurisdiction in which polygraph evidence is routinely admitted before juries in the same fashion as other expert evidence has largely been ignored by the exclusionary courts. In *State v. Dorsey*,[24] the Supreme Court of the State of New Mexico determined that a blanket exclusion of unstipulated polygraph evidence was mechanistic in nature and inconsistent with the thrust of the modern rules of evidence. Polygraph evidence has been admissible in New Mexico State courts since then.

In 1983, the court followed up on its *Dorsey* opinion by promulgating New Mexico rule of evidence 11-707, which provides procedures for pretrial notice, discovery and admissibility of polygraph evidence.[25] After more than a quarter of a century of admissibility in the New Mexico courts, the results have been described as demonstrating that jurors quite capably deal with the evidence just as they deal with other evidence (Daniels, 1997). The evidence has not dominated trials in New Mexico in any regard (Raskin, 1986). In fact, it has been used only occasionally in either criminal or civil cases, although admissible in both (McCall, 1996).

[24] *State v. Dorsey*, 88 N.M. 184, 539 P.2d 204 (1975).

[25] N.M. R. Evid. 11-707 (Michie 2001).

3. WHETHER THE POLYGRAPH IS TOO UNRELIABLE TO BE CONSIDERED

Many courts impose upon polygraph a high burden of accuracy (generally referred to as reliability in the legal literature) that is used against no other form of evidence. The majority of laboratory and field studies place the accuracy rates of the results of a properly conducted comparison question polygraph test in excess of 85%.[26] The court systems in the United States routinely admit evidence with much lower accuracy rates, such as eyewitness identifications, plea-dealing informant testimony, and the like. Lay witnesses are permitted to testify as to sanity and character of another. With regard to scientific testimony in particular, the courts have upheld handwriting comparisons, predictions of future dangerousness, inkblot analyses and other psychiatric diagnoses, even though the data show them to be less reliable, or even more likely than not to be simply wrong (O'Conner, 1988).[27]

Rule 402 of the Federal Rules of Evidence, similar to analogous rules of most State jurisdictions, sets a threshold of evidentiary admissibility in general, providing that evidence need only tend to make the proposition for which it is offered more likely than it would have been without the evidence. That is essentially a more probable than not standard. No polygraph case reported has concluded that the evidence fails to meet that legal standard.

The rationale of lack of reliability often is voiced by judges who simply fear the potential impact of polygraph on the litigation process and who do not express it as candidly as one court did: "Even if the accuracy of polygraph examinations approaches the eighty or ninety percent claimed by the polygraph experts, [the jury's] view of the polygraph as an absolute indicator of truth creates an overwhelming potential for prejudice . . ."[28] A respected American jurist, Justice Hans Lynde of the Supreme Court of Oregon, accurately observed the reality: "I doubt the uneasiness about electrical lie detectors would disappear even if they were refined to place their accuracy beyond question. Indeed, I would not be surprised if such a development would only heighten the sense of unease and the search for plausible legal objections."[29]

4. WHETHER POLYGRAPH EVIDENCE IS TOO TIME-CONSUMING

Many exclusionary opinions rely on the proposition that polygraph issues would simply take up too much court time.[30] None of those cases refer to any empirical study that has ever supported the notion that polygraph evidence is generally more time-consuming than the diverse variety of scientific evidence that the courts deal with in the course of litigation on a regular basis. In fact, the evidence is to the contrary (Peters, 1982). No case has articulated why potential disputes over qualifications, foundations, cross-examination and disagreements among experts need take any more time for polygraph than it does for DNA, psychiatric disputes, legal economics or the issues about hypnotized witnesses that the Supreme Court faced in *Rock v. Arkansas*.[31] The problem of the battle of the experts "is present in every area of expert testimony and the best solution is the discerning judgment of the jury," subject to the trial court's gatekeeping

[26] *United States v. Crumby, supra; United States v. Galbreth, supra.*

[27] *United States v. Scheffer, supra,* at 334.

[28] *Brown v. Darcy,* 783 F.2d 1389, 1396 (9th Cir. 1986).

[29] *People v. Lyon,* 744 P.2d 231, 238 (Or. 1987) (Linde, J., concurring).

[30] *State v. Grier,* 307 N.C. 628 (1983).

[31] *Rock v. Arkansas,* 483 U.S. 44 (1987).

[32] *State v. Mendoza*, 80 Wis. 2d 122, 163, 258 N.W.2d 260, 278 (1977).

[33] *Johnson v. United States*, 780 F.2d 902 (11th Cir. 1986); *Ballou v. Henri Studies, Inc.*, 656 F.2d 1147 (5th Cir. 1981); *Bower v. O'Hara*, 759 F.2d 1117 (3d Cir. 1985).

[34] *Maddox v. Cash Loans of Huntsville II*, 1998 U.S. Dist. LEXIS 14938 (N.D. Al. 1998); *United States v. Pittner*, 969 F. Supp. 1246 (W.D. Wash. 1997).

discretion.[32] In the context of other forms of expert testimony, the courts have acknowledged that the discretion to keep out time-consuming evidence "does not mean that a court may exclude evidence that will cause delay regardless of its probative value."[33]

5. WHETHER THE POLYGRAPHER IS BEING OFFERED AS A CHARACTER EXPERT

One recurring argument, founded on a complete misperception of the nature of polygraph evidence, is that "the polygraph results are inadmissible extrinsic evidence of plaintiff's character."[34]

Rule 608 of the federal rules of evidence, like many corresponding State rules, imposes certain requirements for the use of a witness to testify about someone's good or bad character, which can be used as a basis for an inference by the jury that the person may have acted in conformity with that character on the occasion at issue in the trial. Rule 608(a) allows character witnesses to testify in the form of their own opinion of the person's character or their knowledge of the person's reputation in the community, provided they have a sufficient basis for knowing either. Rule 608(b) precludes character witnesses from testifying about particular instances of misconduct or deception.

The courts employing the character theory for excluding polygraph evidence theorize that when the polygrapher testifies about truthful or deceptive answers of a subject on a polygraph test, he is doing so to show that the test subject has the character of an honest or dishonest person. Since the polygrapher's opinion does not meet the standards for admission as character evidence, the opinion is held to be inadmissible.

Those opinions are simply wrong (Imwinkelreid and McCall, 1997). The polygrapher neither tests nor testifies about a person's overall character. Those considerations are irrelevant to the overriding function of the polygraph test: to provide scientific circumstantial evidence of manifestations indicating consciousness of truth or deception as to particular items of knowledge. Whether the person lies or tells the truth on other occasions has no bearing on the outcome of the test and is of no concern to the polygrapher.

6. WHETHER THE OPPOSING PARTY HAS BEEN PRESENT AT THE POLYGRAPH EXAMINATION

There is nothing in the rules of evidence or other controlling case law which imposes a general requirement that a party must invite the opposing party to be present for any scientific test, medical or psychological examination in order for the results to be offered into evidence. Nevertheless, a substantial number of court opinions exclude polygraph test results on that theory, even where the opponent has been provided an opportunity to conduct its own test or to review the test data and audiotapes or videotapes of the first examination.[35]

7. WHETHER THE OPPOSING PARTY HAS STIPULATED TO ADMISSION OF THE TEST

The frequently encountered stipulation approach, common in State courts (McCall, 1996) and "prevalent in most [federal judicial] circuits,"[36] cannot be justified on any sound jurisprudential basis.[37] If the evidence is relevant and reliable, opposing counsel should not have the unilateral power to decide whether the jury should hear it. Conversely, if it were not relevant and reliable, why should a jury be permitted to use it as a basis for important factual determinations? Surely, courts of law would not countenance using the results of trial by ordeal or combat or the testimony of a ouija board interpreter, no matter how much advance stipulation by the parties had taken place. There is no analogous category of evidence which is subject to this kind of stipulation barrier.

THE *SCHEFFER* OPINIONS AND THEIR IMPACT ON THE FUTURE

The closest the United States Supreme Court has ever come to facing the issues of polygraph evidence admissibility occurred recently in *United States v. Scheffer*,[38] a case which is as narrow in its technical holding as it is broadly significant in its future influence on the exclusion of polygraph evidence from American courtrooms. Anyone who seeks to litigate admissibility of polygraphs must be thoroughly familiar with *Scheffer*.

The case appropriately originated in the military courts. The United States armed forces have for many years studied and used the polygraph, and beginning in 1987 with *United States v. Gipson*,[39] the military courts had officially recognized the scientific reliability of the polygraph and the propriety of its use as evidence. The executive branch of the federal government responded to *Gipson* by issuing a new military rule of evidence to impose a *per se* ban on polygraph evidence for the military courts, precluding any possibility of making a showing of scientific reliability or relevance. *Scheffer* tested the constitutionality of that *per se* ban against the 6th Amendment right of the accused to have his defense evidence heard. That theory had previously been relied on to strike down evidentiary bans on the ability of the accused to introduce exculpatory hearsay statements, accomplice testimony and hypnotically refreshed testimony[40] (Dery, 1999).

An airman charged with using drugs had been administered both a urinalysis

[35] *United States v. Gilliard*, 133 F.3d 809 (11th Cir. 1998); *Conti v. Commissioner*, 39 F.3d 658 (6th Cir. 1994)("unilaterally obtained polygraph evidence is almost never admissible" in the 6th judicial circuit).

[36] *United States v. Crumby* 895 F. Supp. 1354, 1356 (D. Ariz. 1995).

[37] See, e.g., *United States v. Oliver*, 525 F.2d 731 (8th Cir. 1975) (Polygraph evidence reliable enough to be admitted over defendant's objection where he had agreed to stipulate admissibility before taking test).

[38] *United States v. Scheffer*, 523 U.S. 303 (1998).

[39] *United States v. Gipson*, 24 M.J. 246 (C.M.A. 1987).

[40] *Rock v. Arkansas*, 483 U.S. 44 (1987).

and a polygraph by United States Air Force authorities. The urinalysis expert concluded that traces of methamphetamine were found in his urine, and the polygraph expert reported that the airman did not show signs of deception when he denied knowingly ingesting the drugs. As a result of the new exclusionary evidence rule, the court martial equivalent of a jury was not allowed to hear about the polygraph evidence, while the urinalysis analysis was admitted. The airman appealed his resulting conviction, and the court of appeals for the armed forces held that a rule imposing a *per se* exclusion of polygraph evidence violated the Sixth Amendment right to present a defense.[41] The government then took the case to the United States Supreme Court, which reversed the court of appeals and reinstated the conviction.

Those who hoped the *Scheffer* opinion would provide some definitive answers to the issues surrounding polygraph use in the United States courts found little resolution in the decision. There were in fact three separate opinions, none garnering the full support of a majority of the nine-member court. It takes a careful analysis to determine just what the court said and did not say, and the opinion already has been misinterpreted and misused. The only authoritative majority holding from the court's opinion is that a jurisdiction which chooses to keep polygraphs out of evidence is not absolutely precluded by the United States Constitution from making that choice, at least at the present time. That conclusion was shared by the four justices supporting the Thomas opinion ("The Thomas four" – Thomas, Rhenquist, Scalia, and Souter) and the four justices supporting the Kennedy opinion ("The Kennedy four" – Kennedy, O'Connor, Ginsburg, and Breyer).

Only the Thomas four seemed to be firm in their position that the *per se* exclusion was appropriate, mentioning several of the common exclusionary theories analyzed above. The Kennedy four reluctantly joined the Thomas four on the constitutional issue to avoid binding all court systems in the country to a constitutional ruling that they have no power to choose to exclude polygraph evidence. They explicitly based their joinder only on the ground that "the rule of exclusion is not so arbitrary or disproportionate that it is unconstitutional." The Kennedy four went on to say, however, that they did not agree that the *per se* exclusion was wise and that a later case might cause them to re-examine their agreement with the constitutionality of the exclusionary position. The Kennedy four also noted the tension between the *Scheffer* result and the *Daubert* doctrine, as well as the inconsistency between the government's oppositionist position to use of polygraphs by the accused while it makes widespread use of polygraph tests in going about its own business.

Justice Stevens was clear in his separate dissent that the courts should be open to admission of polygraph results and that the Constitution does prohibit a *per se* exclusion.

[41] *United States v. Scheffer,* 44 M.J. 442 (1996).

Synthesizing the three separate opinions, a five-justice majority of the court (Stevens, Kennedy, O'Connor, Ginsburg, and Breyer) made clear their positions on the following issues:

1. A *per se* rule of polygraph exclusion is either unconstitutional (Stevens) or unwise (Kennedy, O'Connor, Ginsburg, and Breyer).
2. Polygraph evidence was not found to be unreliable. In fact, none of the opinions of the nine justices reached that conclusion. The Thomas four and the Kennedy four agreed that in light of the continuing good faith disagreement among experts and courts on the subject, it is possible to "reasonably reach differing conclusions as to whether polygraph evidence should be admitted" as a matter of constitutional law. Justice Stevens found it sufficiently reliable to be admitted.
3. The majority of the court did not find that polygraph evidence invades the province of the jury. The government used this familiar argument, but failed to convince the majority of the court. While the Thomas four accepted the argument, the remaining five judges explicitly rejected it.
4. The court did not say that consideration of polygraph takes too much time in litigation and consideration of collateral issues. This argument had the support of the Thomas four, but not the remaining five justices.

Despite the fact that advocates on all sides of the polygraph issue will find support for their arguments in either the ultimate result or particular language in the various opinions, there are some predictions that are safe to make. There is little doubt that the Thomas four can be expected to remain hostile to the use of polygraph evidence, while the other five justices are likely to be more receptive. In a future case, a majority of the court eventually could hold that admission of polygraph evidence is constitutionally required, though there is no reason to expect that result any time soon. Until the issues may be revisited by the Supreme Court, the lower courts technically remain free to consider the admissibility of polygraph evidence under *Daubert*.

In the period following the issuance of the Supreme Court opinions in *Scheffer*, a growing number of lower court cases purport to have relied on the case. Despite the fact that a majority of the *Scheffer* Court were favorable to consideration of polygraph evidence under the *Daubert* guidelines, the trend of subsequent lower court decisions has been strikingly exclusionary. Language is often taken from dictum in the four-justice opinion of Justice Thomas to support conclusory statements in lower court opinions that the polygraph is in fact unreliable, or is in fact confusing to the jury, or is otherwise excludable under Rule 403.[42] Ironically, an opinion of the highest court of the United States in which a majority of the justices were favorably disposed toward the use

[42] *See, e.g., United States v. Orians*, 9 F. Supp. 2d 1168, 1189 (D. Ariz. 1998); *United States v. Reed*, 147 F.3d 1178, 1183 (9th Cir. 1998); *United States v. Wright*, 1998 U.S. Dist. LEXIS 15127, 15138 (W.D. Tenn. 1998).

of polygraph evidence in the courts has instead been used to bolster the hostile reception traditionally afforded this evidence in the lower courts.

SUMMARY AND CONCLUSIONS

Throughout the history of the treatment of polygraph evidence in the United States courts, there has been a clear pattern of apprehension and exclusion, with only occasional exceptions allowing the evidence to be admitted. The general legal rules and theories of admission of evidence, and of scientific evidence in particular, would seem to favor polygraph admission, but those theories tend to be ignored or applied in unusually stringent ways to exclude polygraph evidence. While proponents will undoubtedly continue to attempt to influence the courts in applying those theories more consistently to polygraph evidence, the historical behavior of courts in the United States provides no reason to expect any significant change in the overall trend of exclusion in the near future.

REFERENCES

Daniels, C. (1997) New Frontiers in Polygraph Evidence. *The New Mexico Trial Lawyer,* 97, 107.

Dery, G. (1999) Mouse hunting with an elephant gun: The Supreme Court's overkill in upholding a categorical rejection to polygraph evidence in *United States v. Scheffer. Am. J. Crim. L.,* 227.

Imwinkelried, E. (1996) *Uncharged Misconduct,* § 3:04.

Imwinkelreid, E. and McCall, J. (1997) Issues once moot: The other evidentiary objections to the admission of polygraph examinations. *Wake Forest Law Review,* 1045.

McCall, J. (1996) Misconceptions and reevaluation – polygraph admissibility after *Rock* and *Daubert. U. Ill. L. Rev.,* 363.

McLaughlin, J. M. (ed.) (1997) *Weinstein's Federal Evidence,* § 401.08[4] at 401-59 (2nd edn).

O'Conner, D. Jr. (1988) The polygraph: Scientific evidence at trial. *Naval Law Review,* 97, 106.

Peters, R. B. (1982) A survey of polygraph evidence in criminal trials. *ABA Journal* ,162.

Raskin, D. (1986) The polygraph in 1986: scientific, professional and legal issues surrounding acceptance of polygraph evidence. *Utah Law Review,* 29, 66.

AUTHOR INDEX

SUBJECT INDEX